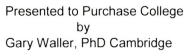

Mary Magdalene
and the Drama of Saints

Mary Magdalene and the Drama of Saints

Theater, Gender, and Religion in Late Medieval England

Theresa Coletti

PENN

UNIVERSITY OF PENNSYLVANIA PRESS

Philadelphia

THE MIDDLE AGES SERIES

Ruth Mazo Karras, Series Editor

Edward Peters, Founding Editor

A complete list of books in the series is available from the publisher.

10   9   8   7   6   5   4   3   2   1

Published by
University of Pennsylvania Press
Philadelphia, Pennsylvania 19104-4011

Library of Congress Cataloging-in-Publication Data

Coletti, Theresa, 1950–
    Mary Magdalene and the drama of saints : theater, gender, and religion in late medieval
England / Theresa Coletti.
        p. cm — (The Middle Ages series)
    Includes bibliographical references (p.) and index.
    ISBN 0-8122-3800-1 (acid-free paper)
    1. Mysteries and miracle plays. English—History and criticism. 2. Theater—England—
History—Medieval 500–1500. 3. Mary Magdalene, Saint—In literature. 4. Christianity and
literature—England—History—To 1500. 5. Women and literature—England—History—To
1500. 6. English drama—To 1500—History and criticism. 7. Christian hagiography—
History—To 1500. 8. Christian saints in literature. 9. Sex role in literature. 10. Women in
literature. I. Title. II. Series.

PR643.M37C65 2004
822′.051609—dc22

                                                                                                    2004043026

Frontispiece: Saint Mary Magdalene, rood screen panel, St. Andrew, Bramfield,
Suffolk. Photo: T. Coletti.

In memory of
Jacqueline Taylor Coletti

Contents

Illustrations

Preface

IN THE PARISH CHURCH OF SAINT ANDREW in Bramfield, Suffolk, fragmented letters against the golden background of a rood screen panel spell out the identity of the elegant female figure that it depicts: "SANCTA MAG" (frontispiece). The most beautiful of all the East Anglian rood screen images of the saint, the Bramfield panel evokes the Magdalene of wealth and status whose late medieval vita found wide circulation through works such as the *Legenda aurea*. At the same time that the woman's luxurious attire alludes to the darker, profligate side of such elegance, it epitomizes tendencies of late medieval hagiography and the visual imagination to represent the saints as familiar and immediate. In the Bramfield panel, the lush drapery and rich fabric of dress and cloak, the jewel-like adornments of headdress and belt, carefully coordinated with the ointment vessel borne before the breast, render this Magdalene as a late medieval aristocratic woman—and thus a worthy patron of noble ladies such as Isabel Bourchier, countess of Eu, who commissioned a life of the saint from fifteenth-century East Anglian friar Osbern Bokenham. If the material splendor of the Bramfield Magdalene bespeaks late medieval habits of representation that linked saintly biography and the contemporary world, the rood screen that privileges the saint's aristocratic image memorializes just as emphatically the biblical foundations of her sacred identity. Appearing to the left of the Magdalene image on the Bramfield screen are panels that depict evangelists John and Luke, whose gospels were the most important sources for Mary Magdalene's scriptural biography. The arrangement and iconography of the images on the Bramfield rood screen thus glance back to biblical meanings that defined Mary Magdalene's significance for centuries, even as they signal the adaptation and appropriation of her vita for late medieval devotional ends. This Mary Magdalene, whose complex spiritual and social identity emerges from symbolic and interpretive processes implicit in the Bramfield screen, played an exceptionally vital role in late medieval East Anglian religious culture; defining that role and exploring those processes form the project of this book.

I invoke the Bramfield Magdalene image as the point of entry into this book not only because of its hermeneutic usefulness for these prefatory remarks but also because it delightfully acknowledges material dimensions of late medieval East Anglian religious culture that have shaped my investigation of the Magdalene figure. This book bears witness to intellectual and emotional ties to medieval East Anglia that go back three decades. In that time it has been my very good fortune to share the passion for these pursuits with other scholars of East Anglia, and I am privileged to recognize them here. I am deeply grateful to Gail Gibson for persuading me to accompany her to Bury St. Edmunds in the summer of 1980, for her support of my work, and for the inspiration of her example. My recent East Anglian travels have been greatly enriched by the friendship and collegiality of Carole Hill, whose discerning eye for the feminine iconography of late medieval religious culture has enlivened our conversations and our "field work." It is also my pleasure to thank Carole Rawcliffe for finding time in a busy schedule to give a captivating tour of the Great Hospital in Norwich and Caroline Cardwell for providing gracious hospitality during a memorable visit to Bramfield Saint Andrew's.

This book has been in the making long enough for me to incur many other debts. My thinking about East Anglian drama and religious culture has been immeasurably advanced by many generous colleagues who shared their work: Kathleen Ashley, Virginia Blanton, Lawrence Clopper, Mimi Dixon, Ruth Evans, Katherine French, Heather Hill-Vásquez, Laura King, Stephen Mead, Judy Oliver, Carole Rawcliffe, Milla Riggio, Catherine Sanok, Victor Scherb, Mary Sokolowski, Lynn Staley, Douglas Sugano, David Wallace, Nancy Warren, Claire Waters, and Nicholas Watson. Kathleen Ashley, Kent Cartwright, and Sarah Stanbury read the entire manuscript and provided encouragement as well as immensely valuable commentary. Virginia Blanton gave crucial assistance with meticulous comments on early chapters. For advice and support at key moments, I thank Jane Donawerth, Donna Hamilton, Gary Hamilton, James Harris, Susan Leonardi, Lynn Staley, and Elizabeth Swayze. I am grateful to Bob Coogan for reviewing my Latin translations, to Meg Pearson and Carissa Baker for able research assistance, and to Herb Ward and Denise Wolff for making me look like a better photographer than I am. A grant-in-aid from the American Council of Learned Societies supported my early investigations into East Anglian religious culture; research leave from the College of Arts and Humanities and General Research Board of the Graduate School at the University of Maryland helped me to bring this project to completion. I am also grateful for the privilege of working with Jerome Singerman and for the efficiency and professionalism of the staff at the University of Pennsylvania Press.

Family and friends offered time away from this project or appealing venues in which to pursue it. For their many kindnesses, I thank my sister and brother-in-law, Marian and Herb Ward, and for patient friendship and support, I thank Angie DeLuca, Tony DeLuca, Aida Martinovic-Zic, Valerie Wilbur, Elizabeth Williamson, and Patricia Yeager.

Portions of this book were presented at the College of the Holy Cross, Colgate University, the Harvard Medieval Doctoral Conference, the University of East Anglia, the University of Toronto, and International Medieval Congresses at Western Michigan University. Except for a few sentences that I have culled from my earlier work, no sections of this book have been previously published.

This book is dedicated to my late stepmother, Jacqueline Coletti, a *mulier religiosa* for our time.

Finally, it gives me great pleasure to acknowledge the unrivaled assistance and incomparable companionship of the unwitting mascot of this project, Madeleine.

Introduction

FOR TWO MILLENNIA Mary Magdalene has maintained an enduring hold on the Western cultural imagination. Emerging from the early Christian Gospels and Gnostic writings, Mary Magdalene by the sixth century had assumed the conflated identity of several scriptural women. The Magdalene whom the canonical Gospels variously place at the Crucifixion, Entombment, and Resurrection was identified with the sister of Lazarus and Martha of Bethany and with the mysterious sinner of Luke 7 who washed Jesus' feet with her tears and dried them with her hair. A few centuries later, legendary elements of an evangelical and ascetic life accrued to the developing biography of the woman named Magdalene. Late medieval understandings recognized her as the sinner-saint who had embraced and then renounced sexual and worldly pleasures and, through her attachment to Jesus, had mingled erotic and spiritual love. Blessed as a sinner, she was a symbol of penance and exemplar of contemplative and passionate devotion to Christ. Because of her witness to and announcement of Christ's resurrection, she had also been designated apostle to the apostles; in this capacity she traveled with a group of Christian companions on a rudderless ship to France, converted the king and queen of Marseilles, and then retired to a hermit's life in the desert. There, cloaked only in her flowing hair, she was sustained on manna fed by angels seven times a day. Since the early Christian era, Mary Magdalene has functioned as a figure who elicits questions about the nature of feminine religious authority, the relationship of spirituality and sexuality, and the social and political positions of women in institutional religions. This book examines the significance of these questions in medieval England at a historical moment when the mythology and symbolism of Mary Magdalene held especially wide cultural currency. It proposes that dramatic discourses, gender ideologies, and vernacular religion converge in late medieval English cultural constructions of Mary Magdalene.

This book had its beginnings as a study of the late fifteenth- or early sixteenth-century East Anglian dramatic text on the life of Mary Magdalene preserved in Bodleian Library MS Digby 133. Otherwise unlocatable in terms of specific cultural and social auspices, the Digby *Mary Magdalene*, as it is called, is perhaps the most theologically ambitious and theatrically eclectic play in the entire corpus of Middle English drama. As my investigation of this text unfolded, I increasingly realized the extent to which compelling issues raised by the Digby saint play were intricately embedded in the discourses and practices of late medieval religious culture as a whole. That this should be so is not surprising. Like all complex cultural symbols, the late medieval Mary Magdalene both generates and attracts a multiplicity of meanings whose very indeterminacy underscores the centrality of the contexts—the social, material, and ideological conditions—that produced them.[1] The symbolic functions of the dramatic Mary Magdalene are elucidated by appeals to late medieval religion and hagiography, conceptions of feminine spiritual authority, ideals of contemplation, constructions of gender and the female body, understandings of sacred representation, and in the case of the Digby saint play, local characteristics of East Anglian religious culture. These symbolic functions also enter into dialogue with devotional and mystical texts, polemical social and religious writings, homiletic and exegetical traditions, and other hagiographic and dramatic works. As I came to see how the commitments of medieval English drama, religious culture, and gender ideologies dynamically converge in the Digby saint play's symbolic representation of Mary Magdalene, my approach to this text and the initial conception of this study evolved accordingly. Although the Digby saint play still provides the analytic focus of this book, the topics identified in its subtitle—theater, gender, and religion—point to the larger concerns of the project as a whole.

The theater investigated in this book is the community and civic religious drama of late medieval England. I employ the word "community" advisedly, as a term capable of embracing various possibilities for the unknown auspices of the dramatic texts on which this discussion focuses. Despite a growing and well-justified tendency to designate pre-Elizabethan drama by the term "early English," I have retained "medieval" to designate this drama because the primary cultural resources that I draw upon to elucidate it are historically identified by that descriptor.[2] While this book pursues a complex cultural reading of the Digby saint play, it also analyzes other East Anglian dramatic texts as well as portions of the northern biblical cycles. Consequently, the arguments of this study address all of the generic "kinds" of drama designated by the highly problematic but still resonant nomenclature "miracle," "morality," and "mystery." At the same time, this book recognizes the limitations of these generic labels and, indeed, the very inadequacy of the terms "drama" and "play" to signify instances of late medieval English cultural performance that melded spectacles of sacred subjects with festive practice, social action, and religious ritual.[3] More specifically, this study responds to the interpretive gap exposed by recent disagreements over the performance of saint plays in England. Lawrence Clopper's contention that there were few saint plays renders conventional generic terminology even more problematic and in so doing invites fuller cultural contextualization of scripted dramas based on saints' vitae such as *Mary Magdalene*.[4]

Contributing to that effort, this project's engagement with issues of gender is an inevitable corollary of its focus on Mary Magdalene, who since her emergence in biblical history has furnished a mythic and symbolic figure intricately bound up with cultural constructions of female identity and femininity. As a gendered symbol, Mary Magdalene in her late medieval incarnations occupies the borders between flesh and spirit, body and word, abjection and privilege, profane and sacred. Her representations in medieval religious drama negotiate the tensions inherent in these binary relationships. In the late Middle Ages the saint's complicated gender identities prompt questions about women's access to spiritual authority, the role of the female body in religious experience, and feminine contributions to salvation history. Drawing upon recent scholarship focusing on the spirituality of medieval women, this book explores historical constructions of gender that shaped the articulation of such questions and demonstrates how Mary Magdalene, as a gendered symbol, provides access to major issues animating late medieval religious culture.

Investigations of religious culture presently constitute an area of immense activity and excitement in Middle English studies. Recent work in the field has produced new historical, critical, and theoretical accounts of a wide range of spiritual, mystical, hagiographical, homiletic, and polemical texts. This work has mapped intersections of secular and ecclesiastical politics as motivating occasions for the development of a specifically vernacular religious culture; it has redefined and broadened historical understanding of the ways in which social and spiritual roles and institutions impinge upon the production of vernacular religious texts. Yet the relevance of this dynamic, conflicted religious culture to medieval English dramatic discourses remains largely unexplored, and the different disciplinary perspectives of literary history and criticism, gender studies, and social and religious history collectively have not yet been brought to bear on a specific local instance of late medieval dramatic practice.

This book aims to fill that gap. My analysis of medieval English theater and the gender issues that constellate around the figure of Mary Magdalene engages the textual forms, social and political contexts, and representational practices highlighted by recent investigations of vernacular religion in late medieval England. In so doing, this project seeks to direct the study of medieval English drama, especially the saint play, away from influential approaches that still focus predominantly on generic typologies and theatrical traditions; alternatively, it places dramatic texts in conversation with the intensely fraught environment of late medieval English religious culture, with its politics of dissent, vernacularity, and sacramentality.[5] This study thus assumes Middle English dramatic texts' contribution, in Nicholas Watson's famous phrase, to late medieval "vernacular theology," a concept whose aims, as defined by Watson, point precisely to the interests pursued here: namely, to undertake "comparative discussions of various kinds of vernacular writing that tend to be studied in isolation or in groupings that are sometimes artificial" and to focus "attention on the specifically intellectual content of vernacular religious texts that are often treated with condescension."[6] By approaching Middle English dramatic texts as a species of vernacular theological writing—one whose public, performative dimensions produce complex intersections of dramatic form and religious ideology—this project relocates medieval English dramatic texts, if not from the margin to the center of English literary history, at least to a more productive critical space where drama's material and discursive intersections with other late medieval cultural texts and practices will be made newly available.

The final term in this book's subtitle, "late medieval England," also calls for elaboration. My discussion of theater, gender, and religious culture is focused principally through an East Anglian lens. Late medieval East Anglia was both the point of origin for a noteworthy concentration of Mary Magdalene texts and, excepting the northern biblical cycles, home to most of the drama extant in Middle English.[7] As Gail McMurray Gibson and others have demonstrated, it was also a region that nurtured an exceptionally vital yet coherent religious culture, manifested in a remarkable melding of monastic and lay pieties and rendered visible in the hundreds of parish churches, many richly appointed, that still dot the East Anglian landscape.[8] Building upon Gibson's foundational work on the social, spiritual, and ritual environments of East Anglian dramatic texts and cultural performances, this book marks a new departure in late medieval East Anglian studies through its focus on Mary Magdalene's many attachments to a feminine religious culture that is amply attested by textual, institutional, political, and iconic preoccupations of the region. I investigate Mary Magdalene's connections with East Anglian cultural artifacts that interpret religious phenomena through the frame of gender, ranging from unique texts, such as Osbern Bokenham's all-female legendary, Margery Kempe's autohagiography, and the N-Town *Mary Play*; to the gendered metaphorics of Julian of Norwich's theology of Incarnation; to evidence of the social and institutional importance of women religious in medieval Norfolk and Suffolk; to the proliferation of feminine sacred symbols in East Anglian parish churches. This valorizing of feminine religious experience and expression is an important signature of late medieval East Anglian society and a distinctive contribution to English religious culture on the threshold of the Reformation.

Mary Magdalene and the Drama of Saints argues that East Anglian dramatic representations of the saint draw upon themes, symbols, and practices of this religious culture to position Mary Magdalene at the center of important late medieval debates about sources of spiritual authority and to articulate a complex vision of feminine contributions to salvation history. Dramatic versions of Mary Magdalene symbolically mediate central tensions within late medieval religious beliefs, politics, and practice: between masculine and feminine religious authority; institutional and individual modes of spiritual expression; authorized and unauthorized forms of revelation and sacred speech. This book concurrently argues that East Anglian dramatic treatments of Mary Magdalene, especially the Digby saint play, shed light on vernacular theater's kinship with influential late medieval religious texts and institutions as well as on the changing climate for sacred representation in the decades before the Reformation. Through an investigation of the symbolic valences and material incarnations of Mary Magdalene, this study revisits the East

Anglian theater of devotion, bringing to center stage the cultural predominance of feminine religion and the contribution that dramatic texts
made to late medieval constructions of gender and religious experience.

My efforts to relate dramatic constructions of Mary Magdalene to
the texts and practices of late medieval religious culture have noteworthy implications for English literary history. By analyzing East Anglian
dramas of Mary Magdalene through a discursive framework that includes texts such as Julian of Norwich's *Revelation of Love*, the *Book of
Margery Kempe*, Osbern Bokenham's *Legendys of Hooly Wummen*, and
Walter Hilton's *Scale of Perfection*, this book embraces mainstream literary history's present preoccupations with women writers and readers
and with audiences for religious literature in the late Middle Ages. By
emphasizing the coincidence of the spiritual investments of East Anglian
dramatic texts and performances with prominent themes of late medieval spiritual writings (for example, their shared focus on contemplative
ideals), this book also underscores the crucial contemporaneity of these
cultural phenomena and thereby renders medieval drama and theater
open to investigation in light of important developments in late medieval textual culture. Although traditional literary history has tended to
isolate dramatic genres from narratives that address mainstream textual
production, distinguishing the radical instability of performative dramatic texts from the sturdier products of early print culture, it is useful
to keep in mind that religious and devotional texts that can be brought
to bear on the Digby *Magdalene*—Hilton's *Scale* and *Epistle on the Mixed
Life*, *Contemplations of the Dread and Love of God*, *The Abbey of the Holy
Ghost*, and *The Chastising of God's Children*—all saw their first publication in the 1490s to 1520s, the very decades within which the saint play
is believed to have been composed and copied.[9] The fact that dramatic
traditions examined in this book are all grounded, as we shall see, in
idiosyncratic codicological environments should not preclude us from
recognizing how they make common, spiritual cause with religious
writings from manuscript and print cultures that furnished the textual
horizons of dramatic audiences.

By arguing for the integral connection of East Anglian dramatic
texts to these broader cultural and literary forces and influences, this
book also seeks to reconfigure the position that religious drama traditionally occupies in medieval English literary history. Here I refer not to
the familiar narrative that made all instances of pre-Elizabethan drama
inferior precursors of Shakespeare but rather to the elision of Middle

English dramatic texts from dominant accounts of late medieval English literary culture.[10] This elision occurs at the gap created by conventional literary history's broader and not always fully articulated division between self-conscious, wide-ranging traditions of vernacular writing struggling for cultural recognition in the fourteenth and fifteenth centuries, and the Chaucer-centered narrative of literary production that established the versatile poet and rhetor as England's response to classical culture.[11] Initiated by Hoccleve and Lydgate in the early fifteenth century and reinforced by later monastic writers such as Bokenham, Barclay, and Bradshaw, this Chaucer-centered, or laureate, account of the history of vernacular literature was subsequently institutionalized by the products of Caxton's press and, in the sixteenth century, recast as part of the nationalist cultural program of Tudor polity and propaganda, whence it has continued to influence accounts of literary history even to this day. As Seth Lerer and others have demonstrated, this narrative fashioned English literary history as the expression of a masculine genealogy, going back to antiquity, with Chaucer as its insular paternal icon.[12]

Hindsight has revealed the high price exacted by the gendering of authorship that accompanied the paternal and genealogical construction of the history of English writing. These processes of authorial and canon formation brought about the woman writer's disappearance from privileged arenas of literary production and, in Jennifer Summit's compelling argument, her re-creation as a figure for the "historical alienation" of English letters itself from an authoritative literary past.[13] By positing English writing as the heritage of "precedent writing of the greatest possible prestige"—Chaucer's "Virgile, Ovide, Omer, Lucan, and Stace"—the laureate narrative also established an origin for English letters that required the virtual obliteration of the polyglot traditions that had nurtured and defined vernacular literary production for several hundred years prior to the emergence of the genealogical paradigm.[14]

Prominent analyses of the theory and politics of the vernacular in recent Middle English studies have substantively challenged the explanatory capabilities of the laureate narrative and the processes of canon formation that it put in place as reliable accounts of the history of writing in late medieval England.[15] These challenges have encouraged the direction of scholarly attention to areas of Middle English textual culture perforce neglected by the laureate narrative, making evident the contemporaneity of its fifteenth-century formation with parallel strands of English writing defined by ties to devotional and performative traditions

of representation and discourse. Notable among these alternatives are
the two major woman-authored texts of late medieval England, all of
the extant fifteenth- and early sixteenth-century drama, a wide range of
religious writing, including contemplative and mystical texts and works
of spiritual guidance, and the endeavors of East Anglian monastic
hagiographers.[16] The texts in this alternative tradition of English writing are just as likely to be gendered feminine as masculine, and not only
because of the rare presence of female authorship in this cohort. Religious writing in Middle English frequently involved some type of gendered transaction, whether through the attribution of the feminine
position to the vernacular itself in familiar constructions of cultural and
textual authority; or through a gendering of the reading process that
analogized lay reception of religious texts to that of female religious; or
through the social auspices and institutional contexts that contributed
to the production of female, principally religious, readers.[17] Comprising
texts such as Lydgate's *Life of Our Lady*, the N-Town *Mary Play*, the
Digby plays of *Mary Magdalene* and *Candlemas Day and the Killing of
the Children of Israel*, the Macro *Wisdom*, Julian's *Revelation of Love*,
Kempe's *Book*, Bokenham's all-female legendary, and Capgrave's *Life of
Saint Katherine*, this other tradition of English, here specifically East
Anglian, writing signals its gendered inflections through direct engage-
ment with feminine subject matter and symbolism.

Given the necessity of a masculine genealogy of literary production
having to come to terms with the feminized "mother tongue" on which
it depended for its articulation, some commingling of these ostensibly
distinct traditions was ideologically inevitable.[18] Such processes of commingling are epitomized in the careers of two prominent East Anglian
regulars, Benedictine John Lydgate from Bury St. Edmunds and Augustinian friar Osbern Bokenham of Clare. Though differently positioned
with respect to fifteenth-century English dynastic political struggles—
Lydgate was a staunch Lancastrian sympathizer while Bokenham threw
his support to the Yorkist cause—each writer articulated his relationship
to his textual forebears and, in part, sought to secure his own place in a
tradition of English writing through literary efforts that significantly
appealed to feminine symbols and subject matter, Lydgate with *Life of
Our Lady* and Bokenham with the *Legendys of Hooly Wummen*. Nancy
Bradley Warren and Sheila Delany have demonstrated how Lydgate
and Bokenham employ the symbolic capital of female saints for complex
literary, linguistic, and political negotiations. The feminine inflections

of language, genealogy, and theology that preoccupied Lydgate and Bokenham inscribed the fifteenth century's emergent masculine literary paradigm with tropes of maternity and incarnation, adumbrating the hybrid gendering of literary models and reception that seems to have characterized encounters with textual culture by a broad spectrum of readers in late medieval England.[19]

The textual perspectives of these communities of writers, readers, and patrons furnish a pathway, albeit circuitous, whereby East Anglian drama might also enter a revised narrative of English literary history. Although little is known about the auspices and provenance of the major extant East Anglian dramas, a great deal is known about the thriving textual community of clerical and lay writers and prosperous gentry and noble readers who nurtured the region's literary culture.[20] Evidence of literary patronage and reception by these readers underscores their simultaneous investment in the cachet of an antique, Chaucerian tradition and the spiritual benefits of feminized, performative devotional reading and practice. Anne Harling of East Harling, Norfolk, borrowed John Paston II's *Book of Troilus* and bequeathed to "my lord of Surrey" Christine de Pizan's classicizing allegory of chivalric virtue, "the Pistill of Othia"; but as Dame Wingfield she also owned a devotional miscellany (British Library MS Harley 4012) that included lives of female saints and indulgences for Syon, and as Lady Scrope, the Foyle manuscript copy of the *Speculum Devotorum*, a work written for cloistered nuns.[21] The literary connections of the wealthy Bury St. Edmunds clothier John Baret further reinforce this portrait of East Anglian readers' hybrid textual commitments. Baret had important ties to the two monastic writers who mediated their laureate aspirations through models of feminine holiness: for at least a decade after 1439 he shared Lydgate's pension; and in his will of 1463 he left a bequest to Osbern Bokenham. Yet Baret was linked by his wife, Elizabeth, to the Drury family of Hawstead, Suffolk, who are notably associated in the sixteenth century with the Ellesmere manuscript of the *Canterbury Tales*.[22]

Anne Harling and John Baret are familiar to students of late medieval East Anglia as prominent exemplars of Gibson's East Anglian "devotional theater," a metaphor that both embraces these individuals' engagement with performative spiritual practices and adumbrates the linkage between such values and practices and those of East Anglian dramatic texts.[23] In Gibson's argument, participation in this devotional theater by East Anglian noble and mercantile elites gives access to

preoccupations of the region's dramatic audiences. In the decade or
more since Gibson first presented these compelling biographies of late
medieval East Anglian cultural patronage, new work in codicology,
manuscript circulation, and literary reception has provided a clearer picture of the ways in which such East Anglian devotional performances
intersect with key texts and players in mainstream literary history.

Although specific connections between these individuals and East
Anglian drama are likely to remain elusive, some elements of this portrait of readers, patrons, drama, and literary history do occasionally come
into sharper focus. Consider, for example, the presentation copy of
Lydgate's very Chaucerian *Siege of Thebes* contained in British Library
MS Arundel 119, an East Anglian manuscript probably produced at Bury
St. Edmunds. Hanna and Edwards speculate that Arundel 119 may be
the copy of "my boke with the sege of Thebes in englysh" bequeathed
in 1463 by John Baret.[24] Probably made for William de la Pole, duke
of Suffolk, whose arms appear in the manuscript, Arundel 119 bears
intriguing resemblances to another manuscript with Baret-Drury connections, the Ellesmere *Canterbury Tales*.[25] The scribe who produced
Arundel 119 is known to have copied three other manuscripts. One of
these, a copy of John Walton's *Boethius* (now MS 615 from the Schøyen
collection in Oslo) bears a signature and declaration of ownership by
Thomas Hyngham, the monk from Bury St. Edmunds who left identical declarations on two major East Anglian play texts from the Macro
manuscript, *Wisdom* and *Mankind*, which he is also thought to have
copied.[26] This brief narrative of scribes and patrons suggests how, at
the point of textual production and circulation, key elements of the
laureate-centered view of English literary history overlapped with performative, devotional traditions of English writing. At the level of reading and patronage, boundaries between areas of English literary culture
that are customarily considered discrete must have blurred more than
scholars and critics have been able to acknowledge. Recognition of this
blurring can begin to carve out a place within medieval English literary
history for an East Anglian dramatic tradition that has largely been seen
as marginal to that history's major commitments.

While this book mobilizes recent developments in the study of late
medieval religious culture and feminine spirituality to reassess the place
of vernacular theater in English literary history, it also implicitly engages
fundamental methodological issues that have dominated Middle English drama studies. The approach to dramatic texts pursued here builds

on the emerging rapprochement in the field between analyses focusing on cultural and literary critique and major scholarly preoccupations of recent decades: namely, advances in editorial and textual activity; the compilation of archival materials related to early drama and theater; and the mounting of contemporary performances informed by historically established conditions of early staging.[27] We increasingly recognize that in the encounter with medieval performances, the construction and interpretation of cultural meaning—for medievals and ourselves—emerges from the complex interplay of ritual events, social sites, the archive, and the text as a material and verbal artifact.[28] We also recognize that for medieval dramatic audiences these acts of cultural interpretation, like the constitutive elements of medieval performances themselves, had to have been diverse and conflicted, both in the synchronic moment of the unique performance's reception and in the diachronic encounter with texts, such as the biblical cycles, composed and performed at intervals over time. Inevitably, then, as social performances and verbal artifacts, medieval plays, in Kathleen Ashley's phrase, "are riven with mixed messages, incompatible world views and multiple voices."[29]

The emergent consensus about the mobility and variety that characterized reception of medieval performances and dramatic texts marks an important departure from prevailing scholarly assumptions about their cultural function that until recently have held sway in early drama studies. William Tydeman offers a typical articulation of these assumptions: "[I]t was the function of drama in the Middle Ages not to conduct a pragmatic exploration of the potentialities of the human condition which might vary from individual to individual, but rather to demonstrate a predetermined theosophy which remained valid for all sorts and conditions of men at all times and in all places. For this reason medieval drama is predominantly celebratory and confirmatory rather than questioning or revolutionary: the *status quo* is more often upheld and justified rather than challenged or subverted."[30] Tydeman's assertion of the ubiquitous and unchanging relevance of medieval theater's theological argument across time, place, and social class invites critique in light of recent understandings of medieval religion and medieval communities, both of which belie the idealized uniformity of significance that he hypothesizes. Medieval dramatic performances can no longer be construed as unreflective vehicles of instruction in a timeless Christian faith, though they surely did convey religious teaching, nor as unchallenged expressions of communal will and sentiment, though drama was deeply implicated in community values and the affective lives of its makers and viewers. When considering the cultural functions of medieval religious drama, we can with profit replace Tydeman's image of a "predetermined theosophy . . . valid for all sorts and conditions of men" with a more mobile notion of the sorts of theological work that medieval theater might do.

Medieval dramatic texts themselves make evident the need for caution in applying Tydeman's critical terms. For instance, the concept of a "status quo" can refer to many different forms of normative order, such as those of societal organization, theological belief, official public rule, or familial and domestic space. As I show in Chapter 4, the Digby saint play's treatment of the Marseilles episode from the saint's vita involves a careful negotiation between, on one hand, a socially conservative vision of familial virtue based on the regulation of desire through heterosexual marriage and lawful procreation and, on the other, a far more fluid conception of the ways that gender roles lay claim to power and authority in the spiritual realm. In fact, I would argue that the play's endorsement of bourgeois family values—one important late medieval version of the status quo—is a rhetorical and representational strategy that enables its bold theological reflections. In this respect the saint play simultaneously supports and subverts the status quo.[31]

This revised understanding of the complex cultural functions of medieval performances draws inspiration and justification from an idea that galvanized medieval English drama studies for much of the second half of the twentieth century: namely, an emphasis on the constitutive role played by local contexts and conditions in the production—as text and performance—of Middle English plays. This emphasis has underwritten the monumental effort of the Records of Early English Drama project, dedicated to identifying and compiling, county by county, all evidence of dramatic activity in Britain up to 1642; and it has provided the informing motivation for the first major critical and historical study to address the pressures exerted by local context on late medieval performance, Gibson's seminal *The Theater of Devotion: East Anglian Drama and Society in the Late Middle Ages*. What made—and still makes—Gibson's account of East Anglian theater so innovative is her multifaceted approach to constructing local conditions of dramatic performance, which by her definition are simultaneously social, institutional, cultic, symbolic, and material. Gibson's study acknowledges the fragmentary evidence of medieval dramatic activity in a range of East Anglian venues already brought to light and offers new information supporting a hypothesis linking known East Anglian dramatic texts to the festive activities and spiritual and social milieu of the Benedictine abbey at Bury St. Edmunds, Suffolk.[32]

Yet the fact remains that unlike the northern biblical cycles and the plays of Coventry, all of the major extant East Anglian play texts—the dramas of the Macro and Digby manuscripts, the N-Town compilation, and the Croxton *Play of the Sacrament*—cannot be tethered to any specific, identifiable cultural context or occasion.[33] Gibson's larger argument about East Anglian devotional theater addresses that gap by positing a late medieval "incarnational aesthetic" as the theological inspiration for the region's dramatic endeavors and then showing its multiple applications in late medieval East Anglian ritual and spiritual practice. My own approach to the issue of localizing East Anglian cultural performances and dramatic texts draws on cultural resources analogous to those adduced by Gibson, but I also approach historical contextualization from the larger discursive perspective of late medieval English religious and spiritual texts, which offer, I contend, an interpretive horizon that establishes some contemporary conditions of intelligibility for ambitious dramatic endeavors like the Digby saint play.[34]

Absent evidentiary sources that can restore East Anglian drama to the specific occasions and auspices of its genesis, then, this study places central focus on dramatic texts as historical resources in their own right, capable of localizing the cultural performances to which they bear witness, if not in relation to a geographical or material site, at least with respect to the dialogues they conduct with the "extratextual world."[35] In the case of the Digby saint play such dialogues include the text's participation in late medieval cultural debates about the authority of women preachers and the authenticity of visionary experiences as well as polemical critiques of sacred drama. By insisting on the centrality of the dramatic text as a key resource for construing the historical and cultural significance of East Anglian drama, this book's manner of proceeding works against the grain of some central assumptions about the analytical function of the text in medieval English drama studies. These assumptions have emphasized the unreliability of medieval dramatic texts as sources of interpretive authority, based on their uncertain authorship and protracted and, in some instances, collective composition over a long span of time; the dynamic and evolving relationship of the verbal artifact to the manuscript context; the problematic relation of extant texts to any particular historical performance; and the incompatibility of medieval dramatic texts with critical concepts such as aesthetic unity and authorial intention.[36] Excepting the Chester biblical cycle and the Macro *Wisdom*, the major Middle English dramatic texts survive in unique copies, each of which represents the idiosyncratic conditions of its preservation.[37] Aside from Henry Medwall's established authorship of *Fulgens and Lucrece* between 1490 and 1500 and the legendary attribution of the Chester mystery plays to Ranulf Higden, no pre–sixteenth-century authors of medieval English plays have been identified; the names of known owners of dramatic texts are nearly as sparse.[38] Medieval English drama, in Peter Womack's phrase, is drama "before the author," that is to say, drama understood principally as a social activity, not a kind of text, an activity in which significance is conferred by "the social occasion of performance," not the thought of an author.[39]

I believe, though, that it is possible to privilege the dramatic text as a resource without necessarily also putting ideas, say, of aesthetic unity and authorial intention back into the mix of methodological issues to be confronted in the effort to establish more precise cultural locations for medieval performances. Rather, we can think of the dramatic text as a kind of "situated knowledge," in Gabrielle Spiegel's phrase, that calls into existence an "authorial consciousness . . . within a historical and textual world defined by place and time," and still eschew "the claim that such knowledge, and its embodiment in textuality, is fully self-aware."[40] Perhaps the interpretive problem presented to us by medieval dramatic texts is not that their notorious instability empties them of clear-cut significance but rather renders them too full. Perhaps such instability is not these texts' epistemological burden, a sign of their weakness as an evidentiary base of knowledge about medieval performance, but a condition of textuality itself as postmodern theoretical perspectives help us to understand it. Medieval dramatic texts, then, provide a special historical instance of such instability, as a function of their existence in language, their social production, and their dialogic and variable reception. They have many things to tell us about the worlds they inhabit, however much they bear witness to cultural performances that remain unknowable. As Paul Strohm observes in a slightly different context, "[o]nly a radical skeptic would conclude that, the entire truth of an event necessarily eluding us, we have no obligation to pursue the various partial truths that an incomplete and treacherously deceptive textual record affords."[41] Texts such as the Digby *Mary Magdalene* are among the few flawed and partial records that can give us any kind of access at all to late medieval East Anglian performative constructions of sanctity.

Despite claims to the contrary, Middle English drama scholars have repeatedly taken positions that paradoxically have reinforced the importance of the text—spoken or written—as a register of meaning. One proponent of the view that medieval plays become completely accessible only through performance has also observed that medieval English dramatic texts are "extremely intellectual . . . written by people whose training was theological and rhetorical"; such texts require "a lot of strenuous thinking" to tease out their meaning.[42] Beadle asserts that the text of the York plays "is essentially a performance script, never intended as reading matter." Yet he also envisions such performance occurring at the York playing stations before audiences small enough to "respond to the subtle patterns of emotional and conceptual interplay set up in the dramatic structures of the cycle." Such audiences, accustomed to hearing rather than reading texts, "were connoisseurs of the remarkable metrical intricacy displayed in many of the plays, which . . . often demand a finely-tuned ear for allusion, wordplay and the verbal embodiments of psychological nuance."[43] Beadle's account of the keeping of the York Register by the common clerk, furthermore, paints a portrait of sixteenth-century interactions with the text guided by concerns for accuracy and authenticity: the clerk checked actors' speaking parts against the register during actual performances and annotated it to signal departures from the text as written.[44] Major revisions of the Chester plays in the early decades of the sixteenth century bear witness to a "conscious attempt to reshape cyclic drama as a textually controlled genre in reaction to models available elsewhere"; early modern copies of the Chester plays, David Mills suggests, may have proliferated because the text "was regarded as suitable for private devotional study."[45] Recent analyses of verse form in East Anglia dramas such as the *Castle of Perseverance* and the N-Town *Mary Play* point to the work of playwrights remarkably alert to the relationship between formal variety, verbal and thematic emphases, and dramatic situation.[46] Dramatic texts thus have overcome the codicological and contextual problems that attend their preservation to assert their viability as sources of knowledge about the cultural meaning and significance of medieval performances.

The Digby *Mary Magdalene* both invites and merits the attention accorded to it in this book because it opens a window onto crucial aspects of late medieval, specifically East Anglian, religious culture. I have employed metaphors of "intersection" and "dialogue" to articulate how this book's analyses of theater, gender, and religion productively overlap, both in the late Middle Ages and in contemporary scholarly discourses that I invoke to elucidate these topics.[47] But given the multifaceted argument and interdisciplinary approach of this study, I think some further clarification of its rhetorical goals and methods of procedure is in order. *Mary Magdalene and the Drama of Saints* does not work toward a single, comprehensive reading of the Digby saint play, nor does it hypothesize an overarching or unified purpose for that text. Instead, this book provides detailed interpretations of different aspects of the play as they are illuminated by, and brought to bear upon, other East Anglian Mary Magdalenes, the region's feminine religious culture, and vernacular religion in late medieval England. Its analyses, then, inevitably toggle back and forth between interpretation of the Digby saint play and discussion of its many contexts, offering detailed readings of issues and questions raised by the play, mapping horizons for its reception, and marking the intellectual and political, social and spiritual investments of this text.

The first and last chapters of this book address formal, historical, and theatrical dimensions of late medieval East Anglian hagiographic drama. Chapter 1 situates the Digby saint play in relation to central issues in medieval drama studies and prominent features of East Anglian religious culture. It identifies methodological problems highlighted in the contemporary encounter with East Anglian dramatic texts and responds to recent scholarly debate on the nature of the English saint play and the usefulness of the generic paradigm to account for the complexities of medieval English theater. Efforts to situate the Digby saint play, I argue, benefit from consideration of the kinds of cultural environments and audiences to which the text bears witness. Hypothesizing one such context, I examine congruencies between the play, the cult and vita of Mary Magdalene, and late medieval ideologies and practices of charity. The spiritually eclectic and international character of late medieval East Anglian society and religion provides an additional lens for focusing a discussion of the Digby saint play.

Chapter 2 investigates evidence of devotion to Mary Magdalene in a region that privileged female communities and religious lifestyles and feminine forms of spiritual expression. These modes of social organization, visual images, and texts bear witness to Mary Magdalene's commanding presence in East Anglia's feminine religious culture.

Representations of the saint in late medieval East Anglian texts and society, I argue, exploit spiritual and symbolic emphases associated with her insular cult from its very beginnings in the Anglo-Saxon period. This chapter considers the contemplative ideals epitomized by Mary Magdalene, examining evidence of such ideals in the social history of Crabhouse Priory in west Norfolk and in the iconography of the neighboring parish church of Wiggenhall St. Mary the Virgin. The ideals and symbols that inspired social institutions and ecclesiastical imagery are also manifested in major East Anglian texts in which Mary Magdalene occupies important roles: hagiographic and mystical works such as Bokenham's *Legendys*, Julian of Norwich's *Revelation of Love*, and the *Book of Margery Kempe*; and dramatic texts such as *Wisdom* and the *N-Town Plays*. These texts inflect the saint's vita with the ideological debates, spiritual preoccupations, and social forms of late medieval religious culture and provide a framework for assessing the Digby saint play's intervention in an expansive regional dialogue about these issues.

Chapter 3 is the first of three chapters that speak directly to prominent issues emerging from the encounter of a medieval English play on the life of Mary Magdalene with well-documented concerns of the larger religious culture. Focusing on discourses of feminine spiritual authority in the later Middle Ages, this chapter argues that the Digby *Magdalene* models the dramatic saint as a late medieval visionary and holy woman whose spiritual example puts at stake major issues of vernacular religious culture. Using Walter Hilton's invocations of Mary Magdalene in the *Scale of Perfection*, I relate the saint play's preoccupation with sources of religious knowledge to the epistemological commitments of late medieval English contemplative texts; the play depicts a dramatic and discursive world that focuses on access to and communication with the sacred. Late medieval understandings of the goals and politics of contemplation, I contend, constitute a major textual and interpretive horizon against which this dramatic hagiography must be viewed. The dramatic text further fashions its heroine's complex spiritual example by invoking resemblances to late medieval women visionaries and by making her a vernacular preacher. Dramatic representations of female encounters with clerical power and vernacular scripture make a daring and timely claim on behalf of feminine spiritual authority.

The Digby Magdalene's relationship to late medieval constructions of gender and sexuality is the principal concern of Chapter 4, which analyzes symbolic, exegetical, and legendary traditions that contributed to the dramatic saint's fashioning as a figure for the complicated role of femininity in salvation history. Interrogating Mary Magdalene's abiding association with sexual transgression, this chapter examines the Digby play's preoccupation with unruly masculine as well as feminine eros. The play represents gender as a crucial category through which forms of power may be differentiated in the earthly and sacred realms. Its vision of the gendering of sacred power, I contend, incorporates a well-developed Christology that highlights the divinity and nobility of Christ in his sapiential aspect and associates his humanity almost exclusively with his mother. As many readers of *Mary Magdalene* have observed, the Virgin Mary receives an unusual amount of attention in the play, especially considering that she never appears as a dramatic character. I trace the logic and genealogy of this perplexing feature of the play to Mary Magdalene, who, in biblical exegesis, liturgy, and sermons was not only identified with the Virgin Mary but also laid provocative claim to a virginity of her own. I argue that the play invokes Mary Magdalene's associations with the mother of Jesus to fashion a saint whose gender attributes as sexual woman and reconstituted virgin pose the possibility of symbolically mediating the differences between a sacred ideal of virginal maternity and the dangers and demands of gendered behaviors in the fallen, secular realm.

In Chapter 5 I revisit the formal dimensions of hagiographic drama introduced in chapter one. The tension between theology and aesthetics that is a central attribute of late medieval uses of dramatic and other religious images, I argue, parallels tensions within the symbolic construction of Mary Magdalene herself, whose late medieval identities are bound up with the questions that dominate a sacramental aesthetic: how can the spiritual be bodied forth in the physical? How can the divine be placed on the same level as the human? Drawing a comparison between the Digby *Magdalene* and the Chester cycle's *Coming of Antichrist*, I demonstrate that both plays employ conventions of the dramatic saint's life to critique the reliability of the dramatic image as a source of knowledge about and contact with the sacred. Versions of the Resurrection in all the English biblical cycles and the Digby saint play further inscribe the defining moment of Christian belief as an intimate, feminine encounter with the sacred. In these cultural texts Mary Magdalene's example signifies the enduring pressures that a corporeal femininity exerted upon understandings of scriptural history, institutional religion, and private devotion.

Subject to urgent questioning on the threshold of the Reformation, these issues are an important preoccupation of changing interpretations of Mary Magdalene by early sixteenth-century biblical commentators and religious reformers such as John Fisher and Jacques Lefèvre d'Étaples. They also figure in the saint's spiritual patronage of Elizabeth Barton, the Benedictine nun, visionary, and prophet who opposed Henry VIII's divorce. My conclusion addresses these emergent perspectives, tracing their affinities with and departures from the East Anglian Magdalenes examined in this study. Like their dramatic counterparts in particular, these early Tudor Magdalenes articulate cultural questions about the sacralizing of the material realm, the feminine role in salvation history, and the biblical foundations of women's religious and evangelical authority. In so doing they also illustrate the special problem that feminine spirituality and authority—legendary, symbolic, or historical— posed to dominant religious and political institutions under the watchful eye of reformers.

In pursuing the cultural significance of Mary Magdalene through the verbal medium of East Anglian dramatic texts, this book draws on a wide range of nondramatic primary resources, invoking biblical commentary from the early Christian period to the sixteenth century; Latin and vernacular sermons; hagiographical writing; Middle English religious and devotional texts; and humanist debates on the Bible. I also draw on the immense fund of visual resources attesting to late medieval understandings of Mary Magdalene, from northern European panel paintings to the painted rood screens and carved bench-ends of East Anglian parish churches. By engaging this variety of textual and visual resources, I hope to make evident the discursive and material ties of East Anglian dramatic texts and feminine religion to a broad tradition of cultural commentary and representation constellating around the figure of Mary Magdalene.

This book's focus on East Anglian theater and religious culture complements the preoccupations of several recent studies of Middle English drama. Sarah Beckwith investigates that drama's theological and sacramental complexity in *Signifying God: Social Relation and Symbolic Act in the York Corpus Christi Plays*; and Lawrence Clopper analyzes traditions of East Anglia theater in light of lay sponsorship of vernacular drama in *Drama, Play, and Game: English Festive Culture in the Medieval and Early Modern Period*. I have also found support and inspiration in Victor Scherb's *Staging Faith: East Anglian Drama in the Later Middle*

Ages, whose timely appearance just as this project was nearing completion galvanized many of my convictions about the dramatic traditions and religious culture of that region. This book's special interest in feminine interventions in religious culture also parallels that of recent studies focusing on feminine texts, representations, practices, and modes of religious experience in late medieval England.[48] Its concentration on the Digby saint play of *Mary Magdalene*, however, makes its general aims most consistent with important work of the past decade that has analogously pursued detailed analyses of major East Anglian texts in which issues of gender and religious culture dynamically converge: Karma Lochrie and Lynn Staley on the *Book of Margery Kempe*, Denise Baker on Julian of Norwich's *Revelation of Love*, and Sheila Delany on Bokenham's *Legendys of Hooly Wummen*.

While pointing out affinities between the aims of this book and recent work on drama, gender, and religious culture in late medieval England, I also want to state what lies outside the scope and interests of this project. *Mary Magdalene and the Drama of Saints* is neither a comprehensive study of the saint's cult in late medieval England nor a survey of Mary Magdalene's incarnations in late medieval religious culture. An exhaustive investigation of the saint whose medieval importance was surpassed only by that of the Virgin Mary can be found in Susan Haskins's *Mary Magdalen: Myth and Metaphor*, which examines biblical, exegetical, literary, historical, and visual materials related to the saint's cult from its origins to the present. More focused but still wide-ranging is Katherine Ludwig Jansen's *The Making of the Magdalen: Preaching and Popular Devotion in the Later Middle Ages*.[49] I share Jansen's attention to the saint's function in multiple late medieval symbolic economies and her construction as a figure who gives access to central theological, social, and political issues of late medieval religious culture. At the same time, the literary, critical, and historical goals of this book differ substantively from those of Jansen's important work.

As I have endeavored to analyze East Anglian dramatic texts as instances of late medieval religious culture, illustrations of theatrical practice, and articulations of a complex symbolism of feminine religion, I have consistently sought to understand dramatic versions of Mary Magdalene in relation to the claims of the historical moments that produced them. But I am also aware that analyzing past significances of a subject as symbolically resonant and overdetermined as Mary Magdalene also has a tendency to bleed into more present concerns, a function, perhaps of the "unruly diachrony" that makes itself evident in efforts to isolate a historical moment and its texts for synchronic investigation.[50] One such manifestation of this bleeding into the present involves the regularity with which contemporary feminist religious scholars invoke Mary Magdalene to point to early Christian traditions of feminine spiritual authority that they seek to recuperate for the contemporary world.[51] In the later part of the twentieth century, the symbolic example of Mary Magdalene was kept alive in popular fiction, music, and film; the early years of the twenty-first century find her the center of interest in electronic websites around the globe.[52] Though disparate in their interpretations and far-flung in time and space, these contemporary versions of Mary Magdalene frequently echo patterns of medieval cultural representation analyzed in this study. Building bridges between contemporary understandings of Mary Magdalene and her late medieval incarnations, this book demonstrates the contribution that historical critiques of gender and religion can make to present social concerns and cultural representations of feminine spiritual authority.

I

The Drama of Saints

ON THE EVE OF THE REFORMATION an anonymous East Anglian
dramatist working under unknown auspices produced the theatrically
demanding play on the life of Saint Mary Magdalene now preserved in
Bodleian Library MS Digby 133. The Digby *Magdalene* play presents the
version of the vita through which knowledge about Mary Magdalene
was principally made available to the later Middle Ages. This vita aug-
mented Gregory the Great's enormously influential sixth-century construction of the saint—which conflated the woman named Magdalene
who witnesses Christ's resurrection in all four gospels, the unnamed
sinner who anoints Jesus in the home of Simon the Pharisee, and Mary,
the sister of Martha and Lazarus—with legendary episodes that had
accrued to Mary Magdalene's biography as her cult expanded in the elev-
enth through thirteenth centuries. The anointer and witness of biblical
narrative and the apostle and hermit of the legendary expansions were
eventually consolidated by Jacobus de Voragine in the *Legenda aurea*.[1]

Ample evidence—in manuscript book and printed text—points to
late medieval familiarity with Jacobus's life of Mary Magdalene. The
1477 will of William Bruyn, chaplain of St. Stephen's, Norwich, provided for his copy of the *Legenda aurea* to be displayed in the parish
church for interested readers, one sign of the "exceptional [. . .] popular[ity]" of the work that Norman Tanner finds among bequests in wills
from late medieval Norwich.[2] The *Legenda aurea* had circulated widely
in Latin and the European vernaculars from the 1270s, and the advent
of printing brought the work into even broader distribution. Caxton's
Middle English version went through ten editions between 1483 and
1527, the very years that span the probable composition and copying of
the Digby saint play.[3]

Although correspondences between the Digby play and the traditional vita associated with Jacobus's legendary have long been acknowledged, the dramatic text's substantive departures from that influential

narrative are sufficiently numerous to prompt some critics to propose
that the playwright either drew upon other, unidentified, sources or, more
likely, imaginatively revised the vita for strategic ends.[4] What importantly emerges from these discussions of the saint play's differences
from Jacobus's vita is not a debate about the dramatic text's possible
sources, which in any case is likely to remain unresolved, but an effort
to map the textual horizons and expectations of late fifteenth- and early
sixteenth-century English dramatic audiences.

In a gesture thoroughly consistent with the rhetorical strategies of
sacred biography, the Digby saint play takes full advantage of the complexities of the biblical and legendary vita popularized by Jacobus and
interprets the life of Mary Magdalene in light of ideological commitments, symbolic interests, and spiritual practices of late medieval religion and society.[5] The Digby play's Magdalene exhibits a piety based on
visionary revelation and angelic communing with the deity that counters the play's representations of the sacramental authority and privilege
of the priesthood. Dramatic images of Mary Magdalene as contemplative and mystical lover of Christ valorize personal knowledge, interior
will, and individual experience as elements of a religious sensibility
in which the institutional church plays a diminished role. The saint's
dramatic roles as visionary and apostle also call to mind spiritual identities of medieval holy women and resonate with late medieval anxieties about feminine authority in mystical experience and the evangelical
sphere.

Much of this book is devoted to investigating the Digby playwright's important interventions in the well-known account of the
sinner-saint turned apostle and hermit. These interventions, I contend,
enter into explicit and implicit dialogues with East Anglian social and
religious traditions and with larger late medieval cultural formations.
This chapter addresses literary, methodological, and cultural contexts
for evaluating these dialogues, situating *Mary Magdalene* in relation
to key issues in medieval English drama studies and central features of
East Anglian religious culture. It proposes analyzing the play through
a revised critical and historical paradigm, one that is shaped by recent
arguments and advances in the study of late medieval religion and
hagiography. This chapter also assesses the interpretive potential of this
paradigm in light of exigencies and constraints involved in addressing
the relationship between East Anglian religious culture and dramatic
texts. As part of a new case for ways that these might profitably be

brought into dialogue with each other, I identify symbolic, institutional, and ideological points of contact between the discourses of dramatic hagiography and late medieval East Anglian society.

The Digby *Magdalene* and Medieval English Drama

By the time her vita came to be the principal subject of a major East Anglian play, Mary Magdalene had been occupying a host of starring and supporting roles in the religious drama of medieval Europe for nearly five hundred years. The Magdalene figure had gotten in on the ground floor, so to speak, of European drama with her appearance as one of the myrrophores in tenth-century performances of the *quem quaeritis* trope; thereafter, changes in her dramatic roles coincided with the expansion of her cult and virtually paralleled the growth of European drama itself.[6] Twelfth-century dramas such as the Tours *Ludus paschalis* and the thirteenth-century Benediktbeuern *Greater Passion* from the Carmina Burana manuscript expanded dramatic representation of Mary Magdalene, creating entirely new scenes for her life based on her role in the gospels and incorporating elements from scriptural exegesis and devotional texts.[7] Vernacular dramas from the later Middle Ages continued to accord a privileged position to the Magdalene: in France she was renowned for her *mondanité*, in Germany for her gossipy reporting of the Resurrection. In England she makes prominent appearances in all the biblical cycles as well as the meditative dramas preserved in Bodleian Library MS e Museo 160.[8]

With the exception of *Il Miracolo di Santa Maria Maddalena*, however, the Digby play is the only extant medieval dramatic text that depicts the saint's entire legendary life as well as her biblical career, and it alone offers such a highly embellished treatment of her vita.[9] Unique among the many medieval dramatic treatments of Mary Magdalene, the Digby play is nearly as anomalous in the annals of its own native English drama: along with its companion piece in Bodleian Library MS Digby 133, the *Conversion of Saint Paul*, it constitutes the sole surviving Middle English specimen of a kind of drama commonly termed saint or miracle plays.[10] In light of this scarcity of extant texts, the Digby saint plays have had to bear some large literary-historical burdens: they have been invoked as model instances of a dramatic genre whose very characteristics are hypothesized on the basis of their own idiosyncratic example.[11]

Suppositions about the generic kinds of early English drama—
morality and mystery as well as miracle—have notably informed interpretation of the Digby *Mary Magdalene*.[12] Because the play exhibits
characteristics of all three recognized "types" of drama, its manipulation
of the formal elements of saint's life, biblical history, and allegorical representation has been assessed in light of its contributions to a develop-
mental narrative of early English drama. Robert Weimann observes, for
instance, that because "*Mary Magdalene* . . . is a late play," its "elements
of synthesis may well reflect a process of decline in the original barriers
between the two genres [saint play and biblical cycle] rather than any
genetic constellation or any transitional link between miracles and mysteries."[13] Other efforts to situate the Digby saint play in English literary
history focus on a discursive and representational variety that makes it
"the most elaborate and demanding" or "most complex and interesting"
play in the extant corpus of early English drama.[14] Weaving together
hagiographical narrative, courtly discourse, mercantile and anticlerical
satire, scriptural texts, and contemplative and mystical idioms, *Mary Magdalene* unfolds on a stage in which dramatic action vacillates between
naturalistic representation, allegory, ritual, parody, and dreamscapes, all
pursued with great mechanical and technical virtuosity. Staging, in fact,
is the aspect of the play's complexity most often singled out for commentary.[15] The play *is* remarkably spectacular, providing for regular jour-
neying of human and divine messengers, sudden appearances and
disappearances of Jesus on earth and in heaven, a cloud that descends
from heaven to set a pagan temple on fire, seven devils that "dewoyde"
from Mary during the feast at the home of Simon the Pharisee, a floating ship that crosses the platea with saintly and regal cargo, visionary processions of Mary and angels scripted by Jesus, and the saint's elevation
into the clouds for her daily feedings with heavenly manna. Critical
approaches attentive more to the matter than the manner of the play's
representation have focused on its larger purposes as hagiographic drama,
framing Mary Magdalene's dramatic function in terms of her saintly
exemplarity. Thus she is figured as a "model Christian, male and female,"
a "representative of mankind," and a "paradigm of God's mercy."[16] More
recently, the Digby saint's role as "everyman" has had to make way for
a gender-oriented critique that recognizes the medieval Magdalene as an
important site for writing the history of the feminine subject.[17]

While it would be foolish to contest the significance of formal
eclecticism, exuberant theatricality, and potent exemplarity in the Digby

Magdalene, I want to suggest that the play's cultural agenda exceeds these important dimensions of text and performance. Much-warranted attention to the play's theatricality has meant that its textual subtleties and multiple registers, though often remarked, have yet to be analyzed in the context of late medieval devotion to the saints and East Anglian society and religious culture. Admittedly, hypotheses on the significance of the saint play as a textual entity in literary history and as a social and material event whose representations unfold in historical time have had a small knowledge base to draw from when constructing both generic and cultural contexts for the development and reception of the English saint play. Unlike the biblical cycles, for at least some of which substantial data survive attesting to the complex functions of these works as cultural performances, there exists little in the way of dramatic records or other documentary materials that might clarify our understanding of the English saint play as a literary genre and as a cultural artifact.[18]

On the basis of scattered extant dramatic records in English sources that make reference to the mounting of *ludi*, *miracula*, plays, games, and pageants on the feasts days of saints and other holy days and seasonal commemorations of the festive year, the saint or miracle play is often assumed to have been the most ubiquitous and long-lived of medieval English dramatic forms.[19] Lawrence Clopper's recent analysis of documentary records believed to furnish evidence of saint play production, however, has set in bold relief the uncertainty that attends reigning assumptions about the late medieval and Tudor saint play. Arguing that the narrative of English literary history that made the saint play the most popular type of medieval dramatic performance is based on critical misreadings of the terminology in which evidence of putative saint plays is articulated, Clopper asserts the unlikelihood that "there were ever many saint plays in England in the later medieval period up through the Reformation or during the reign of Mary." What we have believed to be saint plays, he maintains, were in fact "a variety of lay and clerical activities held on saints' feastdays" that involved festive play or enactment and/or the display of objects, shrines, and mechanical devices. Unlike the Digby *Mary Magdalene* and *Conversion of Saint Paul*, these *ludi*, *miracula*, and "plays" were not scripted dramas on the lives of the saints.[20]

Clopper's contention that the generic boundaries and performative contexts of the medieval English saint play are far less stable than has previously been supposed makes the Digby *Mary Magdalene* newly available as a complex text as well as an instance of cultural performance.[21] While attenuating the hermeneutic utility of the generic approach to early English drama, a revisionary conception of medieval cultural performances of saintly biography implicitly posits a medieval "saint play" of far more fluid and complex aims. The analysis of *Mary Magdalene* pursued here construes the play not simply as the dramatic life of a saint of the universal Church known principally for exemplary and admonitory sin and repentance but rather as text and performance that are, for example, as polemically engaged with questions of ecclesiastical authority as is the Croxton *Play of the Sacrament* and as implicated in contingent constructions of the spiritual life as is the morality *Wisdom*. Paradoxically, once we recognize *Mary Magdalene* and the *Conversion of Saint Paul* not as representative saint plays but as texts that in fact may be even more exceptional in the history of English literature than was previously thought, we can incorporate them into a reconfigured nexus of East Anglian dramatic texts that posits their common engagement with questions about gender roles, spiritual authority, and social and religious practice that were critically important to late medieval clergy and laity.

Looking beyond problematic categories that have slotted the saint play into a principally generic role in literary history, the analysis that I pursue here seeks to formulate new questions about the cultic, social, and ideological function of a unique and specifically situated dramatic text. Its effort to do so coincides with, and is inspired by, recent developments in the study of medieval sainthood and medieval drama. Up to now, studies of *Mary Magdalene* have tended to reproduce medieval ideologies of sainthood that elide historical differences in order to emphasize the larger designs of Christian history, an approach that is epitomized in Gregory of Tours's oft-quoted remark that "it is better to talk about the life of the saints than the lives of the saints."[22] New understandings of the role of the saints in the Middle Ages, however, have stressed ways in which hagiographic narrative and cultic practice, far from simply representing a stable, transhistorical realm of Christian values, participated in crucial ways in the production of social and political power.[23] As Patrick Geary notes, such engagements are possible because the "production of hagiography, that is, not only the authoring of texts but also their copying and dissemination, was intentional action, even if . . . the uses to which these texts were put, were not intended by the producers."[24] Similarly, recent investigations of the cultural functions of the social and ritual practices commonly embraced by the rubric "medieval English drama" have illuminated the complex ideological and political investments of dramatic texts and performances.[25] These developments in the study of both medieval sainthood and medieval drama urge us to view the Digby *Mary Magdalene* as an instance of dramatic hagiography that stands in dynamic relationship to the society that produced it, and to locate this demanding text in the larger analytic context that marks contemporary investigations of both medieval hagiographic materials and cultural performances.

The analytical procedure that I am proposing marks a departure from critical assessments that have emphasized the Digby saint play's congruence with a salvation history based on the authority of the universal Church, the Logos, and the sacraments.[26] According to this perspective, the sacred rites and communications depicted in *Mary Magdalene* contribute ultimately to an eschatological framework and constitute what Bush terms the play's "grand formalism": "[S]peech and action fit into a network of relationships that extends far beyond the history of the christological years and the continuing adventures of one saint. Feasting always bears comparison to the Eucharist and the 'final supper,' flattery and seduction always relate to prayer and preaching, bad rulers are dramatically associated with Satan, and so on." Sacred and secular time, past and present, heaven and earth collapse: "At the end of the play," Bush states, "there is only one place."[27] Scherb identifies a reinscription of salvation history that can be associated with the play's cultural moment: "The dramatist's portrayal of Church history is distinctly medieval in character, emphasizing both the Church's scriptural basis as well as the divinely sanctioned nature of the Church hierarchy."[28]

These characterizations of the larger symbolic and dramatic strategies of the Digby saint play properly identify its preoccupation with the circulation and reception of sacred signs. In privileging the absorption of such signifiers by a corporate and universal eschatological dramatic vision, however, these interpretations—while recognizing the "medieval" character of the play—preclude the posing of other, more historically specific questions about both the dramatic and cultural function of these signs. Bush's comment on the "literary praxis" of the play, in fact, tacitly renders such historical specificity irrelevant: "Events which make up the traditional literary and historical plot . . . are wrenched out of the narrow focus of the plot, and . . . are viewed as existential responses to the demands which God places upon all history. Their specific position within human time before x or after y, is unimportant."[29]

It is precisely the relationship of the Digby saint play's sacred signifiers to "human time" that this study seeks to establish by adding back into the textual equation the historical and material referents elided by the privileging of typology and eschatology. I shall argue that the play's biblicism and typological patterning, as well as its preoccupation with sources of religious authority, can sustain examination as elements of a dramatic discourse that critiques earthly relationships to sacred power. This analysis also responds to the claim that the play's projection of a unified, hierarchical Church founded in scripture and framed by salvation history is an identifying mark of its "distinctly medieval" character. By suggesting that the concept of the Church itself is subject to contestation in *Mary Magdalene*, my argument implicitly makes the "medieval" a locus of contending forces rather than a synonym for a single ecclesiological position.

Considering the extent to which scholars regularly acknowledge the political and social engagement of the so-called sixteenth-century Protestant "saint plays," it seems appropriate to accord similar investments to hagiographic dramatic material of only a few decades earlier.[30] If John Bale and Lewis Wager recognized that the saints functioned as potent signifiers for critical matters of religious belief and practice that had important social and political consequences, the Digby playwright could hardly have been unaware of the heightened and contradictory religious sensitivities that his paradoxical subject could arouse. No less than its reformist successors in the admittedly problematic dramatic tradition of the English saint play, the Digby *Mary Magdalene* bears witness to intensely fraught, highly situated uses of hagiography in the religious climate of late medieval and early Tudor England.

In Search of the East Anglian Saint Play: Methodological Issues

Understanding the Digby saint play's participation in that religious climate requires a double effort of reconstruction and imagination. From fragmentary textual, linguistic, and codicological evidence that may be constellated around the play, we can try to reconstitute something of its cultural context; at the same time we can also critically imagine how text and context mutually informed each other.[31] In the case of *Mary Magdalene*, frustratingly few pieces of information are available that might link the play to a particular place, person, or time. Given the play's theatrical ambitions, the fact that it has left no material traces is surprising, although such circumstances are typical for East Anglian dramatic texts.[32] How then can the Digby saint play be mapped onto the late medieval East Anglian cultural landscape?

Other artifacts of East Anglian religious culture can illuminate the methodological issues at stake in this effort. In his study of the "literary geography" of late medieval Norfolk, Richard Beadle discusses the haunting example of Lambeth Palace Library MS 505, which contains a copy of Michael de Massa's *Vita Christi*, made in 1430 by Edmund Sowthwell at the rectory of Salle, Norfolk:

> A visit to Salle itself, which lies about twelve miles north-west of Norwich, is very revealing, for there is no town or village, . . . only a large and very beautiful parish church in the Perpendicular style, standing alone amongst the fields and woods. Pevsner regarded St Peter and Paul, Salle as an exceptional church even by East Anglian standards, not only for the quality of its architecture, but also because its entire construction can be dated to the decades between about 1410 and 1440. So in 1430 Edmund Sowthwell might have looked up from his work in the now long-gone rectory, and seen the fine new church well advanced in construction; and he might likewise have seen the rector for whom he was working, William Wode, passing to and fro to celebrate divine office before what must have been a substantial congregation, if a church like Salle, with its almost cathedral-like feel, was being built to accommodate it. Today, St Peter and St Paul, Salle and Edmund Sowthwell's manuscript belong together as the most striking reminders of a complex social, economic, and cultural fabric which has otherwise left little trace of its existence.[33]

Beadle's account of Salle's magnificent parish church provides an analytic purchase on the Digby *Magdalene* text, which also now stands singularly removed from the "complex social, economic, and cultural fabric" that would make sense of it.

To a search for the "literary geography" of the East Anglian saint play, though, the parish church at Salle offers up more than the comparative example of magnificent dislocation from its medieval cultural matrix. The analogy between play and parish church can also be drawn in formal terms. Just as *Mary Magdalene* is well known for its eclectic inclusion of virtually every discursive mode, generic attribute, and theatrical device available to the medieval dramatist, St. Peter and Paul,

Salle contains one of just about every architectural feature and interior furnishing that can be found in a late medieval East Anglian parish church (fig. 1).[34] All of the compelling signatures of the region's parochial art and architecture still in evidence at Salle can be found, in more striking or better-preserved form, in one or another East Anglian parish church. Unusually at St. Peter and Paul, Salle, though, they are all there in a single spot. An enormous west tower affords entry to the church through a beautifully carved doorway, decorated by censing angels in the spandrels. At the west end stands an excellent sample of a furnishing that was virtually unique to East Anglian parish churches, the seven-sacrament font.[35] Salle's font is among the few that retain their covers; this one is massive and intricately carved. Still showing signs of the sacred monograms of Christ and Mary that once brightly adorned it, Salle's immense angel roof protects the church's late medieval treasures. The fifteenth-century wine-glass pulpit at the church's east end also retains some of its original paint. Like many celebrated East Anglian parish churches, St. Peter and Paul contains remains of a chancel screen, now in very poor

Figure 1. St. Peter and Paul, Salle, Norfolk. Nave looking west. Reproduced by permission of English Heritage. NMR.

condition, with images of apostles and doctors of the church. Salle also boasts two spacious porches, one of which is decorated with elaborate roof bosses, including an image of the green man, who also appears prominently in the Lady Chapel of Ely Cathedral. The church houses its share of memorial brasses, including one bearing an unusual cadaver image of John Briggs, who died in the early fifteenth century. Throughout St. Peter and Paul, carved in stone and memorialized in glass, are traces of armorial bearings that link the church to prominent East Anglian families such as the Mautbys and Pastons of Norfolk, the de la Poles, and William Bardolf of Suffolk, who fought with Henry V at Agincourt. The student of East Anglian drama is tantalized by fragmentary treasures such as the remains of a Four Daughters of God window in the north transept, a rare iconographic motif whose narrative dimensions figure prominently in the N-Town *Mary Play*.

Beadle's speculation about the substantial congregation that Southwell would have observed in the church at Salle is difficult to verify—the church guide points out that the parish probably never numbered more than two hundred people—but it is clear that families of substance—the Boleyns, Fountaines, and Briggs—employed wealth acquired in the wool trade to endow the building of this remarkable church.[36] Rich in "seeable signs," echoes of late medieval religious practice, and testimonies to individual and community self-expression, St. Peter and Paul, Salle furnishes a poignant allegory for the contextual problems encountered in the contemporary study of late medieval East Anglian theater. That endeavor must come to terms with texts floating free of their geographical and institutional auspices, dramatic manuscripts that laconically bear witness to the processes of their own complicated genesis, and long-lost traditions of dramatic production that possessed the requisite theatrical know-how and material resources to take on the ambitious spectacle of a *Castle of Perseverance* or a *Mary Magdalene*.

Through their common cultural dislocations, these impressive monuments to the late medieval East Anglian "theater of devotion" draw our attention to the ways in which the losses they represent may be conceptualized. Contemporary medieval studies has exhibited a determined interest in pointing out parallels between the losses that constitute the founding condition of studying the medieval past and postmodern theories—semiotic, materialist, and psychic—of cultural representation and the formation of subjectivity.[37] Paul Strohm has recently argued that postmodern theoretical understandings of the operations of language, representation, and cultural production, which underscore the instability of knowledge and truth claims, are fully compatible with historical concerns. Postmodern theory makes a space for historical inquiry, not "to probe the . . . depths but to restore . . . the fully contradictory variety . . . of the historical surface." Such historically minded endeavors do not seek to recover some lost unity of purpose but rather exactly the opposite, that is, to make some particular text or moment of that surface "'thinkable in its specificity.'"[38] The pursuit of historical meaning in a postmodern medieval studies posits neither the total recoverability of the past event nor the certitude of fully rendering up the past to present understanding.[39]

Although these debates about the prospects for historical inquiry in the practice of an inevitably postmodern medieval studies have transpired at some distance from the immediate concerns of medieval English drama scholarship, they impinge on the methodological strategies of a project such as this one, since virtually any approach to East Anglian theater will necessarily require confrontation of the palpable losses that I have invoked through the example of the parish church at Salle. This book's efforts at recuperation employ a variety of materials and modes of analysis to "solicit . . . [the] fragmented inner narratives" emerging from the silences that attend the "once material existence" of East Anglian dramatic artifacts. Guided by Gabrielle Spiegel's idea of the "social logic of the text"—the view that the "power and meaning of any given set of representations derive in large part from their social context and their relation to the social and political networks in which they were elaborated"—this book invokes key features of the Digby saint play's late medieval English and East Anglian environments to hypothesize some conditions of intelligibility for an elusive text that, like most East Anglian drama, has been notably resistant to historicizing.[40]

Not all late medieval East Anglian texts, however, present the same kind of obstacles to historical understanding as the Digby *Magdalene*. Nor do efforts to "solicit . . . [the] fragmented inner narratives" of the contemporary production and reception of these texts always require a self-consciously recuperative methodology. In some instances the pursuit of the "social logic" of East Anglian texts has relied on the idea of the author as a lived, historical person. Scholarly elaboration of the author figure, for example, has characterized much of the modern response to two late medieval East Anglian religious texts, a methodological procedure that can also shed light on cultural analysis of the Digby *Magdalene*.

Both Julian of Norwich's *Revelation of Love* and Margery Kempe's *Book* give the appearance of being comfortably grounded in a geographical context and historical moment. The Short Text of the *Revelation* makes reference to the "devoute womann" and "recluse atte Norwyche" named Julian and reports that in 1413 she is "ʒitt . . . onn lyfe." The text's concern for timekeeping—its notice of its subject's age at the time of the showings (thirty and a half years); of the date they occurred (8 May 1373); of the nearly twenty years that passed between the showings and the inner teaching she received regarding one of them—contributes to its representation of lived, historical experience.[41] The *Book of Margery Kempe* more insistently portrays its protagonist as product of and participant in specific fifteenth-century English and continental communities, peopled by historical personages of her day. Margery's encounters with major English ecclesiastical figures, such as Thomas Arundel, archbishop of Canterbury, and Philip Repingdon, bishop of Lincoln, and influential clerics such as Robert Spryngolde and Richard Caister, are among the many narrative gestures through which the *Book* creates an impression of historical authenticity.[42]

Representations of lived experience and the historical world in these texts have doubtlessly encouraged the scholarly impulse to fill in the late medieval record by fashioning more detailed biographies for the recluse at Norwich and the bourgeois wife and holy woman from Lynn. Thus, Julian becomes the probable nun or possible widow who entered a religious house at a young (or advanced) age and who, despite her claim to the contrary in the Short Text, received a sophisticated theological and biblical education that was completely consistent with traditions of monastic learning. This Julian's historical existence is assumed on the basis of late fourteenth- and early fifteenth-century bequests to an anchoress named Julian—in one instance at the parish church of the same name in Norwich. This is the Julian whose feastday is celebrated on May 8 in some Anglian dioceses and whose historical presence and example are commemorated in the post–World War II reconstructed church of St. Julian in Norwich, where contemporary visitors can contemplate her modern image in the stained glass window that adorns her "cell."[43] The medieval life of the historical Margery Kempe has likewise been embellished. Sanford Meech concluded his introduction to the Early English Text Society edition of the *Book* with a "tentative" chronology of key dates in her life, gleaned from internal references in the text and Hope Allen's expansive glosses. He also appended to the edition seventeen pages of "Extracts from Documents" to validate the historical existence of Kempe and her father, husband, and religious associates.[44]

The reading and interpretive practices that have contributed to the modern construction of Margery Kempe and Julian as medieval historical authors supported by life records and biographies have been encouraged by important, if limited, evidence of the late and post-medieval transmission of their texts that can be harmonized with the themes and interests of the texts themselves. Whereas the single extant version of Julian's Short Text survives in an anthology of late medieval devotional texts and translations that has clear ties to Carthusian production (British Library MS Additional 37790), the multiple versions of the Long Text are the work of seventeenth-century English recusants.[45] Rubrics and annotations in the single text of the *Book of Margery Kempe* (British Library MS Additional 61823) make clear that this manuscript also passed through Carthusian hands and provide important evidence of that text's late medieval reception. Extracts from the *Book* were published in 1501 by Wynkyn de Worde and anthologized in 1521 by Henry Pepwell, who attributed what had become the "*shorte treatyse of contemplacyon*" to "a deuoute ancres Margerye kempe of Lynne."[46] Because these snippets of information locate the texts of Julian and Margery in relation to known readers, copyists, and printers, they further install their authors in the historical world of late medieval England.

Still, the fact remains that the documentary record attesting to the historical existence of these writers and the contemporary production and circulation of their texts is indeed very slim. It was principally twentieth-century scholars and devotees who readily embraced the idea, first advanced by eighteenth-century Norfolk antiquarian Francis Blomfield, that the recluse Julian mentioned in the Short Text's introductory rubric and the medieval anchoress or recluse at St. Julian's in Norwich were the same person. Although Kempe's *Book* reports that its mystic and pilgrim heroine met with many of the prominent religious figures of her day, there is, as Sarah Rees Jones has recently observed, "no evidence outside the text that Margery Kempe, either author or subject, ever existed."[47] There are no contemporary witnesses to either Kempe's *Book* or Julian's *Revelation* as texts, a state of literary and historical affairs that makes Margery Kempe's meeting with Dame Julian, the anchoress in Norwich, one of the most phenomenal coincidences in all of Middle English literary history. The fifteenth-century auspices and circulation of these texts are therefore marked by almost as many lacunae as haunt the Digby saint play's late medieval location; yet these silences have not impeded scholarship from mapping the intricate relationship of their "authors" to late medieval constructions of gender, religion, and society. Moreover, the desire for a historically legible author, especially a female author, has been heuristically valuable in efforts to tease out the ideological and rhetorical complexity of both works. I broach this comparison between English mystical and dramatic texts, then, not to discount the critical processes that have embellished the historical portraiture of both authors but rather to level the interpretive playing field occupied by these three East Anglian works, and especially to suggest how the Digby *Magdalene*, though admittedly more untethered from its late medieval contexts than the other two texts, may provide just as rich and provocative a window on the late medieval literary, religious, and gender issues with which the *Revelation of Love* and the *Book of Margery Kempe* are so regularly affiliated.

Situating the Digby *Magdalene* in East Anglia

The Digby saint play can be assigned to East Anglia on the basis of its language: it contains all the identifying characteristics of the East Anglian dialect, with many inflections specific to Norfolk. The unique text of *Mary Magdalene* was probably copied in the first quarter of the sixteenth century (c. 1515–30), though aspects of its language suggest that the play may have been composed in the late fifteenth century.[48] It is included in a manuscript that contains Latin alchemical, magical, astrological, and religioliterary works; the sole surviving copies of the *Conversion of Saint Paul* and *Candlemas Day and the Killing of the Children of Israel*; and a substantial fragment of *Wisdom*, which is preserved in its entirety in the Macro manuscript (Folger MS V.a.354). A dramatic anthology rather like the Macro manuscript, Bodleian Library MS Digby 133 only achieved its present form in the seventeenth century, when other texts were added to the original volume comprising *Mary Magdalene* and several scientific and alchemical works. The *Magdalene* text is a "poor copy": it may be missing as many as thirty lines; speeches and speakers are confused in four places; lines are out of order; speeches are repeated; stage directions are copied in the wrong place; the rhymes are not always correct; a leaf is skipped. Editors Baker, Murphy, and Hall speculate that the scribe may have had a bad exemplar or that he worked under stressful conditions, even at one point interjecting an exasperated "Jhesu mercy" (f. 129r).[49]

Despite the composite character of the manuscript, the plays preserved in Digby 133 bear important similarities to each other. They are all the work of East Anglian scribes; three of the four—including *Mary Magdalene*—bear the initials or signature of Myles Blomefylde, the sixteenth-century book collector, alchemist, and churchwarden of Chelmsford, Essex who is believed to have inscribed the initials himself. Painstaking reconstruction of Blomefylde's library by Digby editors Baker and Murphy indicates his eclectic taste in books: in addition to the Digby saint plays and other dramas (he possessed the single extant copy of Henry Medwall's *Fulgens and Lucrece*), he owned alchemical and scientific treatises, and works on geography, mathematics, and religious apologetics.[50] Blomefylde's signature on the *Magdalene* manuscript constitutes the single piece of codicological evidence from which we might construct an East Anglian paper trail for the play. This paper trail is intersected by many paths that link the plays in the Digby manuscript with each other and with Bury St. Edmunds, the prosperous Suffolk town not far from the Norfolk border that was home to one of the wealthiest and most powerful Benedictine monasteries in medieval England.[51] One hypothesis about the ownership of the Digby plays proposes that Myles, who was born in Bury, acquired them from William Blomfeld, his senior by many years. The elder Blomfeld was also an alchemist and, more interesting, a monk at Bury. Having achieved notoriety as a dissenting preacher, William was charged with heresy in 1529. The alchemists Blomefylde and Blomfeld obviously knew each other and may even have been related: Myles's notations regarding William's professional and learned accomplishments on his copy of William's alchemical treatise, *The Regiment of Life*, are a major source of knowledge about the elder Blomfeld.[52]

Bury St. Edmunds may have provided a common point of contact for the textual transmission of all of the Digby plays, but the geographical location and cultural auspices of *Mary Magdalene* nonetheless remain an utterly vexed issue. The play's panoramic scope and ambitious theatrical displays have inspired speculations that it hailed from a city "of major size and considerable dramatic experience" or a "prosperous market town" capable of gathering the mixed audience to which it seems to appeal.[53] Chelmsford, Norwich, King's Lynn, Ipswich, and Lincoln have all been suggested as possible homes for the play.[54] To be sure, speculations about origins are fraught with practical as well as theoretical dangers, but they are heuristically useful because they can direct attention to the kind of cultural environment, as well as the kinds of audiences, to which the text seems to bear witness.

One attribute of that cultural environment may be discerned in the Digby saint play's promotion of an image of holiness that is marked by the congruence of religious and economic discourses and practices in late medieval society. These distinctive features of *Mary Magdalene* parallel those of other late medieval East Anglian dramatic texts, which regularly privilege ethical and spiritual dilemmas that also encode social and material concerns. For example, the *Castle of Perseverance*, *Mankind*, and *Wisdom*, and the Croxton *Play of the Sacrament* uniformly yet creatively articulate the self-understandings of a prosperous society in which economic ambitions and religious values could both conflict with and affirm each other. More specifically, the Digby *Magdalene* examines the compatibility of spiritual values and economic interests pursued by prosperous lay groups, exploring the relationship of contemplative piety, religious poverty, and charity to a dynamic social world that embraced the opportunities of the market, the worthiness of commerce, and the responsible use of inherited wealth. As I have argued elsewhere, the play delineates and critiques ways in which economically powerful aristocrats, gentry, and burghers of late medieval England sought an accommodation between such spiritual values and active pursuit of their own material interests.[55] These social groups are precisely those identified by Gibson as comprising the audiences for and patrons of the region's devotional theater; they are also groups whose affiliations with East Anglian dramatic performance are consistently registered in the rhetorical positioning of the extant dramatic texts.[56]

The intersecting material and spiritual values articulated by the Digby saint play furnish an avenue for informed speculation about the play's cultural auspices, on which prominent themes of the cult and vita of Mary Magdalene can also be brought to bear. One intriguing and unremarked possibility involves the congruence of these dramatic values with late medieval ideologies of poverty and charity, particularly as these were expressed for and by lay society in practices of almsgiving and care of the indigent. From its representation of the saint's preaching on the theme *"paupertas est donum Dei"* to its modeling of charitable practices by the king and queen of Marseilles, to its heroine's embrace and then sacrifice of her worldly "lyflode," *Mary Magdalene* is a play saturated with discourses and images associated with late medieval conceptions of poverty and charity. In late medieval England the ideology of charity and the cult of Mary Magdalene converged in the hospital, the cultural institution most devoted to fostering charitable values and practices and to promoting, through its rounds of prayers and almsgiving, the spiritual health of its benefactors while also attending to the bodily sickness of its inmates.[57] Mary Magdalene was a frequent dedicatee of the medieval hospital because of associations with healing, cleansing, and anointing that figured prominently in her conflated scriptural vita: she was the profligate woman linked with leprosy, the disease of lechers; the sinner purged of seven devils; the sister of the dead and resurrected Lazarus; and the follower of Christ who sought to anoint his body at the tomb.[58] Hospital foundations dedicated to Mary Magdalene were established in the major urban centers of late medieval Norfolk, including two of the towns—Norwich and King's Lynn—suggested as possible locales for the Digby saint play.[59]

Mary Magdalene exhibits thematic preoccupations and theatrical images that, viewed collectively, stunningly resonate with the spiritual ideology and activities of the late medieval hospital. Dramatic representation of the saint's life seems designed to underscore the fundamental congruence of physical and spiritual health that medieval religiomedical discourse articulated through the concept of a "heavenly medicine" whose premier practitioner was *Christus medicus*, Christ the physician.[60] This divine medicine underwrote the hospital's practical work as an institution dedicated to healing of souls as well as bodies and its theoretical foundations as a locus of charitable activity redounding to the benefit of its patrons.[61] From the outset the dramatic saint's conversion and repentance are imaged in metaphors of illness and healing: after she anoints Jesus in the home of Simon the Pharisee, he pronounces her "hol [healthy] in sowle" (677), and she affirms her recovery of "[s]owle helth" (693). The converted Magdalene praises Jesus as the "helth and medsyn" against her sickness (681) and the "oyle of mercy [that] hath helyd myn infyrmyte" (759). Martha echoes the idiom of this praise, declaring Jesus "sokour" "[t]o alle synfull and seke" (763); then Lazarus is stricken ill, and his sisters promise to seek "leches" (787) for his "cure" (793), namely, the "Prophe[t] [that] to hym hatt grett delectacyon"

(791). Divided by notice of Lazarus's death and split between two speakers, this stanza picks up the *Christus medicus* trope that also punctuates Mary Magdalene's conversion and repentance:

> LAZARUS. A! In woo I waltyr as wawys in þe wynd!
>> Awey ys went all my sokour!
> A, Deth, Deth, þou art onkynd!
>> A! A, now brystyt myn hartt! Þis is a sharp showyr!
> Farewell, my systyrs, my bodely helth!
>> *Mortuus est.*
> MARY MAGDALEN. Jhesu, my Lord, be yower sokowre,
> And he mott be yower gostys welth! (819–25)

Even the rhyme plays on the metaphoric congruence of physical and spiritual wellness, Lazarus's farewell to "bodely helth" finding acknowledgment in his sister's hope for his "gostys welth." Tropes of physical and spiritual sickness and healing recur in the Marseilles episode, which reprises Christ's raising of Lazarus with Mary Magdalene's preservation of the queen who is left to die in childbed, an outcome that the king acknowledges by conflating the spiritual "sokore" furnished by Christ, the Virgin Mary, and Mary Magdalene: "Heyll be þou, Mary! Ower Lord is wyth the! / The helth of ower sowllys, and repast contemplatyff!" (1939–40).

The arrangement of episodes and stage spectacle reinforce these verbal preoccupations, concretely representing values and charitable practices associated with the late medieval hospital. Such values offer a social and spiritual rationale for the early scene elaborating Mary Magdalene's domestic comfort in the home of her worldly father Cyrus, who, as specified in the saint's traditional vita, is shown dividing his properties among his children in vague anticipation of his inevitable "dysses" (80). Cyrus's wealth is sufficient to set "all . . . [his] posteryte" "in solas from al syyng sore" with the gift of a "lyfelod worthy" (63–64, 87), a gift that promises, according to Lazarus and Mary Magdalene, deliverance from "all nessesyte," release from "peynys of poverte," and a "preseruatyff from streytnes" (88, 96–97). Unparalleled in the Middle English Magdalene literature, this exchange is punctuated by the medieval discourse on poverty that underwrote charitable endeavors: Mary Magdalene and her siblings will be spared all the physical want or "need" whose amelioration sanctioned the mechanisms for, and promised spiritual benefit to, persons performing acts of charity. While Cyrus's gesture inspires the family's momentary celebration of "joye wythowtyn weryauns" (92), it also furnishes an occasion for Martha to consider its more long-term reward: Cyrus's effort to "meyntyn" his children prompts her hope that her father will be "[h]ey in heuen awansyd . . . / In blysse, to see þat Lordys face / Whan ye xal hens passe!" (106–9).

This episode provides a context, in social ideology, for the demise that both Cyrus and Martha have anticipated. After an abrupt switch of scene that takes the dramatic action to the courts of Caesar, Herod, and Pilate (114–264), the play returns just as abruptly to Cyrus as he "takyt hys deth" (s.d. 264). Occurring without warning in the space of two brief stanzas, Cyrus's end epitomizes the horror of the *mors improvisa*, the unforeseen death that caught both body and soul unaware and, it was feared, unprepared: "Her avoydyt Syrus sodenly" (s.d. 276).[62] As a dramatic event, Cyrus's demise also provides the opportunity for graphic portrayal of death's physical realities. Mary Magdalene's traditional vita may have called for the mortal passing of Cyrus and Lazarus, but the Digby saint play has them expire only after displaying symptoms that seem to indicate identifiable illness. The sudden onset of death brings "drede" to Cyrus and renders him "trobyllyd, both bak and syde." "Now, wythly help me to my bede," he asks, lamenting the pain that "rendyt . . . [his] rybbys." (269–71). A little later in the play, Lazarus dies almost as quickly but presents a different set of symptoms. He is struck at the "hart" and complains of weakness, dizziness, buzzing in his head, and what seems to be the approach of unconsciousness: "A, I faltyr and falle! I wax alle onquarte! / A, I bome above, I wax alle swertt!" (779–80).[63] No other medieval English play stages more deaths than the Digby saint play: in the postbiblical, legendary portion of the action, the queen of Marseilles dies in childbirth (1753–65), and at the end of the play Mary Magdalene expires, uttering portions of the liturgical rite for the dying.[64] As physiological, spiritual, and ritual processes, death and dying repeatedly inflect the play's portrayal of the life of Mary Magdalene.

These spectacles of illness and death and the play's investment in ideologies of poverty and charity constitute a meeting ground for dramatic preoccupations of the Digby *Magdalene* and the cultural values and social activities of the late medieval hospital.[65] To be sure, no documentary records connect the Digby play to the hospitals of late medieval East Anglia; nor can any late medieval hospital foundation be linked to the performance of a saint or any other type of scripted play.[66]

But as an institution whose spiritual functions—its maintenance of worship supported by and for its benefactors—were often given priority over its responsibilities for patient care, the hospital as a locus of liturgical and ceremonial activity merits our attention, if not as a space for scripted drama at least as a place where performative aspects of religious expression found a venue in the late medieval theater of devotion.[67] Rawcliffe's magisterial history of the Hospital of St. Giles, or Great Hospital, in Norwich establishes the wealth, cultural sophistication, and artistic excellence of one such foundation, where a string of university graduates served as master and an important late fourteenth-century expansion of the church fabric, including the building of a magnificent chancel, widened the scope and opportunity for ceremony.[68] The richest hospital in the county, St. Giles's rivaled major collegiate churches, with provisions for prayer, service, and ceremony; by 1397 it was home to twelve chaplains and at least seven choristers. Some vestige of this ceremonial life is conveyed in the hospital's late fourteenth-century illuminated processional, which contains nine unique diagrams that show how liturgical processional activities were to be conducted, including the positions of their participants and the location of their liturgical props.[69] The processional affords a rare glimpse of the taste for ritual and spectacle that enlivened the performance of the ideology of charity and religiomedical discourse in one prosperous late medieval urban site.

Like the collegiate church, the late medieval hospital was an institution whose spiritual pursuits epitomized the convergence of material practice, religious intention, and worldly motivation that proved anathema to reformers. Perhaps we can attribute to such animus the destruction of records that might have indicated how developed or extensive the performative activities of such institutions may have been, or how they made formal or informal alliances with their wealthy, influential lay benefactors to pursue modes of ritual performance that would look more like what we would consider "drama."[70] Hence, this hypothesis linking the Digby *Mary Magdalene* to the charitable ideologies and religiomedical values of the late medieval hospital is likely to remain exactly that, and in offering it I by no means want to conflate documented uses of liturgical ceremony, such as those at St. Giles's, with performance of narrative dramas in Middle English. Nonetheless, I have explored this hypothesis at some length because it adds a new prospect to the inventory of cultural auspices invoked as possible venues for the Digby saint play and because it localizes the articulation of a late medieval question—

"why and how can one provide for the needs of body and soul?"—to which the saint play appears to tender an answer.

Positing affinities between the cultural values and social functions of the late medieval hospital and dramatic representation of similar interests and concerns draws support from the hospital's devotional and communal functions in prosperous urban environments, where such institutions represented the commingling of lay and monastic societies and spiritualities that Gibson has identified as a signature of East Anglian religious culture and drama. The fundamental coherence of this culture parallels that of the eremitic movement among clergy, magnates, and gentry that Jonathan Hughes has located in the fourteenth- and early fifteenth-century diocese of York.[71] Just as Hughes attributes important instances of religious cultural production in the late medieval diocese of York to the widely dispersed work and ideals of "pastors and visionaries," the distinctive character of late medieval East Anglian religious culture is now increasingly recognized as a crucial factor in analyzing specific texts, performances, and iconography of the region. Attentive simultaneously to contemplative ideals and to the demands of the material world and social life, the hybrid spirituality of late medieval East Anglia made room for a range of options. It embraced both the exuberant orthodoxy that Tanner situates in late medieval Norwich and an eclectic tolerance that enabled beliefs and habits of polemical nonconformity to exist side by side for decades with mainstream pieties, evidenced by the patronage of religious houses and foundations, the flourishing of parish church and religious guild, the popularity of sacred shrines and images, and fervent devotion to the saints.[72]

This vital, performative hybridity is captured in Tanner's report of the colorful career of Thomas Scrope, who

entered the Carmelite friary in Norwich as an ordinary friar but, according to John Bale, left it and was to be seen around 1425 'clad in a hair shirt and a sack and girded with an iron chain, preaching the gospel of the kingdom of God and proclaiming that the new Jerusalem, the bride of the Lamb, was about to come down from heaven. . . .' Bale said that his eccentric behavior angered Thomas Netter, the prior-provincial of the English Carmelites, and a frightened Scrope returned to the friary. . . . He remained there as an anchor probably for about twenty years. . . . He then reverted to an active life. He went to Rhodes as legate of Pope Eugenius IV, was consecrated bishop of Dromore of Ireland, acted as suffragan bishop in the diocese of Norwich for twenty-eight years and finally, according to Bale, spent each Friday of the last years of his life as a barefoot itinerant preacher in the diocese of Norwich, dying in 1492 aged almost a hundred.[73]

Scrope's histrionic mingling of penitence and prophecy, eremitic private devotion and public preaching, resembles the Digby saint play's complex representation of forms of holiness imaged by the figure of Mary Magdalene. His example invites pursuit of East Anglian explanations for these provocative, mobile pieties.

Aspects of East Anglian society and religious expression can be brought to bear more specifically on distinctive features of *Mary Magdalene*, filling in the picture of local habits and behaviors on which the play seems to capitalize. The very existence of such an ambitious drama devoted to representing the saint's complete biblical and legendary life coincides with the important presence, in Norwich, King's Lynn, and other East Anglian towns, of the Franciscans and Dominicans, whom Jansen terms "the greatest disseminators of the Magdalen cult in Christendom."[74] Both orders had large establishments in Norwich, the scale of which can be discerned from the surviving fabric of the Blackfriars' church.[75] Well into the early decades of the sixteenth century, the Norwich Franciscan friary was still serving as an international *studium*, attracting friars from abroad who came there to learn theology; the school of philosophy at the nearby house of Austin friars also attracted international visitors.[76] Cambridge University provided many opportunities for contact and exchange between English and German Dominicans.[77] The Digby play exhibits an awareness of traditions of learned commentary on the saint and important contemporary debates about visionary experience that suggest its compatibility with the kind of intellectual climate available in late medieval Norwich or Cambridge. Yet the impact of these important intellectual centers upon the formation and dissemination of local late medieval piety and religious practice is rarely taken into account when products of East Anglian popular religious culture such as the Digby saint play are studied. Margery Kempe's idiosyncratic penchant for conversing with doctors of divinity and bachelors of theology notwithstanding, late medieval East Anglia also afforded the average lay person opportunities to come into contact with these purveyors of learning. Thomas Tyard, a bachelor of theology and fellow of Corpus Christi College, Cambridge, who "moved in learned, even humanist, circles," spent his entire clerical living at the parish of Bawburgh, Norfolk, the site of the shrine of local patron of farmers and laborers, Saint Wulstan, and remained close to the parish until his death in 1506.[78] In 1466 well-to-do yeoman John Townshend of Raynham passed his final days in the company of a local doctor of theology, Denys

Holkham, a graduate of Cambridge and friar of the local Carmelite house at Burnham Norton.[79]

A compelling picture of such contacts has recently been brought to light by Mary Erler, whose research on female reading and book ownership fills in this spiritual profile of late medieval Norwich, where a "lively exchange between male and female devout persons whether lay or religious, the high number of parishes, the strong local identity, [and] the influence of continental religious developments . . . produced an atmosphere especially stimulating to the religious life."[80] This "devout society," in Erler's phrase, is exemplified in the wills of prominent widows such as Margaret Purdans (d. 1481) and Katherine Kerre (d. 1497), and the hermit Richard Ferneys (d. 1464). Their bequests—of financial support, books, and sacred objects—reveal patterns of social and spiritual activity that interweave the prosperous late medieval widow with the vowess, anchoress, hermit, and cloistered nun, and identify cultural gestures that are largely focused on feminine roles, spiritual vocations, and communities. At the same time, the will of the exceptional Purdans records her significant relationships with Cambridge doctors of theology. As Erler notes, Purdans's "manifold connections form the outlines of two worlds: a male clerical and learned culture in which she occupied a place, and a female culture running parallel to it, to which she also belonged"—a cultural experience that parallels social forms observable elsewhere in late medieval East Anglia and ideologies of gender and spiritual authority in the Digby saint play.[81]

Mary Magdalene may also bear witness to opportunities available in late medieval East Anglia for cultural and economic exchange with northern Europe.[82] Alexandra Johnston has even suggested that the Digby plays "may owe a debt to the Low Countries" that can be traced from their one-time possessor, Miles Blomefylde, to William Blomfeld, lapsed Bury monk and later vicar of St. Simon and St. Jude in Norwich who was known for his "facility with the Dutch language."[83] The only extant late medieval plays on the saint's life that approach the ambitions of the Digby *Magdalene—Il Miracolo di Santa Maria Maddalena* and *La vie de Marie Magdaleine par personages*—are continental dramas, and the spectacular visual effects of the East Anglian saint play bear more resemblance to continental traditions of staging than they do to English ones.[84]

Of the international influences making a mark on late medieval East Anglian religious culture, however, none is more relevant to *Mary*

Magdalene than the region's ties to devotional traditions identified with continental holy women. The extraordinary dependence of Margery Kempe's *Book* on themes and anecdotes from the devotional texts and vitae of these women is perhaps the most famous illustration of this important feature of the late medieval East Anglian religious land- scape.[85] Pondering how the pious woman from Lynn would have en- countered such influences, Susan Dickman suggests that Margery Kempe's "inspiration must have been in the air"; but enough is known about the actual human conduits of continental traditions of feminine piety to postulate that their influence in East Anglia was neither amorphous nor haphazard.[86] In the late fourteenth and early fifteenth centuries, East Anglian clergy figured prominently in efforts to advance the cult and works of the two most influential continental holy women of the late Middle Ages, Catherine of Siena and Bridget of Sweden. Augustinian friar and Cambridge bachelor of theology William Flete was a close friend and hagiographer of Catherine of Siena. Cardinal Adam Easton, a former monk of the cathedral priory of Norwich, played an influential role in Bridget's canonization.[87] Carmelite and Cambridge doctor of divinity Alan of Lynn compiled indices for the *Revelationes Brigittae* and the *Prophetiae Brigittae*; he is probably best remembered, however, as the "Master Aleyn" whose friendship Margery Kempe records in her *Book*.[88] The attraction to continental models of feminine piety in late medieval East Anglia is stunningly memorialized in the depiction—extremely rare for England—of both Bridget and Catherine on the rood screen of the parish church at Horsham St. Faith, Norfolk (figs. 2 and 3).[89]

Margery Kempe's devoted friendship with the Cambridge doctor of theology and indexer of St. Bridget represents a form of cultural exchange that was nourished by these rich and productive traditions of local female piety.[90] Insular devotion to continental holy women such as that exemplified in the saintly images of the Horsham St. Faith rood screen would have found a hospitable venue in the East Anglian clerical and lay communities whose investments in feminine pieties were as deep as they were wide-ranging.[91] Late medieval East Anglia laid claim to more anchoresses and female recluses and a greater concentration of female religious houses than any other area of England. It was home to the only known medieval English female mystics and a vital center of the insular cults of the Virgin Mary and her mother, Saint Anne.[92] In the fifteenth century it emerges as an unacknowledged hub for the production of texts linked to female devotion and feminine constructions

Figure 2. Saint Bridget of Sweden. Rood screen, St. Andrew and the Blessed Virgin, Horsham St. Faith, Norfolk. Reproduced by permission of English Heritage. NMR.

Figure 3. Saint Catherine of Siena. Rood screen, St. Andrew and the Blessed Virgin, Horsham St. Faith, Norfolk. Photo: T. Coletti.

of the sacred: Bokenham's unique all-female legendary, Capgrave's *Life of Saint Katherine*, Lydgate's *Life of Our Lady*, and dramas such as the N-Town *Mary Play*, the Digby *Candlemas Day and the Killing of the Children of Israel*, and, of course, *Mary Magdalene*. The rood screen images of Horsham St. Faith reinforce what local cultic practices and these extant hagiographic and dramatic texts also underscore: that in their devotions, rituals, dedications, and offerings, late medieval East Anglians promoted and honored feminine sources of sacred power.

To express these commitments they turn frequently to Mary Magdalene. Julian of Norwich and Margery Kempe draw inspiration from her rejection of sin and her intimacy with Christ. Bokenham makes her vita the centerpiece of his legendary. The morality *Wisdom* appropriates the image of Mary Magdalene's corporeal purgation to figure the plight of every sinful soul. While the N-Town *Passion* foregrounds the saint's apostolic role, her contemplative identity modeled the ideals of women's religious communities across the region. The next chapter examines this extraordinarily diverse yet ideologically coherent assembly of East Anglian Magdalenes.

Some East Anglian Magdalenes

Here shall entyr þe þhre Mariis arayyd as chast
women, wyth sygnis of þe passyon pryntyd ypon þer
brest. . . .

—Digby *Mary Magdalene*

THE STAGE DIRECTION FROM the Digby saint play that furnishes the
epigraph for this chapter simultaneously captures the moment preceding the discovery of Christ's resurrection in all the gospels and emphatically moves the dramatic agents of that discovery into the late medieval
world.[1] Like other occasions in *Mary Magdalene* when clothing signals
important developments in the saint's unfolding spiritual biography, the
stage direction encodes the narrative and symbolic complexity of the
Magdalene figure whom the gospels preeminently identified as anointer
of Christ's body.[2] The stage direction's notice of the "sygnis of þe passion," or *arma christi*, emblazoned on the breasts of the three Marys
invokes that body with an incisive iconic condensation of events that
the play does not stage.[3] Despite the great interest in the life of Christ
shown by the Digby saint play, its dramatic action eschews representation of the Passion. Instead, the play moves quickly from the raising of
Lazarus to the visit to the tomb and first acknowledges the Crucifixion
through the defeated devil who reports both the Harrowing of Hell and
the Resurrection (963–92). The dramatic image of the three Marys who
approach the sepulcher bearing the *arma christi* on their breasts thus
stands in for the entire Passion narrative.

Critical commentary on the Digby stage direction has stressed its
relation to the play's larger spiritual and narrative strategies. Jerome
Bush states that the imprinting of the "sygnis of þe passyon" on the
breasts of the three Marys contributes to a dramatic emphasis on personal, immediate testimony to faith.[4] Scott Boehnen finds in the Marys'
arma christi an implicit reference to the badges recommended to late

medieval pilgrims returned from Jerusalem.[5] Neither of these interpretations addresses the direction's evocative specification for costuming: the three Marys are to be "arayyd as chast women." A straightforward simile articulates a cluster of cultural codes that appear to require no elaboration. The phrase assumes common knowledge about who such women are and what they would look like, and in so doing aligns the biblical Marys with late medieval modes of living and constructions of social identity.

Mary Erler's important work on intersecting religious and social identities available to late medieval women illuminates the social classification and the attire recognized by the Digby stage direction.[6] In late medieval England the term "chaste woman" most commonly designated the vowess, a lay woman, often but not always a widow, who had chosen to pursue a chaste life in the world by taking a formal vow in the presence of a bishop or other ecclesiastical authority. The vowing ceremony focused on the woman's pledge and her assumption of symbolic apparel—the veil, wimple, mantle, and ring that marked her social and spiritual state, the very sort of "array" highlighted by the stage direction. The vowed state of chastity appears to have been an appealing option for increasing numbers of women in late medieval England; it had the potential to secure spiritual capital, social power, and economic—and possibly psychological—independence.[7] For the well-to-do widows in particular who were its most common adherents, the vowed state provided opportunities to cross social categories and identities. The ceremony that established the widowed vowess's vocation resembled that of religious profession, but she was neither nun nor wife; she was chaste but not virginal. The vowess typified the "permeable partition" between lay and religious spheres in the late medieval female social formation.[8]

Even more relevant to the Digby stage direction are the larger patterns of late medieval female spirituality in which the social category "vowess" was implicated. Recent work on the social organization of female religious life in the diocese of Norwich has identified a "disproportionately large population of religious women" in that region. Roberta Gilchrist and Marilyn Oliva cite women living communally as cloistered nuns and hospital sisters, individually as anchoresses and vowesses (they count as many as seventy-three of the former and twelve of the latter), and informally in small groups, thus underscoring how the diversity of East Anglian female religious vocations extends the potential application of the term "chaste" to women other than vowesses.[9]

Adherence to chastity was expected, for example, of the "sisters" who provided care in many medieval hospitals and also received from those institutions alms and other types of support. The foundation charter of the Hospital of St. Giles, Norwich stipulates that there "shall . . . be three or four women . . . of good life and honest conversation, . . . being fifty years old or a little less, to take good care of all the infirm." The "array" of these "chaste women" included "white tunics and grey mantles and . . . black veils." In addition to vowing continence, the sisters observed the monastic life of the hospital foundation.[10] Gilchrist and Oliva cite evidence of women engaged in this quasi-religious capacity in thirteen different hospital establishments in the diocese of Norwich, including locations in major towns such as King's Lynn, Bury St. Edmunds, and Yarmouth, and smaller centers such as Swaffham, Walsoken, and Beccles.[11]

The situation at St. Paul's or Norman's Hospital in Norwich sheds light on the social roles and functions of these hospital sisters. They were a vital focus of charitable giving in the late medieval city; nearly one-third of the citizens making wills between 1370 and 1532 left them at least a small bequest.[12] St. Paul's was the only hospital in Norwich that catered to pregnant women and nursing mothers, groups often excluded by statute from other charitable establishments because they were imagined to carry with them the threats of defilement elaborated by misogynist discourses.[13] In the overlapping religious and medical ideologies of these institutions, the requirement for chastity and continence on the part of hospital sisters also was bound up with traditional views about women as sources of physical pollution and temptation.[14] The "chaste women" at St. Paul's and the pregnant women and mothers who numbered among their charges thus make that institutional environment a rich locus for female experience and feminine symbolism in late medieval Norwich.

In addition to women living as vowesses and hospital sisters, Gilchrist and Oliva have drawn attention to a number of small female religious communities in Norwich and Ipswich, whose existence is attested by bequests to "sisters dedicated to chastity," "sisters under religious vow," *mulieres paupercule* and *sorores commeranti*. As Tanner first pointed out, such designations suggest these groups' resemblance to the continental beguinages, informal communities of women dedicated to labor, poverty, and charity who formed an important part of the urban landscape in northern France, the Low Countries, and the Rhineland in the later Middle Ages.[15] Cultural ties between East Anglia and north-ern Europe were sufficiently frequent and important to allow for migra-tion, across the channel, of the "religious creativity" demonstrated by continental *mulieres sanctae*.[16] The informality and ambiguity of these East Anglian communities make them difficult to categorize; Gilchrist and Oliva cite their apparent social fluidity as evidence of "a possible indigenous tradition of female piety, which flourished outside the theo-logical and spiritual practices ordained by the Church."[17]

This newly emergent portrait of that piety points to the range of associations that the Digby saint play's "chaste women" would have activated for lay and religious audiences in the region. Teasing out the cultural semiotics of that stage direction enables us to see how East Anglia's rich and varied traditions of female piety offered occasions in which the conditions of women's religious experience could be assimi-lated to the figure of Mary Magdalene, whose example "bound to-gether" the penitence and asceticism that were central attributes of late medieval women's traditional and alternative religious vocations.[18] The overlapping values of these vocations echo in the spiritual portrait of the Digby play's saint, the well-born daughter of a wealthy family who eventually embraces a quasi-religious life *in herimo*, dedicating herself to humility, patience, charity, and "abstynens, all dayys of my lyfe" (1994).[19]

The Digby stage direction thus urges attention to the embedding of dramatic iconography and saintly identity in the signs, discourses, and social formations of late medieval religious culture. The announce-ment that Mary Magdalene and her companions appear as "chaste women" signals the play's effort to make its version of the saint con-gruent with late medieval possibilities for imagining feminine holiness. As a cultural gesture, the stage direction participates in late medieval hagiography's larger effort to resignify the vitae of biblical and legend-ary saints to suit the values and desires of new, devout publics. John Capgrave's *Life of Saint Katherine* and Osbern Bokenham's *Legendys of Hooly Wummen* furnish two other important East Anglian illustrations of that effort: Capgrave modeled Katherine's learning and her piety in accordance with contemporary religious and political anxieties, and Bok-enham adapted the concept of the legendary itself to promote ideas of feminine spiritual authority and dynastic power that were keenly sensitive to ecclesiastical and secular politics in mid-fifteenth-century England.[20]

This chapter follows the lead provided by the Digby stage direc-tion's "chaste women," investigating social, iconographic, and textual evidence of devotion to Mary Magdalene in late medieval East Anglia. I preface my study of this evidence with a look at the saint's distinctive appearances at earlier moments in the history of the medieval English Church, moments that presage her later prominence in East Anglia. Recuperating the cultural dialogue between textual constructions of Mary Magdalene and the regional landscape of feminine religion, this chapter argues that late medieval East Anglian versions of the Magdalene figure foreground the relationship between virginity and sacred power, the spiritual and material valences of the female body, feminine contributions to salvation history, and feminine spiritual authority. These preoccupations demonstrate Mary Magdalene's symbolic and ideological centrality to major themes of late medieval religious culture, and thereby establish crucial historical and cultural contexts for aspects of the Digby saint play analyzed in this book.

Early English Traditions of Mary Magdalene

By the time the Digby playwright set to dramatizing the life of Mary Magdalene, this popular medieval saint may well have been, after the Virgin Mary and the Eucharist, the most overdetermined symbolic construction in western Christendom. At her cultic centers in France, claims to possess her relics had made first Vezelay and then Saint Baume major European pilgrimage sites and international centers of Magdalene devotion. The ubiquity and power of the saint's international cult were attested in church dedications (over 180 in England alone) and religious foundations. Her scriptural roles, narrative vita, and symbolic identities were ceaselessly invoked in the liturgy; Latin hymnody; vernacular lyric; homiletic, exegetical, and devotional texts; liturgical and vernacular drama; folk traditions; and all the medieval visual and plastic arts.[21]

In the long shadows cast by Vezelay and Saint Baume, it is easy to overlook both Mary Magdalene's prominent role in the historical development of Christianity in England and important early English contributions to the formation of the saint's cult. The very first textual evidence of that cult in the West is, in fact, insular: Bede's martyrology (c. 720) identifies July 22 as the "Natale [sanctae] Mariae Magdalenae."[22] Fuller documentation of early English veneration of the saint appears in the ninth-century *Old English Martyrology*, where Mary Magdalene is remembered as the woman whose great longing (*micelre longunge*) for

Christ made her flee to the desert after his ascension, where she remained for thirty years.[23] The *Martyrology*'s use of the vita *eremetica* as a source attests to early English knowledge of the saint's nonscriptural identities and may also reflect the influence of an ascetic eighth-century Irish Church.[24] These eremitic associations account for Mary Magdalene's representation on the late seventh-century Ruthwell Cross, where her appearance in the posture of Luke's penitent and contemplative (7:37–8) may echo insular traditions of female asceticism.[25]

Mary Magdalene's inclusion in ninth- and tenth-century English calendars reinforces these early textual and visual testimonials to her Anglo-Saxon veneration, providing further evidence of the saint's cult in Britain before its diffusion in the West and her first appearances in continental calendars.[26] The "preeminence of the English cult of Mary Magdalene," in Veronica Ortenberg's phrase, is best illustrated by an image in the late tenth-century *Benedictional* produced for Æthelwold of Winchester. The opening pages of the manuscript depict the choir of virgins; figured prominently on the right folio and identified by inscriptions on their books are Æthelthryth, the Anglo-Saxon virgin saint and founder of Ely, and Mary Magdalene.[27] The two saints are identically attired in a garment that strongly resembles one worn by the Virgin Mary in the *Benedictional*'s illustration for the Annunciation. Among the choir of virgins, only Æthelthryth and Mary Magdalene wear large gold nimbi, a detail that further emphasizes their likeness to each other.[28]

The *Benedictional* places Mary Magdalene at the head of the choir of virgins, an honored location that is consistent with the order of saints found in litanies of virgins from Winchester and other Anglo-Saxon foundations.[29] Rather than reinscribing the sexual sin for which she was so well known from the time of Gregory the Great, Æthelwold's book instead reflects traditions of scriptural commentary that emphasized Mary Magdalene's reattainment of purity through her associations with the human Christ and her related appropriation of Marian roles. This assumption of virginal attributes and specific paralleling with the Virgin Mary herself were distinguishing features of the early insular cult of Mary Magdalene, which also highlighted the saint's identities as loving penitent and apostle of the Resurrection.[30]

Significantly, another English service book furnishes the first Western pictorial representation of Mary Magdalene in her most controversial role, that of "apostle to the apostles," a distinction accorded to her because she bore witness to Christ's resurrection.[31] The *St. Albans*

Psalter is thought to have been made for Christina of Markyate, the late Anglo-Saxon virgin recluse turned abbess, for whom the image of Mary Magdalene's apostolate may have provided an exemplary yoking of ideals of physical purity and spiritual authority. Images of the saint in the psalter, which also depicts Mary Magdalene's anointing of Christ and her presence at his deposition, enable its likely dedicatee to assimilate the saint's "spiritual personality," her roles as penitent, contemplative, and witness to Christ's humanity and divinity.[32] Such contemplative, penitential ideals were actively promoted for female and male monastics: Aelred of Rievaulx's *De institutione inclusarum* invoked Mary Magdalene to model the female recluse's spiritual and affective life, and French monastic counterparts of Aelred regularly turned to the Magdalene figure to model their own spiritual experiences.[33] Mary Magdalene seems to have been especially important to early English female monastic communities. Jansen's inventory of spiritual dedications for European convents of contemplative nuns finds England leading the way in the twelfth century with six foundations dedicated to Mary Magdalene.[34] The saint was also a popular dedicatee for male monastic houses; between 1151 and 1216, eighteen foundations chose her as titular saint, making her the fifth most popular; among female saints only the Virgin Mary exceeds her in number of monastic dedications.[35]

While offering evidence of a precocious and vital cult of Mary Magdalene during and after the Anglo-Saxon period, these signs of early English veneration of the saint can also be linked more directly to East Anglian religious traditions. By all conventional measures, medieval East Anglia could not claim to be a center of devotion to Mary Magdalene; still from the twelfth through fifteenth centuries it was the home of a significant number of foundations dedicated to her.[36] Their establishment parallels a broader diffusion of the spiritual ideals associated with Mary Magdalene and her availability as a cultural symbol that was regularly employed to sanction identities, beliefs, and practices embraced by religious communities and the larger society.

Mary Magdalene's placement alongside Æthelthryth in Æthelwold's choir of virgins illuminates these symbolic functions by pointing to the larger complex of cultural values informing the association of the two holy women in medieval East Anglia. One of the holy daughters of Anna, seventh-century king of the East Angles, Æthelthryth (her Latin name was Etheldreda) was a preeminent East Anglian saint. Among the exceptional cohort of Anglo-Saxon saintly women Æthethryth stands out for her exemplary virginity and asceticism, the very qualities that Bede praised when he likened her to the Virgin Mary in his "Hymn to Æthelthryth."[37] As an attribute of East Anglian royal, feminine piety, that virginity receives special attention in the *Benedictional*, where Æthelthryth occupies a full-page illustration for her own feast day, bearing the sprig of golden blossoms that identified her as one of the "virgin flowers" that, in Bede's words, sprang from the Virgin Mary's worthiness.[38]

As Æthelthryth's cult developed, her celebrated reputation for preserving her virginity through two marriages was complemented, symbolically and practically, by her ecclesiological associations. As the founder of an important cathedral monastery at Ely, she was identified with an institution that eventually controlled a large portion of the county of Suffolk. Ely shared that power with the large Benedictine house at Bury St. Edmunds, the other influential monastic foundation dedicated to an East Anglian saint.[39] Æthelthryth's institutional authority as abbess and bodily authority as virgin converged at Ely itself, where the presence of her incorrupt physical remains furnished both a token of her sanctity and the source of the abbey's power.[40] This complex symbolic identity probably contributed to Æthelthryth's enduring popularity through the end of the Middle Ages, when she makes frequent appearances on rood screens of East Anglian parish churches. Adorned in her habit and bearing crosier and book, Æthelthryth is memorialized by the lay patrons of these screens as a regional icon of the convergence of female sanctity, virginity, and abbatial power.[41]

Æthelthryth was the subject of more medieval vernacular lives than any other native English woman saint, including one of the three Anglo-Norman vitae known to have been composed by women.[42] The sole copy of *La vie seinte Audrée* by Marie, possibly of Chatteris abbey near Ely, survives in a late thirteenth-century Anglo-Norman legendary (B.L. MS Additional 70513) produced at or for the wealthy Augustinian priory of nuns at Campsey Ash, Suffolk. Highlighting Anglo-Saxon virgin princesses and royal abbesses, English male ecclesiastical authorities, virgins, and ascetics, the lives collected in the Campsey manuscript exhibit notable connections to male and female saints having prominent East Anglian cults and ties to monastic communities and noble families in Essex, Suffolk, and Norfolk.[43] Jocelyn Wogan-Browne's work on Anglo-Norman women's literary culture emphasizes the importance of the Campsey manuscript as an index to individual and communal female patronage and to the multiple uses of hagiographic narrative by aristocratic religious, semireligious, and lay women at communities such as Campsey. For this mixed community of religious women, Marie's life of Æthelthryth/Audrey offered a congenial illustration of pious patronage, chaste living, and social and spiritual authority.

The Campsey legendary focusing on East Anglian cults, female saints, virgins, and ascetics, includes the life of a single biblical saint: Mary Magdalene. One of only three non-British saints contained in the collection, Mary Magdalene earns her place in it through her association with the major spiritual values that the legendary's vitae espouse. Like Æthelthryth, Mary Magdalene also appears regularly on East Anglian rood screens, directly following the Anglo-Saxon virgin and monastic foundress in frequency of representation.[44] Mary Magdalene is able to keep company with Audrey in the Campsey Ash manuscript and Æthelthryth on East Anglian rood screens because of their shared participation in a tradition of female sanctity that focused on virginity and the spiritual authority of feminine purity. These key emphases of the early English cults of both saints contributed to East Anglian religious culture an image of feminine holiness that appealed broadly to monastic and lay patrons and audiences.[45] The pairing of Æthelthryth and Mary Magdalene in Æthelwold's *Benedictional*, then, adumbrates a vision of feminine sanctity whose relevance reaches far beyond the tenth-century Anglo-Saxon choir of virgins to embrace not only the themes of Anglo-Norman hagiography but also the values, roles, and identities articulated by East Anglian traditions of piety and representation that accord symbolic and cultic centrality to the figure of Mary Magdalene.

The Sociology and Iconography of Female Religious Communities

East Anglian commitments to women's eremitic spirituality and traditions of female sanctity converge in the social history and iconography of the west Norfolk parish church of Wiggenhall St. Mary the Virgin. The most impressive of the Wiggenhall churches, St. Mary the Virgin is best known for the carved bench-ends, or poppyheads, that adorn the center aisle of the nave.[46] Because of their completeness and near-perfect original condition—Cox called them "the very best in the kingdom"—

the panel carvings on the northern block of benches are especially celebrated; they have been dated circa 1500 on the basis of the headdress
worn by Mary Magdalene (fig. 4). Joining her on the relief panels
facing the nave aisle and the carved figures flanking the poppyheads,
among others, are images of apostles Paul, Andrew, and Peter, virgin
martyr Saint Agatha, and Edward the Confessor.[47] Less artistically distinguished but more intriguing are the panel carvings that face this holy
lineup on the nave aisle's south side (fig. 5). Probably a century older
than their counterparts, the more crudely executed bench-ends on this
side display symbols of the church's patron, such as the lily, and female
figures who evoke Marian iconography of the virgin in an aureole, or
radiance, but whose variety calls to mind a range of pious female spiritual vocations (fig. 6). A badly damaged carving bearing remnants of a
kneeling annunciate virgin and angel Gabriel suggests that the poppyheads on the nave aisle's south side were decorated with scenes from the
life of Mary; saints Margaret, Æthelthryth, and Leonard appear here too.
The carved panels of the last row of the southern block of benches, on
both the nave and south aisle sides, further complicate the iconography
of Wiggenhall St. Mary. Each depicts a pair of nuns holding rosaries:
their heads are covered by veils, their hands folded in prayer (figs. 7 and
8). Whereas the other bench-ends invoke the saints as guardians, models,
and sources of sacred power, these figures seem to commemorate the
church's relationship with an actual community of religious women.[48]

Gilchrist and Oliva observe that the presence of these figures, along
with the predominance of female saints in the church's iconographic
program, may signal the interests of patrons who "wished to identify
with the nearby female monastery" of Crabhouse priory and documented anchorholds for women in its immediate vicinity, phenomena
that contributed to the high "profile of religious women in the Wiggenhall parishes."[49] The surviving medieval register for Crabhouse priory
makes clear that this Augustinian foundation was connected socially and
economically to all the Wiggenhall communities; it seems to have had
especially strong ties, however, to the parish of St. Mary the Virgin.[50]
After flooding forced the nuns to move the original site of their twelfth-
century foundation at Wiggenhall St. Mary Magdalene, they put themselves under the protection of a lord Alan, from the parish of Wiggenhall St. Mary.[51] Crabhouse priory had noteworthy ties to the Kervile
family, who held the chief manor in Wiggenhall St. Mary from the

Figure 4. Saint Mary Magdalene. Bench-end, Wiggenhall St. Mary, Norfolk. Photo: T. Coletti.

lords Bardolph.[52] Joan Kervile was a nun at Crabhouse in November 1436, when she testified along with prioress Joan Wiggenhall at divorce proceedings for Thomas Tuddenham and his estranged wife Alice Wodehouse, herself a professed nun at Crabhouse.[53] The first entry in the Crabhouse register reports the September 1476 marriage of Margaret Kervile to Thomas Hunston.[54] The Kervile family were also major patrons of Wiggenhall St. Mary the Virgin parish church, which is still adorned by a number of Kervile monuments, including a brass commemorating the burial of the heart of Sir Robert Kervile (c. 1450). Other local families whose arms appear in the church's heraldic painted glass—Bardolf, Ingaldsthorpe, Howard, and Scales—also figure prominently in the Crabhouse register's account of nearby lands given to and held by the priory.[55]

Given their close ties to the parish, the Crabhouse nuns may have memorialized themselves in the benches of this parish church. Looking at these late medieval portraits today, we can easily imagine them as the brainchild of prioress Joan Wiggenhall, who with lay and clerical

Figure 5. Female figures and women religious. Bench-ends, Wiggenhall St. Mary, Norfolk. Photo: © Crown copyright. NMR.

Figure 6. Female figure. Bench-end, Wiggenhall St. Mary, Norfolk. Photo: T. Coletti.

Figure 7. Female religious. Bench-end, Wiggenhall St. Mary, Norfolk. Photo: T. Coletti.

Figure 8. Female religious. Bench-end, Wiggenhall St. Mary, Norfolk. Photo: T. Coletti.

support undertook an ambitious rebuilding program during her twenty-five-year stewardship of Crabhouse (1420–45).[56] Lay patrons of Wiggenhall St. Mary would have had good reason to welcome into the local parish church visual reminders of the women religious in their midst, who appealingly modeled a devotion that for a long time had linked the Wiggenhall parishes with feminine piety. Crabhouse was located on the western end of a region that nineteenth-century antiquarian Augustus Jessopp dubbed "the Holy Land of Norfolk" because of the nine medieval religious houses bordering a twenty- or thirty-mile stretch of the River Nar.[57] From its twelfth-century foundation in the fenland parish of Wiggenhall by "a maiden whose heart the Holy Spirit moved to seek a desert place where she might serve God without disturbance of any living thing," Crabhouse had been identified with female eremitic devotion.[58] When the female religious community that developed around the recluse's original foundation moved because its house was overwhelmed by flooding that routinely plagued the area, one stayed behind as a recluse in the cemetery of Wiggenhall St. Mary Magdalene.[59] Organized as an Augustinian convent by the thirteenth century, the nuns of Crabhouse held the advowson of this hermitage; an anchoress was still residing there in 1492 when the wealthy Bury St. Edmunds widow Margaret Oldham left twelve pence to "every nunne" in most of the convents of Norfolk and Suffolk, including one at "Wygnale."[60] Crabhouse priory itself supported recluses within its walls in the thirteenth and fifteenth centuries, reinforcing the convent's and the Wiggenhall community's identification with female eremitic piety through the late Middle Ages.[61] Evidence that Crabhouse was also home to at least one documented vowess helps to make it a nodal point for considering the range and significance of women's religious vocations in the region.[62]

Never a large or prosperous foundation, Crabhouse priory as a religious and social institution exhibits the demographics and patterns of activity and interaction that were characteristic of female monasteries in late medieval East Anglia.[63] The close relationships with the local community evidenced by the Crabhouse register were typical of these foundations; like its sister houses, the Wiggenhall priory drew its population largely from the local parish gentry who, along with yeoman farmers, also constituted the primary patrons for these foundations.[64] The overlapping populations of convent and community doubtlessly contributed to a "tight web of interactions which both sustained the

religious women and spiritually nurtured lay society."[65] As illustrated by
the marriage services for Margaret Kervile and Thomas Hunston, Crabhouse shared its church with the local gentry and also allowed them to
be buried there. The local guild of the Trinity, "whiche Neybores helde
in this same chirche," gave twenty-one marks to the building program
undertaken by Joan Wiggenhall in the 1420s and 1430s. Like other East
Anglian female monasteries, Crabhouse also took in lay boarders or corrodians, persons whose support by the convent was secured, in this case,
by rents from donated lands.[66] Despite its geographical isolation in the
low-lying fens, Crabhouse attracted the attention of distinguished
donors such as Richard Steynolf, a mayor of Norwich who gave 40
pounds in 1427 for the roof of Joan Wiggenhall's new church, and Henry
VI, who made a grant to the prioress and nuns when he visited nearby
Lynn in 1434.[67] Even a small and relatively poor foundation such as
Crabhouse sustained ties to influential and powerful East Anglian clergy.
The register reports the assistance that Prioress Joan received for her
building projects from her cousin John Wiggenhall, a doctor of canon
law and parson at Oxborough who later served as official of the bishop
of Norwich, archdeacon of Sudbury, and dean of the collegiate foundation of St. Mary's at the Chapel in the Fields, Norwich.[68] It is precisely
this web of worldly and economic entanglements that are preserved in
the Crabhouse register's charming introduction to the changing fortunes of the convent as if they were material for verse romance: "Lords
and ladies, old and young / Freemen and serfs and the whole commons,
/ Who wishes to hear and attend / In this writing may learn / How the
convent of Crabhouse / and all its possessions and holdings began."[69]

Such involvements would seem to be at odds with the eremitic
ideals of Crabhouse's recluse founder and its early community. Yet, as
Gilchrist and Oliva maintain, "regular interactions with local communities neither violated the integrity of the cloister, nor compromised the
verisimilitude of the nuns' vocations." On the contrary, the nuns' piety
"attracted gifts and favours" and "formed the basis" for the "symbiotic
relationship" that defined connections with the local community by
female houses such as Crabhouse. Such "interactions placed the monasteries for women firmly within the context of lay society."[70] This "symbiotic relationship" was sustained by material as well as spiritual ties.
Benefactors from all levels of society, hoping for assistance in securing
the good of their souls, sought the support of the nuns' intercessory

prayers. For example, in her will of 1498 Anne Harling bequeathed forty shillings to Crabhouse to engage its sisters "to pray for me and my frendes," specifying three shillings and four pence for the prioress, twenty pence "to yche ladyes" and "the residue to the well [weal] of the place."[71] This is exactly the relationship that the Digby saint play invokes when Mary Magdalene promises the king and queen of Marseilles that she will "have rememberavns" of "yow and yowers . . . And dayly [y]ower bede woman for to be" (1965–66).[72] Just as the Digby play's Magdalene offers her spiritual assistance and gives her blessing to the king and queen ("Ille vos benedicatt, qui sene fine vivit et regnat" [1971]) at the very moment that she departs the world for the wilderness, the poverty and physical austerity of foundations such as Crabhouse added value to the spiritual efficacy of the nuns' prayers. The eremitic dimensions of the nuns' vocation were "vital aspects" of East Anglian female piety."[73]

Local affinities for such piety—and the example of the Crabhouse nuns—may gloss the iconographic program of Wiggenhall St. Mary's other famous appointment, an early sixteenth-century rood screen depicting, from left to right on the north side (fig. 9), Saints Mary Magdalene, Dorothy, Margaret, and Anne (?); and on the south side (fig. 10), Saints Catherine and Barbara, the Virgin Mary and infant Jesus, and John the Baptist. The screen is one of the few surviving East Anglian examples to bear the names of probable donors: Humphrey Kervile, identified as "armiger," and Thomas Lacy, a member of an influential local family who had dealings with Crabhouse.[74] Recent work on East Anglia's famous late medieval rood screens points out various factors influencing the choice of saints depicted and the corporate and private motivations that underwrote these choices.[75] The saints at Wiggenhall are among those represented most frequently on East Anglian rood screens, on which images of virgin martyrs and biblical saints and penitents were especially popular.

The presence of John the Baptist among this group solicits further attention, especially in light of his position on the south end, where he balances Mary Magdalene on the north. John the Baptist and Mary Magdalene "were frequently paired off together in medieval art" because of their common association with asceticism.[76] The Wiggenhall screen's spatial juxtaposition of the saints creates a visual and symbolic frame for the images of virgins that they flank. Here representations of Mary Magdalene and John the Baptist draw upon these saints' shared penitential, contemplative, and eremitic identities to physically enclose images of feminine virtue—the purity of virgin martyr and virgin mother, the heroism of virginal sacrifice, the modeling of the chaste female life. Known for his perfect holiness and virginity, the Baptist offers an especially complementary image to the screen's visual celebration of feminine purity.[77]

A twelfth-century Magdalene vita that circulated in the later Middle Ages further illuminates the symbolic roles that Mary Magdalene and John the Baptist occupy on the Wiggenhall screen. Mary Magdalene

showed she was equal to John the Baptist in being more than a prophet. Just as John surpassed all the saints in his conversion in the desert and his holiness from the womb, so Mary had no equal in her wonderful conversion to Christ and her incomparable intimacy with Christ. . . . Her deeds are equal to his,

Figure 9. Saints Mary Magdalene, Dorothy, Margaret, and Anne. Rood screen, Wiggenhall St. Mary, Norfolk. Photo: T. Coletti.

write the four evangelists. He is praised because he heard the voice of the Father and saw the Holy Spirit; she, because she loved the Son of the Virgin greatly, ministered to his needs diligently, stood nearby when he was crucified, and embalmed his body, and was the first to see his resurrection from the dead and to believe it. Christ praised and commended John's angelic life; he defended Mary against the murmuring Pharisee; he excused her to the complaining Martha, he praised her before the angry Judas, and destined her to be apostle to his apostles. Among the sons of women, only the King of Heaven is equal to and greater than the Baptist; among the daughters of men, only the Queen of Heaven is equal to and greater than Mary Magdalene.[78]

Inscribing the parallel significance of the holy man and holy woman as witnesses to Christ's godhead and manhood, intimate friends of the deity, and persons whose comparable worthiness is surpassed only by Christ and the Virgin, the text's careful rhetorical balancing of the Baptist and Mary Magdalene precisely articulates the spiritual attributes that the spatial arrangement of the Wiggenhall screen also invokes.

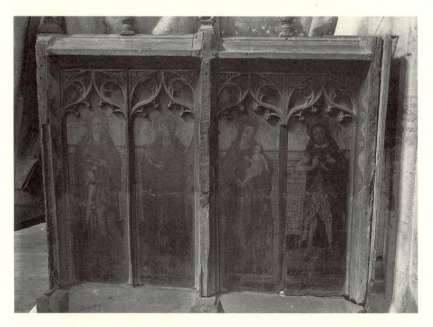

Figure 10. Saints Catherine and Barbara; Mary and Jesus; and John the Baptist. Rood screen, Wiggenhall St. Mary. Reproduced by permission of English Heritage. NMR.

The juxtaposition of Mary Magdalene and John the Baptist on the Wiggenhall screen not only provides a reminder of the eremitic ideals of the female religious foundation in its nearby parish but also underscores identifications that redound especially to the vision of feminine spiritual authority that the Wiggenhall rood screen, and the church as a whole, projects. From opposite ends of the screen, these images of Mary Magdalene and John the Baptist concretely embrace feminine icons of spiritual discipline, physical purity, and love of Christ, conveying ideals that are perfectly consistent with those of the female religious community of Crabhouse and that at some level surely inspired the lay patrons of both convent and parish church.

The potential for the iconographic program of Wiggenhall St. Mary to encourage identification between the lay and religious it served is suggested by yet another detail of the rood screen. Saints Barbara and Catherine are depicted with open books; Catherine glances up from hers and looks out of the picture while Barbara remains engrossed in reading (fig. 11). A relatively rare motif in late medieval English representations of virgin martyrs, this image of reading transforms the saints into mirrors of the lay readers who avidly consumed hagiographic and other devotional texts.[79] The screen's highlighting of a specifically female pious reading may also reference more local preoccupations of the religious women who left their spiritual imprint on the Wiggenhall church. Oliva speculates, for example, that Anne Harling's many financial bequests to houses of religious women in Norfolk parallel her gifts of books, possibly signifying a "high level of literacy among the nuns there."[80]

Paul Binski's recent work on the English parish church as a medium of communication provides a useful framework for assessing the appointments and iconography of Wiggenhall St. Mary in light of ideals of feminine piety circulating in late medieval East Anglia. Noting that the practical and intellectual problems posed by the parish church still constitute a frontier of research in late medieval art, Binski posits that the "inner world" of these churches, in other words, their images and installations rather than their architecture and archaeology, "needs to be regarded . . . not as the sum total of the media in concert but as an ontological whole."[81] Binski addresses the ways in which the internal spatial and visual organization of the parish church—for example, its screening systems, placement of squints, and arrangement of images—

Figure 11. Saints Catherine and Barbara. Rood screen, detail, Wiggenhall St. Mary, Norfolk. Photo: T. Coletti.

"form a cognitive map of religious experience" that contributed to the construction of the religious sensibility of the church's congregations.[82] He also points out how "concentrated and focused schemes" of representation may signal "the presence of the 'invisible complement' of social groupings, including gender groupings, within the parish as surely as does the location of altars or, later, family pews."[83]

The carved and painted images of Wiggenhall St. Mary the Virgin provide ideal material in support of Binski's emphasis on the "theme of integration as a priority in the design and decoration of medieval churches."[84] If, as Binski suggests, the images and installations of medieval English parish churches "had a constitutive, rather than representational, role in the making of religion itself," what sort of religion is made by the prominent display—from chancel screen to the nave's west end—of these figures of feminine spiritual authority and female religious experience?[85] Bearing witness to local female religious vocations as well as the larger landscape of late medieval East Anglian feminine piety, these images memorialize lay and religious investments that are intriguingly compatible with the Digby play's elusive provision that Mary Magdalene be arrayed as a "chaste woman." Binski's observation that "we need a richer sense of activity, of movement, of performativity" within the late medieval parish church than that "to be derived from liturgical reconstruction alone," prompts consideration of material artifacts such as the iconographic program of Wiggenhall St. Mary and its attendant cultural links to the eremitic piety of Crabhouse priory as evidence of "a highly determined" aesthetic environment, a "theater of religious allegory" that, in Binski's tantalizing comparison, has "principles of taste and structuring of ideas in common with contemporary theater."[86]

The parish church at Wiggenhall St. Mary the Virgin epitomizes East Anglian preoccupations with feminine figures, symbols, and forms of religious expression. The commitments articulated in its social history and iconographic program were regularly reproduced in late medieval East Anglian religious institutions and regional politics, in sacred images and cultural performances. These commitments correspond especially to the interests of East Anglian texts in which Mary Magdalene figures prominently. Diverse in their auspices, these Magdalene texts speak to the flexibility and influence of the saint's symbolic construction in the region where writers busily invoked her life in verse hagiography, vernacular mysticism, and allegorical, scriptural, and hagiographic drama.

Mary Magdalene in East Anglian Hagiography and Mysticism

Eamon Duffy has suggested that Osbern Bokenham's *Legendys of Hooly Wummen* "reads like program notes" for any one of a number of East Anglian rood screens upon which female saints are prominently represented.[87] Not only does this all-female legendary assemble vitae of saints who appear regularly on these rood screens, such as Margaret, Catherine, Mary Magdalene, and Dorothy, but Bokenham's own chatty prologues to the legends disclose devotional investments by the clerical author and his prominent patrons in the female subjects and feminine ideals that the vitae inscribe. Bokenham's remarks locate the production of the legendary in East Anglian networks of religious patronage and lay dedication to the eremitic, feminine spiritual ideals that also characterize the relationship of Crabhouse priory to the Wiggenhall parishes. The colophon of the single manuscript witness of the legendary, British Library MS Arundel 327, reveals that the vitae which the friar originally prepared for his noble and gentry patrons were eventually collected for a "holy place of nunnys."[88] Widening the circle of Bokenham's readership, this attribution also extends the reception of his text to an actual community of East Anglian religious women contemporary with the sisters of Crabhouse.

Pride of place in Bokenham's legendary must go to the longest of its thirteen legends, the "Lyf of Marye Maudelyn." Probably written between 1443 and 1447 when Bokenham resided at the Augustinian priory at Clare, Suffolk, the "Lyf of Marye Maudelyn" closely follows Jacobus's *Legenda aurea*. Like the Digby saint play, Bokenham's life offers a full account of Mary Magdalene's biblical history as anointer of Christ and witness to his resurrection, apostle to Marseilles, and desert contemplative. Though other late medieval English texts, such as John Mirk's *Festial*, also present the saint's composite biblical and legendary vita, these two East Anglian texts stand out for their expansive, leisurely articulation of that story and especially for the attention they accord to Mary Magdalene's transformation from sinful woman and anointer to apostle and preacher.[89]

This is precisely the identity of the saint invoked by Bokenham's patron, Isabel Bourchier, countess of Eu and sister of Richard, duke of York, in the poet's account of the commissioning of his text: "'I haue,' quod she, 'of pure affeccyoun / Ful longe tym had a synguler deuocyoun /

To þat holy wumman, wych, as I gesse, / Is clepyd of apostyls þe apostyllesse'" (5065–68). The noblewoman fixes on the saint's authority and privilege, attributes with which Isabella herself was likely to feel some kinship.[90] The countess of Eu was Bokenham's "most socially exalted patron"; in reporting Isabella's request that he compose a life of Mary Magdalene, the poet acknowledges "how hard it is to denye / A-statys preyer" (5082–83).[91] However flattered Isabella may have been "by the celebrity of appearing in verse as a devout character in eloquent command of the threshold into a hagiographic text," Bokenham's "prolocutorye," or preface, to the "Lyf of Marye Maudelyn" has a more complex rhetorical agenda than simply offering praise of his patron.[92] Rather, the prolocutory furnishes literary and social glosses on the vita that it introduces and on the uses of female hagiography in late medieval East Anglia.

Sheila Delany argues that Bokenham's prolocutory to the "Lyf of Marye Maudelyn" states his "poetic credo." Here he mounts an attack on the literary ethics and excesses of courtly classicism typified by the works of Chaucer, Gower, and Lydgate and their French influences, proposing as an alternative the moral superiority of an Augustinian theory of reading and writing, a Christian aesthetic that focuses on doctrine rather than classical learning, plain speaking in pursuit of grace rather than eloquence.[93] Bokenham's decision to place that critique in the prefatory materials to the life of Mary Magdalene, Delany posits, makes that vita the aesthetic and doctrinal center of the legends as a whole.[94] Mary Magdalene's celebrated witness to the human Christ and her intimacy and familiarity with his physical person—epitomized in the somatic preoccupations of Bokenham's text—present an especially appropriate site for the friar's literary and religious musings. Her personal history clearly illustrates how the "theological-corporeal semiotics of . . . the female body" that Bokenham devised to respond to courtly constructions of femininity enabled his legendary to resignify the feminine and the physical for Christian ends.[95]

Delany's analysis of the legendary correctly stresses the importance of Bokenham's "Lyf of Marye Maudelyn" to the ideological design of the project as a whole; I want to examine other aspects of the saint's vita that contribute to that effort. Bokenham reserves his most serious literary and philosophical statements in the legendary for the vita of its most important saint, commissioned by his most distinguished patron, as if the elevated status of his immediate audience and the spiritual prominence of his subject together call up his most heightened reflections on his enterprise. The poet's hagiographical and literary projects converge in the prolocutory to the life of Mary Magdalene in an intensely personal fashion when Bokenham renounces the temptations of the classical muses and the courtly poetic that they underwrite with the vehemence of one of his virgin martyrs refusing to worship pagan gods: "Wherefore, lord, to þe alone I crye / Wych welle art of mercy & of pyte, / And neythyr to Clyo ner to Melpomene, / Nere to noon oþir of þe musys nyne, / Ner to Pallas Mynerue, ner Lycyne, / Ner to Apollo . . . / But all þem wyttyrly I denye, / As euere crystene man owyth to do, / And þe oonly, lord, I fle on-to" (5214–24). Paradoxically, though, Bokenham presents his extended critique of courtly discourse in the very prolocutory in which he also reports the circumstances—the Twelfth Night celebration at Isabella's aristocratic household—that evoke his most courtly language and demeanor. The prolocutory to the "Lyf of Marye Maudelyn" thus creates a tension between the circumstances and occasion of the vita's commission and the Christian aesthetic that Bokenham elsewhere propounds.[96]

This tension is epitomized in resemblances between the language Bokenham employs to describe his patron's "foure sonys ying" (5023) and the words with which he condemns the "gay speche eek & . . . eloquencye" of "curyals" who compose deceitful "baladys or amalettys" "for þere ladyis sake" (5221, 5226–30). "Besy . . . wyth reuel & wyth daunsyng," Isabella's sons are "in þere most fressh aray / Dysgysyd, for in þe moneth of may / was neuyr [wyth] floris [whyt], blewe & grene, / Medew motleyid freshlyere . . . / Than were her garnementys" (5024–29). The courtly poets, in their turn, produce a "centens / So craftyd up, & wyth langwage so gay / Uttryd, þat I trowe þe moneth of may / Neuere fresshere enbe[l]shyd þe soyl wyth flours / than is her wrytyng wyth colours / Of rethorycal speche both to & fro" (5234–39). Juxtaposing the material colors of courtly attire and the figurative colors of courtly rhetoric, Bokenham establishes a connection between aristocratic youth and courtly language; both involve imitations of a more natural world.[97]

The use of the figure in such different contexts—in the service of social flattery on the one hand and an ethical poetic on the other—implicates not only the productions of courtly poets but also Isabella's courtly sons in the dangerous ambiguities of courtly representation. Set up by the prolocutory's social and rhetorical musings, Bokenham's life of the saint emerges then as a direct response to such verbal, and an implicit response to such physical, adornments. Felicitously rhyming his stylistic preferences with the name of the saint herself, the poet resolves to "translate in wurdys pleyne / In-to oure langwage oute of latyn / The lyf of blyssyd Mare Mawdelyn" (5252–54). As the setting for not only the genesis of his life of Mary Magdalene but also the statement of his Christian poetic, the entire festive occasion that Bokenham describes, with its gaiety and "daunsyng . . . [a]boute þe chaumbyr" (5035–36) is at far remove from the ascetic retreat, with "no solace / To hyr bodyly counfort in no degre" (6159–60) toward which Mary Magdalene's spiritual progress tends, and from the models of corporeal abjection and renunciation articulated by the legends as a whole. As the subject of the poet's translation into "wurdys pleyne," the life of Mary Magdalene thus becomes a textual and symbolic agent of both rhetorical and moral correction.[98]

As if the very thematic compendiousness of Mary Magdalene's vita afforded opportunities for such complex cultural mediation between poetry and religion, poet and patron, Bokenham enlists the saint's life to navigate the intersecting literary, religious, and social commitments of late medieval East Anglian readers. He dramatizes his delicate negotiation of the social intricacies of these patronage systems when he reports his audience with Isabella Bouchier. As they walk together Isabella notes the "dyuers legendys" (5038) that he has already translated, a point that leads up to her commissioning the poet to produce a life of Mary Magdalene. But with the mention of Saint Elizabeth of Hungary, "[w]hos holy legend as at þat tyme / I newly had begunne to ryme" (5049–50), Bokenham interrupts his account of Isabella's rehearsal of vitae in midsentence, momentarily suspending this narrative of commission in order to acknowledge his present involvement with another, that of Elizabeth de Vere, countess of Oxford (5051–61). Although Bokenham describes his relationship with each of these noble patrons with commensurate respect—he cannot say no to either of them—his preempting of Isabella's conversation in order to praise Elizabeth de Vere for ten lines strikes an odd note. The normally meticulous poet here only clumsily covers all his social bases.[99] In a gesture that seems designed to advertise the great demand for the literary services of the Augustinian poet, the prolocutory's mention of the intersecting hagiographical interests of Elizabeth and Isabella also invokes politically resonant networks of East Anglian literary patronage into which Bokenham's commissions were woven. Two of Bokenham's other patrons—the Denstons and Flegges—were among the retainers of Isabella's brother Richard, duke of York. Elizabeth de Vere's social contacts included some of the best-known East Anglian book-collecting figures of the fifteenth century: the Pastons, John Fastolfe, and Miles Stapleton.[100]

Bokenham's account of the role that commissioned hagiographies played in specific devotional practices of Countess Isabella, Elizabeth de Vere, Katherine Howard, Katherine Denston, and Agatha Flegge underscores the important involvement of East Anglian female readers in the late medieval literary subculture that Felicity Riddy has characterized as "women . . . 'talking about the things of God.'"[101] Even as the contemporary picture of late medieval women's textual culture—its involvements with devotional and contemplative writings, its patterns of book owning and book giving—has come increasingly into detailed focus, specific instances when late medieval English women speak directly about forms of religious understanding and belief are nonetheless lamentably rare.[102] Such scarcity complicates interpretation of the few extant textual witnesses because our recognition of their idiosyncratic survival must be balanced by awareness of their relationships to larger cultural formations and meanings.[103] In Julian of Norwich's *Revelation of Love* and Margery Kempe's *Book*, the textually distinctive and the culturally normative converge in the significance each work accords to Mary Magdalene. We should not be surprised to find that when these East Anglian women writers "talked about the things of God," they also talked about Mary Magdalene. East Anglian appropriations of the saint discussed in this chapter identify specific and local contexts for the emphasis on Mary Magdalene in the only two mystical texts known to be authored by women in late medieval England.

At two important moments in both the Short and Long Texts of her *Revelation of Love*, the late fourteenth-century anchoress and visionary from Norwich invokes Mary Magdalene. Julian includes the saint among the group of "Crystes loverse" whose direct experience of the Passion stirs her longing to have been present at that event. Mary Magdalene also appears among the biblical saints—David, Peter, Paul, Thomas of India—who, because they are "knawenn in the kyrke of erth with thare synnes to thayre wirschippe," play an illustrative role in Julian's effort to reconcile a compassionate God with the realities of human sinfulness.[104] The appeal to Julian of Mary Magdalene's example can be understood in terms of the medieval woman's own spiritual life.

Because of her personal devotion to Jesus, Mary Magdalene provides an emblem of the affective, participatory spirituality that medieval religious women and lay people were encouraged to pursue, the spirituality that initially grounds Julian's mystical experience.[105] Julian's social position as anchoress further invites identification with Mary Magdalene; women committed to reclusion and other alternative religious vocations emphasizing penitence and asceticism subscribed to ideals that the saint embodied.[106]

These invocations of Mary Magdalene, however, also point beyond devotional traditions and Julian's self-reference to suggest the saint's symbolic significance for Julian's visionary project as a whole. Because she represents the longing for participation that pervades much medieval mystical and devotional literature, Mary Magdalene's example underscores, for Julian, the importance of experiential knowledge at a foundational moment of a text that increasingly engages epistemological concerns: "Me thought I wolde haue bene that tyme with Mary Mawdeleyne and with othere that were Crystes loverse, that I myght have sene bodylye the passionn of oure lorde that he sufferede for me. . . . whare yn y myght have more knawynge of bodelye paynes of oure lorde oure savyoure, and of the compassyonn of oure ladye and of alle his trewe loverse that were be levande his paynes that tyme and sythene; for I wolde have beene one of thame and suffrede with thame."[107] As she longs to witness just as "Crystes loverse" did at "that time," Julian declares her desire for the bodily sight and knowledge that had made Mary Magdalene an emblem not only of compassionate suffering but also a corporeal theology of presence. More than any other of Jesus' followers, Mary Magdalene was the devotee whose role in sacred events was inextricably bound up with the bodily witnessing of divinity imaged mostly directly in the risen Christ's admonition to her in John 20: *noli me tangere*.

Mary Magdalene occupies this role in both the Short and Long Texts of Julian's *Revelation*, even though the revised text attenuates the importance of both affective participation and penitential suffering in the mystical quest, as Julian's earlier address to like contemplatives yields to robust theological argument directed to all of her "evyn Christen."[108] The Long Text retains Julian's commitment to this theology of presence; but it transfers the locus of this commitment from the historical moment of the Passion, in which Julian longed to participate, to a more broadly formulated conception of the incarnational likeness that makes God always present to—and in a sense at one with—humanity. For example, when Julian's Long Text reprises the Short Text's reference to Mary Magdalene among the cohort of biblical sinners, the anchoress further clarifies the saint's theological significance. In both versions Julian's vision of the ultimate "behoveliness" of sin transforms Mary Magdalene's most negative attribute—her sinfulness—into a mark of glory. Of these sinners, the Short Text asserts: "[I]t is to thamm no schame that thay hafe synned—na mare it is in the blysse of heven—for thare the takenynge of synne is tourned into wirschippe."[109] In the Long Text, however, Julian shows more interest in explaining the sacred logic of their eternal rewards rather than condemning the lapses of these famous sinners. Anticipating that text's exploration of sin in terms of differences between divine and human sight and understanding, she draws a distinction between earthly human apprehension of those rewards and their heavenly significance: "[O]ure curtesse lorde shewyth for them here in party, lyke as it is ther in fulheed."[110]

Though brief, Julian's references to Mary Magdalene enact in miniature several larger strategies of her theology, telescoping foundations of her visionary quest articulated in the Short Text and the exploration of sin that receives so much attention in the Long. Whereas other English mystics such as Walter Hilton and the author of the *Cloud of Unknowing* looked to Mary Magdalene to model the contemplative's spiritual identity, Julian principally recognizes the biblical saint's epistemological, affective example and her transcendence of sin. Grounded in her composite scriptural identity, Mary Magdalene's transformation from a sinful to a blessed state was a common theme of traditions of commentary on the saint and her medieval cult. Significantly, Julian's inclusion of Mary Magdalene among those whose "takenynge of synne is tourned into wirschippe" makes no mention of the gendered terms in which that transformation was regularly framed. Rather, Mary Magdalene's recuperation as one of the blessed provides scriptural support for Julian's daring revision of the theology of redemption, an effort that is fully consistent with her refusal, as she probed the significance of her visions, to privilege an identificatory feminine suffering with Christ.[111] While invoking Mary Magdalene's traditional attributes, Julian thus also colors those associations with her own corporeally grounded vision of salvation history.

If Julian found in Mary Magdalene's example an empirical, bodily "knawing" that she longed to experience herself, her fellow East Anglian

holy woman, contemporary, and sometime confidante Margery Kempe
goes one better, giving corporeal and narrative shape to Julian's more
laconically expressed desires. Whereas Julian only wishes that she had
been "with Mary Mawdeleyne and . . . others that were Crystes loverse,"
Margery Kempe's visions locate her precisely in that place and role. As
many of her readers have noted, Kempe's *Book* fulfills the spiritual and
rhetorical imperatives of late medieval devotional practices enjoined by
Pseudo-Bonaventure's *Meditationes vitae Christi*.[112] In Kempe's quirky
appropriation, that text's promptings to experience the truth of biblical
events by making oneself present to them emerge in the audacious
personalization of sacred encounters for which the *Book* is so well
known. Kempe does not simply occupy the meditative space of imaginative presence before sacred sights or model herself after Mary Magdalene's example as preeminent lover of Christ; instead, she scripts a
role for herself in her own devotional theater, tracking the Virgin Mary's
responses to the Passion, eavesdropping on her conversations with the
risen Christ and Mary Magdalene, and accompanying the Magdalene,
"in hir contemplacyon," to the tomb.[113] Margery Kempe may have med-
itatively occupied the role of handmaiden to the Virgin Mary and enacted, as both devotional subject and aspiring saint, her own *imitatio
christi*, but among the scriptural figures who populate her visions, it is
Mary Magdalene who provides Kempe with the fullest occasion for
articulating her own religious subjectivity. For the burgher wife, mother,
and businesswoman of Lynn, Mary Magdalene serves as mystical companion and fellow traveler, rival for Christ's affections, and source of
hope that she too might one day be accorded the status of honorary virgin in heaven.

The similarities between the lives of the biblical and legendary saint
and the fifteenth-century bourgeois holy woman are so numerous and
Margery's identifications with Mary Magdalene so specific that Susan
Eberly has argued that Kempe directly modeled her own contradictory
hagiographical aspirations upon the life of the saint.[114] More recently,
Rosalynn Voaden has linked Kempe's "special devotion" to Mary Magdalene to their shared identification as sexual sinners.[115] The second of
the two proems to Kempe's *Book* notes that its priestly author began "to
wryten in þe ȝer of owr Lord a m. cccc.xxxvj on þe day next aftyr Mary
Maudelyn," or 23 July 1436, demonstrating the medieval habit of marking secular narrative time by anniversaries and holy days in the liturgical and festive year.[116] The proem's notice that the writing of the book

began on the day after Mary Magdalene's feast implicitly invokes the saint's power and authority to sanction the vita that follows, and perhaps also implicates her in the contested production of the *Book* that the proems record.[117]

Mary Magdalene's biblical and legendary reputation as a sexual sinner "who reformed, lived chastely and loved Christ" offered Margery Kempe a spiritual model aptly suited to her own preoccupations with sexual sin.[118] The very likeness of Kempe's own physical and moral self-conception to the situation of Mary Magdalene, particularly in relation to their recuperated purity and closeness to Jesus, provided the occasion for Kempe's competitiveness with the biblical woman.[119] A closer look at the context of that competition underscores how Mary Magdalene functions in Kempe's *Book* not merely as a member of her devotional peer group but a touchstone for her spiritual development. Mary Magdalene's first appearance in the text occurs in an exchange in which Jesus tries to allay Margery's guilt over her sexual activity by assuring her that "contynuly to thinkyn" on God's love will secure the grace to overcome her sin: "'Haue mend, dowtyr, what Mary Mawdelyn was, Mary Eypcyan, Seynt Powyl, & many oþer seyntys þat arn now in Hevyn, for of vnworthy I make worthy, & of synful I make rytful. & so haue I mad þe worthy to me.'"[120] Recalling Julian's use of Mary Magdalene to exemplify the transformed sinner in heaven for whom "the takenynge of synne is tourned into wirschippe," Kempe's invocation of the saint here simultaneously reinforces her own tainted sexual identity and confirms the surety of her eternal rewards in spite of it.

Kempe's sustained effort to come to terms with that identity takes a step forward when Jesus once again cites the example of Mary Magdalene, only this time not among a cohort of sinners but rather among the heavenly company comprising the Virgin Mary, the apostles, and the virgin martyrs Saints Catherine and Margaret.[121] As Kempe's narrative chaotically unfolds, recording her increasing confidence in her own spiritual authority, the figure of Mary Magdalene takes on increasingly personal significance for her. When Kempe's Passion meditations provoke a dialogue with Jesus in which she expresses the longing to be "worthy to ben sekyr of thy lofe as Mary Mawdelyn was," she receives prompt assurance that her need has already been met and that the saint does not mind one bit: "'Trewly, dowtyr, I loue þe as wel, & þe same pes þat I ʒaf to hir þe same pes I ʒeue to þe. For, dowtyr, þer is no seynt in Heuyn displesyd thow I loue a creatur in erde as mech as I do hem.'"[122] Despite such assurances, Kempe nevertheless has trouble abandoning a rivalry that even Jesus at times appears to encourage. Jesus complicates the equality with Mary Magdalene that he has elsewhere declared for Margery by suggesting that she also benefits from the saint's intercessory efforts: "'[D]owtyr, I knowe . . . how þu clepist Mary Mawdelyn in-to þi sowle to wolcomyn me, for, dowtyr, I wot wel a-now what þu thynkyst. Þu thynkyst þat sche is worthiest in þi sowle [and] most þu trustyst in hir preyerys next my Modyr, [and] so þu maist ryth wel, dowtyr, for sche is a ryth gret mene to me for þe in þe blysse of Heuyn.'"[123]

While underscoring the convergence of its protagonist's behavior, affect, and moral identity with those of the biblical saint, the *Book* also employs Mary Magdalene to articulate the text's larger theological and spiritual investments. As she does in many of her late medieval incarnations, Kempe's Magdalene signals the blurring of boundaries between the spiritual and material, the sacred and profane, staking out the position that Kempe herself uneasily occupies. The biblical saint plays a prominent role in the sequence of extended meditations on the Passion that culminate in Kempe's impatient account of Christ's resurrection appearance to Mary Magdalene (chapters 79–81). Inspired by the example of Mary Magdalene, who in Kempe's vision solicits the Virgin Mary's permission to do "worschip & reuerens" to the dead Christ's feet, Kempe is overcome with sorrow, "as it had be a woman wythowtyn reson." Her urge to mourn is so great that she wants to have "þe precyows body be hir-self a-lone þat sche myth a wept a-now in presens of þat precyows body, for hir thowt þat sche wolde a deyid wyth wepyng & mornyng in hys deth for loue þat sche had to hym."[124] Kempe's competitive edge shows here in her desire to have Christ's body "be hirself a-lone," in other words, without Mary Magdalene in the picture, and looks ahead to the tense moment at the end of chapter 81 in which she gives the biblical woman the visionary elbow as she rescripts her encounter with the risen Christ told in John's gospel.

In a sense Margery has already rehearsed this scriptural moment. Her book reports that during her pilgrimage to the Holy Land "sche stode in þe same place þer Mary Mawdelyn stode whan Crist seyd to hir, 'Mary, why wepyst þu?'"[125] She is thus well prepared for the vision that places her "in . . . contemplacyon wyth Mary Mawdelyn, mornyng & sekyng owr Lord at þe graue." Although Kempe's version of the biblical scene omits the angels who query Magdalene (John 20:12–13), making her first and only interlocutor Christ himself ("'Woman, why wepist þu?'"), her account generally follows the dialogue of the scriptural text and its Pseudo-Bonaventurean expansions.[126] At the point when Mary Magdalene recognizes Jesus and he utters his famous "'Towche me not,'" however, Kempe sets off on her own independent narrative course. Her text defers both Jesus' reference to his ascent to his father (John 20:17) and his command that Mary Magdalene announce his resurrection to the disciples, and also eliminates the dialogue between Mary and Jesus that Pseudo-Bonaventure adds to their scripturally based exchange. In a reversal of the logic of saintly *imitatio* that provided for the devotee to model herself after the holy person, Margery Kempe remakes Mary Magdalene in her own resistant image, giving her the words to talk back to Jesus: "'A, Lord, I se wel ȝe wil not þat I be so homly wyth ȝow as I haue ben a-forn.'" Only after Mary's challenge elicits Jesus' assurance that he will never forsake her does Kempe allow the historical significance of the biblical scene to seep back into her vision: "Go telle my bretheryn & Petyr þat I am vp-reson." Even then, Kempe does not relinquish her resistant reading. She reports that she "marveled" over the joy that Mary Magdalene seemed to feel, observing that "sche cowde neuyr a ben mery" had "owr Lord . . . seyd to hir as he dede to Mary." Instead, she says that she experienced such great sorrow whenever she heard the words "Touch me not"—as she frequently did in sermons—that she could only weep "as sche xulde a deyd for lofe & desir þat sche had to ben wyth owr Lord."

Carolyn Dinshaw's discussion of this important moment in the *Book of Margery Kempe* points to the theological issues at stake in Kempe's revisionary account of Mary Magdalene's meeting with the risen Christ. Reviewing interpretations of *noli me tangere* in scriptural exegesis that reinforce the line between humanity and divinity that Jesus draws with his admonition, Dinshaw notes that meditative writers such as Pseudo-Bonaventure "seem to have felt its potential harshness."[127] Kempe multiplies their discomfort, destined as she is to repeat "many tymys" over the pain she felt at the "[s]heer physical withdrawal and distance" that the words "Touch me not" signified for her. To the extent that Margery Kempe "is marked," in Dinshaw's phrase, "by this visionary experience of corporeal rejection," she is marked by the experience of the biblical Mary Magdalene, pursuing an utterly tactile religious epistemology, forever at odds with the deeper spiritual implications of the *noli me tangere*.[128]

Mary Magdalene looms large in the *Book* as a symbolic signature for the "unresolved tension between the spiritual and the corporeal" that was central to Kempe's spiritual self-conception and to the spiritual and social ideologies of her vita.[129] Yet, if Kempe's fixation on *noli me tangere* narcissistically identified Mary Magdalene's example with the limits that the medieval woman's own corporeal preoccupations placed on her spiritual possibilities, still other late medieval East Anglian texts invoke the saint to articulate symbolic meanings and reinforce devotional practices that promote the corporeal as a source of spiritual power and authority.[130] Exploring the productive tension between the spiritual and corporeal realms is a crucial function of late medieval East Anglian dramatic representations of Mary Magdalene. In the Macro *Wisdom*, the *N-Town Plays*, and the Digby *Magdalene*, this tension is figured in spectacular stage images of the sinful woman's bodily purgation. Kempe's ingenious appropriation of Mary Magdalene thus recognizes symbolic dimensions of the saint's late medieval construction that are particularly relevant to the theology and aesthetics of East Anglian dramas in which the saint appears.

"Very temple of Jhesus": Mary Magdalene in Morality and Biblical Drama

At three different textual moments East Anglian drama represents Christ's expulsion of seven devils from a feminine body, a frequency of occurrence that prompts Alan Fletcher to call the episode "a popular scene" in the dramatic corpus of the region.[131] In the Digby saint play and N-Town *Passion Play I*, Mary Magdalene is the subject of the exorcism; in the Macro morality *Wisdom*, the sinful feminine soul, Anima. Inspired by scriptural notice of Mary Magdalene as the woman from whom Christ cast out seven devils (Mark 16:9; Luke 8:2), the scene makes for sensational theater. For example, after the Digby play's Christ expresses his forgiveness of Mary Magdalene, the stage direction provides for "seuyn dyllys" to "dewoyde from þe woman, and the Bad Angyll [to] entyr into hell wyth thondyr" (s.d. 691).[132] The scene's frequent appearance in East Anglian drama, however, suggests that it offered more than graphic and pleasurable exploitation of the medieval stage's special effects. Rather, these dramatic images of feminine purgation take advantage of theater's requirements for material embodiment in order to explore the spiritual significance of the feminine body. Staging the expulsion of Mary Magdalene's demons palpably exposes that body's capacity for purity and pollution, closure and permeability, and interrogates the relationship between gender, corporeal form, and sacred identities—themes that were central to the symbolic construction of the saint in late medieval England.

In a deliberate allusion to the biblically reported exorcism of Mary Magdalene, *Wisdom* provides for its central character, Anima, to be purged of seven devils.[133] Anima's association with the Magdalene figure is grounded in the allegorical hermeneutic that identified both the biblical woman and the human soul, or anima, with the Bride of the Song of Songs.[134] Anima prominently occupies this role in *Wisdom*, a text whose large debt to the Song of Songs is evident in its allegorical narrative of the loving soul's relationship with Christ and in numerous verbal echoes of the scriptural text. More than traditions of scriptural exegesis, however, link *Wisdom*'s Anima and Mary Magdalene. In particular, the play's characterization of Anima as both feminine and fallen seems to have invited her association with the biblical woman whose spectacular signature was bodily purgation of sin. Anima's appearance as a Magdalene figure at the climactic moment of *Wisdom*—when the corrupt antics of the soul's three masculine Mights are brought to a sudden halt by the admonitions of Wisdom—underscores the complex dramatic construction of a character who also exhibits shifting gender identities and ambiguous relationships to the material and spiritual realms.

In *Wisdom* the purgation of Anima occurs in two phases. After a long absence from the dramatic scene as the beautiful allegorical maiden and lover of Wisdom introduced early in the play, Anima later returns to the stage at Wisdom's command: "Se howe ye haue dysvyguryde yowr soule! / Beholde yowrselff" (901–2). The transformation of the image of her former self—arrayed in her white robe and adorned with golden hair and chapelet—is absolute: "Here Anima apperythe in þe most horrybull wyse, fowlere þan a fende" (s.d. 902). Although Anima's hellish appearance graphically sums up the spiritual state into which her three Mights have fallen since her departure from the stage (s.d. 324), the extent to which she has "defoule[d] Godys own place" (906) is made fully manifest only when her sinful condition is theatrically incarnated in the Magdalenian image: "Here rennyt owt from wndyr þe horrybyll mantyll of þe Soull seven small boys in þe lyknes of dewyllys and so retorne ageyn" (s.d. 912). Of the three instances of feminine corporeal purgation in East Anglia drama, only in *Wisdom* are the bodily demons first expelled and then reincorporated, as the small boys who represent the devils "retorne ageyn," presumably to be covered once more by Anima's "horrybyll mantyll." The grim spectacle of seven demons moving out of—and back into—Anima's body is glossed by Wisdom: "As many dedly synnys as ye haue vsyde, / So many deullys in yowr soule be. / Beholde wat ys þerin reclusyde! / Alas, man, of þi Soule haue pyte!" (909–12). Only after Anima expresses contrition—"I wepe for sorow, Lorde!" (977)—do her devils permanently depart: "Hic recedunt demones" (s.d. 978). Wisdom confirms the success of this "purger and clenser": "Lo, how contrycyon avoydyth þe deullys blake! / Dedly synne ys non you wythin" (962, 979–80). In the interval during which Wisdom reprimands her three guilty Mights and she learns that penance requires "sorowe of hert" as well as acknowledgment of fault, the unrepentant Anima stands exposed as a silent, gruesome container of sin —alternatively open and closed, permeable by demons who flee from and occupy her body at Christ's command, but "reclusyde" or "shut up" until contrition opens her again.

By figuring Anima's ethical and spiritual dilemma—and in a sense symbolically condensing the conflict of the entire play—through the visual image that displayed the spiritual plight of Mary Magdalene, *Wisdom* invokes medieval culture's familiar association of a corporeal femininity with a corruptible sensuality.[135] Yet the play's engagement with gendered images and discourses is neither traditional nor straightforward. The ambivalence of Anima's bodily image is, in part, a function of the paradoxical construction of the dramatic character herself: although "Anima, cast as the Soul, . . . metaphorically represents the body . . . it is the three male Mights, paradoxically housed in Anima's flesh . . . who actually fall into bodily corruption."[136] Marlene Clark, Sharon Kraus, and Pamela Sheingorn have argued that the play's representation of that fall is consistently orchestrated through constructions and discourses of gender: *Wisdom* stages the demise of Mind, Understanding, and Will in a homosocial political and juridical realm where corrupt social practices are accompanied by a disordering of gender categories that is imaged in homophobic affect, homoerotic behaviors, and excessive and mobile sensuality. This slippage is epitomized in the stage direction that introduces the dancers whom Will calls forth as his "company": "Here entreth six women in sut, thre dysgysyde as galontys and thre as matrones, wyth wondyrfull vysurs congruent" (s.d. 752). According to Clark, Kraus, and Sheingorn, the characterization of Anima's constitutive masculine Mights (and their fragmentation from Anima herself) challenges the unity of the gendered subject, exposing, in Judith Butler's phrase, "the constructed character of sexuality."[137] This challenge, they contend, is not fully overcome even in the final scene of reconciliation, where, despite the play's effort to restore normative power relations, gender categories, and sexual identities, the fluidity of these established by the antics of Mind, Will, and Understanding "leaks into" that effort.[138]

What is the relevance of these unstable gender categories to Anima's own ambiguous bodily image and to the play's evocation of Mary Magdalene? I want to suggest that these moments of slippage also contribute to a gender-specific critique that calls into question traditional associations of sensuality and feminine weakness, making femininity available for other significations. To the extent that the play's dramatic action makes Anima's male Mights both principal targets of desire and agents of sin and sexual disorder, it shifts the burden of cultural association, imaging the masculine realm, not the feminine, as a site of riot. The three Mights' acquiescence to temptation makes permeable "the boundaries protecting their sex/gender identities," and the spiritual implications of that permeability are figured in the body of Anima.[139]

By presenting Anima's Magdalene-like purgation in two phases, *Wisdom* focuses dramatic and visual attention on the ambivalent feminine figure of containment itself. Anima's devils move out, and in, and back out again, their presence or absence signaling her moral and spiritual valence as container.[140] Paradoxically, the very permeability that permits Anima's devils to reveal themselves as the deadly sins "reclusyde" within her also allows her to be emptied of their devastating effects ("Lo, how contrycyon avoydyth þe deullys blake! / Dedly synne ys non yow wythin"). Though horrifying, her permeability is thus also a salutary agent of change, enabling a spiritual transformation which is depicted, like that of Mary Magdalene, in graphic corporeal terms. Imaging the soul's capacity to be open to the effects of both sin and grace, Anima's theatrical body, permeable and feminine, is also the dramatic figure for the idealized, feminine "clean" soul that is "symylytude of Gode abowe" (284) and, as the play's important verbal figures of containment suggest, his habitation.[141] The "clene sowll," Anima declares, "ys Godys restynge place" (176). Understanding invokes a biblical image of containment to illustrate his teaching about the mutual indwelling of God and the soul through charity: "Blyssyde ys þat sowll þat þis speche spellys: 'Et qui creauit me requieuit in tabernaculo meo'" (275–76; "And he who created me rested in my tabernacle"). At the conclusion of the play Wisdom confirms that Anima's cleansing of sin has made her the "very temple of Jhesus" (1108). These tropes of enclosure and containment, to be sure, participate in the conventional association of the chaste feminine body and virtue—Anima is first introduced in the play as a "mayde" (s.d. 16). But through its dramatic performance of her permeability (Anima's loss of "virginity"), Wisdom also enacts her Magdalene-like recovery of purity through its very engagement with the entice-ments of worldly sensuality: "Ye were neuer so leue to me verelye. / Now be ye reformyde to yowr bewtys bryght" (1091–92), Wisdom tells Anima. Like Julian's Magdalene, Anima's sin is "behovely": its reforma-tion makes her even more beloved, more worthy of God's blessing. As the riotous gender play of the secular, masculine realm yields to closure and stability in the feminine soul, the image of Anima's transgressivity lingers, her theatrically spectacular bodily purgation made compatible with the indwelling of the deity.

In view of the play's fascination with Anima as ambivalent figure of containment, the assertion that she is "empty of [a] signification of her own" invites qualification.[142] The elaborate allegorical interpreta-tion that Wisdom accords Anima is relevant here because it glosses the ambivalences imaged in her bodily purgation. Anima is not passive, as some might contend; as a figure for the soul, rather, she is double: "[A] sowle ys bothe fowlle and fayer," Wisdom explains to her, "Fowll as a best be felynge of synne, / Fayre as an angell, of hewyn þe ayer" (157–59).[143] Anima's double nature as a creature of sensuality and reason is imaged in Wisdom's description of her attire:

Thes tweyn do sygnyfye
Yowr dysgysynge and yowr aray,
Blake and wyght, fowll and fayer vereyly,
Euery sowll here, þis is no nay,
Blake by sterynge of synne þat cummyth all-day,
Wyche felynge cummythe of sensualyte,
Ande wyght by knowenge of reson veray
Off þe blyssyde infenyt Deyte. (149–56)

In an important departure from the masculine gendering of the soul that appears in the play's major source, Suso's *Orologium Sapientiae*, *Wisdom* constructs Anima in distinctly feminine terms, thereby according a feminine identity to "euery sowll."[144] Far from being empty of a meaning of her own, Anima signifies the most basic connections between body and soul, humanity and God.[145] Anima's very doubleness— an inevitable consequence of her foul and fair nature—both requires and enables her bodily purgation. The materiality of dramatic performance images her as a permeable body in order also to remake her as the "clene sowll [that] ys Godys restynge place."

The paradoxical aesthetic requirement that sacred drama render abstract spiritual concepts such as Anima in decidedly corporeal terms felicitously coincides with the fundamental issues of *Wisdom*'s symbolic action and moral plot. The play's vision of the inevitable conflict between the material and the spiritual within the "anima" of the individual Christian also posits their symbolic and practical mediation. Anima may bear the "dyrke schadow . . . of humanyte" (166), imaged in her black mantle, but it is, after all, the covering for the garment of "wyght clothe of golde gysely purfyled wyt menyver" (s.d. 16) that signifies the splendor of the "clene" soul's aristocratic queenship united in allegorical marriage to Wisdom. As Milla Riggio has argued, the social inflections of Anima's aristocratic identity must have lent concrete assurance of attractive spiritual possibilities to the materially well-situated "souls" who seem to constitute the ideal audience addressed by the play.[146] When the conflict between the material and spiritual, within and for the individual Christian soul, is most at stake—that is, when Anima is most exposed to the world by her gender-bending masculine Mights, her symbolic boundaries most violated, her angelic fairness nearly overcome by bestial foulness—the *Wisdom* playwright turns to Mary Magdalene as a symbolic resource. The play's iconic condensation of the spiritual identities of Anima and the Magdalene relies on the biblical woman's association with the transgression of bodily boundaries and remakes her image of corporeal femininity into a dramatic sign of the "clene" soul's relationship to matter, spirit, and God.

As the figure renowned for her worldly engagements, corporeally signified penitence, and intimacy with Jesus—the figure who was not simply made right after sin but made better because of it—Mary Magdalene shadows the allegorical plot of *Wisdom*. The biblical woman

makes a still more commanding appearance in the East Anglian dramatic compilation known as the *N-Town Plays*, in which she assumes unusual narrative and symbolic roles in the staging of Christ's Passion and
its aftermath. As is the case with its counterpart in *Wisdom*, the dramatic
image of feminine bodily purgation in the *N-Town Plays* importantly
contributes to East Anglian drama's elaboration of Mary Magdalene's
spiritual and ideological significance for late medieval religious culture.

N-Town *Passion Play I* conflates the exorcism of Mary Magdalene,
reported in Luke 8:2 and Mark 16:9, with the biblical episode from Luke
7 in which a sinful woman anoints Christ; the play then relocates this
narrative and symbolic amalgamation to the scene of the Last Supper,
which here occurs in the home of Simon "leprows."[147] Approaching
Jesus in Simon's house, Mary Magdalene declares her bodily sin through
a series of devotionally resonant metaphors:

> A mercy, Lord, and salve my synne!
> Maydenys floure, þu wasch me fre.
> Þer was nevyr woman of mannys kynne
> So ful of synne in no countré.
> I haue be fowlyd by fryth and fenne
> And sowght synne in many a ceté.
> But þu me borwe, Lord, I xal brenne,
> With blake fendys ay bowne to be! (270.639–46)

Mary Magdalene adopts the N-Town plays' propensity to figure the
female body through tropes of purity and pollution.[148] Linking public
notice of her own sin with Jesus' incarnation, the woman's petition
simultaneously identifies his salvific power with his virgin birth and
contrasts her own sinful state with the Virgin Mary's purity; she implies
that Jesus is able to "wasch" her, the most sinful of women, clean because he is himself the "maydenys floure."[149]

Mary Magdalene's metaphoric naming of Jesus in terms of his corporeal tie to his mother introduces an association of bodies—filial and
maternal, pure and impure, holy and sinful—that Jesus further elaborates in his speech of exorcism:

> [F]ro vii develys I xal þe fende [defend].
> Fendys, fleth ȝoure weye!
> Wyckyd spyritys, I ȝow conjowre,

Fleth out of hire bodyly bowre!
In my grace she xal evyr flowre
Tyl deth doth here to deye. (270–71.659–64)

Ordering the fiends to depart from Mary Magdalene's "bodily bower"—
a corporeal metaphor employed elsewhere in the N-Town plays to signify the enclosure of the Virgin Mary's body—Jesus here echoes the
woman's own metaphoric characterization of him as the "maydenys
floure."[150] Like her counterpart in *Wisdom*, Mary Magdalene experiences
a tearful spiritual contrition (270.652–53) that is concretely realized in a
corporeal transformation; her body "so ful of synne" is now metaphorically likened both to the enclosed space of the Virgin Mary's body and
to the fecundity—she shall "flowre" in Jesus's grace—that the penitent
woman has just attributed to Jesus and his mother. What was permeable
by demons is now rendered open to Jesus' own productive, flowering
grace.

Mary Magdalene's immediate response to her purgation further
highlights the ambiguity of her transgressive body:

I thanke þe, Lorde, of this grett grace,
Now þese vij fendys be fro me flytt, . . .
Now I am brought from þe fendys brace,
In þi grett mercy closyd and shytt,
I xal nevyr returne to synful trace
Þat xulde me dampne to helle pytt. (271.665–66, 669–72)

Mary Magdalene here shifts the tenor of the enclosure metaphor that
made a "bower" of her body: now Jesus becomes the container, she the
contained. Acknowledging her substitution of a sacred lover for a diabolical one, she thanks Jesus for having rescued her from the sinister
enclosure of "þe fendys brace" and rejoices that she is now in his "grett
mercy closyd and shytt."

In the aftermath of the Passion, Mary Magdalene repeatedly rec-
ollects the act and scene of her bodily purgation. In terms of the
metaphoric patterns that we are examining, the most significant instance
occurs when she approaches the tomb with the other Marys. The slippage between encloser and enclosed, container and contained, exhibited
in Mary Magdalene's thanksgiving speech after her exorcism, returns
here in a touching image of her celestial inhabitation:

Vii develys in me were pyght.
My loue, my Lord, my God almyght,
Awey he weryd þe fyndys wight
With his wyse wurde.
He droff fro me þe fendes lees,
In my swete sowle his chawmere I ches,
In me beleveth þe Lorde of Pes. (360.9–15)

Electing to establish ("I ches") Jesus' "chawmere" in her soul, Mary
Magdalene is once again metaphorically figured as the encloser or container, a trope that is consistent with her statement in the next line that
the Lord of Peace "beleveth," or "dwells" within her.[151] Her reference to
having Jesus' "chawmere" in her own soul recalls the familiar trope that
made Jesus himself the enclosure that the devout soul could occupy or
inhabit. Mary Magdalene's recollection at the sepulcher thus reinter-
prets her transgressive body—from which the "fendes lees" have been
spectacularly and graphically driven—as the metaphorical locus of her
soul's mutual indwelling with the deity.

Dramatic elaboration of Mary Magdalene's bodily exorcism
through tropes of enclosure and inhabitation places that event, and the
episode from her narrative vita that it appropriates, in dialogue with
an important symbolic and interpretative tradition that had particular
currency in medieval women's mystical and religious discourse. Elaborating exegetical traditions, deriving from John 7:38 and Song of
Songs 2:14, that encouraged devotion to Christ as sheltering enclosure,
celebrated mystics of the community at Helfta, Gertrude the Great,
Mechtild of Hackeborn and the beguine Mechtild of Magdeburg, represented the divine, especially the idea of the Sacred Heart, through
images of feminine interiority.[152] Mechtild of Hackeborn's *Liber specialis
gratiae*, translated into Middle English as the *Booke of Gostlye Grace*,
includes a vision that resembles the mutual indwelling of soul and deity
praised by N-Town's Mary Magdalene in her speech before the sepulcher. Mechtild depicts Christ's heart as an enclosure, a great house, that
contained within it a little house, the mystic's own heart, where Christ
sits.[153] The author of *Ancrene Wisse* exploits the semiotic resonances of
the anchoress's literal enclosure, articulating an analogy between the
anchoritic cell and the recluse's own heart: "'hard on the outside, with
thorns that prick, and . . . on the inside soft and yielding. . . . Place
[Christ] in your nest, that is, in your heart.'" At the same time, the guide

enjoins the anchoress to make herself a worthy habitation for Christ by encouraging her to enter his body and dwell in his wounds: "'My dove,' He says, 'come and hide thyself in the holes in my limbs, in the hole in my side.'"[154] Figures of enclosure help Margery Kempe envision her marriage to the Godhead, who "toke hir be þe hand in hir sowle."[155] In its meditation on Mary Magdalene's "homli" relationship with God, the female-authored collection of prayers and meditations known as the *Faites and the Passion of Our Lord* employs the trope of enclosure to praise Jesus' charity to contrite sinners: "[Y]e make hem fair and brith and famuliarli in hem ye make youre habitacion."[156]

It is Julian of Norwich's *Revelation of Love*, however, that articulates with the most dazzling originality the symbolic and theological implications of such devotional constructions of mutual indwelling. Julian exploits the metaphoric potential of the analogy between anchorhold and womb in a theology that privileges feminine images and attributes as well as female experience, a theology that defines sacred acts of enclosing and being enclosed as central to the process of salvation itself. In this "involved series of reflections and inversions, of bodies engendered and gestating within other bodies," Christ enters his mother's body in order to become mother himself—"in this lowe place he arayed hym and dyght hym all redy in oure poure flessch, hym selfe to do the service and the officie of moderhode"; the adornment with flesh that resulted from that act of enclosure, in turn, enables the mutual indwelling of Christ and the human soul.[157] Dependent, in Maud McInerney's phrase, on the "fruitful hollowness of three bodies—that of the Virgin, that of Christ's body, which was contained therein, and that of . . . the lover of Christ who both contains and is contained by Him," Julian's profoundly incarnational theology is rooted in a "biological imaginary" that resignifies the female body as "not divided and divisive but the ultimate agent of union" of human and divine.[158]

The intricate metaphorics of enclosure, containment, and inhabitation through which Mary Magdalene's exorcism is represented in the N-Town *Passion* sequence thus participates in a larger symbolic system that elaborated intersubjective, corporeal relationships between Christ, the Virgin Mary, and the devout soul. The N-Town *Passion* dramatist may have taken advantage of the opportunity to bring the scriptural and legendary episode of Mary Magdalene's bodily purgation into semiotic congruence with that system, in part, because of the theological and semiotic commitments of the N-Town compilation as a whole. Through their selection of scriptural episodes, theatrical spectacle, and dramatic language, these plays repeatedly engage the subject of the Virgin Mary's bodily purity and her sharing of maternal, maiden flesh with her son in the sacred enclosure of her womb.[159]

The symbolic triangulation of Mary Magdalene, Christ, and his mother that occurs in the dramatic dialogue about the purgation, moreover, is reinforced by unusual testimonials at the sepulcher offered by the "other Marys." Whereas Mary Magdalene uses that dramatic moment to invoke her spiritual and corporeal permeability, remembering how Christ drove out the seven devils that were "pyght" within her and installed himself in her "swete soul" in their stead, Mary Jacobi offers a brief reprise of the Incarnation and Nativity. Stressing her familial ties to the one she seeks ("My systerys sone I woot he was"), her speech recalls Jesus' miraculous conception and virginal birth. With a slight realignment of a familiar incarnational metaphor, she anticipates the resurrection of the one who "lyth in here [Virgin Mary] as sunne in glas" (360.17–18). The contrast between the two women's speeches emphasizes the difference between the types of feminine enclosure that they reference, one transgressive and permeable, the other perfectly intact and resolutely unbreachable; yet both are imaged as containers of divinity. Mary Salome in her turn asserts a more complex familial tie, adding to her announcement that she is the Virgin's sister this affectionate genealogical note: "Annys dowterys we be all thre; Jesu, we be þin awntys" (360.25–28).

Peter Meredith has suggested that the "repeated mention of relationships" in these speeches before the sepulcher "trivialises a potentially moving episode."[160] But the Marys' notice of familial connections and feminine enclosures at this moment anticipates their discovery of Christ's resurrection in a way unparalleled in the other English biblical cycles. Their reflections on Marian involvement, enclosure, and sacred genealogy make a fitting prelude to the angel's notice that "3oure fleschly Lorde now hath lyff" (361.67), marking these testimonials at the sepulcher not simply as familial responses to the death of Christ but as spirited reminders of the feminine role in the Redemption.

The unique dramatic placement of Mary Magdalene's purgation at the scene of the Last Supper makes a crucial contribution to the N-Town compilation's effort to foreground such theological and symbolic possibilities, expanding her significance in sacred history. Analysis of codicological evidence of the processes that produced the N-Town collection reveals that the imaginative relocation of Mary Magdalene's bodily exorcism occurred as the manuscript was being compiled into its present form.[161] By establishing Mary Magdalene's presence at the Last Supper and the institution of the Eucharist, the N-Town Passion sequence inaugurates her discipleship from these moments rather than her later, canonical, witnessing of Christ's resurrection, thereby placing the saint in an early apostolic community that recalls traditions of women's spiritual authority dating back to the early Christian era. Known largely through extracanonical writings such as the *Gospel of Mary*, *Pistis Sophia*, *Gospel of Philip*, *Gospel of Thomas*, and *Dialogue of the Savior*, this tradition articulated women's role in religious teaching, prophecy, and leadership through the figure of Mary Magdalene, whom these texts represent as a favorite of Christ and repository of spiritual authority.[162]

Of special relevance to medieval English drama is the way writings such as the *Gospel of Mary* stage a conflict between Mary Magdalene and the male disciples, especially Peter, a conflict that represents a struggle between a conception of ecclesiastical authority based "on feminine principles of vision, prophecy, and spiritual understanding . . . as embodied by Mary Magdalen" and one "vested in the male principles of apostolic tradition, hierarchy and acquired knowledge . . . as represented by Peter."[163] By the later Middle Ages, centuries dominated by the Gregorian construction of Mary Magdalene as a sexual sinner had significantly diluted the claims for women's religious leadership accorded to her in these early Christian writings. But the idea of Mary Magdalene's spiritual authority retained currency in the tradition of her apostolate, which "popular devotional literature, sacred poetry and drama, religious art, the liturgy, and sermons" made "ubiquitous" from the twelfth century to the Council of Trent.[164] As Jansen asserts, "the problem of female ecclesiastical leadership, whose authority derives from spiritually attained knowledge as distinct from knowledge acquired from tradition, did not die with Gnosticism, nor did it move outside the church into heresy; it remained a paradox at the very heart of Christian experience, and the figure of the Magdalen embodied it."[165]

With its rich traditions of devotional writing, sacred iconography, and religious vocation manifesting profound preoccupations with feminine spiritual authority, East Anglian religious culture provided a congenial arena for exploring this paradox. The plays brought together by the N-Town compiler furnish one of its fullest articulations, making an extracanonical space for the feminine presence in and perspective on signal events in sacred history. More than any of the other English biblical cycle plays, the N-Town *Passion* sequence presents Mary Magdalene as disciple, weaving her experience into post-Resurrection testimonies of doubt and belief and foregrounding her relationship to Peter. Whereas early Christian texts put the two at odds with each other, the *N-Town Plays* suggest the possibility of their rapprochement.

From the announcement by the angel at the tomb to the resolution of Thomas's doubt, N-Town's Resurrection sequence repeatedly places Mary Magdalene and Peter in dialogue. The play follows Mark 16:7 in having an angel tell the women at the tomb to "goth forth fast, all thre, / To his dyscyplys fayr and fre. / And to Petyr þe trewth telle 3e" (362.71–73). Among the gospel accounts and the English biblical cycles, however, only N-Town shows the women acting on this request, as confirmed by both a stage direction ("Maria Magdalene dicit Petro et ceteris apostolis"; [s.d. at 362.94]) and Mary Magdalene herself ("An aungel us bad ryght þus, sertayn, / To þe, Petry, þat we xulde telle / How Cryst is resyn" [363.99–101]). Exhibiting the disbelief attributed to the disciples by the Gospels (Mark 16:11; Luke 24:10–12), Peter questions the women's announcement: "Sey me, systeryn, with wurdys blythe, / May I troste to þat 3e say?" (363.111–12). When Peter and John race to the tomb (John 20:3–10), John is the first to profess the truth of the Resurrection that the discarded shroud proclaims: "Now may I wele knowe and wete / Þat he is rysyn to lyve ageyn! / . . . As women seyd, so haue we fownde" (364–5.137–38, 151). Peter makes a similar announcement to "all the disciples gathered together" ("Hic petrus loquitur omnibus apostolis simul collectis" [s.d. at 364.146]). N-Town's Mary Magdalene reports her meeting with the risen Christ to the presumably assembled "bretheryn": "For, trost me trewly, it is ryght thus / . . . I spak ryght now with Cryst Jesus" (368.91, 93). Her announcement prompts this lone and utterly unscriptural response from Peter: "A woundyrful tale, forsothe, is this" (368.94).

Peter's unusual affirmation of Mary Magdalene's experience of the risen Christ prepares for his conspicuous advocacy on her behalf in the exchange that precedes Christ's appearance to Thomas. Here Peter tries to engage Thomas in a joyful response to the "gode novell" that they have just received from Luke and Cleophas, namely that "[o]ure Lord is resyn his se[r]uauntys to saue" (379.300). When Thomas dismisses these "wantowne and ryght vnwyse" words regarding how a "deed man" could become "qwyk flesche and blood . . . ageyn," Peter counters his fellow's doubt by invoking "[r]ecord of Mawdelyn and of here systerys too" (379.302–4, 306). When Thomas remains adamant in his refusal to believe, Peter again references Mary Magdalene's speech, recalling that his inspection of Christ's tomb was prompted by what "Mawdelyn dede tell us" (379.313).[166] Thomas avers that neither the "prechynge of Petir" nor knowledge "þat Mary Magdalyn in Cryst dede sone beleve" could move him to the faith that he can embrace only through his direct probing of Christ's bloody wounds (381.377, 385). The doubting disciple thus articulates his need for an immediate, corporeal knowledge in terms of the common evangelical work in which Peter and Mary Magdalene have been engaged, even as he differentiates between the persuasion of Peter's "preaching" and the experiential force of Mary Magdalene's faith.

Thomas's speech calls to mind the early Christian tradition that debated rival claims to spiritual authority represented by Peter and Mary Magdalene. Like that tradition, the N-Town Resurrection sequence acknowledges the possibility of feminine access to spiritual truth; but it also departs from it, not simply to diminish the potential for conflict between the two disciples but to suggest the parity of their evangelical influence. While the N-Town plays were probably never performed in their achieved state, the compiler's book that has come down to us bears signs of a developed commitment to articulating such feminine interventions in salvation history. Its preoccupations with Incarnation and maternal genealogies, in manuscript text and marginalia, give evidence of this commitment. Its incorporation of a life of the Virgin Mary paralleling its life of Christ, moreover, introduces opportunities to parallel their respective demonstrations of spiritual authority, such as that produced by the juxtaposition of precocious children in *Mary in the Temple* and *Christ and the Doctors*. The relocation of Magdalene's anointing and purgation to the scene of the Last Supper further extends this emphasis and lays foundations for her expanded role as disciple in events of the Passion and Resurrection.

"Record of Mawdelyne"

In *Wisdom* and the *N-Town Plays* the motif of feminine purgation, then, is intricately bound up with social, spiritual, and symbolic constructions of gender. Dramatic renderings of female bodily exorcism invoke the role of the feminine in spiritual identity formation, underscore feminine capacity for the indwelling of the deity, and identify corporeal foundations of feminine spiritual authority. These themes, and not simply a report of Christ's Resurrection, constitute the "record of Mawdelyne" in East Anglian drama and religious culture; and that "record" is most ambitiously and creatively expressed in the Digby saint play. It *is* remarkable, if not entirely surprising, that the resonant moment of feminine exorcism, associated with Mary Magdalene from the time of Gregory the Great, appears in three different late medieval East Anglian plays. The symbolic commitments and spiritual idioms of these Magdalene dramas may owe their commonality to the likelihood that they were all copied, and probably composed, within relative geographical proximity of each other during the late fifteenth and early sixteenth centuries.[167] The fact that a substantial fragment of *Wisdom* appears in the Digby manuscript and that the Macro manuscript, source for the only complete text of that morality, bears what Gibson calls an "incestuous relationship" to the manuscript containing the single extant version of *Mary Magdalene* invites comparative assessment of the plays' respective aims and emphases.[168]

Wisdom reads and plays like an allegorical dress rehearsal for the more elaborate biblical and legendary treatment of related themes in the Digby *Magdalene*. Both plays present a feminine figure whose symbolic mediation of corporeal desires, spiritual longings, and relationship to Christ are informed by exegesis of the Song of Songs. Seduced by evil in the guise of their respective gallants, the feminine "heroines" of both plays are each made right through contrition. The morality and the saint play also exhibit similar preoccupations with knowledge of self, suspicion of learning, the mediation of the active and contemplative lives; and, as I shall argue, they reveal a common debt to spiritual ideologies propounded by late medieval devotional texts. These similarities are reinforced by substantial verbal echoes.[169] Even the sixteenth-century marginalia of the Macro copy of *Wisdom* acknowledge Mary Magdalene: a ballad written on folios 111v and 112 speaks of "iii lowely" who go on pilgrimage: "[T]he fyst was marymaudellen whom cryst forgaue her syn a—marya / the secunde was mary regytpe next of all hyr kyn a—marya / ye therde owr bllyssyde lady ye flower of all women a—marya."[170]

The marginalia's association of the sinful woman forgiven by Christ and the sinless "flower of all women" recalls the connection between the two elaborated in the N-Town *Passion Play*'s exorcism of Mary Magdalene, and just as important, points to a theological congruence highlighted in the Digby play's purgation scene, where the saint's spiritual and symbolic preoccupations echo those of her N-Town counterpart. In the speech that leads up to her exorcism—her first direct address to Christ—the saint play's heroine praises the deity in terms of his mother: "O, blessyd be þou, Lord of euyrlastyng lyfe, / And blyssyd be þi berth of þat puer vergynne!" (678–79). Invoking Christ's virgin birth to highlight his sacredness rather than her contamination, Mary Magdalene's allusion to the deity's maternal generation brings to the moment of her bodily purgation the triangulation of sacred identities that the N-Town scene of exorcism also exhibits. Mary Magdalene's notice here of these overlapping identities introduces an important element of the Digby play's theology of redemption and anticipates its provocative elaboration of other prominent themes that also shape representations of the Magdalene figure in *Wisdom* and the *N-Town Plays*: the formation of feminine religious subjects and subjectivities, the female body's relationship to sin and sacred power, and the nature of female apostolic authority.[171]

Like the stage direction that provides for Mary Magdalene and her companions to be "arrayed as chaste women," these aspects of the Digby saint play bear witness to representational and interpretative strategies that securely located the saint's dramatic vita within an East Anglian social and spiritual climate that fostered feminine religious subjects, symbols, and experience. As the following chapters shall demonstrate, these features of the play underscore its recognition—and promotion—of feminine interventions in salvation history and inscribe the dramatic life of Mary Magdalene with the ideological debates and spiritual preoccupations and practices of late medieval religious culture. The portrait of the play to be educed from this evidence has important implications for English literary history and late medieval vernacular religion.

3

Mystic and Preacher

Nevertheless, yif it so be that this maner of feelynge lette not thyn herte fro goostli occupacion, but it maketh thee the more devoute and the more fervent for to pray, it maketh thee more wise for to thenke goostli thoughtes. . . . Bi these tokenes may thu knowe thanne that it is of God, maad bi the presence and the touch- inge of the good angil, and that is of the goodnesse of God in confort of symple devoute soulis for to encrese ther trust and there desire to God . . . or ellis, yif thei be perfight, that thei fele suyche a delite: it semeth than that it is an ernest, and as it were a schadewe of glori- fyynge of the bodi which it schal have in the blisse [of heuen]. But I not whether ther be ony siche man lyvande in erthe. This pryvylegie hadde Marie Mawde- leyn, as hit seemeth to my sight, in tyme whanne sche was visited, whanne sche was aloone in the cave thritti wyntir and iche day was born up with angelis into the eyr, and was feed bothe bodi and soule bi the presence of hem. Thus we reden in the legend of hire.
— *Scale of Perfection*, 1.11

AT THREE DIFFERENT POINTS in the *Scale of Perfection*, a work remark- ably lacking in reference to specific human example, Walter Hilton departs from his characteristic idiom to identify the achievements, assurances, and challenges of the accomplished contemplative with the biblical and legendary experience of Mary Magdalene. Hilton first in- vokes the saint's ecstatic angelic feedings in her desert hermitage to illus- trate the perfect soul made privy to heavenly mysteries. In the *Scale* Mary Magdalene also bears witness to the promise of full knowledge and love of God in heaven that is presaged in the contemplative's earthly experience.[1] Because devotion to Christ's humanity, rather than his divinity, distinguished Mary Magdalene's response to the risen Savior, she also signifies for Hilton the contemplative's ongoing struggle to know and love god "as a God and man godli not as man manli" (2.30).[2] The only individual—other than Jesus, the Virgin Mary, and the authors of scripture—whom Hilton designates by name, Mary Magdalene elusively presides over the arduous and disciplined pursuit described in the *Scale of Perfection*.

Like this popular theological and mystical text, the Digby saint play similarly parallels the experience of its saintly heroine with the contemplative's progress toward perfection. This similarity stems in part from the basic debt of both texts to scriptural commentary and spiritual writings that by the late Middle Ages had long identified Mary Magdalene as an exemplary figure of the contemplative life. Her reputation as the sinner who lovingly anointed Jesus, quietly listened to his words despite the protests of her industrious sister Martha, and first witnessed his resurrection had made her renowned for intimacy with the human Christ before and after his death. Scriptural exegesis associated Mary Magdalene with the Bride of the Song of Songs, designating the saint as a type of the mystical lover of Christ.[3] Mary Magdalene's sorrowful vigil before the empty tomb was easily conflated with the longing expressed by the Song's Bride; her lament for Jesus, as Michel de Certeau points out, made her the "eponymous figure of the modern mystic."[4] Mary Magdalene's affective and contemplative example offered a spiritual model to devout late medieval religious and lay people of both sexes. In addition to the *Scale of Perfection*, she serves that function in Love's *Mirror of the Blessed Life of Jesus Christ*, the *Cloud of Unknowing*, and, as we have seen, Margery Kempe's *Book* and Julian's *Revelation*.[5] As the archetypal contemplative and mystical lover, Mary Magdalene provided a powerful exemplar for medieval holy women in particular, who embraced her as guide in their quests for spiritual perfection.

By invoking Hilton's paradigmatic contemplative in this analysis of the Digby play, however, I mean to appeal to more than the traditions of scriptural commentary and late medieval strategies of spiritual identification upon which both Hilton and the East Anglian playwright importantly and perhaps inevitably draw. Rather, what interests me in the relationship of drama to devotional text are strong resemblances between the spiritual journeys that each outlines for the contemplative subject. Analyses of the Digby text have more frequently emphasized the penitential side of the saint's double identity as penitent *and* contemplative, in the process overlooking many signs that the Digby dramatist gave priority to the saint's mystical and contemplative authority rather than her penitential biography.[6] Although several scholars have recognized the Digby play's attention to Mary Magdalene's contemplative and mystical vocations, the contemporary late medieval context informing such investments has yet to be fully investigated.[7] This chapter argues that the saint play draws upon prominent texts, themes, and practices of late medieval religious culture to construct the dramatic Mary Magdalene as a figure of contemplative and visionary authority. I use Hilton's *Scale of Perfection* as a touchstone for eliciting the Digby saint play's congruence with the epistemological interests and terminology of late medieval contemplative and mystical discourses.[8] Encounters with the sacred are a staple of saintly biography, to be sure, but the Digby play uniquely makes visionary authority and modes of sacred communication dominant topoi of its rewriting of the saint's vita. Late medieval understandings of the goals and politics of contemplation, I contend, constitute a major textual horizon for interpreting this dramatic hagiography.

A signal feature of late medieval vernacular religious culture was the important role occupied by women, as addressees, producers, and consumers of religious writing and as subjects of the contemplative and mystical experiences that were increasingly memorialized and promoted by vernacular texts. Accordingly, this chapter also examines the Digby play's representation of Mary Magdalene in light of visionary and charismatic women whose example and experience evidence late medieval preoccupations with gender and spiritual authority. These visionaries were both revered and held suspect—revered because they bore witness to forms of religious experience that spoke meaningfully to the spiritual needs of both religious and laity; held suspect because those very innovative forms cast these women in roles that challenged traditional religious thinking and clerical authority. Late medieval anxieties about women's religious authority frequently focused on their ability to serve as teachers and preachers. Because the Digby *Magdalene* unmistakably presents its saint as a public preacher of vernacular scripture, I also examine the play's participation in late medieval debates about the nature and scope of women's public spiritual authority.

Drama and Contemplative Texts:
Intersections

My claim that *Mary Magdalene* articulates themes and terms of late medieval vernacular religious culture draws support from another East Anglian dramatic text. Walter Smart's 1912 source study of the Macro *Wisdom* established that play's primary debts to the Middle English version of Suso's *Orologium Sapientiae*, known as the *Sevene Poyntes of Trewe Love and Everlastynge Wisdame*, as well as to Hilton's *Scale of Perfection* and *Epistle on the Mixed Life*. Smart judged the sections of *Wisdom* deriving principally from vernacular religious texts as lacking interest and originality, especially in comparison to parts of the play where the dramatist used "his own language" to satirize contemporary social and political abuses.[9] Recent studies of *Wisdom*, however, have more favorably assessed its appropriations of vernacular religious texts as crucial indices to the cultural disposition of its intended audience and to the interweaving of monastic and lay spiritualities in late medieval England.[10] The play's dependence on vernacular works by Suso and Hilton offers evidence of the varied transmission and dissemination of late medieval mystical and devotional writings, signaling how theological texts originally circulated among devout religious and lay audiences migrated from their destined milieu of individual, devotional reading to the social and public realms of theater. *Wisdom*'s dramatic debts to vernacular religious writing and to Hilton's *Scale* in particular establish an East Anglian precedent for the kind of intertexual and cultural grid within which the Digby *Magdalene* is also firmly embedded.

The dialogic relation between the Digby saint play and the contemplative discourses of the *Scale of Perfection* that I am hypothesizing draws a different kind of support from abundant evidence that Hilton's text provided a "powerfully articulated" model of lay instruction in late medieval England.[11] Although Hilton had addressed book 1 of the *Scale* to an anchoress, by the time he wrote book 2 (c. 1390), he clearly had in mind the broader purpose of presenting the contemplative life as suitable for and available to laypeople, a goal that coincides with the spiritual ideologies of the Digby saint play.[12] One of the popular English vernacular theological works having wide currency through the fifteenth and early sixteenth centuries, the *Scale of Perfection* survives in an impressive number of manuscripts (book 1 in forty-five; book 2 in twenty-six).[13] Testamentary and codicological evidence indicates that the *Scale* was a favorite among religious as well as lay audiences, ranging from the aristocracy to the merchant classes, whose taste for spiritual reading was nourished by literary efforts of the Carthusians and the program of translation and textual production that constellated in the fifteenth and early sixteenth centuries around the Brigittine monastery at Syon.[14] After achieving the status of a religious classic by the late fifteenth century, the *Scale of Perfection* became the first vernacular work on contemplative practices to be printed in England; at the request of Margaret Beaufort, Wynkyn de Worde published it along with Hilton's *Epistle on the Mixed Life* in 1494.[15]

The late medieval popularity of Hilton's *Scale* and other works of contemplation and religious instruction, including *The Abbey of the Holy Ghost, Contemplations of the Dread and Love of God, Dives and Pauper, The Chastising of God's Children*, and numerous writings by and attributed to Rolle, bears bibliographical witness to the democratization of devotional reading and conceptions of the religious life that Nicholas Watson identifies as a key feature of late medieval English spirituality.[16] Typified in Hilary Carey's idea of the "devout literate layperson," this aspect of late medieval religious culture has attracted ever-increasing attention in recent years; its larger context, in Michael Sargent's characterization, involved ecclesiastical and historical as well as literary "adaptation to secular ends or audiences of what was originally or primarily monastic or heremitic."[17] The permeation of late medieval lay society by contemplative ideals originally associated only with professed religious is one important indicator of a gradual shift of power toward lay interests in the late medieval church, a shift that is also attested in the breakdown of the opposition between *literatus* and *illiteratus* and in the politically contested use of the vernacular as a medium of religious expression and instruction.[18]

Democratization of devotional reading and conceptions of the religious life in late medieval England also involved their feminization. The feminine gendering of lay, vernacular religious culture stemmed in part from the gendering of the vernacular itself, the *lingua materna* whose opposition to Latinity provided a central binary in a nexus of relationships that also opposed the masculine realm of clerical learning, theological complexity, figural hermeneutics, the spiritual sense, and Christ's divinity, to lay ignorance, intellectual simplicity, literalness, carnality, and Christ's humanity.[19] The growth of vernacular literacy increasingly placed the laity in "a position in the educational hierarchy similar to that which had long been occupied by women religious," whose "less fully developed capacity for independent reading and meditation," compared to those of their male counterparts, encouraged the development of new modes of devotional reading as alternatives to monastic *lectio divina*. As the "intellectual and pastoral assumptions" of vernacular spiritual guides originally addressed to nuns, anchoresses, and recluses were increasingly appropriated for new, lay audiences, the conception of the religious life that these texts first sought to model retained feminine symbolic valences.[20]

If the intersection of lay and monastic values and cultures is a crucial informing context for late medieval East Anglian drama, as Gibson has argued, one distinctive feature of the drama it helped to produce is a predilection for imaging the relevance of monastic contemplative ideals to "every Christian life" in feminine symbols of spiritual progress.[21] Dramatizing the apocryphal story of how the young Virgin Mary was offered as "servaunt of God" in fulfillment of her parents' vow, the N-Town "Mary in the Temple" figures the Virgin's ascent of the temple stairs as an allegorical progression, through the fifteen gradual psalms, to "Hevynly Jherusalem."[22] This ritual action links the process of Mary's enclosure in the temple with monastic virtues and, through the image and allegory of ascent, reinforces the spiritual pattern of the contemplative's journey. At the same time, the young Mary's humility, concern for the "holy felachepp" of her temple maidens (90.202), and interest in performing "dedys of mercy" for "[p]ore folk" (94.291–92) also offer a "recognizable and emulatable model for [the] lay piety" that the play's emotional portrait of parent and precocious child obviously manipulates. Gibson usefully observes that the modeling of contemplative experience in Mary's allegorical "journey to purity of soul" provides "an ideal type" of the one accomplished in the morality *Wisdom* by Anima, who "makes a stumbling and painful journey into sin and despair before finally attaining her own spouse and crown at the top of the Temple steps."[23] These East Anglian dramatic narratives of feminine spiritual progress find a counterpart, I submit, in the experience of the Digby play's Mary Magdalene.[24]

Many of the Latin manuscripts of Hilton's *Scale of Perfection* contain a summary of book 2 of that work that reads like an outline of the spiritual development of the Digby play's protagonist, reinforcing correspondences between the dramatic vita and late medieval models of the contemplative life.[25] The summary explains the text's four-part presentation of its subject: "how the human soul is reformed to the image of God." The first part relates the reformation of the soul in faith alone, a state that pertains to spiritual novices (*ad status incipiencium*), while part 2 discusses those who want to advance in grace to achieve reformation of the soul in feeling. It is the account of parts 3 and 4 that resonates most deeply with the spiritual narrative of the Digby play. Part 3 relates what happens

> when, through the grace of the holy spirit, the conscience is cleansed of all stirrings of sin and the inner eye of the soul is opened, the soul is reformed in the stirring of virtues, so that it truly feels humility of heart, perfect love and charity toward all those near to it, peace and patience, purity and cleanness, with comfort and joy for them and glory in its conscience. And this pertains to the state of the perfect who, through the grace of God and great sustaining of effort, and through struggling with sin night and day, have conquered the bitter stirrings of sin and received the sweet sensations of virtue through the grace of the most beloved Jesus Christ. And thus they are truly reformed in feeling. In the fourth part I touched upon certain souls who are not only reformed to the image of God in the stirring of virtues but are elevated even higher. Thus they are reformed by perfect love of God, and they are filled up by what they feel in their hearts, and perceive secret inspirations of Jesus Christ, and spiritual illuminations, heavenly comforts and gracious thoughts, marvelous contemplations of good spirits and hidden knowledge of heavenly joys.[26]

Mary Magdalene's dramatic itinerary maps a similar spiritual progress in which the heroine acquires virtues that mark an inner disposition leading to contemplative perfection. By her own report, the saint is first "temtyd . . . wyth tytyll of trew perfythnesse" by the "speryt of goodnesse" who prompts her repentance (602–3). When she encounters Christ in the house of Simon, she responds to his dramatic pronouncement of her forgiveness by declaring her commitment to spiritual virtues: "And for þat I haue synnyd in þe synne of pryde, / I wol enabyte me wyth humelyte. / Aȝens wrath and envy, I wyll devyde / Thes fayur vertuys, pacyens and charyte" (681–85). Later when she withdraws from her worldly apostolate to pursue an ascetic life in the desert, she reaffirms her commitment to the virtues she had embraced at the moment of her conversion, resolving to

> evyr abyte me wyth humelyte,
> And put me in pacyens, my Lord for to love.

In charyte my werkys I woll grave,
And in abstynence, all dayys of my lyfe.
Thus my concyens of me doth crave;
Than why shold I wyth my consyens st[r]yffe? (1991–96)[27]

Determining to pursue the humility, patience, charity, and abstinence of the contemplative life and follow the dictates of her conscience, Mary Magdalene here echoes the description of the "state of the perfect" in the summary of the Latin *Scale*, as she does only a few lines earlier when she declares her intention to "labor forth, God to plese, / More gostly strenkth me to purchase!" (1959–60).[28] The spectacular rewards she receives for her spiritual pursuits—she is elevated and fed by angels, filled with bliss, made privy to angelic "gle and game" and "gret mesteryys shewyd from heven"—bring her experience squarely into line with that promised by the Latin *Scale* for only the most advanced contemplatives. The conclusion of the Digby play finds Mary Magdalene accomplished in both the state and the virtue that mark the true contemplative: she thanks God "wyth speryt of perfythnesse" for her angelic visitations and is lauded as the "blyssyd woman, inure [practiced] in mekenesse" by the hermit priest who brings her final communion (2100–01).

The dramatic shaping of the life of Mary Magdalene as a progress conforming to the spiritual journey set out for contemplatives in texts such as the *Scale of Perfection* also resonates in the play's characterization of the heavenly mysteries to which the hermit saint is privy. The penultimate scene of the Digby play stages Mary's desert colloquy with the priest who witnesses her elevation and feeding by angels. Summoned by "grett myrth and melody" of angels (2040) to a spectacle of heavenly mysteries, he eagerly "spye[s] Mari in hyr devocyon": "Þe joye of Jherusallem shewyd þe expresse, / Þe wych I nevyr save þis thirty wyntyr and more! / Wherfor I know well þou are of gret perfy[t]nesse, / I woll pray yow hartely to she[w] me of yower Lord!" (s.d. at 2045; 2049–52).[29] Invoking the scriptural commonplace of the heavenly Jerusalem, the priest here draws a more direct connection between the contemplative's privileged access to the deity ("show me the lord you've seen," he beseeches Mary) and the "joy of Jerusalem," here a term that ambiguously designates both the subject of the contemplative's divine revelation as well as its source. Jerusalem is also the name by which Hilton, in a well-known allegory in the *Scale* (2.21–26) designates the goal of the contemplative's spiritual pilgrimage: "Jerusalem . . . bitokeneth contemplacion in perfighte love of God. For contemplacion is not ellis but a sight of Jhesu, the whiche is veri pees. Than yif thou coveite for to come to this blissid sight of veri pees and be a trewe pilgrim to Jerusalemward, though it be so that I were nevere there, neverthelees as ferforth as I can I schal sette thee in the weie thedirward" (2.21).[30] Significantly, Hilton identifies a position for himself that resembles the one that the hermit priest occupies in relation to Mary Magdalene; both are outside the privileged place of divine revelation.

Faced with the necessity of inventing testimonials for Mary Magdalene about which her narrative vitae could remain silent, the dramatist turns to biblical language and metaphors that circulated in well-known contemplative texts. Whether or not these similarities suggest the direct influence of the devotional upon the dramatic text, as in the case of *Wisdom*, they unambiguously point to intertexual relationships that signal the play's commitment to making Mary Magdalene's contemplative experience conform to values and ideals that late medieval vernacular religious texts similarly sought to inculcate.[31] To the extent, however, that Hilton's text also promoted an antispeculative contemplative theology intended to strengthen orthodox clerical positions in the face of the circulation of Lollard doctrines and increasing use of the vernacular as a medium of religious instruction, these intersections with the Digby play also raise important questions about the drama's own participation in contested arenas of late medieval religious culture.[32] Dramatic appropriation of themes and terms appearing in the *Scale of Perfection* is further rendered problematic because that work's contemplative program avers the priority of spiritual over carnal forms of accessing religious truths, a stance that is at odds with both Mary Magdalene's biblical and symbolic identities and the aesthetics of late medieval religious drama.[33]

The Digby saint play's encounter with political, aesthetic, and epistemological issues raised by the *Scale of Perfection* thus offers a critical lens focusing on a neglected moment in the history of the reception of vernacular religious texts by late medieval dramatists. Recent work on these texts has established that they could be differently read, construed, and used, depending on the social circumstances of their audiences and the historical and cultural moment of their reading. In the early fifteenth century, *Dives and Pauper*, for example, was confiscated from an East Anglian charged with heresy; yet its orthodoxy was otherwise attested by the commissioning of a copy of the text by the abbot of St. Albans.[34]

The Middle English translation of Catherine of Siena's *Il Dialogo,* known as the *Orcherd of Syon,* adapted the Italian ecstatic's mystical activism into a meditative devotional guide suitable for contemplative nuns, while Bridget of Sweden's *Revelations* were recast for a variety of late medieval purposes and audiences.[35] Alphonso of Jaén's treatise on the discernment of spirits supporting Bridget's visionary experiences, *Epistola solitarii ad reges,* became in its Middle English incarnations a statement of exactly the opposite: it was incorporated into *The Chastising of God's Children* to warn the visionary of susceptibility to diabolical influence.[36] Wynkyn de Worde's 1501 publication of extracts from *The Book of Margery Kempe* exemplifies the vulnerability of devotional text and author to the vagaries of late medieval textual transmutation. *A shorte treatyse of contemplacyon taught by our lorde Jhesu Cryst / or taken out of the boke of Margery kempe ancresse of Lynne* turned Kempe's worldly, noisy religion into a private, quiet spirituality.[37]

Just as the translation of works of religious instruction from one language or audience to another gave rise to new interpretations and new textual forms, the medieval English vernacular theological work that most consistently invoked Mary Magdalene's exemplary contemplation was selectively appropriated for a late fifteenth- or early sixteenth-century dramatic occasion to make a new and different vernacular statement about religious experience in late medieval England. While *Mary Magdalene* approvingly appeals to much of what Hilton's account of contemplative experience prescribes, it by no means reproduces all of Hilton's spiritual values. Rather, it employs contemplative themes and terms that the *Scale of Perfection* in a sense epitomized to make its own late medieval case about the relationship between contemplation, gender, and spiritual authority, a case with the potential to resist the kind of orthodoxies propounded by texts such as Hilton's.

The Digby saint play omits the episode in Luke 10:38–42 that had provided the scriptural foundation for Mary Magdalene' association with contemplation. Considering that the dramatic text otherwise so encyclopedically incorporates virtually every narrative episode and symbolic motif with which its heroine was customarily associated, the neglect of this scene is a striking omission. Rather than represent Christ's declaration to Martha that her sister Mary has elected the *optimam partem,* which Hilton described as "the loue of god in contemplacion," the Digby playwright, I suggest, chose instead to make the saint's well-known exegetical identity the subtext of the entire dramatic narrative.

When Mary Magdalene twice "enhabits" herself with humility, she allies her experience with the spiritual foundations of Christian asceticism as a whole. The saint play reaches beyond these devotional commonplaces, however, to incorporate Magdalene's embrace of humility into a larger dramatic portrait that privileges the contemplative's progress, an experience that the play itself represents as subject to the same epistemological probing regularly accorded to visionary phenomena described in vernacular religious texts.

Contemplative and Dramatic Christologies

The Digby saint play devotes an extraordinary amount of attention to the life of Christ. We might expect a faithful rendering of the composite biblical life of Mary Magdalene to include scriptural moments involving the saint's critical encounters with the deity: her anointing of Jesus in the house of Simon, the raising of Lazarus, the visit of the three Marys to the tomb of the Resurrection, and the hortulanus episode. But *Mary Magdalene* also dramatizes events from the life of Christ whose inclusion does not obviously further the *imitatio Christi* that was one goal of Christian hagiography. For example, the play devotes over 10 percent (312) of its 2,143 lines to episodes involving the earthly rulers' conspiracy against Jesus.[38] Far from simply making Christ, rather than Mary Magdalene, the focus of the play, as one critic has argued, these additions to the saint's traditional vita underscore a dramatic preoccupation with elaborating the attributes of the deity.[39] In the Digby play Christ occupies a role even larger than the one that scripture and the life of the saint provided for him because his divine nature and human being are intricately connected to the Magdalene's capacities for contemplative insight and spiritual understanding.

The play's treatment of the Passion and Crucifixion provides a framework for assessing its christological emphases. Although *Mary Magdalene* dramatizes attempts by Caesar, Herod, and Pilate first to apprehend Jesus for preaching against their law and their gods (121–28) and then to hide the outcome of his death (1249–1335), it stages no direct confrontation between Jesus and his persecutors nor any incident from his Passion. Instead, the play represents these temporal rulers as deeply concerned about the exchange of information about Jesus, making him the object of a plot from which he is oddly removed and to which he is dramatically never shown to be vulnerable. While its characters talk all around the Passion of Christ, the Digby play never represents the deity in anything but a triumphal or divine mode. In good Aristotelian fashion, the gruesome elements leading up to the confirmation of Christ's divine nature at the Resurrection all happen offstage. The Passion figures in the play only by the report of a devil who declares what the Crucifixion has accomplished: "Now ar we thrall þat frest wher fre, / Be þe passyon of hys manhede. / O[n] a crosce on hye hangyd was he, / Whych hath dystroyd ower labor and alle ower dede!" (971–74).

This oblique account of Christ's Passion soon yields to direct testimony offered by the three Marys. As the women pause at the site of the Crucifixion on their way to anoint Christ in his tomb, they recollect moments from the procession to Calvary. Their speeches move quickly from lament to affirmation of Christ's divinity and his victory over sin:

[MAWDLEYN]. Alas, alas, for þat ryall bem!
A, þis percytt my hartt worst of all!
For here he turnyd aȝen to þe woman of Jerusalem,
And for wherynesse lett þe crosse falle!
MARY JACOBE. Thys sorow is beytterare þan ony galle,
For here þe Jevys spornyd hym to make hym goo,
And þey dysspyttyd þer Kyng ryall.
That clyvytt myn hart, and makett me woo.
MARY SALOME. Yt ys intollerabyll to se or to tell,
For ony creature, þat stronkg tormentry!
O Lord, þou haddyst a mervelows mell!
Yt is to hedyows to dyscry!
[s.d.] *Al þe Maryys wyth on woyce sey þis folowyng*:
[THE THREE MARYYS]. Heylle, gloryows crosse! þou baryst þat
      Lord on hye,
Whych be þi myght deddyst lowly bowe doun,
Mannys sowle from all thraldam to bye,
That euyrmore in peyne shold a be [boun],
Be record of Davyt, wyth myld stevyn:
      "*Domine inclina celos tuos, et dessende!*" (993–1011)

Here it is not the body of Christ that emerges as central signifier of the Passion but the "gloryows cross" itself, the "ryall bem" for which the memory of kingship and triumph, as in the Anglo-Saxon *Dream of the*

Rood, supercedes all other emblems of suffering. Mary Salome invokes the horrors of the Crucifixion only by not speaking of them, as the inexpressibility topos here leads to the Marys' worshipful regard, totally without biblical precedent, for the spiritual and historical significance of the event to which the "ryall bem" bears witness, the divine victory authorized by the prophetic "record of Davyt." Rather than offer an occasion for meditating on Christ's suffering humanity, as did many late medieval plays, lyrics, and devotional texts, the Crucifixion in *Mary Magdalene* emerges instead as one of many moments in which the play foregrounds Christ's divine and kingly nature.[40]

The christological emphases of this treatment of the Passion are reinforced by the striking variety of ways in which the dramatic text invokes the divinity of Christ through references to his power, rule, and authority.[41] These references are verbally inventive—they contribute significantly to the play's aureate diction—and they are noteworthy for their frequency and distribution among the play's characters. The playwright assigns the majority of these testimonials to Mary Magdalene, who, even before her fall and repentance, reveals her predilection for signifying the deity in regal terms. At Cyrus's death, for example, she seeks help for her father from "the inwyttyssymus God þat euyr xal reyne," the "most mytyest governowre" (285, 289). At subsequent moments in the play, Mary Magdalene refers to Jesus as "Lord of euyrlastyng lyfe" (677); "repast contemplatyf" (680); "Thys Kyng, Cryste" (753); "þat Lord [who] relevyd me be hys domynacyon" (755); "gloryus Lord" (815); "rythewys regent, reynyng in equite" (889); "dereworthy Emperowere, . . . hye devyne!" (1086); "þe hey and nobyll inflventt grace" (1096); "gloryous Lord of heuen regyon" (1125); "good Lord in Deite" (1390); "Lord in eternall glory" (1393); "Son of þe mythty Trenite" (1457); "þe Secunde Person, þat hell ded conquare" (1472); "Lord of lorddys, of hye domenacyon!" (2031); and "mythty Lord of hye mageste" (2105). When Mary Magdalene arrives in Marseilles, she declares her intention to show the "sentens" "[o]f my Lordys lawys . . . [b]othe of hys Godhed and of hys powere" (1452–53). When later summoned by the king, she expresses the hope that the "mythe and þe powere of þe heye Trenyte, / The wysdom of þe Son, mott governe yow in ryth!" (1646–47).

Declarations about Christ's divine nature by the play's other characters accord with Mary Magdalene's verbal portrait of the deity's power and authority. Simon Leper desires to welcome Jesus into his home

because of the "report of hys hye nobyllnesse" (584). The Good Angel
rejoices at Magdalene's conversion with a Trinitarian hymn that invokes
the "hyest . . . omnipotency" and "inperall glorye" of God and the
"soverreyn sapyens" of "delectabyll Jhesu," who illuminates ignorance
with his "devynyte" and is called "Redempcyon of sowlys defens" and
"*Lux vera*" (705–21). Mary and Martha seek help for the ailing Lazarus
from "Lord Jhesu . . . / . . . grettest Lord in glorie!" (794–95). When
Jesus prompts Martha to respond to his "I am the resurreccyon of lyfe"
speech, she departs from the gospel account to praise his divine nature
and power: "3e, forsoth, þe Prynsse of blysch! / I beleve in Cryst þe Son
of Sapyens, / Whyche wythowt eynd ryngne xall he" (885–87).[42] Jesus
himself anticipates his passion as "the soferons of my deite" (864) and
at the raising of Lazarus distinguishes the "hey paternyte" of the "Fathy-
rod in glory" from his own "humanyte" (903–5). Even the devil who
reports the harrowing of hell refers to that event as the work of the
"Kyng of Joy" (967). At Jesus' post-Resurrection appearance to the three
Marys, he is greeted by Mary Salome as the "gracyus Lord" whose
"blyssyng of . . . hye deyte" will provide spiritual sustenance for their
souls (1112, 1114). The converted king of Marseilles petitions Jesus, "þat
is hye justyce," for guidance as he and his wife prepare for their pilgrimage to the Holy Land (1710), while the angels whom Jesus dispatches to feed Mary Magdalene with heavenly manna praise him as
"precyus palme of wytory" (2012).

How are we to understand this proliferation of epithets and attributes focusing on the divine nature and power of the incarnate Christ?
The play's exuberant riff on the possibilities of naming the deity coincides with Wolfgang Riehle's observation about mystical language's
"constant attempts to describe God."[43] By making Jesus a prominent
reference point for the hierarchy of spiritual values and powers that
they repeatedly stress, these invocations collectively produce a Christ
who is abstracted from the human nature that in biblical, legendary, and
symbolic lives of Mary Magdalene constituted the basis of the love and
devotion that connected her to him. The play's verbal representation of
a Christ whose divine nature is one of its indisputable preoccupations
has the potential to contradict its lavish depiction of the life of a saint
whose identity was intricately tied to physical intimacy with the human
Christ. The fact that the Digby playwright risked such a contradiction
suggests that the christological interests advanced by the play contribute
crucially to its involvement with larger religious questions.

The *Scale of Perfection* once again offers an analytic purchase on *Mary Magdalene* because Hilton's contemplative program involves a conception of Christ that similarly abstracts the incarnate God from his human nature. Hilton develops his Christology through his account of the path that the aspiring contemplative must follow. In the *Scale* (2.30) he outlines three progressively valuable degrees of love of God available to the soul seeking reformation. The first "cometh oonli with feith, withouten gracious imaginacioun or goostly knowynge of God"; least of the three, it is nevertheless sufficient for salvation. The second kind of love "is that a soule feeleth thorugh feith and by imaginacion of Jhesu in His manhede." It is better than the first because grace stirs the imagination, and the eye of the spirit "is opened in bihooldynge of oure Lordis manhede." The third, superior degree, which is perfect love, "is that a soule feeleth thorugh gosteli sight of the Godhede in the manhede"; it is achieved only by those who can move beyond the impulse to meditate upon Jesus "al manli and fleschli."[44]

At issue in Hilton's analysis of the three kinds of love is the role that sensible devotion can and should play in the aspiring contemplative's effort to approach a deity who is both god and man. Although Hilton presents an Anselmian interpretation of the atonement (2.2), which maintained that the Son of God was incarnated to perform full restitution and satisfaction for the sins of humankind, he nevertheless makes clear his preference for a Jesus abstracted from what Tarjei Park terms his "anthropomorous particularity."[45] Hilton concedes that devotion to Christ's humanity is not only good but also necessary for those who must be "tendirli norischid as children, til thei ben able for to come to the fadris boord and taken of his hande hool bred." But such sensible imaginings of God "with manli affeccions and with bodili liknesse" are, in Hilton's view, only "a maiden," serving the "ladi" understanding, which is "oolde breed, mete for perfite soulis" (2.31).[46] For Hilton, knowledge of Christ as God is superior to knowledge of him as man: "Than right as the Godhede is more sovereyne and more worthi than is the manhede, right so the goostli biholdynge of the Godhede in Jhesu man is more worthi, more goosteli, and more medful than biholdynge of the manhede aloone, whethir he biholde the manhead as deedli or as glorified. And right so be the same skile the love that the soule felith in thenkynge and bihooldynge of the Godhede in man, whan it is graciouseli schewid, is worthiere, goostliere, and more medful than the fervour of devocion that the soule feelith bi imaginacion oonli of the manhede. . . ." (2.30).[47]

The incarnate Jesus is a shadowy presence in the *Scale of Perfection*. Hilton declares that Christ's "precious deeth is the ground of al the reformynge of mannes soule" (2.2), yet he in fact gives little notice to the suffered Christ.[48] Although he follows Saint Bernard's lead in conceding the value of meditating on Christ's humanity or Passion as a step to a more spiritual devotion (1.35), Hilton's account of such meditation, as Park observes, "produces a certain confusion."[49] In Hilton's disjunctive meditative sequence, the appearance of God "in bodili likness as He was inn earth" occurs only when the soul draws its thought "from alle worldli and fleischli thinges" (1.35). Thus meditation on the "fleshly nature of Christ," as Park points out, "is acceptable in that it does not involve *our* flesh"; such sight of Christ's humanity in the soul is non-physical.[50] Indeed, one early annotator of the *Scale of Perfection* seems to have been sufficiently troubled by Hilton's distinct preference for the nonhuman qualities of the deity that he was prompted to augment the text with what have come to be known as the "Christocentric additions." Offering "variations on a set of formulae referring to the manhood of Christ," these two dozen marginal and interlinear corrections and additions to book 1 suggest an effort on the part of an influential reader to punctuate the theocentric emphases of Hilton's text with a greater recognition of Christ's human nature.[51]

Hilton finds important support for his argument about the superiority of Christ's Godhead to his manhood—and scriptural validation for his text's discomfort with "the mind's fixation to embodiment"—in Christ's admonition to Mary Magdalene in John 20:17: *Noli me tangere*.[52] Hilton makes the hortulanus episode a measure of the spiritual progress that Mary Magdalene, who "schulde be contemplatif," has yet to achieve; he also has the resurrected deity ventriloquize his work's own christological priorities. Hilton's Jesus reprimands Mary Magdalene's urge to touch for its lingering fixation on his human form, in which he is not equal to his father: "Touche me not so, but sette thi thought and thi love into that forme in the whiche I am evene to the Fader (that is, the forme of the Godheede) and love Me, and knowe Me and worschipe Me as a God and man godli, not as man manli" (2.30). Because Mary Magdalene's love was, in Hilton's assessment, "moche bodili and litil goostli," her experience speaks not only to the hierarchies of perception and love that structure the contemplative's path to perfection but also the hierarchical construction of Christ himself.[53]

The Digby play's version of the *hortulanus* scene provides some of

the most compelling evidence that the playwright was working through—
and against—christological emphases of texts such as Hilton's. Mary
Magdalene's problem was the inability to transfer her devotion from the
"man manly" to the "god and man godly," a transfer required, Hilton
implies, for the attainment of contemplative perfection. The Digby playwright takes advantage of the dramatic power of Christ's reproof—
"Towche ne natt, Mary! I ded natt asend / To my Father in Deyyte, and
onto yowers!" (1074–75)—and has Mary Magdalene answer back in a
manner that would have removed all of Hilton's reservations about the
woman's ability to distinguish worship of the God from love of the man:

> O, þou dereworthy Emperowere, þou hye devyne!
> To me þis is a joyfull tydyng,
> And onto all pepull þat aftyr vs xall reyngne,
> Thys knowlege of þi deyyte,
> To all pepul þat xall obteyne,
> And know þis be posybyll[yt]e. (1086–91)

Given the opportunity to invent a response for Mary Magdalene beyond the brief dialogue of John 20, the Digby playwright shows her
forcefully articulating the christological emphases that the dramatic text
and Hilton's work independently inscribe. She makes clear that she no
longer harbors any lingering attachment she may have had to Christ's
humanity, as she boldly explicates the spiritual impact of the Resurrection upon herself and its historical significance for "all pepull that aftyr
vs xal reyngne." If devotion to the "god and man godly" rather than the
"man manly" is a requirement of the true contemplative, the Digby
play's Magdalene fully meets that qualification.

In the same chapter in which Hilton discusses the *hortulanus* episode, he further asserts the priority of Christ's divine over his human
nature through the metaphor of the flesh "as mantle or blind" covering
the godhead of Jesus.[54] "[O]ure Lorde Jhesu," Hilton states, "tempereth
His unseable light of His Godhede, and clothid it undir bodili liknesse
of His manhede. . . . [O]ure Lord Jhesu in His Godhede is a spiret, that
mai not be seen of us lyvand in flesch as He is in His blissid light. Therfore we schulle lyven undir the schadwe of His blissid manhede as longe
as we aren heere."[55] The figure of the flesh as veil also resonates in
the hymn with which the Good Angel celebrates Mary's repentance,

addressing Jesus as "Redempcyon of sowlys defens, / Whyche shal ben obscuryd be þi blessyd mortalyte" (713–14). One of the playwright's more unusual interpolations into the traditional life of Mary Magdalene, the Good Angel's hymn furnishes the clearest statement about the devotional emphases that the play accords to the figure of Christ, emphases that the christological priorities of Hilton's text illuminate. The loving, nurturing, healing, but distant Savior who is the object of the Digby saint's increasingly contemplative devotion bears a striking resemblance to the "god and man godly" that Hilton's *Scale* offered to a wide range of aspiring contemplatives, religious and lay, in the late Middle Ages.

Why does a play on the life of Mary Magdalene offer a hospitable framework for examining the respective claims made upon the devout soul by Christ's divine and human natures? Because the saint's biblical and legendary experiences epitomized the differences between what Hilton identified as imaginative apprehension and understanding of the deity, Mary Magdalene's life was at each of its crucial phases implicated in christological issues. The Digby play stages the tensions between her symbolic grounding in body, flesh, and experience and a Christology that abstracted the god from the man. Her dramatic example thus challenges the spiritual commonplace that distinguished between devotion to the manhood and the Godhead of the deity, which was often invoked to characterize differences in devotional practice along gender lines.[56] The playwright further addresses that tension by constructing Mary Magdalene herself as a figure of notable spiritual authority. In the Digby resurrection scene, Mary's affirmation of the "hye devyne" nature of the human Christ whom she has just mistaken for Simon the gardener is one among many dramatic moments in which the saint interprets the significance of her contact with the sacred. Mary Magdalene's complex relationship to the christological emphases of the Digby play thus directs attention to the drama's interest in the sources, instruments, and effects of spiritual knowledge.

Contemplation as Dramatic Action

Two textual features of *Mary Magdalene* signal the playwright's effort to situate the saint's biblical and legendary religious experience in the context of late medieval debates about sources and interpretations of sacred knowledge. First, the play alludes to late medieval discourses that cautioned the devout soul on the discernment of spirits or *discretio spir-ituum*, that is, admonitions and guidelines for assaying the truth or falsehood, authenticity or inauthenticity, sacred or demonic origins of spiritual visitations that sometimes took the form of unusual physical sensations, voices, and apparitions. Late medieval cultivation of interior pieties that included ecstatic and visionary experiences made discern-ment of spirits a major concern for both the writers of devotional and contemplative literature and for practitioners of the personalized pieties that these texts espoused. One important treatment of the subject, Alfonso of Jaén's *Epistola solitarii ad reges*, circulated in Latin copies of Bridget of Sweden's *Revelations* and was translated into Middle English around 1435, approximately forty years after portions of the text had been adapted and translated by the author of *The Chastising of God's Children*.[57] Familiarity with the discourse of spiritual discernment was widespread; the topic was formally addressed in a variety of works for religious and lay readers, such as *The Chastising*, *Ancrene Wisse*, and the *Cloud of Unknowing*; informal treatments appeared in biblical stories, hagiography, exempla, admonitory tales, manuals of advice, and other pastoral materials.[58] The Middle English *Tretis of Discrecyon of Spirites*, originally written for contemplative religious, was included in common profit books owned by London merchants; Pepwell reproduced it in an anthology of contemplative works printed in 1521.[59]

Walter Hilton introduces the subject early in book 1 of the *Scale of Perfection*, making suspicions about spiritual visitations foundational to his contemplative program: "[V]isiones or revelaciouns of ony maner spirite, bodili apperynge or in ymagynynge, slepand or wakand, or ellis ony othere feelinge in the bodili wittes maad as it were goosteli . . . though it be never so comfortable and lykande, aren not verili contem-placion. . . . [Y]if a spirit bodili appere to thee as hit were an angel for to conforte thee and teche thee; or ony swich feelynge which thu woost weel it cometh not of thiself ne of noo bodili creature—be thanne waar in that tyme or soone aftir and wisili bihoold the stirynge of thyne herte" (1.10–11).[60] Hilton concludes his lengthy discussion of the dis-cernment of spirits with his text's first reference to Mary Magdalene, whose visionary privileges "whanne sche was aloone in the cave thritti wyntir" offered an authentic preview of the perfect soul's experience of heavenly bliss: "[T]hus we reden in the legend of hire," he adds. Hilton's reference to what is known from the saint's legend suggests a desire to qualify his prior assertion of her contemplative achievement, linking his text to other late medieval efforts to challenge women's visionary authority. Concerns about the discernment of spirits posed both institutional and personal problems for women contemplatives in particular, whose carnal natures, weak moral sense, and limited mental capacities—in prominent theological and scientific formulations—were said to make them unlikely conduits for authentic spiritual revelations.[61] Alfonso of Jaén may have authored his *epistola* to endorse the veracity of Bridget's visions and advance her case for sainthood, but the work's Middle English redactors had no difficulty reversing that intention, turning his promotion of female visionary experience into an effort to discourage it. Anxiety about such experiences consistently inflects the best-known Middle English illustration of *discretio spirituum*, Margery Kempe's habitual concern for the authenticity of her visions and her constant "dred for illusyons & deceytys of hyr gostly enmys."[62]

The Digby play alludes to the discernment of spirits and to the sources of visionary revelation in four episodes in which the dramatist either adapts or invents scenes that make Mary Magdalene the recipient of angelic communications. The first occurrence involves the "Good Angyll" who warns Mary where her pursuit of "fleschly lust" will lead and advises her to seek mercy for her soul (588–601). This angelic intervention is usually seen as evidence of the saint play's debt to traditions of morality drama. Given Mary's emergent identity as a contemplative, however, it seems just as appropriate to recognize this visitation as inaugurating a series of spiritual encounters that stress, at the great transitional moments of the saint's life, the reliability of her angelic messages.[63] The discourse of the discernment of spirits, in fact, frequently warned the contemplative that the spirit of malice or the devil "somtyme . . . wol . . . chaunge his licnes into an aungel of liȝt, þat he may, under colour of vertewe, do more dere."[64] The Digby angel identifies itself as a good spirit ("I am þe gost of goodnesse þat so wold þe gydde" [601]), and Mary links this identity to the spiritual journey on which she is about to embark: "A, how þe speryt of goodnesse hat promtyt me þis tyde, / And temtyd me wyth tytyll of trew perfythnesse!" (602–3). Appearing later to rejoice at Mary Magdalene's repentance, the Good Angel once more invokes sacred knowledge and the truthfulness of spiritual visitations, petitioning Jesus to "[i]llumyn ower ygnorans wyth your devynyte." In a striking echo of Christ's promise to Mechtild of Hackeborn when she inquired about the truth of her visions—"Tu etiam toties me rogasti, ut te non permitterem spiritu erroris seduci"—the angel seeks a "lucense" from the "*Lux vera*" so "[t]hat wyth þe spryte of errour I nat seduet be!" (712, 715–16).[65]

The need to authenticate the source of spiritual visitations, to assure that the vulnerable soul is not led astray by the "spryte of errour," helps explain why Jesus himself appears at all the other moments in the saint play when Mary receives communication from angelic messengers. In a spectacular scene entirely of the dramatist's own making, the heavens open to reveal Jesus (s.d. 1348), who announces that Mary will convert the "land of Marcyll" and sends "Raphaell, myn angell" to bring her this news (1366–84).[66] Raphael's words to the neophyte evangelist, "Abasse [fear] þe novtt, Mary," recall Gabriel's address to Zacharias (Luke 1:13), which one fifteenth-century preacher invoked for a lay audience to illustrate the importance of discerning spirits.[67] A related effort to authorize Mary Magdalene's angelic visitations occurs in an episode adapted from the legendary vita calling for the saint to appear in the dreams of the king and queen of Marseilles when they refuse to provide her with food and shelter. The Digby playwright turns this event into a heavenly embassy ordered by Jesus to assist his "lovyr," Mary. Angels descend to "lede hyr to the prynsses chambyr," tell her what to say, and describe how they will accompany her wearing "a mentyll of whyte" and bearing "solem lyth" (1586–1605). Mary actively interprets the visitation as she expresses confidence in its message: "O gracyus God, now I vndyrstond! / Thys clothyng of whyte is tokenyng of mekenesse. / Now, gracyus Lord, I woll natt wond, / Yower preseptt to obbey wyth lowly-nesse" (1606–9).[68]

Mary's final spiritual visitation, based on the episode in her legendary life that called for her daily elevation by angels, furnishes the surest evidence, however, that the dramatist sought to link the play's representation of the saint as ecstatic and visionary with late medieval anxieties about discernment of spirits. The playwright fashions the whole spectacular scene as the deity's answer to Mary's prayers for "contemplatyff" food: Jesus hears her petition from the wilderness and dispatches heavenly messengers to feed her with manna. His parting words to the angels establish the spiritual authenticity of what she is about to experience: "Byd hur injoye wyth all hur afyawns, / For fynddys frawd xall hur non deseyve" (2009–10).[69] Jesus ensures that Mary Magdalene, unlike Margery Kempe, will be not be plagued by fear of "deceytys & illusyons" masquerading as "revelacyonis" that prove "it is not expedient to ȝeuyn redily credens to euery steryng but sadly abydyn & preuyn yf þei be sent of God."[70] Mary's final visitation is presented as "fode by revelacyon" sent from god "wyth hevenly synys" (2024, 2020), a gift whose incontrovertibly divine origin she readily confirms: "O gloryus Lord, in þe is no fravddys nor no defame" (2034).

Mary's angelic colloquies, to be sure, give theatrical image and form to the most celebrated events of her life. But nothing in these episodes from the narrative vita requires that these experiences be so completely facilitated by angelic messengers, nor that sacred communications, and the sources, authenticity, and truth of "revelacyons" be the subject of these conversations between heaven and earth. By figuring Mary Magdalene as the recipient, not of "fynddys frawd" but rather of "hevenly synys," the play positions the dramatic saint's contemplative and visionary example within contemporary cultural discourses that harbored suspicions about spiritual visitations. While bearing witness to late medieval anxieties about such visitations, the play's representation of Mary Magdalene's experience also constitutes an argument on behalf of their authority and truth.

The Digby saint play also acknowledges late medieval debates regarding sources of sacred knowledge when it shows Jesus anachronistically critiquing clerical learning for its inability to comprehend and communicate sacred mysteries. With their brother Lazarus on death's door, Mary Magdalene and Martha seek Jesus' aid for the sick man in his time of dire need. Before complying with their request, Jesus poses the resurrection of Lazarus—and the heavenly joy that it portends—as divine mysteries unavailable to rational demonstration and clerical knowledge:

> Of al infyrmyte, þer is non to deth.
> For of all peynnes, þat is impossyble
> To vnderstond be reson; to know þe werke,
> The joye þat is in Jherusallem heuenly,
> Can nevyr be compylyd by covnnyng of clerke—
> To see þe joyys of þe Fathyr in glory,
> The joyys of þe Sonne whych owth to be magnyfyed,
> And of þe Therd Person, þe Holy Gost, truly,
> And alle thre but on in heuen gloryfyed! (802–10)[71]

Divine recognition of the inadequacy of clerical "covnnyng" recurs in a wholly original post-Resurrection scene in which the heavens open to disclose Jesus preparing to send Mary Magdalene an angelic dispatch ordering her apostolic mission to Marseilles. He prefaces his charge to the angels with a two-stanza encomium to his mother (1349–63). The encomium is rich in tropes made familiar through scriptural exegesis of Marian purity and the virgin birth, tropes that articulated the inscrutability of the Incarnation through an allegorical hermeneutic: Mary is the "onclypsyd sonne," the "tempyll of Salamon," the "fles of Judeon," the "wessell of puere clennesse." Concluding this densely allegorical passage with a telling variation on the inexpressibility topos, Jesus asserts: "The goodnesse of my mothere no tong can expresse, / Nere no clerke of hyre, hyre joyys can wryth" (1364–65).

Jesus' notice of a specifically clerical inadequacy in the face of divine mystery signals the saint play's appropriation of late medieval discourses that challenged established clerical claims to power and authority based on knowledge. Expression of such doubts was a staple feature of late medieval mystical and contemplative literature, whose very existence, as Karma Lochrie notes, signaled a rejection of "institutional discourse, including learning, letters, and textual authority, whether it explicitly criticizes them or not."[72] Rolle offered his *Incendium Amoris* "for the consideration not of philosophers, not of the worldly-wise, not of the great theologians enwrapped in endless *quaestiones*, but of the simple and untaught who strive more to love God than to know many things."[73] The author of the *Cloud of Unknowing* minces few words when he advises his reader to be wary of evil uses of "kindely witte," "when it is swollen wiþ pride and wiþ coriouste of moche clergie & letterly conning as in clerkes."[74] In comparison to the understanding that God grants to the soul reformed in feeling, clerical pursuit of learning, in Hilton's view, is similarly deficient because the clerk operates "blyndly and nakedly & unsauourly . . . thrugh myght of hys naked reason" (2.32).[75] Margery Kempe's clerical interlocutors expose their own inadequate knowledge as compared to hers: "We han gon to scole many ʒerys, & ʒet arn we not sufficient to answeryn as þu dost. Of whom hast þu þis cunnyng?"[76]

The Digby playwright boldly punctuates Mary Magdalene's quest for contemplative perfection with divinely authenticated communiqués and places a critique of clerical intellectual authority in the mouth of Jesus himself. Dramatic representations of spiritual discernment and a problematic clerical "cunning" stake out controversial positions that align the interests of the saint play with those of late medieval debates about the acquisition of sacred knowledge. Forms and processes of knowledge are recurring concerns of the Digby *Magdalene*. Variations on the words "knowing" and "understanding" appear frequently in the text, especially in relation to sacred beings and events. The earthly rulers' plot against Jesus is depicted largely as a problem of knowledge and belief. "Lett me ondyrstond whatt can ye seyn!" (166), Herod insists as he seeks unsuccessfully to extract confirmation of his sovereignty from his philosopher-advisors, only to learn that "skreptour gevytt informacyon" (171) of a mighty ruler against whose "worthynes [no king] xall opteyn" (182). A preoccupation with knowing and understanding appears in encounters with Jesus. "Godamercy, Symont, þat þou wylt me knowe! / I woll entyr þi hows wyth pes and vnyte" (619–20), Jesus declares in the scene based on Luke 7:36–50. His remark looks ahead to Mary Magdalene's repentance, which the woman similarly describes in terms of personal knowledge: "Thow knowyst my hart and thowt in especyal— / Therfor, good Lord, aftyr my hart reward me!" (639–40). The Good Angel who celebrates Mary Magdalene's conversion identifies Jesus as an agent of sacred knowledge— "Illumyn owyr ygnorans wyth your devynyte!" (712)—a role that he assumes for himself as he prepares to raise Lazarus from the dead: "Tyme ys comyn of very cognyssyon" (846).

Mary Magdalene serves as both reporter and recipient of Jesus' illuminations. "Of all maner tonggys he 3af vs knowyng, / For to vndyrstond every langwage" (1343–44), she says of the Pentecostal gift of tongues. When she is down and out in Marseilles, she recognizes the angelic visitation she receives as a vehicle of knowledge: "O gracyus God, now I vndyrstond! / Thys clothyng of whyte is tokenyng of mekenesse" (1606–7); and she sums up the import of the king of Marseilles's pilgrimage to the Holy Land in epistemological terms: "[N]ow have 3e a knowle[ge] of þe sentens / How 3e xall com onto grace!" (1955–56).

The Digby saint play's attention to spiritual cognition and sacred knowledge is metatheatrically realized in its demonstrable self-consciousness about the respective capacities of language and spectacle to communicate sacred truth. Best known for its dramatic spectacle, the play also exhibits enormous linguistic variety, ranging from the doggerel Latin of its pagan priest, to the aureate diction of evil spirits, to the saint's plain-spoken articulations of scripture in Marseilles. While the legendary life of Mary Magdalene—with its falling idols, sea voyages, penitential histrionics, and miraculous resurrections—provided episodes tailor made for performance, it also presented the challenge of giving dramatic form to contemplative experiences that are, the dramatic text asserts, beyond language and material representation.

These metatheatrical issues have figured prominently in recent studies of the play, which have analyzed its preoccupations with the communicative powers of writing and speech as well as its ostensible privileging of a visual hermeneutic.[77] Yet *Mary Magdalene*, I think, does not represent the verbal and the visual as rival foundations of religious knowledge as much as it identifies words and theatrical images as parallel sources of sacred truth or illusion. The play deploys its metalinguistic and hypertheatrical resources to represent how its dramatic subject and the dramatic medium itself are variably positioned in relation to the sacred. As resources of religious and dramatic epistemology, word and spectacle in the Digby play dynamically interact and mutually reinforce each other.

Mary Magdalene's colloquy with the hermit priest who encounters her heavenly elevation in the play's penultimate scene extends this interest in the verbal and visual resources of religion and drama. In Jacobus's account the priest who witnesses the saint's elevation by angels wants to know who she is. Magdalene reveals herself as "the renommed synful woman, whiche wesshe the feet of our Sauyour with her teeris, and dryed them wyth the heer of here hede, & deserued to haue foryeueness of her synnes"; she then dispatches her interlocutor to tell her former companion, the priest Maximin, that she is about to die and will seek him in his "oratorye."[78] Altering both the substance and purpose of the episode in the *Legenda aurea*, the playwright transforms the encounter into a conversation about access to sacred knowledge. The scene omits all reference to Magdalene's sinful past and her biblically-recorded deeds. Instead, saintly hermit and desert priest discuss visionary experience. The priest has witnessed one of the most visually spectacular moments of the entire play, Magdalene's wafting up into the clouds to be houseled "wyth reverent song" of angels (s.d. 2030). Far from being preoccupied with the ecstatic woman's identity—he already knows it—the priest instead seeks knowledge of her spiritual experience, previewed in the "gret mesteryys shewyd from heven" (2040) that inspire his wonder:[79]

Heyl, creature, Crystys delecceon!
Heyl, swetter þan sugur or cypresse!
Mary is þi name be angellys relacyon;

Grett art þou wyth God for þi perfythnesse!
Þe joye of Jherusallem shewyd þe expresse,
Þe wych I nevyr save þis thirty wyntyr and more!
Wherfor I know well þou art of gret perfy[t]nesse,
I woll pray yow hartely to she[w] me of yower Lord! (2045–52)[80]

Whereas the priest's petition focuses on a visual revelation ("shew me"), Mary Magdalene's response concentrates instead on verbal communication:

Be þe grace of my Lord Jesus
Þis thirty wyntyr þis hath byn my selle,
And thryys on þe day enhansyd þus
Wyth more joy þan ony tong can telle
Nevyr creature cam þer I dwelle,
Tyme nor tyde, day nore nyth,
Þat I can wyth spece telle,
But alonly with Goddys angyllys brygth. (2053–60)

Magdalene counters the priest's plea for a "showing" with a speech on the impossibility of saying what heavenly joy is.

By turning Magdalene's verbal exchange with the hermit priest into a dialogue about acquiring sacred knowledge, the Digby play allies the saint with a position that Jesus has previously articulated: both the deity and the contemplative pronounce the limitations that human language and intellect impose upon the communication of heavenly joy. The priest's association of Mary Magdalene with the "joye of Jherusallem" further recalls Jesus' assertion that "the joye that is in Jherusallem heuenly, / Can nevyr be compylyd by covnnyng of clerke." Magdalene's visionary exposure to such joy also implicitly counters the inadequacy that Jesus had observed of clerical attempts to represent the joy of his mother, "Quewne of Jherusalem, that heuenly cete" (1359). What clerical cunning fails to "compile" is openly revealed to Mary Magdalene.

The dramatic rendering of this episode from Mary Magdalene's legendary life underscores the play's construction of the saint as a contemplative whose visionary experience is a source of spiritual and charismatic power.[81] The play builds upon the saint's biblical identity as witness to Christ's divinity, and her celebrated legendary familiarity with Christ in his more human aspects, in order to represent her life as a drama of encounters with sacred experience, the "joys of Jerusalem." Among the late medieval English lives of the saint, the Digby play uniquely fashions Mary Magdalene as the recipient of sacred messages articulated through visions in which the saint converses with angels who purvey "hevenly synys" (2020). Sacred communication is also transmitted through the medium of scripture, in Magdalene's preaching, and in her dynamic, potent prayers. And it is inscribed on the body of the saint herself, in her spectacularly corporeal purgation and her angelic transport into the heavens. In *Mary Magdalene*, heavenly mysteries may elude the "connyng" of clerks and the longings of the hermit priest, but they are firmly located within the realm of everyday occurrence for the penitent and apostolic saint.

The dramatic Magdalene's privileged access to the sacred is founded upon the interiority of her personal experience.[82] The play presents her conversion and forgiveness as the workings of a private process in which Jesus examines her heart and discovers her true intent: "Thow knowyst my hart and thowt in especyal— / Therfor, good Lord, aftyr my hart reward me!" (639–40). Jesus acknowledges Magdalene's conversion as the valorization of an inner power— "Woman, in contryssyon þou art expert, / And in þi sowle hast inward mythe" (686–87). At his resurrection he reaffirms his relationship to her inner being: "Mannys hartt is my gardyn here. / Þerin I sow sedys of vertu all þe зere. / Þe fowle wedys and wycys I reynd vp by þe rote! / Whan þat gardyn is watteryd wyth terys clere, / Than spryng vertuus, and smell full sote" (1081–85).[83] The theatrical image of seven devils "devoiding" from Mary Magdalene's infamous body (s.d. 691) commandingly conveys the dynamic relationship of outward sign and inner experience that consistently marks the dramatic saint's association with sacred power.

These representations of Mary Magdalene's personal connection to the sacred also signal the Digby saint play's congruence with late medieval religious discourses devoted to elaborating epistemological and spiritual dimensions of the category "experience." The development of these discourses is marked by an increasing valorization of the concept of experience against increasingly embattled conceptions of authority. Although "certain forms of personal experience" were accorded significance. throughout the Middle Ages, Nicholas Watson observes, "in the fourteenth century, this sense of significance was reserved especially for private and affective experiences, which, under the proper conditions, could come to be regarded as having importance for everyone."[84]

The theoretical bases for the increased late medieval prestige of personal experience and affective devotion reside in the distinction, first formulated by Augustine, between intellective knowledge, or *scientia*, and affective knowledge, or *sapientia*. Whereas intellective knowledge characterized the practice of human science, affective knowledge involved divine science, epitomized in the Bible, and was associated by Franciscan thinkers such as Bonaventure with the affective appeals of the literary modes of scripture, which were deemed superior to appeals made through ratiocination. Eventually the distinction between *scientia* and *sapientia* came to apply not only to the modes for apprehending scripture but also "to the kinds of understanding possessed by individual Christians," a shift that coincided with increasing lay investments in an accessible, vernacular theology.[85] Margery Kempe's struggle to establish the validity of spiritual knowledge that came to her as feeling provides a celebrated illustration of the role increasingly occupied by experience as an epistemological and spiritual category in late medieval culture. Revelations, her book concedes, "be hard sum-tyme to vndirstondyn," but "as to þis felyng of þis creatur, it was very trewth schewyd in experiens."[86]

The Digby saint play's culturally specific representations of inner experience and access to sacred knowledge contribute to the dramatic fashioning of Mary Magdalene as a visionary whose personal spiritual authority resonates with late medieval mystical and contemplative texts.[87] It is late medieval visionaries who principally evidence the process by which private, affective experiences came to be accorded significance with respect to traditional clerical and ecclesiastical authority.[88] *Mary Magdalene* exploits the potential of sacred biography to address these relationships.

"Approved Women"

The tradition of female sacred biography was an important resource in late medieval efforts to critique spiritual and institutional dimensions of the Church.[89] Over the past two decades an ambitious, cross-disciplinary scholarly investigation has made evident gender's constitutive role in late medieval struggles over the sources, languages, and exercise of religious authority. Late medieval religious controversies, as we have seen, were articulated through gendered systems of representation that figured the dominant, orthodox position as Latinate, allegorical, rational, intellectual and masculine, and the subordinate position as vernacular, literal, affective, experiential, and feminine. But oppositional discursive strategies and material struggles for power only partially disclose the significance of gender for later medieval religious belief and practice. The history of the medieval "feminization of Christianity" identified by Barbara Newman and others recounts multiple, complex ways that feminine piety intersected with masculine institutional and ecclesiastical authority.[90] Women's very exclusion from sites of spiritual and institutional power at all levels of the ecclesiastical hierarchy, inevitably, may have lent an oppositional cast to expressions of feminine piety, but that stance was also facilitated by internal divisions that rendered the authority of the Church itself vulnerable in many areas.[91] Like Elisabeth of Schönau and Hildegard of Bingen before them, later medieval visionaries such as Bridget of Sweden and Catherine of Siena directly addressed the moral and political failings of the Church and its leaders, filling the perceived vacuum of leadership created by these failings. In the epilogue to Angela of Foligno's *Book of Instructions*, her confessor alludes to a necessary realignment of spiritual authority and power, noting that doctrine was transferred to women because its guardians had shamefully transgressed its law, thus requiring the translation of the gift of prophecy to the female sex.[92] In most cases the reported experiences of late medieval holy women remained well within the realm of orthodox piety and practice. But like the mystical texts and voices with which this feminine piety was so firmly associated, these women's frequent trafficking in spiritual power underscored ambivalences within orthodoxy itself as well as the inherent contradictions of a church whose hegemonic claims to universal truth and clerical privilege officially excluded female experience and authority even as its foundational narratives made an important space for feminine participation.[93]

The example of Mary Magdalene offered opportunities to mediate these contradictions, influencing the spiritual self-fashioning of a far-flung cohort of late medieval holy women whose experience bridged the temporal and cultural distance between the saint's biblical and legendary attributes and contemporary spiritual behaviors and discourses.[94] Speaking to the "approuyd wymmon" whose revelations were commended by the *Speculum Devotorum* as well as to condemned heretics, Mary Magdalene's scriptural identities and capacious symbolic associations as model contemplative, intimate of Jesus, and apostle of his resurrection lent precedence and authority to women's ecclesiastical politics,

visionary pronouncements, and somatic pieties.[95] Twelfth-century recluse Christina of Markyate attributed the preservation of her chastity
to Mary Magdalene, who made a visionary appearance to deliver an
aggressive warning to the priest who threatened her.[96] Through her
identification with Mary of Bethany in Luke's gospel, Mary Magdalene
represented the exemplary contemplative life that Christ promoted to
Bridget of Sweden.[97] Catherine of Siena invoked the sins of Mary Magdalene to admonish women about excessive vanity but also found in the
saint's apostolate and ascetic life models more akin to her own spiritual
ambitions.[98] Margaret of Cortona's alliance with the saint relied on a
different aspect of her polyvalent identity: Christ promised the sexually
tainted Margaret that like the fleshly sinner turned saint, she too would
be restored to virginal purity.[99] To Ivetta of Huy, the prosperous urban
patrician widow turned beguine, Mary Magdalene offered a devotional
role model and patron through her own complicated sexual and social
identities.[100] As Christ's beloved, Mary Magdalene also inspired the
mystique courtoise of Hadewijch, Mechthild of Magdeburg, and condemned heretic Marguerite Porete.[101] Although charges of heresy only
shadowed Margery Kempe, her effort to place herself, as a kind of devotional proxy, in Mary Magdalene's biblical roles brought a fervor to that
identification that easily rivaled Porete's more challenging formulations
of spiritual love.

The Digby saint play capitalizes on the propensity of late medieval
holy women to invoke Mary Magdalene's patronage and example to
authorize their own spiritual impulses and acts, endowing the dramatic
portrait of the saint with attributes that recall the experiences of these
women. In late medieval East Anglia, in fact, it may have been difficult
to depict the life of Mary Magdalene without the example of more contemporary contemplatives and visionaries coming to mind, especially in
view of continental religious influences that crisscrossed the region. As
we have seen, late medieval East Anglia was home to important cham-
pions of Catherine of Siena and Bridget of Sweden. The rare depictions
of both of these holy women on the rood screen in the parish church
of Horsham St. Faith near Norwich represents them in specifically
visionary and ecstatic postures: Bridget of Sweden receives divine inspiration for her writings, and Catherine of Siena holds her flaming heart
(figs. 2 and 3). The experience of the dramatic Magdalene mirrors that
of Bridget, who was chosen by divine election to be the channel of god's
word and teaching.[102] Whereas the Magdalene of the legendary vita was

set adrift at sea with her companions by persecutors of Christians, the dramatic saint travels alone to Marseilles in response to the "heuenly masage" (1367) that initiates her apostolic mission. The experience of the Digby saint also echoes that of twelfth-century visionary Elisabeth of Schönau, whose works circulated in England through Cistercian channels.[103] Like Elisabeth, the dramatic Magdalene not only regularly receives heavenly communications through angelic intermediaries but also casts her experience in terms of that of biblical prophets: when the king of Marseilles refuses her food and shelter, she seeks divine aid by comparing her plight to that of Daniel, who was "relevyd wyth sustynovns" by the messenger and prophet Habbacuk (1582–83).[104]

The Digby playwright invents other occasions to probe the spiritual authority of the late medieval woman visionary in relation to clerical power. Mary Magdalene's relation to clerical mediation of the sacred through official rites and ceremonies is first addressed in the episode involving the heathen priest and his "clericus" (1150), who perform rites for the king and queen of Marseilles in honor of "Sentt Mahownde" (1133–1248). Their pagan worship bears some stunning similarities to Christian ceremonies, providing dramatic images whose resemblance to late medieval liturgical rite and religious practice would have been readily recognized by the dramatic audience: the ringing of bells, the donning of vestments, the displaying of relics (Mahownde's "yeelyd" and "nekke bon"), and the extending of pardon. Like the crude banter exchanged between Prysbyer and his boy over the preparation of the altar (1143–77), the priest's garbled Latin *lectio* exposes spiritual and sexual transgressions of priests.[105] The polyglot idiom in which the priest pronounces the pagan rite contrasts with Mary Magdalene's own lucid linguistic hybridity, which moves easily between Latin and the vernacular, working into her speeches passages from the psalms and the Gospels. When Mary Magdalene visits Marseilles, she is brought by the king before the same idols of "Sentt Mahownde" to which the pagan priest makes his petition. There she unambiguously bests her spiritual rival, when her unadorned scriptural preaching and her psalmic plea for divine aid—*Dominus, illuminacio mea, quem timebo?*—not only stand in stark contrast to the form and language of pagan rite but also produce an immediate response: "Here xal the mament tremyll and quake" (s.d. 1553). The triumph of Christian ways over pagan may be a staple feature of hagiographic narrative, but the care with which the Digby playwright makes Mary Magdalene's heathen opponent resemble his contemporary

Christian cohort inscribes the saint's triumph with a historical critique reminiscent of that propounded by Angela of Foligno's confessor to justify the transfer of spiritual power to women.[106]

At the dramatic moment of Mary Magdalene's repentance, the saint play also alludes to her relationship to clerical mediation of the sacraments. Although Mary articulates her sinfulness before encountering Jesus in the house of Simon ("Alas, how betternesse in my hert doth abyde! / I am wonddyd wyth werkys of gret dystresse" [604–5]), it is her gestures of weeping, washing, and anointing that prompt his declaration: "Woman, in contryssyon þou art expert" (686). Her silent encounter with Jesus doubtlessly made for effective theater, but the idea that her penitence was unspoken posed notable challenges to a religious establishment that emphasized the necessity of auricular confession. Penitential doctrine stressed the importance of interior sorrow, *amaritudo cordis*, and gestures of tears and lamentation that communicated that inner condition; still it was the act itself of confession to a priest that constituted an "essential moment" of penance, signifying "that clerical mediation was indispensable to the penitential experience."[107] Troubled by the lack of any record of Mary Magdalene's confession, influential medieval clerics such as Odo of Cluny and Innocent III simply invented one for her.[108] Although examples of Mary Magdalene's hypothetical confession eventually made their way into popular devotional texts such as the *Meditationes vitae christi*, the Digby play does not follow their lead, a notable choice in view of the playwright's tendency to invent at other key moments of the saint's life.[109] Instead, the saint play mirrors the more circumspect opinion of thirteenth-century Dominican Aldobrandino Cavalcanti, who maintained that Mary Magdalene's confession is not discussed in the Gospels "because it was not necessary for her. . . . [T]he priest who absolved her knew simply and clearly all her sins and all the circumstances, and he also saw sufficient contrition in her heart for destroying her sins."[110] The dramatic example of Mary Magdalene's confession circumvents the problem of clerical ministration of penance by showing how Jesus fulfills the priestly role himself.

Although the saint play follows the traditional vita by acknowledging the clerical role of Saint Peter, who baptizes the king of Marseilles and serves as guide during his sojourn in the Holy Land, it makes no mention of the legendary Magdalene's priestly companion, Bishop Maximin. His absence from the evangelical phase of her life also facilitates his removal from the penultimate episode of her dramatic vita, where he usually appears. Whereas Jacobus's contemplative Magdalene requests that the hermit priest inform Maximin of her imminent passing and hence her desire to meet him in his church at an appointed time—an encounter in which she receives the Eucharist from the Bishop's hands and stretches "her body tofore the aulter"—the Digby play conflates the duties of the hermit priest with those usually assigned to Maximin and makes Mary's desert interlocutor the bearer of her final communion, administered not in a bishop's church but in her desert hermitage.[111] The nameless priest who stands in for the institutional authority signified by Maximin in other versions of the saint's life is a revealing character in his own right. When he seeks illumination about the nature of the saint's heavenly revelations, Mary Magdalene replies cautiously, welcoming the encounter: "Yf thou be of good conversacyon. / As I thynk in my delyth, / Thow sholddyst be a man of devocyon" (2062–64).[112] Reversing the terms of the exchange that appear in the *Legenda aurea*, where the saint reveals her identity at the priest's request, here Magdalene's reservations prompt the priest to establish his own spiritual credentials: "In Crystys lav [law] I am sacryed a pryst, / Mynystryyd be angelys at my masse. / I sakor þe body of ower Lord Jhesu Cryst" (2065–67).

The dramatic saint's complicated relationship to clerical power is also imaged in her participation in the eucharistic sacrament. Like the traditional vita, the play provides for Mary Magdalene to receive the Eucharist near the end of her life. In the Digby drama, however, it is Jesus' own expressed intention to reward Mary Magdalene with a crown "be ryth enirytawns" (2074), not the saint's request to the desert priest, that prompts this scene, thereby supplanting the customary reunion of the ascetic woman and Bishop Maximin with an encounter that emphasizes her personal ties to the deity, outside the ecclesiastical authority of church and clergy. It is Jesus who orders his angelic messengers to deliver "from heven region" (2085) the command that the desert priest bring the sacrament to Magdalene: "3e xall go hosyll hys servont expresse, / And we wyth you xall take mynystracyon / To bere lyth before hys body of worthynesse" (2086–88). Rather than present the Magdalene's final communion in a church before "alle the clerkes and the prestes" mentioned by Jacobus, the Digby play stages a private ceremony in which the eucharistic viaticum is brought to the saint for her last rites in a quasi-visionary spectacle that functions as an extension of the ecstatic feedings that sustained her for thirty years in her desert hermitage.[113]

In representing angelic transport of the Sacrament to Mary Magdalene, the saint play allies itself with the personalized eucharistic piety cultivated by many late medieval holy women. Indeed, Mary Magdalene's legendary associations with ecstatic feedings doubtlessly furnished a model upon which these idiosyncratic expressions of female devotion could draw.[114] The play's focus on themes of feeding and nourishment, feasting and fasting, recalls both the idiom of late medieval women's eucharistic piety and more fundamental tensions between masculine liturgical and ecclesiastical power and the private, visionary charisma of feminine devotion that this piety inscribed.[115] The dramatic image of the desert priest's presentation of the Sacrament, accompanied by two angels bearing "lyth before hys body of worthynesse," occurs only after the play has shown Magdalene herself in a virtually identical ritual performance: she makes her visionary appearance to the king and queen of Marseilles accompanied by two angels who "go before . . . wyth solem lyth" (1603). Through this visual echo, the hermit saint's encounter with the desert priest establishes their analogous relationships to sacred power, hers through angelic feedings with heavenly manna, his through the "sakoring" of the body of Christ.[116]

Mimi Still Dixon astutely observes that the Digby saint play "relishes Mary's appropriation of male power" yet does not show her transgressing male clerical authority; baptism and administration of the Eucharist remain the exclusive offices of Saint Peter and the hermit priest. In comparison, Mary Magdalene's "spiritual forte . . . [is] visionary and charismatic . . . deriving from a personal relationship with God."[117] Relationships between the spiritual authority of the late medieval holy woman (legendary or historical) and the ecclesiastical figures and institutions on which she was ultimately dependent were inevitably ambivalent, marked by gestures that could be construed simultaneously to challenge as well as reinforce traditional clerical authority.[118] For instance, Margery Kempe's preoccupations with frequent reception of the Eucharist in one sense underscore priestly transubstantiation of the Sacrament. Yet her eucharistic piety, as Beckwith states, "is more a singling out, a mark of special religiosity." Like that of the Digby saint, "it comes by special request from Christ, bypassing the clergy, who become the mere medium by which God is to work his special grace in her."[119]

The Digby saint play embraces these ambivalences and represents

Mary Magdalene as a figure whose reception of divinely authorized revelations and circumvention of clerical control of the Eucharist constitute channels of access to sacred power rivaling those of institutional
religion. In the dramatic figure of Mary Magdalene, the play models an
image of devotion that emphasizes the independence of the religious
subject from clerics but not from God; it lends authenticity and authority to the inner spiritual life and inflects that image as feminine. Gender
is an important aspect of the play's construction of a devotional ideal, I
suggest, not because the drama seeks to model female behavior, but
rather because the play associates femininity with a spiritual ideal that
was broadly available in late medieval culture. Based in the individual's
personal relationship with the deity, this ideal cultivated an inner spiritual disposition, stressed the power of prayer, and acknowledged the
importance of but was not defined by ritual observances. Dramatic
articulation of such an ideal illustrates larger patterns of late medieval
reception of hagiographic narrative, in which saintly "*imitatio*," as Catherine Sanok observes, was "filtered . . . through contemporary discourses of ethical and spiritual behavior."[120] Like Hilton's *Scale of Perfection*, the Digby saint play envisions possibilities for lay devotion through
the figure of Mary Magdalene. But it departs from Hilton's image of
the paradigmatic contemplative whose example reinforced hierarchies
of spirit over flesh and the antispeculative bias of a spiritual program
that was intended to remove matters of faith from the realm of public
debate. In the narrative, symbolic, and exegetical complexity of the saint's
vita, the dramatist finds opportunities to associate Mary Magdalene
with gestures that trouble the conservative impulses of Hilton's text.

"Woman, thou hast many resonnys grett"

Within the religious culture of late medieval England, Mary Magdalene's
expanded ideological register as feminine visionary and charismatic is
further elaborated in the Digby play's representation of her vernacular
scriptural preaching. The saint play's heroine delivers two sermons
based on biblical texts. In the first instance, her preaching responds to
the king of Marseilles's insistent query: "Woman . . . answer me! /
Whatt mad God at þe fyrst begynnyng?" (1477–78). Invoking the opening of John's gospel (*In principio erat verbum*), Mary Magdalene gives
an account of the creation that closely follows Genesis. The second

instance occurs as the newly converted king and queen return home
from their pilgrimage to Rome and the Holy Land; after their ship
"goth . . . owt of the place" (s.d. 1922), the scene shifts to display Mary
Magdalene preaching on the theme *paupertas est donum dei* (1923–38)
and paraphrasing the Sermon on the Mount (Matt. 5:3).

Though as old as her identity as "apostle to the apostles," the tradition of a preaching Mary Magdalene was consolidated by the development of legendary expansions of the saint's vita that had reported her
ministry to the people of Marseilles. In the late Middle Ages this expanded version of the saint's life was known most widely through the
Legenda aurea.[121] According to the legendary life, Mary Magdalene,
Lazarus, Martha, Maximin, and other companions were put to sea in a
rudderless ship by enemies of Christ and eventually found safe harbor
in Marseilles. There the holy woman promptly began to convert the
people through her preaching. The Digby play emends the legendary
life to foreground the saint's apostolic role, dramatizing her ministry as
divinely inspired and orchestrated by a command from Jesus' angelic
messenger: "Kyng and quene converte xall ȝe / And byn amyttyd as an
holy apostylesse. / Alle the lond xall be techyd alonly be the, / Goddys
lawys onto hem ȝe xall express" (1379–82).

Neither Jacobus's account nor any of the other late medieval English lives of Mary Magdalene indebted to the *Legenda aurea* specifically
identifies the saint's ministry with scriptural preaching.[122] Jacobus
focuses on the style—her "glad visage" and "discrete tongue"—rather
than the substance of her preaching in Marseilles; he observes that it
is "no merueylle" that Mary Magdalene, with her "beaute, . . . reson,
and . . . fayr spekyng" was so successful in her preaching, nor that
the "mouth that had kyssed the feet of our Lord so deboneyrly and
so goodly shold be enspyred with the worde of God."[123] Bokenham's
verse life of the saint casts in sharp relief the playwright's innovative
reworking of the same material.[124] His Magdalene's vaguely defined exhortations to the king, queen, and people of Marseilles are not readily
distinguishable from those of the virgin martyrs whose lives dominate
the Augustinian friar's legendary. They function frequently as spiritual
teachers, offering basic Christian doctrine and reproof of pagan customs, but not even Saint Catherine of Alexandria, celebrated for her
learned besting of pagan philosophers, engages directly with the scriptural text.[125]

Other aspects of the saint play underscore its attention to the role of scripture and preaching in the transmission of sacred knowledge. The text shows an interest in scriptural hermeneutics that far exceeds the reminiscences of biblical language that might be expected of a drama whose narrative has a scriptural basis.[126] Encounters with the sacred text are central to the play's characterization of Mary Magdalene, who is both its mouthpiece and its living witness. The dramatist employs such encounters to establish the saint's identification with Christ (2115–18), her resemblance to the prophet Daniel (1582–84), and her personal testimony to the accuracy of Old Testament prophetic announcements about the Savior (697–98). The play further emphasizes the authority of the biblical text in several early scenes that show Tiberius Caesar, Pilate, and Herod composing a counternarrative that seeks to falsify events attested by scripture. These ruling figures, as Scherb notes, impose political strictures that "are specifically directed against preachers."[127] Finally, *Mary Magdalene* exhibits a special interest in the gendered dimensions of preaching when the pagan priest's boy provocatively alludes to the medieval commonplace that identified women as the favored audience for sermons. "Whan woman comme to here þi sermon," he boasts to his master, "[p]ratyly wyth hem I can houkkyn" (1159–60).[128]

An early sixteenth-century northern European panel painting by the Master of the Magdalene legend provides a striking contemporary visual analogue to the Digby saint's scriptural preaching (fig. 12). The painting depicts Mary Magdalene poised on an improvised, outdoor wooden structure, addressing a well-attired gathering of men, women, and children.[129] The preaching scene is situated in a wooded area; visible in the background on the left, the image of a sailing vessel alludes to the holy woman's legendary transport to Marseilles and thereby situates the panel's representation of the saint's preaching in relation to her entire life. Appearing in the background on the upper right is an astonished male clerical figure, gazing at what in the original triptych must have been an image of the saint levitated by angels for her feedings with heavenly manna.[130] The importance of Mary Magdalene's preaching is suggested by the central position of the saint's image on the panel, which privileges her apostolic role over other signal attributes of her legendary life. Jeanne Tombu's reconstruction of the Magdalene Master's work stresses the complexity of that role by proposing that the original triptych balanced an image of the preaching woman on the right with a depiction of the worldly Magdalene at the hunt on the left.[131]

Figure 12. *Mary Magdalena Preaching*. Master of the Magdalene Legend. Reproduced by permission of the Philadelphia Museum of Art: The John G. Johnson Collection.

Other features of the now-detached panel underscore the social and spiritual complexity of the preaching Mary Magdalene. Although the woman preacher has traded a modestly fashioned veil for the stylish headdress of the huntress, she still sports the elegant attire that she wears in all scenes of the reconstructed triptych, providing a visual continuity that underscores the paradoxical identity of the profligate turned preacher.[132] With one hand resting on a crossbar of her outdoor pulpit and one lifted gently in the air in what seem to be the gestures of the preacher, Mary Magdalene casts her eyes downward so as to suggest humility as well as reflection upon what she is saying, a pose that creates a tension with her physical prominence in the picture. Spatially segregated by gender—the women sit, the men stand—her audience exhibits a range of responses to her preaching. While two women in the foreground give their rapt attention, four men on the right side of the picture converse among themselves. One in front raises a hand in a gesture paralleling the Magdalene's; another, with the index finger of one hand extended upward, appears to be making a point of his own.[133]

The painting's image of earnest yet ambiguous reception of Mary Magdalene's teaching directs attention to the prestige and power of its central subject: an elegant yet humble woman who occupies a public role and acts as figure of spiritual authority for lay society. The late medieval East Anglian saint play similarly highlights the spiritual authority of the woman's preaching office: what the painting conveys through the very scale of the figure who performs it, the play accomplishes through the vernacular scriptural medium in which she speaks. Both painting and play bear witness to the heightened late medieval sensitivity to a feminine "ministry of the Word," in André Vauchez's term, and to the cultural attraction to and discomfort with the public voice of the woman preacher.[134]

These scenes of Mary Magdalene's sermonizing in dramatic text and devotional painting signal awareness of exegetical and homiletic traditions that forcefully examined the saint's legendary identity as a figure of spiritual authority and preacher. Although the power accorded Mary Magdalene in the early Church had been diminished through the transformations wrought by Gregory the Great's conflated scriptural biography, the saint's long history in the medieval West was regularly punctuated by acknowledgment of the authority deriving from her foundational contributions—as witness to and messenger of Christ's resurrection—to the Christian tradition of women's sacred speech. In the twelfth century Mary Magdalene's claim on that authority was realized in increased veneration of her apostolic identity, signified in the use of the terms *apostolorum apostola* and *praedicatrix* to articulate her teaching role.[135] Abelard's letter to Heloise on the origins of women's religious orders invoked the example of Mary Magdalene and other followers of Christ to establish the importance of women in the early Church, arguing from evidence of their special privileges with the deity and superior loyalty to the Savior that such resolute devotion earned them the honor of being appointed "Apostles over the Apostles . . . so that the Apostles might first learn from these women what afterwards they would preach to the whole world."[136]

Abelard may have been willing to trace back to Mary Magdalene a heritage of feminine spiritual authority, but his clerical cohort more frequently labored to suppress the challenges to the pastoral office posed by the prospect of her preaching. Although the saint's legendary evangelical mission to Marseilles was well known by the early thirteenth century, a cycle of images glazed for the nave of Chartres cathedral displaces her apostolic identity by representing Bishop Maximin rather than Mary Magdalene in the role of preacher. This interpretation of her life reflects the view promulgated by late eleventh-century hagiographers of Vezelay, who reported that the saint knew it was forbidden to women to speak of the word of God in public.[137] Jacques de Vitry understood Christ's famous interdiction of Mary Magdalene's desire for fleshly contact, *noli me tangere*, to contain in its "mystical sense" a prohibition of women's preaching and ministration of the sacraments, a prohibition that was reenforced by the *Glossa ordinaria* as well as canon law.[138]

The specific terms in which medieval homilists and exegetes approached Mary Magdalene's biblical and legendary involvements with preaching participate in a larger contemporary debate that focused on feminine access to public spiritual authority.[139] Originating with Saint Paul's famous interdiction of women's preaching and public teaching (1 Tim. 2:11–12, 1 Cor. 14:34–35) and sanctioned by the Fathers, the discourse on women's right to teach and preach religious doctrine came to renewed prominence in the thirteenth century. It coincided with the increased visibility and social authority of feminine religion through the growth of the beguine movement, the emergence of influential holy women from those beguine communities and other social contexts, and the expanded interest in religious doctrine and spiritual teaching that inspired the mendicant movement and motivated lay reform initiatives whose very existence was seen to court heresy. All of these strengthened concern among Church officials and the clerical community to reassert the "principle of a male prerogative over preaching" at a time when the authority and office of the preacher were themselves receiving renewed attention because of interclerical struggles for preeminence.[140] Questions about women's right and power to preach were never far removed from the broader issue of lay involvement in religious study and teaching; the assertion of clerical authority over preaching sought control over both groups.[141]

In its scrutiny of the scriptural text and traditions of commentary, the late medieval debate on women's right to preach turned frequently to the example of Mary Magdalene to puzzle over the potential for an officially sanctioned conception of female spiritual authority. The saint's public ministry in Marseilles emerged as a point of contention in learned sermons and university disputations such as Henry of Ghent's *quaestio, Utrum mulier possit esse doctor, seu doctrix huius scientiae*.[142] In his *Speculum Historiale*, Vincent of Beauvais attempted to resolve the contradiction between Paul's prohibitions and Magdalene's legendary demonstration of apostolic behavior by reporting that the saint drew a timely halt to her preaching in Marseilles as soon as she learned that Paul had ordered women to keep silent in church.[143] Less ingenious considerations of the issue distinguished between forbidden preaching and allowable private teaching and exhortation. One thirteenth-century dispute on the office of preaching assessed the teaching and preaching of Mary Magdalene and Saint Catherine as exceptional events that were permitted only because they transpired during the early Church's struggle to strengthen the faith.[144] Thirteenth-century interpretations of canon law concluded that preaching was the province of the clergy alone, but women, and the laity in general, could engage in other forms of well-intentioned instruction, provided that these occurred in the limiting contexts of religious communities or the domestic realm. Despite the specificity of evidence to the contrary in popular versions of Mary Magdalene's vita, Jacques De Vitry invoked the distinction between *praedicatio* and *exhortatio* to account for the teaching activity conducted by the saint in Marseilles, maintaining that she had converted the people through exhortation rather than preaching.[145] Late medieval clerical censure of women's preaching and public teaching had important consequences. It produced an increased dependence of holy women on clerics, who could perform the sacramental and sacerdotal

offices forbidden to the female sex, and displaced to the sphere of consumption women's potential agency as teachers of scripture: clerics en-
thusiastically approved women's participation as audiences for male
clerical teaching.

When the pagan priest's boy in the Digby saint play declares his
desire to "houkkyn" with the women who come to hear his master's
sermons, then, he alludes to ecclesiastical and political debates that had
linked concerns about the authority of preachers to issues of gender—
debates in which Mary Magdalene was prominently figured. As Alcuin
Blamires observes, these debates inscribed contradictions and paradoxes
within the medieval church's own doctrine, "alternately seeming to
disallow and promote a woman's right to preach." Despite the qualifi-
cations the Parisian university masters attached to her legendary public
teaching—and the prohibitions of women's preaching in scriptural
commentary, canon law, and preaching manuals—Mary Magdalene provides this discourse with a "cogent" and ubiquitous "witness to a possible female preaching role."[146] Her example indicates the availability, to
some late medieval communities, of the ideal of "a public apostolate for
women."[147] Blamires asserts that the *Legenda aurea*'s emphasis on the
"conspicuous evangelizing" of Mary Magdalene and Catherine of Alexandria evidences a "climate of renewed awareness of women's religious
aspirations," upon which this seminal hagiographic text helped to confer authority.[148]

In late medieval England central questions about the authority of
preachers were invigorated by challenges that the Wycliffite movement
posed to ecclesiastical control of sacerdotal power and the institutional
church: who is permitted to preach? what are the differences between
public and private instruction? in what form should scripture be made
available to the faithful? Traditional prohibitions against women's
preaching were specifically invoked by opposition to Lollardy. Like many
medieval reform movements, Lollardy was hospitable to women; by
the late fourteenth century the reputed involvement of Lollard women
in scriptural reading and teaching keenly focused the major challenges
that the movement presented to traditional ecclesiastical authority.[149]
Women Lollards who were directly engaged with the English scriptures
as preachers and teachers were doubly transgressive: they not only violated strictures against women's religious speech that had prevailed
since the early Christian Church, but in so doing also engaged the forbidden medium of the vernacular as a fit vehicle for communication

about the sacred. Official opposition to the preaching and teaching of women Lollards, as Copeland has shown, bears witness to a larger cultural formation, a gendered hermeneutics of reading and textuality that elided literalism, the vernacular, and the laity under the sign of the feminine, thereby attributing to women's reading (and preaching and teaching) symbolic violations not only of religious tradition but also of contemporary textual, political, and social order.[150] The debate about women preachers conducted by adherents and opponents of Lollardy thus has bearing on some of the most fundamental civil and ecclesiastical controversies in late fourteenth- and fifteenth-century England.[151]

In these contested historical intersections of gender, language, and religion, Mary Magdalene once again emerges as a touchstone for thinking about women's access to spiritual authority as preachers and teachers. Lollard William Brut invokes Mary Magdalene in his defense of women's ability—and right—to preach as well as perform other priestly sacramental ministrations.[152] The *quaestio*, *Utrum liceat mulieribus docere viros publice congregatos*, a work bearing the mark of Henry of Ghent's earlier formulations on the same issue, unequivocally asserts: "It is confirmed, for we read that the blessed Mary Magdalene preached publicly in Marseilles and in the surrounding area, which she converted to Christ through her preaching. Because of this she is called the 'Apostle of Apostles.'"[153] In a related *quaestio* on women's ability to administer the eucharistic sacrament, Brut more pointedly cites the historical precedent of "many women [who] steadfastly preached the word when priests and other [men] did not dare to speak a word, and this is shown by Magdalene and Martha."[154] At times Brut is careful to concede some details to the opposition. He notes, for example, that "women may not be allowed to teach in public" (*non liceat mulieribus publice docere*) except in three special circumstances. One of these involves a situation in which many people need to receive religious instruction but few are available to provide it. Such was the case, he maintains, when Mary and Martha were permitted to preach publicly.[155] But he also tackles the opposition in lexical maneuvers, observing that whereas Paul "does not permit a woman to teach or to exercise authority over men," he "does *not* state that women are *not able* to teach or to exercise authority over men—nor do I presume to affirm it."[156]

Brut's claims on behalf of women's ability to serve as preachers and priests are probably more noteworthy for the theory they advance about women's spiritual equality than for any historical witness they may bear to women's actual engagement with preaching.[157] But records of opposition to Lollardy in fifteenth-century East Anglia—where documented feminine challenges to ecclesiastical structures and traditional Christian doctrine occur more frequently than in any other region of late medieval England—demonstrate that views investigated in the rarified academic community that examined Brut's claims were part of a broader cultural conversation that also engaged Norfolk women Lollards such as Margery Baxter and Hawisia Moone, both of whom were reported to endorse women's equal participation in sacred rite as priests.[158]

Among East Anglia women, however, it is Margery Kempe who most famously illustrates how a challenge to Paul's strictures might be mounted. Kempe's accounts of her confrontations with clerical interlocutors over her preaching and scriptural knowledge as well as her frequent verbal triumphs over clerks in the context of her public religious speaking seem expressly designed to convey the apostolic and moral superiority of women's speech articulated by Abelard and the heterodox Brut. For example, at the moment when Kempe's bible talk is most severely challenged by a clerk of York who "browt forth a boke & leyd Seynt Powyl for hys party a-geyns hir þat no woman xulde prechyn," the narrative turns quickly to Kempe's trenchant anticlerical allegory of the bear and the pear tree. When confronted directly with Pauline prohibition of her activity, furthermore, Kempe provides a self-justification for her public religious speech that echoes the very terms that circulated in earlier clerical assessments of the preaching that Mary Magdalene was reputed to have performed in Marseilles: "I preche not, ser, I come in no pulpytt. I vse but comownycacyon & good wordys."[159] The East Anglian mystic's response to the dilemma posed by Pauline prohibition of women's speech is far more daring than the quiet retreat that Vincent of Beauvais had imagined for Mary Magdalene under similar circumstances. Kempe tells how Christ sent Saint Paul directly to her "to strengthyn . . . & confortyn" her. Roundly contradicting one of the evangelist's most influential pronouncements, Christ urges that she should "boldly spekyn in my name fro that day forward." Ventriloquized through Christ in Kempe's imagination, Saint Paul promises her a reward of grace as generous as the reproof she has suffered because of him, and he implies regret for causing her tribulation through his writings in 1 Timothy.[160]

In the real world of late medieval ecclesiastical politics, Paul's ingenious apology was surely the exception. Other female proponents of vernacular scriptural reading and teaching were more likely to be greeted with the rancorous contempt of ecclesiastical officials who, like Kempe's accusers in York, railed against the scripturally engaged who wanted to "smater se de summa divinitate" in order to mount "so hye in litteratura et clerimonia," and especially against the women who "cum suis Anglicis libris smateren hem of clergi."[161]

The East Anglian saint play portrays its principal subject engaged in the very behaviors that at various moments had attracted such vociferous opposition in fifteenth-century England. How would these dramatic representations of vernacular scriptural paraphrase and teaching have been viewed?[162] Were they susceptible to the anxious critique with which official culture met feminine incursions into the realm of clerical prerogative, immeasurably complicated in this instance by the biography of the speaker herself, who was not simply a profligate turned saint but profligate turned preacher? Or would the female speaker's reputation for sanctity, her celebrated devotion to Christ, and her high social class have conferred upon the Digby Magdalene's preaching the sanction of authority rather than the mark of transgression?[163] Might the play's revision of her vita to emphasize the divine mandate of her apostolate be seen as a direct response to opponents of women's spiritual teaching who, like Robert of Basevorn, maintained that "no woman, no matter how learned or saintly, ought to preach" and that those who claimed they were commissioned by God to do so had to prove it?

In view of the degree to which churchmen regularly either served as grudging apologists for Mary Magdalene's legendary preaching or tried to drain it of symbolic and political significance through inventive glossing, the saint play's representation of a woman's vernacular preaching of scripture, especially the gospel, must seem a bold move. The dramatic image is rendered even more provocative in light of continuing religious controversies during the historical period (c. 1490–1530) in which the Digby saint play was composed and copied. It is tempting to historicize the play in light of these controversies as well as the known evidence of East Anglian Lollardy in the late fifteenth and early sixteenth centuries.[164] Arundel's 1409 *Constitutions* were still generating anxieties about vernacular religious teaching over a hundred years after their promulgation, anxieties that were only heightened by the difficulty of distinguishing "lollard" from orthodox writing in the context of lay desire for access to scripture.[165] Although the Norwich heresy trials

(1429–31) mark the earlier decades of the fifteenth century as the high point of reformist activity in East Anglia, the region continued to be a flashpoint for heterodox practices well into the sixteenth century. On the eve of the Reformation, East Anglian women were involved in vernacular religious teaching: in 1523 Agnes Pykas of Bury St. Edmunds gave her son a book of Paul's epistles in English and told him to follow the way of the Gospels.[166] Between 1499 and 1512, seven people in East Anglia were burned for heresy, and many more were under suspicion.[167]

The Digby saint play discloses its affiliations with this regional climate of religious contestation, embroidering the saint's vita with details that have the potential for polemical interpretation. The dramatic Magdalene's private confession, for example, illustrates the Wycliffite view that auricular confession to a priest and clerical absolution were unnecessary because God alone can forgive sin. One Wycliffite sermon invokes her washing of Christ's feet in precisely these terms: "He[e]re may we see hou pryuey shrifte is autorisid of oure Iesu . . . ȝif man haue ful sorowe for his synne, ȝif he speke not aftir o word but do wel and leeue to synne, God forȝyueþ þis synne, as he forȝaf þis wommanus synne."[168] The setting of Mary Magdalene's dramatic preaching, which takes place in unspecified, presumably outdoor, locales in Marseilles, corresponds to the open-air venues with which Lollard preachers were identified— preaching, that is, without a pulpit, as Margery Kempe emphasized, and without ecclesiastical accoutrements.[169] Tokens of heterodox rhetoric elusively echo in the king of Marseilles's response to Mary Magdalene's sermon paraphrase of Genesis. His sharp critique—"Herke, woman, thow hast many resonnys grett!" (1526)—of her declaration that "skryptur declarytt pleyn, / Þat al shold reverens make / To hyr Makar that hem doth susteyn" (1521–23) resembles the charge leveled against London Lollard Robert Plat and his wife, who were "accused of being 'great reasoners in scripture.'" The prominence given to Matthew 5:3–11 in the dramatic Magdalene's sermon on poverty also has transgressive resonances. Foxe's accounts of proto-Protestants include notice of Agnes Ashford of Chesham, who in the early sixteenth century taught James Morden the Sermon on the Mount, and of Alice Brown of Burford, who knew by heart "the beatitudes and other sayings of Jesus."[170]

The dramatic invention of a preaching Magdalene who paraphrases the Sermon on the Mount foregrounds the Digby play's investment in vernacular scripture and religious speech. This investment is apparent

See Modland for mother Mag. I might have investigated local list.

146   Chapter 3

in the text's manifest awareness of specifically linguistic dimensions of sacred communication. The play stages the saint's miracle working in Marseilles as the combined result of Latin scriptural petitions and focused vernacular prayer (1552–61); depicts her sister Martha negotiating linguistic difference in the act of divine praise ("Now worchepyd be þat hey name Jhesu, / The wyche in Latyn is callyd Savyower!" [760–61]); and, through the religious antics of the pagan priest, destablizes the authority of Latin as the language of sacred ritual (1186–97). Pointing to the flexibility of the linguistic encounter with the sacred, these verbal gestures reinforce the potential of the vernacular to effect such an encounter, to function, as Mary Magdalene says to the king, as a "pleyn" vehicle of religious knowledge (1521–25).

The saint play's investment in vernacular preaching, though, is best articulated in Mary Magdalene's recollection of Pentecost:

> Of alle maner tonggys he ȝaf vs knowyng,
> For to vndyrstond every langwage.
> Now have þe dyspyllys take þer passage
> To dyvers contreys her and ȝondyr,
> To preche and teche of hys hye damage—
> Full ferr ar my brothyrn departyd asondyr. (1343–48)[171]

Here Mary Magdalene declares her membership in the community of disciples ("he ȝaf *vs* knowyng"; "*my* brothyrn") and anticipates the apostolic mission that she will receive from Jesus in the very next scene.[172] The speech also effects a transition between the biblical and nonbiblical portions of the saint's vita by invoking Mark 16:15: "Go ye into the whole world and preach the gospel to every creature."

Even as the Digby saint's reminiscence of Pentecostal heteroglossia establishes that her preaching is already divinely authorized, the text's allusion to Mark 16:15 also renders the disciples' dispersal "to prech and teche" the Passion in "every langwage" more immediately relevant to late medieval discourses on uses of the vernacular in sacred teaching. Mark 16:15 "was the favourite text of supporters of lay access to the gospel in sermons": "'Criste sente hys dyssypulles into alle the worlde, ande badde hem prechen the gospelle to euerye creature.'"[173] The friar who wrote MS Longleat 4 in the wake of Arundel's *Constitutions* expressed the connection directly, using Mark 16:15 to challenge injunctions against vernacular teaching and writing of scripture: "And þerfore leue frend sitthe crist bad hese disciplis & oþere prechouris & techeris of godys lawe techin þe gospel to euery man & womman in euery language þer may non prelat artin ne lettin preching & teching of þe gosepel in eng-lych." To urge his lay reader to "spekith of crist gospel & of goddys lawe," the Longleat author calls upon the witness of female saints—"of seynt katerine of seynt lucye & of seynt margarete of seyn agneys & of many oþer"—who "in here ȝougthe were wol connyng in crists lawe."[174] Though he does not mention Mary Magdalene in the group of virgin martyrs, the devotionally savvy reader would most likely have included her in the "many other" mentioned here. By any measure, the connection that the Longleat author establishes between scriptural knowledge, teaching, and feminine spiritual agency and authority is remarkably consistent with the one that the Digby playwright would employ nearly a century later to initiate Mary Magdalene's preaching mission.

Late medieval religious politics—of gender, preaching, and the vernacular—unquestionably shadow the public teaching of the Digby play's Mary Magdalene. Commenting on the medieval reception and interpretation of "hagiographical descriptions of women preaching," Blamires ponders whether "they required delicate explanation in some ecclesiastical contexts beyond that of academic debate." Perhaps, he speculates, "*all* such descriptions were more fraught than we are accustomed to suppose." Even Chaucer inscribes a "doctrinally provocative dimension" in his tale of Saint Cecilia, who "gan . . . bisily to preche" about Christ to Tiburtius, "and of his peynes teche."[175] Emphasizing the ways in which late medieval hagiography intersected with fifteenth-century rhetorics of dissent, Karen Winstead finds similarities of rhetoric and logic in the ways that virgin martyrs critique false religion and early fifteenth-century heretics ridicule material religious practices and ecclesiastical authorities. Hagiography, she asserts, "provided an ideal venue for . . . social criticism . . . [and] theological deliberation: what safer place to flirt with dangerous ideas than within a genre whose uncontested authority and orthodoxy" were unlikely to invite scrutiny and attack?[176] Lollardy itself retained the usefulness of the idea of female sanctity, particularly as attested by preaching and teaching the gospel.[177] The potential for "doctrinally provocative dimensions" to emerge from hagiographic representation becomes still more complex and allusive when we move from narrative text to an embodied, communal theater.

Religious Culture, Hybridity, and the
East Anglian Saint Play

The decades that separate the Longleat friar's endorsement of feminine teaching of a vernacular gospel and the saint play's staging of this phenomenon were marked by contested and fluid allegiances in ecclesiastical and textual politics. It is against this background that we must assess the Digby playwright's representation, at century's end, of a version of feminine scriptural authority that the Longleat author invoked at its beginning to model lay religious knowledge. Recent work on late medieval religious texts and lay reading habits has highlighted the difficulty of determining the orthodox and heterodox investments of these texts and their audiences, particularly in view of incentives for fifteenth-century religious writers to resort to strategies of indirection in the prevailing climate of censorship established by Arundel's *Constitutions*.[178] The religious allegiances and sympathies of late medieval laity and clergy alike were far from uncomplicated; the emphasis on individual piety that was such an important aspect of late medieval orthodoxy was not only perfectly compatible with but also preparatory for the emphases of reformed religion in the sixteenth century. One of the most valuable developments in recent studies of the history of late medieval religion and spirituality has been the elucidation of the vital hybridity that characterized English religious culture in the period that Anne Hudson has termed the "premature Reformation."[179] Such hybridity was exceptionally active in East Anglia, where the religious culture sustained a wide range of options and behaviors, showing itself relatively tolerant of the nonconformity it harbored and bred while clinging at the same time to habits and beliefs of what Duffy has called "traditional religion."[180]

The spiritual experience, textual interests, and social connections of Katherine Manne, anchoress of the Norwich Dominican friary in the 1520s and 1530s, illustrate these hybrid religious allegiances in the very period when *Mary Magdalene* was copied into the manuscript that became part of Digby 133. Manne is best known as a spiritual familiar of Thomas Bilney, the ambiguous East Anglian champion of reform from whom she received copies of Tyndale's New Testament and *Obedience of a Christian Man*. But she also numbered among her supporters the economic and political elites of the city of Norwich as well as distinguished intellectuals and clerics from Cambridge University who located themselves on the orthodox side of contemporary religious disputes. Reinforcing gendered models of spiritual advice from less politically contentious contexts, Manne's example evidences "the extremely fluid nature of religious positions" during this period and more importantly documents the presence of the female ascetic "as intellectual participant[] in the tense debates just before the break with Rome."[181]

Rather than argue that the Digby *Magdalene* stakes out particular allegiances in the contested realm of its contemporary ecclesiastical politics, I claim that it is precisely the conflicted climate of late medieval religion itself that the text puts at issue. Granting the evidence pointing to the play's transgression of official religion and ecclesiastical authority, we must also acknowledge the degree to which the text unequivocally reinforces traditional late medieval religious culture.[182] The saint's dramatic vita represents an array of beliefs and practices that heterodox opinion identified as principal signifiers of what was wrong with traditional religion: it endorses pilgrimage and clerical performance of sacred rite and ritual processions, emphasizes visions and angelic visitations, and accords to a female saint powers that a reformed religion would attribute to God alone. In one sense, these dramatic images of traditional religion are simply elements called for by narrative elements in the saint's life. Still, the Digby playwright's exploitation of the symbolic and theatrical power of such spectacles urges us to view them not as unproblematic signifiers of the tenacity of late medieval religion but rather as evidence of a consciously chosen strategy of engagement that acknowledges the ideological investments of late medieval religious experience. From this perspective the saint play's representations of traditional religion can be seen to parallel the larger late medieval project of reinscribing orthodoxy, a project that Spencer also finds at work in the copying of certain sermon collections and in the printing of so-called "safe books," such as the English version of the *Legenda aurea* and Mirk's *Festial*.[183] The Digby saint play's intervention in that project resides in the bold interplay between orthodox pieties and gender-based challenges to them that the text articulates, furnishing evidence of the "surprising proximity of orthodox and oppositional meaning" that Sanok hypothesizes as "the most salient and unsettling feature of civic drama" in late medieval England.[184] The controversial subjects entertained by the Digby play—the critique of clerical learning, the nature of sacerdotal sacramental and pastoral authority, the authenticity of visionary experiences, vernacular preaching and teaching—are all inflected by questions of gender. Through these concerns the drama of female saints in *Mary Magdalene* discloses its dynamic relationship to vernacular religion in late medieval England, illustrating at the same time the contributions that vernacular theater made to the production, critique, and renewal of religious culture.

4

Gender and the Anthropology of Redemption

Needs to ask question
Machonism question silence, absence

In honor of St. Margaret, St. Mary Magdalene, and all
Holy Virgins
            —Dedication of Margery Kempe's
                parish church, King's Lynn

THE DRAMATIC STRUCTURE AND verbal texture of the Digby *Mary Magdalene* rely heavily on typology, repetition, and parallelism for their most powerful effects. Scholarship has typically evaluated these features of the text as formal devices contributing to dramatic unity or as evidence that the play seeks to reproduce universal Christian history. Yet the playwright also used these structural and verbal techniques to exploit ambiguities that arise from such moments of symbolic and narrative convergence.[1] One important instance of this ambiguity appears in the encomium uttered by the queen of Marseilles upon waking from the "grevos slepe" of death suffered in childbirth:

> O *virgo salutata*, for ower savacyon!
> O *pulchra et casta* cum of nobyll alyavns!
> O almyty Maydyn, ower sowlys confortacyon!
> O demvr Mavdlyn, my bodyys sustynavns!
> Þou hast wr[a]ppyd vs in wele from all waryawns,
> And led me wyth my lord i[n]to the Holy Lond! (1899–1904)

Whereas the version of this episode in the *Legenda aurea* creates no doubt about the queen's addressee, the Digby text, by contrast, is far from straightforward about identifying her deliverer.[2] The queen's speech combines celebrated attributes of the Virgin Mary with references to events that the saint's life credited to Mary Magdalene. The queen's mention of a "worshipful virgin" (*virgo salutata*) appears out of keeping with traditional understandings of Mary Magdalene's sexual identity, as does her description of her rescuer as chaste (*casta*). Although the saint play has firmly established Mary Magdalene's beauty and "nobyll alyauns," as well as her patronage of the queen's maternal experience, these worthy attributes do not add up to the appellation "Maydyn," a designation complicated by the queen's address to "Mavdlyn" in the next line.

The Digby playwright's conflation of attributes of the Virgin Mary and Mary Magdalene in this recognition scene is not the only point when the text establishes symbolic congruence between the two most important women in Christian tradition. At a moment when Jacobus's *vita*, for example, has the king of Marseilles directly address Mary Magdalene, his Digby counterpart anticipates his queen's ambiguous praise by asking blessing on the "puer vergyn" who bears responsibility for his wife's revival (1895). The royal couple further intertwine the identities of Mary, mother of Jesus, and Mary, the Digby heroine, when they greet Mary Magdalene upon their return to Marseilles:

> [REX]. Heyll be þou, Mary! Ower Lord is wyth the!
> The helth of ower sowllys, and repast contemplatyff!
> Heyll, tabyrnakyll of þe blyssyd Trenite!
> Heyll, covnfortablyll sokore for man and wyff!
> REGINA. Heyll, þou chosyn and chast of wommen alon!
> It passyt my wett to tell þi nobyllnesse!
> Þou relevyst me and my chyld on þe rokke of ston,
> And also savyd vs be þi hye holynesse. (1939–46)

The king and queen laud attributes that were regularly associated with the Virgin Mary (her enclosure of the "blyssyd Trenite"; her privilege of being "chosyn and chast" among women) and employ distinctive Marian language echoing Luke's annunciation (1:28). Nevertheless, they clearly addresses their remarks to Mary Magdalene, even kneeling, as the stage direction indicates, at her feet (s.d. 1938).

This "assimilation" by the Digby play's Magdalene of "characteristics and powers of God's mother" is evidenced in still other scriptural, allegorical, and liturgical allusions that associate the dramatic saint with the Virgin Mary.[3] Gabriel's address to the Virgin in Luke 1 ("Ne timeas Maria") resonates in Raphael's announcement to Mary Magdalene that she convert the people of Marseilles: "Abasse [fear] the novtt, Mary" (1376). In each case an angel delivers to a female auditor news of a divine imperative that cannot be refused. At an earlier moment in the play, Luxuria's salutation—"Heyl, lady most lavdabyll of alyauvns!" (440)— begins the process of Mary Magdalene's seduction even as it ironically echoes Gabriel's "Ave" and anticipates the "Heyll be thou, Mary" uttered by the king and queen. In the diabolical plot leading up to Luxuria's greeting, a scheming Mundus ascribes to the still virtuous Magdalene powers comparable to those that biblical typology attributed to the Virgin Mary, the maiden who, according to Genesis 3:15, would crush the serpent's head: "Yf she in vertu stylle may dwelle," claims Mundus, "[s]he xal byn abyll to dystroye helle" (419–20). At the play's conclusion angels raise Magdalene aloft for her feedings with heavenly manna to strains of *Assumpta est Maria in nubibus*, a hymn associated in the Middle Ages with the feast of the Virgin Mary's assumption.

Critics of the Digby saint play have paid little attention to the gender politics inscribed in the play's sustained conflation of Mary Magdalene and the Virgin Mary.[4] This oversight is a function, I believe, of the critical inclination to ground analyses of the saint's gender identity—and gender issues in the Digby play—in her overcoming of a sexual sin that was usually gendered feminine. Just as critical emphasis on the dramatic Magdalene's penitential example has overshadowed substantial textual evidence that the playwright was more interested in her role as model contemplative rather than sinner, so too the impulse to privilege the saint's fallen, feminine sexuality has obscured other signs that the dramatist saw that attribute as but an aspect of a complex spiritual anthropology.[5] This chapter demonstrates that, far from being idiosyncratic, the Digby saint play's frequent fusion of Mary Magdalene and the Virgin Mary draws upon medieval exegetical and spiritual traditions that both asserted and interrogated linguistic, symbolic, and corporeal congruences between the penitent saint and the mother of Jesus. It further proposes that this identification furnishes a point of access to the play's gender politics. In *Mary Magdalene* constructions of gender and the relationships of power and authority that produce them are reinforced, and in a sense determined, by differences between the sacred and profane realms in which they occur. The play's profane constructions of masculinity and femininity are conventional, constricting, and, as dramatic treatment of Mary Magdalene's fall illustrates, often sinister in their implications. Sacred categories of gender, by contrast, are more fluid, less bound to predictable binary constructions, and grounded in the complicated incarnational relation of spirit and flesh. Gender issues in the Digby saint play, then, encompass far more than Mary Magdalene's notorious identification with a feminized sexual sin. Rather, they resonate in the play's energetic critique of a sex-gender system that excoriated a predominately feminine lust and the social ideologies that accompanied it. Gender categories are also central to the play's theology of redemption, constituting some of the most challenging revisions that the Digby dramatist made to the saint's traditional vita.

Investigations of the theology and politics of *Mary Magdalene* have frequently argued that the play is ideologically invested in the reproduction of Christian knowledge. In this view secular interests of earthly political power yield to the prerogatives of the spiritual realm, pagan beliefs to Christian, diabolical shenanigans to divinely authorized miracle, flawed human communication to the sacred word, and quotidian reality to the eternal present.[6] Although the fundamental orthodoxy of the play's theology is hardly in doubt, I believe that it provides a bolder vision of the anthropology of redemption than these critical constructions will allow. Assessments of the transformation from profane to sacred power in *Mary Magdalene* must take the play's nuanced critique of gender squarely into account. One reason the Virgin Mary, though never appearing as an actual character in the text, so consistently shadows dramatic representation of the lives of Christ and Mary Magdalene in the play is that she provides a continual reminder of the feminine contribution to Christ's human flesh, and hence to the Redemption. The saint play articulates the cosmological shift from profane to sacred power in terms of a gendered theology of atonement in which Mary Magdalene, by virtue of her legendary and symbolic convergences with the Virgin Mary, is herself deeply implicated.

Gender Politics and the Profane Realm

The Digby saint play maps the interplay of gender categories in the secular and sacred realms. The dramaturgy of the secular, earthly realm inscribes gender differences as both products and producers of social and political relationships. This is the realm of the tyrants; Cyrus and his family; the fallen Magdalene and her suitor, Curiosity; the king and queen of Marseilles; and low-status comic characters such as the pagan priest, Nauta, and their boys. In the play's sacred dramaturgy, gender categories and identities are more variable and elastic, allowing the conflation of the sexual and the chaste woman and enabling frequent crossings between Christ, his virgin mother, and Mary Magdalene. The play juxtaposes this fluidity, which recognizes the feminine as a cocreative component of the deity, to the hypermasculinity and sexualized femininity that it locates in secular public rule and domestic life.

In the earthly realm such hypermasculinity is manifested in a public preoccupation with juridical power.[7] As the play dramatizes worldly sovereignty, it consistently employs the trope of judgment to articulate the earthly rulers' desire to project an image of absolute power. So frequently is the word "jugge" used to name these representatives of worldly sovereignty that juridical authority may be said to characterize masculine power itself in *Mary Magdalene*.[8] These allusions to judgment culminate in a mock trial conducted by Rex Diabolus to punish the Bad Angel (Malinus Spiritus) and the seven demons who have failed to keep Mary Magdalene in a state of sin. Epitomizing the type of justice about which the earthly rulers boast, Rex Diabolus's trial establishes their juridical kinship with him and enacts the diabolic nature of judgment as they understand it. "Settyng in judycyal-lyke astate," Rex Diabolus conducts a "jugment of harlottys" (727–28). He hears the transgressors' excuses, only to punish "þese felons" by beating them ("thys hard balys on þi bottokkys xall byte!") and then burning them up (744, 735).

This image of secular, masculine juridical power furnishes an important counterpoint to the play's representation of Christ's parable of the debtors in the scene of Mary Magdalene's repentance. Provoked by Simon the Pharisee's objection to the unnamed penitent woman of Luke 7:37–50 who anoints Jesus in his home, the parable appears in one of the major biblical texts contributing to the medieval Magdalene's composite identity. Jacobus omitted the parable of the debtors from his vita, but the Digby playwright seems to have reinserted this important biblical episode into the saint's life in order to exploit an ironic convergence between the juridical preoccupations of the play's earthly rulers and Jesus' very different response to the loving penitent.[9] He queries Simon's understanding of the two debtors—one owing little and one much, but both forgiven equally of their debt—when he asks his host, "Whych of þes to personnys was most beholddyn to þat man?" (658). To

Simon's reply ("He þat most owt hym" [660]), Jesus provides a response that echoes the secular rulers' preoccupations: "*Recte iudicasti*"
("You have judged correctly" [661]). Although representatives of earthly
power in the play regularly threaten to punish offenders who transgress
their law, it is Jesus whom the play shows in the role of judge (the trial
of Rex Diabolus notwithstanding) and Mary Magdalene whom it casts
in the role of transgressor.[10] Morever, the play stresses that Jesus' substitution of grace and mercy for the retributive justice exercised by its
masculine ruling figures is also inflected by a gender difference that
highlights the feminine dimensions of his redemptive actions. At the very
moment when Jesus declares Mary Magdalene forgiven of "wrecched-
nesse," and directly after he fulfills his role as arbiter of correct judgment, she identifies his maternal conception as a source of his divine
power: "O, blessyd be þou, Lord of euyrlastyng lyfe, / And blyssyd be
þi berth of þat puer vergynne!" (678–79). Mary Magdalene's address
links her forgiveness to her redeemer's virgin birth and hence to a
"right," and in her characterization, feminized, form of justice.

Paralleling the saint play's dramatic construction of the juridical
power and authority of earthly masculinity is its comparably precise
representation of masculinity's attachment to a troubling and unruly
desire. In light of its heroine's reputation for sexual transgression, this
dimension of the play's gender politics is especially important, I think,
and it is consistent with other textual evidence pointing to the playwright's effort to attenuate Mary Magdalene's notoriety as a sexual sinner. The text labors to distance her from that reputation, for example,
by suggesting that she fell victim, not to a weak feminine nature, but
to demonic forces still trying to avenge Lucifer's demise (365–67); that
her lapse was occasioned by grief over her father's death (452–55); and
that her sin was as much a social transgression as it was a moral fault.[11]
These interpretations of the saint's traditional vita problematize the link
between sin and female sexuality that Mary Magdalene was habitually
said to exemplify. It is not that the play absolves the saint of sexual sin
nor that it renders female sexuality untainted. Rather, it renders it unin-
teresting, especially compared to the text's far more compelling display
of male bodies and representations of masculine desire.[12] Instead of
simply reinscribing Mary Magdalene's conventional associations with
sexual sin, the saint play recognizes gender as a complex system of shifting identities and relationships in which idealized roles for men and
women come under strain from many directions; economic and political

factors influence the structure of the "family and other social institutions"; and masculinist ideologies foster and maintain "power through the oppression of both men and women."[13]

Mary Magdalene ubiquitously figures the sinister and violent, if at times comic, aspects of masculine constructions of femininity as the object of desire. Luxuria may single out Mary Magdalene as her prime target, but Curiosity, the king of Flesh, the king of Marseilles, and the low-status male characters also come under her spell. Cyrus addresses his daughters in a courtly idiom that accords with his family's gentle status: "Here is Mary, ful fayur and ful of femynyte, / And Martha, ful [of] beute and of delycyte, / Ful of womanly merrorys and of benygnyte" (71–73). But his speech also eerily anticipates the king of Flesh's reference to Mary Magdalene's allegorical temptress, Lady Luxuria, as "flowyr fayrest of femynyte" (423) and the king of Marseilles's praise of his queen, who "is full fayur in hyr femynyte" (943).[14]

This masculine discourse of desire, articulated as "courtesy," also furnishes the idiom in which Mary Magdalene is seduced by Curiosity, whose temptation of Cyrus's daughter, the play intimates, may succeed in part because it verbally echoes her father's praise. In league with the king of Flesh, whose own amorous repartee with Luxuria epitomizes the menacing workings of masculine desire masquerading as courtesy, Curiosity exposes the duplicitous nature of his courtly wooing of Mary Magdalene when he enters the scene announcing his hot pursuit of "sum praty tasppysstere" (494) but quickly turns his sights higher up the social ladder to take a crack at the "jentyll women" the Taverner introduces to him (513–14):

A, dere dewchesse, my daysyys iee!
Splendavnt of colour, most of femynyte,
Your sofreyn colourrys set wyth synseryte!
Consedere my loue into yower alye,
Or ellys I am smet wyth peynnys of perplexite! (515–19)

Curiosity's advances come closer to their author's true intentions, however, when he more crudely asserts, "So wold to God ʒe wold my loue fele!" (522). Magdalene chides his haste—"Qwat cavse that ʒe love me so sodenly?" (523)—and when Curiosity protests that he cannot resist the power of her "womanly" person (525), she ambiguously reproves his cheeky come-on and suggests that she has begun to soften to his overtures: "Syr, curtesy doth it you lere!" (527).

Tony Davenport calls the scene of Magdalene's seduction by Curiosity a "neat little pastiche of courtly love."[15] What does the Digby playwright's innovative use of courtly repartee in this scene signify in relation to traditional emphases of the life of Mary Magdalene? What does it contribute to the text's constructions of gender? The social resonances of Mary Magdalene's courtly exchanges with her suitor imply that she succumbs as much to flattery and to Curiosity's ability to speak to her own sense of social superiority as she does to sexual desire. The Digby dramatist's use of the courtly idiom to mask the evil or less-than-honorable intentions of Curiosity and the kings of Marseilles and the Flesh establishes a discursive identification among these characters based on their shared preoccupation, not simply with the worldliness and pride with which they are regularly credited, but with "fayur . . . femynyte" (943), thereby suggesting how courtly discourse elicits feminine vulnerability to masculine sexual overtures even as it promotes an idea of "femynyte" as the embodied, coveted object of desire.[16]

The Digby play thus complicates traditional interpretations of Mary Magdalene as a so-called prostitute by designating masculinity as a preeminent dramatic locus of erotic energy and behavior. This alteration of the standard narrative of the saint's life is provocatively underscored in several comic scenes of the playwright's own invention that develop an image of clerical life and ritual in pagan Marseilles and create characters for the elusive seamen of Jacobus's account who ferry the converted king and queen to the Holy Land and back. These scenes abandon the patina of courtliness through which the play's high-status masculine authority figures relate to their feminine objects of desire in favor of a crude, aggressive, and violent image of masculine sexuality that draws its excitement from fantasy women but in the end focuses on relations between men. These queer moments in the dramatic action have gone largely unremarked in scholarship on the Digby saint play; yet they are of crucial importance to its representations of gender in the earthly realm.[17] Focusing principally on conflicts between male masters and subordinates over absent women, these scenes emphasize a masculine sexual imaginary, creating for the gender politics of the earthly realm a kind of shadow role for women that parallels that occupied by the Virgin Mary in the sacred realm.[18]

In relation to the theological issues of the Digby text, the garbled macaronic rituals of the pagan priest of Marseilles and his clerk serve as foils for Mary Magdalene's Christian miracles (1143–1201), but in the limiting context of the play's attention to masculine eros, the priest's encounter with his clerk, Hawkyn, more immediately establishes an analogy between religious ritual and sexual practices. When the priest orders Hawkyn to prepare his "awter" and ring a bell for the "grett solemnyte" at which he will preside, the clerk responds with this non sequitur: "Whatt, mastyr! Woldyst þou have þi lemman to þi beddys syde?" (1144, 1147, 1149). Though the priest contends he has spoken of no such thing, Hawkyn persists in pressing his symbolic substitution of the bed for the altar: "Wether þou ded or natt, þe fryst jorny xall be myn," he replies, in an apparent allusion to a sexual act (1153). Hawkyn further presses his case by taunting the priest for having become so fat— "grett as þe dywll of hell" in fact—that he fails to attract the "woman [who] comme to here þi sermon," leaving all the women for Hawkyn himself: "Pratyly wyth hem I can houkkyn, / Wyth Kyrchon and fayer Maryon— / Þey love me bettyr þan þe!" (1157–62).[19] Having brooked enough threats to his masculinity, the priest tries to put an end to Hawkyn's rivalry and fantasies of sexual conquest and reasserts his own authority by threatening violence: "I xall whyp þe tyll þi ars xall belle!" [swell?] (1169). But the clerk does not readily abandon his insubordination; instead, Hawkyn counters the priest's threat with an insult that still locates the terms of their conflict below the belt: "A fartt, mastyr, and kysse my grenne! / Þe dyvll of hell was þi emme! / Loo, mastyrs, of swyche a stokke he cam! / Þis kenred is asprongyn late!" (1171–74).

Besides hinting at the pagan priest's diabolic heritage through an image that echoes Rex Diabolus's beating of his subordinates on the "ars" (735), the clerk's retort intimates a more complex dynamic for this relationship of dominance and subservience. It is difficult to dismiss the homoerotic cast of Hawkyn's provocative "kysse my grenne," glossed as "groin" by the Digby editors and, in light of the genealogical references, the still more ambiguous connotations of "this kenred . . . asprongen late." What, if anything, is "asprongen" in this scene, and what gesture would accompany this assertion? Here conflict arising from rivalry over imaginary women concludes in a violent act of dominance between men. "Stryppys on þi ars þou xall have, / And rappys on þi pate!" the priest exclaims; the stage direction ("Bete hym") confirms his aggression (1174–75). It might be argued that the king of Marseilles in his earlier appearance has already established a kind of local predilection for unruly male desire, a predilection whose cruder forms are here displaced onto pagan religious error. But the confrontation between pagan priest and youthful clerk also illustrates on its own terms the extent to which masculine desire problematically—and ironically—haunts the dramatic life of Western Christendom's most famous exemplar of feminine sexual transgression.[20]

The Digby playwright also invented a comic interlude for the shipmaster and his boy that reprises the major emphases of the Hawkyn episode: fantasy woman, youthful sexual aggressor, demonic associations, and violent subjugation. In this scene the dominant male is ostensibly cast in the role of helper rather than sexual rival. The boy complains of illness ("[S]wyche a cramp on me sett is, / I am a poynt to fare þe worse"), and the shipmaster inquires about his needs ("Now, boy, whatt woll þe þis seyll?" [1407–8, 1411]). But the boy's declaration that "[n]othyng butt a fayer damsell" will cure him (1412) quickly arouses the master's wrath: "Be my trowth, syr boye, ȝe xal be sped! / I wyll bryng hyr onto yower bed! / Now xall þou lern a damsell to wed— / She wyll nat kysse þe on scorn!" [in mockery] (1415–18). The shipmaster immediately proceeds to beat the boy (s.d. 1418), making clear the identity of the "damsell" that he has promised to deliver to him: the boy will be "wed" to the whip and its "kisses." As the spectral femininity of the "fayer damsell" once again evaporates in an act of violence between men, the shipmaster's boy ambiguously confirms the expiration of his own desire: "A skorn! No, No, I fynd it hernest! / The dewlle of hell motte þe brest, / For all my corage is now cast! / Alasse! I am forlorn!" (1419–22).

Directly after this altercation, Mary Magdalene approaches the shipmaster seeking her passage to Marseilles. Her sudden entrance at first seems to place her in the role of the "fayer damsel" whom the boy desires, that is, in a role for her old, rather than her new, converted self, a social construction of femininity she here resists. The shipmaster's eagerness to respond to her request for a word with him ("All redy, fayer woman! Whatt wol ȝe?" [1424]) suggests that the libidinal energies of the previous scene are still at play. In this respect, then, Mary Magdalene's encounter with the shipmaster charts her ethical and spiritual evolution since her meeting with Curiosity. But occurring as it does immediately after the shipmaster's boy declares his "corage" all "cast," the scene also makes a timely association between the woman saint and the subjugation of a male desire that has been channeled, in ironic anticipation of Mary Magdalene's involvement with the king and queen of Marseilles, into a symbolic "marriage" with an instrument of dominance and discipline—a whip. The disciplining of that desire is further confirmed by a telling detail of the saint's exchange with the shipmaster. The terms of that exchange offer a direct rebuttal to the life of Saint Mary of Egypt, with whom Mary Magdalene was frequently identified because of their common association with sexual profligacy. The legendary lives of both women provide for them to travel by sea. Whereas Mary of Egypt had only her body to offer as collateral in exchange for her passage, the dramatist shows Magdalene able to pay good money for that service: "Syr, may I natt wyth yow sayle? / And ʒe xall have for yower awayle" (1431–32).[21]

The first encounter between the king of Marseilles and the ship-master, or Nauta, further elaborates the play's preoccupation with masculine eros. When the king, accompanied by his wife and directed by Mary Magdalene to seek Saint Peter in the Holy Land, approaches the shipmaster in quest of passage, Nauta accuses him of abduction and adultery: "I trow, be my lyfe, / Þou hast stollyn sum mannys wyffe! / Þou woldyst lede hyr owt of lond!" (1733–35). The situation of the king, who is bound on Christian pilgrimage with his pregnant queen, comically exposes the shipmaster's charge as a case of mistaken identity. By once more invoking a feminine presence ("sum mannys wyffe") as the occasion for a conflict between men, Nauta's accusatory projection that the expectant royal couple represent illicit sexual relations also mirrors the trafficking in imaginary women that subtends the homosociality of priest and clerk, shipmaster and boy. This time the conflict is quickly resolved through money rather than violence (1739–41), but the gratuitous sexual challenge with which the Digby playwright punctuates the exchange between shipmaster and king suggests how resistant to containment such unruly masculine desire may be.

By juxtaposing Mary Magdalene to these illustrations of the male erotic imagination, the dramatic text hints at her elusive identity as a figure capable of containing or controlling the terms of masculine power itself. She overcomes the pagan priest and his boy with her own Christian miracles, redirects the energies expressed by the shipmaster and his boy from sex to commerce, and engages the king in a conversion imaged in a movement from lust to procreation.[22] By punctuating Mary Magdalene's passage to Marseilles and the royal couple's voyage to the Holy Land with these representations of masculine desire, the Digby play extends the sex and gender thematics of the saint's scripturally based life into the legendary narrative that figured so prominently in her late medieval vita.[23]

If some of the Digby playwright's most important additions to the dramatic life of Mary Magdalene put the masculine erotic construction of femininity at issue, still other scenes establish that femininity is itself a complex sign that resists containment by this masculine imagination. Granted, most of the meanings that the text ascribes to femininity reproduce the traditional system of gender differences.[24] For example, femininity signifies the willfulness and variance castigated in misogynist discourse. This is the femininity that the king of Marseilles invokes, though does not name, when he tries to dissuade his wife from undertaking a pilgrimage to the Holy Land: "Alas! Þe wyttys of wommen, how þey byn wylld! / And þerof fallytt many a chanse!" (1701–2). The queen of Marseilles's "wild" womanly wits epitomize the familiar association of femininity and irrationality in misogynist discourse. When the woeful "chans" that befalls the queen at sea appears to fulfill the king's prediction and ensure her death in childbirth, she calls upon a femininized conception of nurturer and deliverer, hailing Mary Magdalene, "flowyr of wommanned" (1747), and lamenting the absence of a midwife's assistance: "For defawte of wommen here in my nede, / Deth my body makyth to sprede" (1762–63).[25] The queen's plight at sea also invokes the dark, dangerous side of the maternal feminine as the site of pollution and death; it is the presence of her dead body that stirs up the storm and threatens the lives on the ship bearing the king to the Holy Land: "Cast hyr owt," the shipmaster's boy exclaims, "or ellys we synke ond[yr]!" (1780). In *Mary Magdalene* femininity *is* an unstable category but not solely in the ways that the king's complaint implies. Rather, it is a site where masculinity inscribes its anxieties about sexuality, social and domestic control, and the taint of mortality.

Drawing upon a complex gender politics that was grounded in Mary Magdalene's multiple identities, the Digby playwright reworks the legendary narrative about the royal couple of Marseilles not simply as a story about the spread of Christianity but as a cautionary tale about the disciplining and redirecting of gendered sexuality in the earthly realm. The traditional vita's linkage of the conversion of the king and queen to their conception of a child takes on added significance in light of the text's many illustrations of riotous hetero- and homoerotic desire: the rulers of Marseilles bear witness to the channeling of unrestrained sexuality into lawful procreation. As Laura King suggests, it is to the "vexed marital relationship with its conflicting imperatives to procreate but abstain from concupiscence" that the ruler of Marseilles seems to allude when he hails the saint as "covnfortabyll sokore for man and wyff!" (1942) at the conclusion of his harrowing but ultimately restorative pilgrimage.[26] The king and queen overcome both the threats of unruly masculine desire and the dangers of feminine pollution through the beneficent influence of Mary Magdalene, whose own embrace of chastity signals her transcendence of these constraints of earthly gender categories. Coming to aid the queen just when she thinks that "wommannys help is away" (1759), Mary Magdalene's feminine power reestablishes order in the heteronormative family, an order that includes placing the queen on an equal spiritual footing with the king (1905–10). The saint's timely ministrations also reinforce that family's claim to social and dynastic power. She preserves the royal child "conseyvyd" on the queen "by ryth" (1758) and welcomes the "yong prynsse of dew and ryth" to repossess with his parents their "own erytage wythowt othe" (1948–49).

To the extent that the Marseilles episode both critiques and models the private and public values of lay society through the family, it comes to look less like a conversion narrative and, as was the case with many saints' lives, more like a romance. The newly Christianized royal couple of Marseilles emerge as the lay hero and heroine of the drama, confirmed in faith, secure in their property and lineage, and eager to engage in pious worldly practices such as church building.[27] In social, material, and spiritual terms Mary Magdalene navigates the gender politics of this earthly realm. She first embraces, then rejects, construction as the feminine object of Curiosity's desire; redirects the libidinal energies of the king and queen of Marseilles to the establishment of Christian dynastic power; and enters the frail realm of maternal flesh, purifying it of pollution and death. Representing Mary Magdalene's success in all these problematic negotiations of profane gender categories and identities, the Digby play thereby establishes the saint as a worthy participant in the nexus of sacred gender relations that link her to both Christ and his mother, and make her, in fact, a bridge between constructions of gender in the secular and sacred realms.

Gender Politics and the Sacred

Nothing in either the biblical or the legendary life of the saint prepares for the post-Resurrection dramatic episode in which the heavens open

to disclose Jesus (s.d. 1348), who dispatches his angel to Mary Magdalene with this prefatory encomium to the Virgin Mary:

> O, þe onclypsyd sonne, tempyll of Salamon!
> In þe mone I restyd, þat nevyr chonggyd goodnesse!
> In þe shep of Noee, fles of Judeon,
> She was my tapyrnakyll of grett nobyllnesse,
> She was þe paleys of Phebus brygthnesse,
> She was þe wessell of puere clennesse,
> Wher my Godhed ʒaff my manhod myth;
>
> My blyssyd mother, of demvre femynyte,
> For mankynd, þe feynddys defens,
> Quewne of Jherusalem, þat heuenly cete,
> Empresse of hell, to make resystens.
> She is þe precyus pyn, full of ensens,
> The precyus synamvyr, þe body thorow to seche.
> She is þe mvske aʒens þe hertys of vyolens,
> Þe jentyll jelopher aʒens þe cardyakyllys wrech.
>
> The goodnesse of my mothere no tong can expresse,
> Nere no clerke of hyre, hyre joyys can wryth.
> Butt now of my servantt I remembyr þe kendnesse;
> Wyth heuenly masage I cast me to vesyte;
> Raphaell, myn angell in my syte,
> To Mary Mavdleyn decende in a whyle,
> Byd here passe þe se be my myth,
> And sey she xall converte þe land of Marcyll. (1349–71)

Christ's elaborate praise of his mother is both dramatically and linguis-
tically out of place at this juncture of the play. His catalog of Marian
epithets and symbolism abruptly shifts the focus from Magdalene's
account of the apostles' evangelical work, and the rich typological language of his speech sharply contrasts with the imperative mood into
which he quickly slips as he orders Raphael to charge the new apostle
with her mission.

This unusual Marian reverie, however, is both relevant to the thematic investments of the Digby play that I have been examining and
consistent with other evidence that East Anglian dramatists were keenly

attuned to the relationship of the adult Christ and his mother. For example, the encomium to Mary is reminiscent of a speech delivered by Christ Dominus as he prepares to raise his mother bodily into heaven in the N-Town *Assumption*, a play whose representation of the complicated tie between human mother and divine son provocatively echoes in *Mary Magdalene*.[28] In this passage Christ's recognition of his mother's "demure femynyte" once more foregrounds a gender category that the play otherwise elaborates in terms of a system of earthly sexual identities. At this juncture, however, femininity signifies the sacred enclosure of Christ's own double nature. Like the play's other invocations of feminine physicality, the Virgin Mary's femininity is associated with the material body, the vessel and tabernacle of her pure flesh where Jesus' Godhead empowered his manhood. Stressing the physicality that he shares with his mother, Christ praises Mary's "demure femynyte" and thereby signals the Digby play's commitment to elaborating a gendered deity whose feminine ties are central to his salvific humanity.[29]

Although the Virgin Mary never appears in the text as a speaking character, she occupies an important spiritual and symbolic role in the Digby saint play because the Savior's human generation is a central element of the text's christological emphases. At crucial moments in the text the dramatist returns to the substance and spirit of Christ's encomium in order to acknowledge the fleshly, feminine aspects of his exceptional divine nature. The very first words that Mary Magdalene addresses to Jesus in the play when he declares her "hol in sowle" speak directly to his masculine divinity and femininized humanity: "O, blessyd be þou, Lord of euyrlastyng lyfe, / And blyssyd be þi berth of þat puer vergyne!" (677–78). Jesus' declaration of forgiveness issues in Mary Magdalene's confirmation of the maternal, feminine character of his generation, making gender categories themselves central elements in their relationship and her redemption. By speaking to Christ's double identity at the moment of her forgiveness, Magdalene also establishes the sacred triangle of reformed saint, deity, and virgin mother whose symbolic and physical relationships provide an important subtext of this hagiographical narrative's vision of the role of gender in salvation history.

At other key moments the Digby play acknowledges Jesus' double nature. In a post-Resurrection encounter based on Matthew 28:9, Mary Magdalene greets Christ: "O þou gloryus Lord of heuen regyon, / Now blyssyd be þi hye devyntye, / Thatt evyr thow tokest incarnacyon" (1125–27). About to be raised into the clouds for her angelic feeding with heavenly manna, she momentarily dispenses with the recognition of the Godhead that she elsewhere in the play so consistently avers, in favor simply of "[l]avd and preyse to þat blyssyd byrth!" (2029). This shifting of emphasis to the incarnational, feminine sources of Christ's sacred power, his "blyssyd byrth," is highly appropriate for the dramatic scene of Mary Magdalene's spectacular heavenly levitation, which is modeled on the Virgin Mary's assumption. The angelic messengers that Christ dispatches to bring Mary Magdalene's "gostly fode" (2005) also underscore the feminine aspect of his divine nature: "O þou redulent rose, þat of a vergyn sprong! / O þou precyus palme of wytory! / O þou osanna, angellys song! / O precyus gemme, born of Ower Lady!" (2011–14).

By calling attention to the Virgin Mary's corporeal, spiritual, and symbolic role as the generator and bearer of the deity, the Digby playwright balances the text's assertive identification of Christ as divine ruler with regular acknowledgments of the fleshly feminine nature he received from his mother. These other references to Jesus' birth and incarnation in the Digby play reinforce the dominant trope of Christ's encomium to the Virgin Mary, recalling enclosure in a feminine space. Without precedent in the scriptural episodes and legendary elements on which the vita of Mary Magdalene was based, this emphasis bears witness to the playwright's interest in establishing how symbolic and soteriological dimensions of gender relate to conceptions of the deity. It constitutes a sacred parallel to the play's detailed critique of the workings of gender in the earthly realm.

The dramatist further complicates the Marian dimensions of the text's christological preoccupations by carefully elaborating Jesus' hypostatic nature as God in trinity. The Good Angel celebrates Mary Magdalene's contrition and forgiveness, for example, with a trinitarian hymn that recognizes the "imperall glorye" of the "hyest" God "of omnipotency," the "soverreyn sapyens" of "delectabyll Jhesu," and the benignity of *Spiritus Alme*" (705–21).[30] Mary Magdalene echoes the trinitarian idiom of this angelic rejoicing when she seeks alms from the king of Marseilles by calling upon the "mythe and þe powyre of þe heye Trenyte, / The wysdom of þe Son . . . / [and] The Holy Gost. . . ." (1646–48). Responding to Mary and Martha's plea for help for the ailing Lazarus, Jesus invokes the divine inscrutability of "þe joyys of þe Fathyr in glory, / The joyys of þe Sonne whych owth to be magnyfyed, / And of þe Therd Person, þe Holy Ghost" (807–9). As the risen Christ, he identifies fully with his hypostatic nature when he speaks to the three

Marys ("We blysche yow—Father, and Son, and Holy Gost. . . . Be ower powyr of mytys most" [1117, 1119]), whereas Mary Magdalene, on her apostolic mission to Marseilles, recognizes Christ *Salvator* as the "Secunde Person, þat hell ded conquare, / And þe Son of þe Father in Trenyte" (1471–73).

The terms in which the Digby play alternately identifies Christ as the "blyssyd byrth" of the virgin womb on the one hand and the triune god of a divine hypostasis on the other are in themselves far from unusual, and together they contribute to the play's densely textured portrait of the deity. How do these alternating dramatic figurations of Christ relate to each other, and what role does the construction of such a labile deity play in the Digby drama's broader engagement with gender issues in the sacred realm? What exactly is contained by the Virgin Mary's "demure femynyte"? Although the Marian language of *Mary Magdalene* never becomes as explicit on this issue as does that of the N-Town plays, which specify that Mary's gestation of Jesus involved her containment, as both "trone" and "tabernakyl," of the "hyȝ Trinite," the Digby play's punctuation of its divinity-focused idiom with references to Christ's virgin birth nonetheless points to a similarly crucial role for the Virgin Mary in regard to the persons of the Trinity.[31]

In the constellation of sacred and human identities and origins that the Digby play attributes to Jesus, the Virgin Mary seems at times to occupy a position of importance equal to that of the Holy Spirit. This is, at least, the role that Jesus intimates for her when he remarks on his own impending death at the raising of Lazarus:

My Fathyr, of nemyows charyte,
Sent me, hys Son, to make redempcyon,
Wyche was conseyvyd be puer verginyte,
And so in my mother had cler incarnacyon;
And þerfore must I suffyre grewos passyon
Ondyre Povnse Pylat, wyth grett perplexite,
Betyn, bobbyd, skoernyd, crownnyd wyth thorne—
Alle þis xal be þe soferons of my deite. (857–64)

Jesus interrupts his proleptic account of the "grewos passyon" to identify the pure, feminine origin of his suffering humanity, as if father, son, and virgin mother here together accomplish the deity's redemptive work. The grouping of sacred beings that he describes calls to mind late medieval attraction to alternative conceptions of the Trinity that appear to place the Virgin Mary in the role of the Holy Spirit and venerate her as a goddess. These so-called Marian Trinities, which appear frequently in the visual arts, make Mary an "honorary female member" of the Trinity conceived as a family, feminizing the Godhead and divinizing the family.[32] As Barbara Newman observes, from a doctrinal perspective "the dogmatic assertion of a hypostatic union between Mary and the Holy Spirit" would have seemed heretical. But it "would hardly have been surprising if laypeople, unschooled in the niceties of Trinitarian dogma, 'read' such images as revealing the true objects of Christian worship: the Father, the Son, and the Virgin Mother."[33]

The spiritual anthropology developed in the Digby play imposes on the saint's traditional vita a complicated nexus of topoi whose configuration in the drama has no precedent in any of the lives of the saint known to have been available to the Digby playwright. These include the hypostasis of the Trinity, Christ's double nature as man and god, the divine kingship as product of "demvre femynyte," the human generation of Christ by the Virgin Mary, and the Virgin Mary as sacred enclosure of the divine hypostasis. Through these preoccupations, the saint play articulates a vision of gender roles and relationships in the sacred realm that offers a counterweight to the social and ethical problems that gender differences are seen to produce in the human, social world. It is not that sacred gender roles and identities are presented as simple alternatives to the predatory hierarchies, pollution, lust, and violence that the play ascribes to the performance of gender in the earthly realm. Rather, the ambiguity and excess that the play associates with gender categories in the secular world—the troubling suggestions of effeminate males, homosocial rivalries, and women and men out of control—are corrected by the idealized image of salvific fluidity that characterizes gender relationships in the sacred realm. Although the play at times seems to stress the gulf that separates secular and sacred as far as issues of gender are concerned, the very possibility of relationship between the two realms is necessitated by the dense and overdetermined biography of Mary Magdalene herself.

In the remainder of this chapter I argue that the Digby playwright draws upon symbolic, exegetical, and legendary traditions that constructed Mary Magdalene as a capacious figure for thinking through the relationship between femininity and salvation history. The play elaborates this relationship by developing two important themes of the late

medieval saint's life: Mary Magdalene's ambiguous identification with
the Virgin Mary and her provocative claims to a virginity of her own.
The play takes advantage of exegetical and spiritual resources that highlighted the Virgin Mary and Mary Magdalene as the women who nego-
tiated the manhood and Godhead of Jesus at the two moments when
the deity's double nature was simultaneously revealed and tested: his
nativity and his resurrection. This is one reason, I believe, the Digby
play transfers the locus of Christ's salvific power from the Passion,
which it only reports, to the Incarnation, which it symbolically re-
creates. The playwright draws upon the spiritual resources implicit in
the identification of Mary Magdalene and Mary, the mother of Jesus, to
construct a saint whose gender attributes as sexual woman and reconstituted virgin pose the possibility of symbolically, if not humanly,
mediating the differences that marked the workings of gender in the
secular and sacred realms.

"Venit Maria Magdalene, et Altera Maria"

When the king and queen of Marseilles address Mary Magdalene immediately upon praising a "*virgo salutata*" and greet the saint in language
that directly echoes Gabriel's speech to the annunciate Virgin Mary, they
articulate the exegetical complexity and symbolic multivalence that gen-
erations of biblical commentators and spiritual writers had accorded
Mary Magdalene. Contemporary analyses of medieval sex and gender
roles more commonly situate Mary, the mother of Jesus, and Mary
Magdalene in a binary relationship signifying the opposition of sexual
purity and pollution, spirit and flesh, madonna and whore. But medieval understandings were just as likely to construct these potent symbols
as ambiguous mirror images of each other, reflecting a nuanced play of
likeness and difference. It is precisely the tensions and possibilities of
that relationship that the Digby *Magdalene* explores through its identification of the two Marys.[34]
    From the early Christian centuries through the end of the Middle
Ages, permutations in Mary Magdalene's spiritual meanings illustrate
what Sarah Beckwith has observed about the production of complex
symbols: they always occur "in the context of specific social and political relations" and "mobilize meaning in the service of power."[35] The history of Mary Magdalene's symbolic production in the West reveals how

a figure from the canonical and apocryphal Gospels who represented the personal and apostolic authority accorded to women in the early Church was displaced by the paradigmatic sinner. Hippolytus of Rome (c. 170–c. 235) may have identified Mary Magdalene with the Bride or Shulamite in his early commentary on the Song of Songs and been the first to recognize her as "apostle to the apostles," but by the third century those identifications had already become necessary anachronisms to the male-dominated Church's effort to suppress feminine intrusion into spheres of ecclesiastical authority. Despite the fact that Matthew, Mark, and John establish Mary Magdalene as first witness to Christ's resurrection, Peter's competing claim to that privilege would prevail in the Church's determination of male apostolic succession.[36] In his famous thirty-third homily on Luke's gospel (c. 591), Gregory the Great established the dominant attributes of the Mary Magdalene figure for centuries to come when he conflated the witness to Christ's resurrection with the Mary from whom Christ cast seven devils in Mark; Mary of Bethany, sister of Martha and Lazarus; and the unnamed sinful woman who anoints Jesus in Luke 7.[37] Haskins asserts that the model penitent resulting from this conflation was so "'exegetically untenable'" that it has to be seen as a "wilful misinterpretation" suiting the "purposes of an ascetic Church" in need of an image of the converted sinner as a moral paradigm. Given the Church's increasing emphasis, well before the time of Gregory, on clerical celibacy and female virginity, it was also fitting that the sin of the composite Magdalene should be identified with what the Church deeply feared: female sexuality.[38] By the High Middle Ages, Mary Magdalene appears ubiquitously as the exemplary penitent recommended by pastoral literature to religious and lay audiences, male and female.[39]

Despite the dominance of this interpretive model, as a cultural symbol Mary Magdalene never fully relinquished her association with the allegorized Bride of the Song of Songs and Ecclesia, and later medieval variations on her symbolic construction reflect the ongoing effort by Western spiritual writers and biblical exegetes to think through the contradictory identities of the biblical woman who was simultaneously Gregory the Great's paradigmatic sinner and the allegorical beloved and first witness of Christ's resurrection. In that process of symbolic production Mary Magdalene's example may have been invoked to model both male and female penitential behaviors, but the pressure to reconcile her corporeal femininity with her biblical and allegorical roles was clearly central to efforts to resolve her contradictory attributes. The saint further complicated that effort because as a cultural symbol of the feminine, she stood outside traditional systems of classification based on sex and gender categories. Although the beloved Bride, she was neither sealed nor silent. Her holiness required neither sexual purity nor martyrdom; her social role was not that of virgin, wife, or widow.

In the evolution of Mary Magdalene's symbolic identities, nothing confounds her problematic connections to these traditional categories more than her relationship to the Virgin Mary. The two women do, indeed, have quite a lot in common. Scripture established that each occupied a unique position in relation to Christ's human and divine natures and especially to his physical body. Biblical exegetes understood both the Virgin Mary and Mary Magdalene as playing special roles in Christian soteriology: in different senses each undoes and completes what Eve was believed to have begun in the history of humankind. Even the similarity of their names, which was further complicated by the Magdalene's conflation of several other scriptural Marys, enhanced their overlapping identities. The Virgin Mary's own symbolic multivalence also contributed to her congruence with the witness to Christ's resurrection, since the mother of Jesus herself occupied with notable fluidity roles that were also associated with Mary Magdalene: Bride, Mother, Church, and Christian soul.[40] Elaborated in the Western Church from the time of Isidore of Seville, symbolic paralleling and metaphoric identification of the Virgin Mary and Mary Magdalene occur in monastic, episcopal, liturgical, cultic, and pastoral contexts, and appear in meditative prayers, scriptural exegesis, Latin hymns, vernacular lyric, and the visual arts.[41] The Digby saint play bears witness to textual and iconographic traditions that came to terms with the complex hermeneutics of Mary Magdalene by elaborating the "bienheureuse polysemie" that marked her affinities with the mother of Jesus.[42]

The linguistic ambiguity that linked the two Marys provided scriptural exegetes with a compelling basis upon which to elaborate connections between them. A fourth-century sermon on the Resurrection by Peter Chrysologus exploits the significance of their identical names suggested by Matthew 28:1: "[V]enit Maria Magdalene et altera Maria videre sepulchrum." Playing on the ambiguity of the "altera Maria," he comments on both Mary Magdalene's likeness to the Virgin Mary and her own interior transformation: "Venit Maria. This is the name of the mother of Christ; therefore the mother came in name, the woman came. . . . *Venit Maria et altera Maria*. It does not say they came, but she came; under one name the two came in mystery, not by chance. . . . *Venit Maria et altera Maria*. She herself came but one of the two; but the other [also] herself, came, so that the woman might be changed with respect to her life, not her name; with respect to her goodness, not her sex."[43] The identification of the two women that Peter Chrysologus elicits from the ambiguity of "Maria" takes a different twist in Ambrose's interpretation of Mary Magdalene's name in *De virginitate*. Citing John 20:15–17, Ambrose proposes that Jesus addressed the Magdalene as "woman" when she did not believe but recognized her by her name "when she began to be converted." Then "Mary is named, that is, she takes the name of her who brought forth Christ, for it is the soul that gives birth to Christ spiritually."[44] Peter Comestor also takes up the linguistic ambiguity of the two Marys. After urging his audience to seek the help of the "Blessed penitent" before God, the homilist justifies his recommendation by arguing that Mary Magdalene's likeness to the Virgin Mary more than qualifies her for this intercessory role: "Not without weight is the patronage of this penitent; just as she is called the same as the Blessed Virgin in name, so in the same way she is comparable to her in example. Nor did the Lady, the Queen, the Mother of God disdain to bear the same name as the servant, the girl, she who had been a sinner; for, indeed, each was named 'Maria,' which signifies *maris stella* and applies to them both because of their example. For in this great and spacious sea each shows us a guiding way to the light."[45]

It is not always easy to tell from these illustrations whether the conflation of the two Marys is caused by the equivocation of their names or whether other typological and symbolic connections between the two women enhanced opportunities to exploit the linguistic ambiguity that linked them. Scriptural exegetes frequently invoked, either individually or as a pair, the relationship of Mary Magdalene and the Virgin Mary to Eve in salvation history.[46] Odo of Cluny's famous sermon *In veneratione sanctae Mariae Magdalenae* illustrates both types of linkage:

Because death had been brought into the world through a woman, lest the feminine sex might ever be held in reproach, [God] wished to announce to men the joy of the resurrection through the feminine sex. . . . And just as through the blessed Mary, ever Virgin, who is the only hope of the world, the gates of paradise have been opened to us and the curse of Eve denied entry, so through the blessed Mary Magdalene the dishonor of the female sex has been annihilated. . . . Whence Mary [Magdalene] is properly interpreted as *stella maris*.

Although this interpretation is especially suited to the mother of God, through whose virgin birth the Sun of justice has shown brightly to the world, nevertheless it can also suit the blessed Magdalene, who coming with aromatic ointments to the sepulchre of the Lord, first announced to the world the splendor of the Lord's resurrection.[47]

The rapprochement of Eve, Mary Magdalene, and the Virgin in this sermon illuminates the dominant logic of the penitent's symbolic construction in biblical typology. She is, as Iogna-Prat points out, a "bridge" between extremes that are customarily marked by feminine figures.[48]

The linking of Mary Magdalene and the Virgin Mary through biblical typology, however, did not always depend upon their shared relationship to Eve. Thirteenth-century Dominican Peter of Reims, for example, identifies the two women with the *mulier fortis* of Proverbs 31:10. Christ put strength in each of them so that one could be an exemplar of innocence, the other of penitence, one a greater light to the righteous, the other a lesser light to sinners.[49] Nor did symbolic condensation of Mary Magdalene and the Virgin Mary in scriptural exegesis always require a linguistic or typological base. In creative formulations of this relationship, biblical commentators link the two women through tropes that invoke similarities in their roles and functions at central moments in the life of Christ. Peter Chrysologus images Mary Magdalene at the tomb as a surrogate mother for Christ's second "birth": "Mary came to the sepulcher, she came to the womb of the resurrection, she came to the birth of life, so that Christ who had been born from the womb of flesh would be born a second time from the sepulcher of faith; and the one whom sealed virginity had brought forth into the present [life], the sealed sepulcher might restore to eternal life."[50] Peter of Celle employs tropes of maternity and gestation more daringly, relocating them from the scene of Christ's resurrection to that of Mary Magdalene's tearful repentance in the house of Simon the Pharisee: "Mary waters the shoots born from the garden of Mary; but Mary, mother of God, sowed those shoots from her own flesh and blood. . . . Mary, the great sinner, watered them from the fountain of her innermost heart; she watered thoroughly, and the other, not with water, but with the oil of grace. Indeed, the Father of heaven sowed in Mary's womb the one whom Mary Magdalene moistened with water, and anointed with unguent when he rested in the house of Simon."[51] Peter's elaborate agriculture trope links the Virgin Mary and Mary Magdalene in sequential acts of planting and watering, emphasizing the material source of those acts in the bodies of the two women: the Virgin's "own flesh and blood" and the Magdalene's "fons internorum viscerum," literally the spring of her inmost part or gut. Whereas Chrysologus's metaphor plays on the relationship between womb and tomb to place Mary Magdalene in the symbolic role of "mother" to Christ's resurrection, Peter of Celle asserts the difference between the Virgin and the sinner even as he insists on the mutually sustaining gestures of planting and watering that link their own physicality to the body of Christ. Implicit in both of these metaphoric substitutions is the saint's identification with a spiritual and corporeal fecundity that brings forth life from the tomb and gives nurturing moisture to living shoots from within her own body.[52]

Joseph Harris observes that the medieval "mode of thinking in parallels, contrasts, and typological relations often brought the two Marys together." The foregoing examples and Harris's own analysis of a community of images joining the women in sermons, hymns, and scriptural commentary demonstrates that such connections were posited on symbolic as well as cognitive bases, even arriving in some cases at the kind of "mystical union" of the two figures that characterizes the "Magdalenian background and Marian foreground" of the elusive Middle English lyric "Maiden in the mor lay."[53] Occasionally, the paralleling of the two figures resulted in the elevation of the penitent witness to the Resurrection over the mother of Jesus. An eighth-century Irish homilist, for instance, asserts that the evangelists relate more about Mary Magdalene than they do about the Virgin Mary: no one had more distress over Christ's passion than the Magdalene (his mother did not mourn because she knew through the Holy Spirit that her son would reign in heaven).[54] The unusual stature granted to Mary Magdalene in this sermon probably reflects veneration for a saint whose eremitic tendencies were sympathetically regarded by Irish Christians, while the characterization of the aloof Virgin Mary, whose confidence in her son's heavenly kingship preempts suffering for his earthly ordeal, obviously predates the twelfth-century shift in Western spirituality that emphasized Mary's great *compassio*.[55] Peter Comestor's sermon for Mary Magdalene's feast compares the penitent saint even more favorably to the Virgin Mary, especially regarding each woman's relevance to the experience of sinners. Comestor argues that more people gain something from Mary Magdalene's example because "there are more people in the Church who have corrected their faults than there are those who have not lost the way:

more, I say, justified than just." Mary Magdalene, he suggests, is more useful to the sinner: "Should I speak of the help of the two or should I be silent? Without a doubt it is true that the help of the Virgin Mary is matchless. . . . She intercedes for us, as it were, from a lofty height. But this woman [Mary Magdalene] who knows our very makeup, totally pours herself forth in prayers; she is completely prostrated at the feet of the Lord; nor is she ashamed to petition recklessly until she will have obtained what she asked. Therefore let her call upon the Lord on our behalf. . . ."[56] Just as the Irish sermon emphasizes the great *labor* of Mary Magdalene's grief over the Passion and death of Christ, Comestor foregrounds the woman's connection to the experience of sin, making her intercessory powers more desirable to the petitioning sinner not because she is necessarily more effective than the Virgin Mary, whose help is "matchless," but because she is proximate and familiar to the sinner.

Whether homilists and scriptural commentators invoked the two women to suggest that Mary Magdalene's own worldly involvements could in some contexts make her superior to the Virgin Mary or, as was more often the case, to sketch their ambiguous ethical and maternal mirroring of each other, Dominique Iogna-Prat properly asserts that the equivocation attending the medieval paralleling of the two figures has not received the attention it deserves.[57] The Digby play's conflation of the "almyty Maydyn" and the "demur Maudlyn" offers an important late medieval illustration of the theological and spiritual implications of such equivocation. In the dramatic moments cited at the beginning of this chapter, Mary Magdalene and Mary the mother of Jesus are ambiguously merged in terms of the criteria and circumstances we have just examined. The confusion over the name Mary here must be seen, I think, as evidence of a studied awareness of the symbolic and theological import of such verbal identification. The king of Marseilles's "Heyll, be þou, Mary! Ower Lord is wyth the" (1939) conflates the annunciate Virgin and the fledging apostle, drawing an implicit analogy between the Virgin's bearing of Christ and Mary Magdalene's bearing of the word. The ambiguous thanksgiving speeches of the king and queen of Marseilles also invoke the tacit intercessory rivalry that Comestor attributed to Mary Magdalene and the Virgin Mary: the play portrays the royal couple as familiars of Mary Magdalene's sin, making the penitent apostle's intercession on their behalf especially appropriate because they have indeed shared in her worldly experience.

Shadowing these verbal maneuvers on the part of scriptural exegetes and the Digby playwright simultaneously to identify and distinguish the two women is the attribution of purity and chastity to this ambiguous double Mary (1895–96, 1900). Whereas the king's thanksgiving prayer to the "puer vergyn" who has revived his wife from "grevos slepe" could refer either to Mary Magdalene or the mother of Jesus, there is little ambiguity in his petitioning of Mary Magdalene's "puere blyssyng" (1969). The play goes one step further, however, by directly attributing to the penitent apostle the very state or condition that centuries' worth of commentary on her sinful identity would have rendered deeply contradictory to it. One of the angels who feeds Mary Magdalene with heavenly manna near the end of the play descends into the "wyldyrnesse"and announces:

> Mari, God gretyt þe wyth hevenly influens!
> He hath sent þe grace wyth hevenly synys.
> Þou xall byn onoryd wyth joye and reverens,
> Inhansyd in heven above wergynnys! (2019–22)

Among the extant late medieval English lives of the saint, the Digby play uniquely specifies the particular favor by which God will honor Mary Magdalene. The *South English Legendary*, Bokenham's *Legendys of Hooly Wummen*, and Caxton's translation of the *Legenda aurea*, for example, make no mention of an eternal reward that seems to defy the saint's sinful reputation. Though atypical in Middle English hagiography, the angel's promise that the saint will be elevated in heaven "above virgins" is hardly unique in the medieval theology of the Magdalene. In this tradition the attribution of virginal purity to the sexual sinner encodes a complicated cultural conversation about the relationship of sanctity and sexuality.

Michel Lauwers singles out the difficulty of reconciling sinner and virgin as one of three problems encountered by thirteenth-century clerics who sought to make Mary Magdalene a model for beguines and other "semi-religieuses."[58] Just as exegetes and homilists struggled to reconcile the saint's legendary apostolate with clerical prohibitions of women's preaching, so too did they seek a rapprochement between the much-publicized physical facts of a body and what was believed to be true of a life and a soul. Despite this obvious contradiction, reinventing the sexual sinner as virgin was a fairly frequent occurrence in medieval liturgy, scriptural commentary, and homiletic writings. As Joce-lyn Wogan-Browne points out, this gesture reconstituting purity recog-nized that the "spiritual aspirations and life-styles of virginity are not exclusive to the technically intact but apply to the chastity undertaken by a range of women (consecrated nuns, lay and religious recluses and vowesses) and to the behavioural ideals offered to married women and widows. . . . [V]irginity is gradable and negotiable."[59] Available from the time of Jerome and Augustine, these definitions persisted through the Middle Ages.[60] But particularly from the thirteenth century on, renewed interest was shown in them as clerics articulated spiritual values and models affirming the lives of increasing numbers of women who chose the religious life outside of the cloister as *mulieres sanctae*.

Mary Magdalene figures prominently in these clerical reassessments of purity and the social phenomena that they sought to explain. In a *sermo ad status* intended to illustrate the principle that "humility with-out virginity can be pleasing to God" but virginity without humility cannot, Jacques de Vitry tells of a proud virgin who bragged "that she did not want to be like Mary Magdalene." Within a month of speaking such presumption, she became attached to the vilest of lechers, "who deprived her of her virginal honor."[61] In a sermon based on Proverbs 31:10, Eudes de Châteauroux states that Mary Magdalene was placed first in the litany of virgins "because she was an apostle, a martyr in compassion, and a preacher of truth. She deserved this not in respect to purity of body but purity of soul. . . . The blessed Virgin," he observes, "said 'the Lord regarded the humility of his handmaiden'"; she did not say, "'He regarded the virginity of his handmaiden (Luke 1:48).'"[62] In another sermon Eudes de Châteauroux identifies Mary Magdalene's virginity as but one of the three female *status* exemplified by her life: she was a virgin in spirit, a wife in the spiritual marriage she contracted with Christ, and after his passion, she suffered his absence like a widow.[63] Mary Magdalene's example also inspired Ivetta of Huy, the prosperous late twelfth- and early thirteenth-century urban patrician mother, widow, and *mulier sancta* whose piety and humility are con-sistent with models of spiritual virginity available to her.[64] Recalling Comestor's notice of Mary Magdalene's intercessory superiority to the Virgin Mary, Mulder-Bakker suggests that Mary Magdalene furnished Ivetta with a model more relevant and immediate than that provided by the remote Queen of Heaven.[65] Mary Magdalene's honorary virginity also provided a powerful precedent for Margaret of Cortona, whose appropriation of the saint's reconstituted purity was but one of many ways in which the thirteenth-century Tuscan reformed adulteress self-identified with the penitent and ascetic woman. When Margaret doubted her own prospects for eternal reward, Christ assured her in one of her visions that after the Virgin Mary and Catherine of Alexandria, "there is none above Magdalen in the choir of virgins."[66] Margery Kempe's long pursuit of honorary virginity parallels her equally long fixation on Mary Magdalene. Jesus makes a clear connection between the two when he promises that she shall have a heavenly reward comparable to that received by the Virgin Mary, the apostles, "Seynt Kateryne, Seynt Margarete, Seynt Mary Mawdelyn, & many other seyntys," a company that he later identifies as the "holy maydens & virgynes" with which she shall dance in heaven.[67]

Homiletic and hagiographical discourses thus frequently invoked Mary Magdalene to sanction as well as promote the appropriation of a virginal identity by late medieval *mulieres sanctae*. Yet the saint's identification with spiritual virginity also resulted from a kind of circular logic related to her specific paralleling with the Virgin Mary through the linguistic and symbolic channels we have already examined. The linguistic ambiguity that contributed to Gregory the Great's conflation of several scriptural Marys also linked Mary Magdalene to the mother of Jesus through a liturgical text that provided a reading for the feast of the Assumption of the Virgin, the story of Mary and Martha told in Luke 10:38–42. Heiric of Auxerre's ninth-century homily on the Assumption pursues the connection between Luke's Mary, understood since Gregory the Great as the Magdalene, and the Virgin, finding a link in the "better part" chosen by the sister of Lazarus in the scriptural text, which he allegorizes as the fecund virginity of the mother of God. The confounding of the two Marys that results from this "liturgical coincidence," according to Iogna-Prat, explains how Mary Magdalene came to be included in the choir of virgins and why liturgical pieces from Marian feasts and the common of virgins were also associated with her.[68] It is precisely this kind of liturgical migration that explains the Digby play's use of *Assumpta est Maria in nubibus*, an antiphon for the Feast of the Assumption, to accompany Mary Magdalene's ecstatic feedings in her desert hermitage (s.d. after 2030).[69] By a similar chain of overlapping associations, this scene also alludes to the Virgin's heavenly reward when Jesus declares that "Mary [shall] have . . . [b]y ryth enirytawns a crown to bere" (2073–74). The crowning of Mary Magdalene here parallels the coronation of the Virgin Mary, but it may also signal the superiority of a reconstituted virginity that earned the saint's inclusion in the choir of virgins. For instance, Eudes de Châteauroux invokes Mary Magdalene (*hec beata*) as proof that "the tainted through humility, patience, and charity can attain a crown equal to or greater than that of virgins."[70]

The Digby play's allusion to Mary Magdalene's inclusion in the choir of crowned heavenly virgins draws on iconographic and liturgical traditions that had a venerable English heritage. I have previously noted a double-page illumination in Æthelwold's *Benedictional* (c. 970) that shows Mary Magdalene at the head of the choir of virgins, where she is depicted alongside Saint Æthelthryth.[71] Mary Magdalene's appearance in the *Benedictional* and other tenth- and eleventh-century liturgical texts is clear evidence of the early English cult of the saint discussed in Chapter 2. It was the Anglo-Saxon custom to venerate holy women as virgins, even those who were mothers and widows or who, like the Magdalene and Mary of Egypt, had repented their sexual sins. By clothing Mary Magdalene in the same garments worn by the annunciate Virgin elsewhere in the manuscript, the illumination in the *Benedictional* represents a symbiosis between the two Marys that bears witness to liturgical influences such as the collect for the feast of the Assumption, *Optima pars*, based on Luke 10:38–42.[72] Nearly five centuries later, and much nearer in time to the Digby play, a sermon for the feast of Mary Magdalene revisits the symbolic logic that linked Magdalene's "better part" and her virginity: "But the Marie aforesaid chese the beste parte, for sche sete by the feete of oure lord and herde his holy wordes, and sche folowyd hym to the crosse and sche ʒede in the day of Paske to his sepulcre for to a-noynte hym. And after þat he was vp resyn, sche was the firste þat sawe hym. And þerfore in oure letanie we take hure before alle virgines except the moder of God, þe whiche noʒt onely is set and prayede afore virgines but also afore alle other seyntis after hire sone."[73]

"Covnfortabyll Sokore for Man and Wyff"

The medieval discursive and iconographic traditions that remade Mary Magdalene as an ambiguous mirror image of the mother of Jesus provide a necessary context for understanding the saint's dramatic vita as a narrative about gender roles and relationships that had social and spiritual currency for late medieval audiences. As an illustration of East

Anglian theatrical tradition and feminine religious culture, *Mary Magda-lene* bears witness to drama as a medium for the circulation of spiritual values involving feminine roles and agencies that Jocelyn Wogan-Browne identifies as a broader spiritual movement in late medieval culture.[74] What do Mary Magdalene's complex linkages to virginity and Jesus' mother contribute to the Digby play's constructions of gender and sexuality in the earthly and sacred realms?

Dramatic assimilation of Mary Magdalene to the Virgin Mary gives ultimate spiritual sanction to the role as maternal patron that the saint increasingly assumes in the legendary portion of her vita, bearing witness to the fact that "in the development of her cult and the kinds of miracles ascribed her, [the saint] is as importantly associated with maternal care and responsibility as she is with transgressive sexuality."[75] Mary Magdalene's transformation from the gallant Curiosity's "dere dewchesse . . . daysyys iee! / . . . most of femynyte" (515–16) to the "flowyr of wommanned" (1747) lauded by the queen of Marseilles charts the evolving significance of the play's representation of feminine sexuality. This transformation resonates in the experience of the king and queen of Marseilles, who enter the drama after Magdalene's fall and repentance are already accomplished and thoroughly replay the seduction of Cyrus's daughter by Curiosity. The king gazes hungrily on his "delycyows" and "favorows fode," "ful fayur in hyr femynyte" (942–43, 946), while his queen's carnal excesses, veiled in aureate diction, offer a more ornate version of the very sentiments expressed to Curiosity by a submissive Mary Magdalene: "Yower dilectabyll dedys devydytt me from dyversyte. / In my person I privyde to put me from polucyon— / To be plesant to yower person, itt is my prosperyte!" (955–57).[76] Just as Mary Magdalene is transformed from sexual profligate to patron of regal Christian maternity, under her influence the language and sentiments of these paragons of pagan lust are displaced by prayers and Christian procreation, as they simultaneously convert, and conceive, the child for whom they had yearned for "many ʒerys" (1566). The decadent erotic language of their introductory speeches yields to the idiom of Christian praise: "A ʒe! I fel ytt ster in my wombe vp and down! / I am glad I have þe in presens! / O blyssyd womman, rote of ower savacyon, / Þi God woll I worshep wyth dew reverens!" (1668–71).

Contemporary assessments of the significance of Mary Magdalene's sexuality, for medieval culture and the Digby play, commonly emphasize the nature of the individual sin (illicit sex) and the individual sinner (a woman). According to this view, Mary Magdalene mediates the impossible fecundity and absolute purity of the Virgin Mary, whose singular attributes as virgin mother "have a deleterious effect upon the status of [the] real women" from whom she is so far removed. Susan Haskins articulates this position: "It was into this niche that the medieval Magdalen . . . fitted, a figure who could play the part which the Virgin, because of her sinlessness, could not, as a model for mere mortals who could sin and sin again, and yet through repentance still hope to reach heaven. . . . [S]he represented the sexuate feminine redeemed, and therefore rendered sexless."[77] Haskins's acknowledgment of Mary Magdalene's exemplarity for sinners underscores the parallels that the Digby play establishes between the saint's experience and that of the ruling couple of Marseilles. Yet the play's representation of the significance of not only the saint's sexuality but also sexuality more generally complicates Haskins's assessment of what the redeemed, individual, feminine sinner accomplishes. The Digby saint's renunciation of sexuality—and her recuperated virginity and eventual fusion with the Virgin Mary—must all be seen in light of the play's portrait of erotic relationships. In the aftermath of succumbing to Curiosity, when Mary Magdalene rejects the "halsing and kissing" (571) of "valentynys" and turns from awaiting lovers in "þis erbyre, / Amons . . . bamys precyus of prysse" (568–69) to pursuing "þe Prophett whereso he be" (610), she abandons an oddly passive sexual identity that the play has exposed as largely the creation of Curiosity's hyperactive male desire. When she embraces the humility and charity (683–85) that clerical commentary on Mary Magdalene identified as the true tokens of her purity, she acquires spiritual, social, and political power.

The import of that renunciation is imaged in the visionary moment when Mary Magdalene, seeking alms to relieve her "hongor, threst, and chelle" (1613), appears to the sleeping king and queen of Marseilles. Most late medieval English versions of the legendary life include this narrative episode, but the saint play takes special advantage of its spectacular potential by conveying Mary Magdalene's spiritual authority in the multivalent sign that Margery Kempe long desired: she wears white clothes.[78] Mary Magdalene's appearance is directed from on high by Jesus himself, who orders two angels to guide the saint to the "prynsses chambyr" (1591). Accompanied by "solem lyth," they supervise her change of clothing: "In a mentyll of whyte xall be ower araye" (1603–4). Mary Magdalene interprets this performative gesture as a sign of humility—

"O gracyos God, now I vndyrstond! / Thys clothyng of whyte is tokenyng of meekness" (1606–7)—but the significance of the "token" exceeds even her own reading. As commentary on Margery Kempe's quest for white clothes has made clear, spiritual virginity figures prominently among the multiple symbolic meanings that white garments convey.[79] At this point in the action, Mary Magdalene has yet to be identified with either the Virgin Mary or virginity, but the play's unique handling of this visionary moment nevertheless looks ahead symbolically to these aspects of her dramatic portraiture and especially to the significance they will have for the king and queen. The vision links the heavenly resources that are available to Mary Magdalene with the humility and purity that are epitomized in her white clothes, making the display of those attributes fundamental to her conversion of the royal couple. Indeed, the king invokes her special attire when he comments on the power of the "shewyng": "A fayer woman I saw in my syth, / All in whyte was she cladd" (1622–23). In a sense Mary Magdalene's "mentyll of whyte" is predictive of the spiritual and sexual cleansing that the king and queen are about to undergo, a transformation to which her visionary appearance is pivotal. The vision inspires the royal couple to give alms to Mary Magdalene and receive her evangelical message, actions that result in the conception of the child they have desired. "From God above comit þe influens, / Be þe Holy Gost into þi brest sentt down, / For to restore þi offens, / Þi sowle to bryng to ewyrlastyng salvacyon. / Thy wyffe, she is grett wyth chyld!" (1662–66), Mary Magdalene announces, in language that associates the royal couple's conception with the incarnational emergence of their Christian souls.[80] Her appearance in white—and the spiritual virginity that it signals—thus becomes central not only to their conversion but also to the couple's newly acquired, proper alignment of Christian revelation and sexuality. Whereas the king had retired to his bed suspiciously "seke" from erotic excess, he emerges from it the grateful progenitor of a Christian dynasty.[81]

Through the characterization of the king and queen, the sexual indulgence and renunciation so familiar from Mary Magdalene's biblical life thus also resonate in her legendary vita, thereby underscoring the dramatist's commitment to probing the dynamics of gendered sexuality in the earthly realm. Curiosity's seduction of Mary Magdalene in the play is not the singular work of a lone tempter but rather one important moment in a larger narrative of troubling erotic relations. Eros is a problem common to high-status as well as low-status characters. The examples furnished by Mary Magdalene and Curiosity, the king and queen of Marseilles, Nauta, the priest and their boys suggest that carnal eros itself is dangerously out of control in the Digby play. Its transgressions, significantly, are imaged principally as masculine disturbances of social order, whether it be the status climbing displayed by Curiosity's wooing, the homoerotic valences of the altercations between the priest and his boy and Nauta and his, or the challenges to customary master and servant hierarchies enacted in these two social relationships. Hence it is not just Mary Magdalene's renounced sexuality that exemplifies the potential benefit of a much-desired discipline but a more broadly based, equal opportunity sublimation of earthly eros that the play seems to admonish, and over which the saint's acquired virginal purity presides.

In addition to redirecting carnal eros toward ends that reinforce prevailing norms of sex and gender and ensure orderly social reproduction, the Digby saint play depicts the transmutation of physical desire to a spiritual plane.[82] The hierarchical relation of spirit and flesh that informs this redirection is consistent with rhetorical conventions of mystical and contemplative texts that drew upon traditions of bridal mysticism derived from Bernard's commentary on the Song of Songs. Such a gesture is not surprising in light of Mary Magdalene's identification with the Bride of the Song of Songs, the scriptural text whose traditions of commentary mark the most celebrated discursive instance of sexual sublimation in Western culture.[83] The play signals the transmutation of Mary Magdalene's erotic desire by representing her tavern seduction and sinful attachment to lovers in the same language and imagery that it employs to figure her devotion to Jesus.[84] Thus the "erbyre" or bower in which she awaits "valentynes" anticipates the "garden" that the resurrected Christ will make in her heart; the "bamys precyus" that grow in that bower look forward to the "bamys sote" with which she attempts to anoint the risen Jesus; the "halsing and kissing" she expects from carnal paramours become the kisses that Jesus rejects with his "Towche me natt, Mary"; and the "ardent lowe" of which Luxuria claims to be full is rejected in favor of the "ardent love" with which the eremitic saint prepares to meet her maker—and lover.[85]

Despite the unease with carnal expressions of eros that the Digby *Mary Magdalene* exhibits and its consequent transmutation of fleshly longings into spiritual ones, the play neither dismisses the body nor enjoins a flight from the material world. Rather, it recuperates the flesh—

and worldliness—in other terms. The text's consistent reminders that Christ is a god of flesh as well as spirit, of maternal generation and enclosure as well as regal heavenly authority, contribute to this recuperation, as does Jesus' privileging of the "demure femynyte" where the Godhead "ȝaff . . . myth" to his manhood. The play's insistence on Jesus' fleshly, feminine nature repeats an important theme of late medieval theology and piety identified by Caroline Walker Bynum: that physicality was the feminine contribution to the Redemption, and Christ's humanity was in an important sense to be understood as feminine.[86] Physical gestures—anointing, touching—figure prominently in Mary Magdalene's scriptural biography, attesting to her "privileged tactile relation to Christ."[87] But the Digby saint's persistent identification with the Virgin Mary, her symbolic conflation, in the king of Marseilles's words, with that "tabernakyll of þe þe blyssyd Trenite" (1941), deepens that bodily connection and makes Mary Magdalene herself a participant in the fleshly, feminine bond that united Christ and his mother, a bond that underscored the capacity for intimacy with the sacred that was available to feminine flesh, and to the material world as a whole.[88]

Mimi Still Dixon has argued that the Digby play's central paradox is the "association of woman's body with divine power."[89] While granting Dixon's point, I have argued that the gendering of sacred power in the play pertains not only to Mary Magdalene but also to the elaborate constellation of bodily identities, divine and human, that we have been examining. The saint's instantiation of such power achieves authority and distinction from her symbolic fusion with the Virgin Mary and her recuperated virginity, just as Jesus' identity as redeemer is bound up, by his own characterization, with his "cler incarnacyon" in his mother's "puer verginyte" (859–60). It is this tie to the fleshly "femynyte" of the Virgin Mary that the Digby saint and the play's Jesus hold in common. The resulting triangulation among the Virgin, Mary Magdalene, and Jesus, I suggest, involves a more broadly formulated gendering of sacred power and authority than Dixon's characterization of the play's central paradox can admit, a gendering that embraces the incarnate God as well as the reformed sexual sinner. If the play insists on Christ's feminine origins, it also shows Mary Magdalene laying claim to masculine roles and attributes. Whereas its secular constructions of gender polarize and exaggerate masculine vengeance and dominance as well as feminine submission and absence, the sacred manifestations of gender associated with the Virgin Mary, the reformed Mary Magdalene, and Jesus supplant conventional, hierarchical constructions of masculinity and femininity with a salvific crossing of roles and attributes, embracing all three participants in a dramatic rendering of a more extended holy family romance.

"Heyll Be Þou Mary! Ower Lord Is Wyth The!"

A confraternal banner created by Spinello Aretino for a late fourteenth-century brotherhood of flagellants dedicated to Mary Magdalene strikingly illustrates the potential for the saint to absorb complex gender identities. The banner shows her seated on an elaborate platform of decorated tile: a large and majestic figure, she holds in her right hand the ointment jar that was her most recognizable signature in medieval iconography. Her left hand grips a much larger crucifix, positioned so that the slumping body of Christ hangs directly in front of her torso (fig. 13). In relation to the crucifix, the posture and scale of the banner's Magdalene call to mind two distinct medieval iconographic constructions that employed similar proportion and arrangement to communicate theological concepts: the Throne of Grace and the *Vierge ouvrante*. The Throne of Grace depicts the Trinity as an enthroned God the Father; resting in front of him is a crucifix on top of which lights the dove of the Holy Spirit. The three-dimensional sculpted image of the *Vierge ouvrante* conveys the idea of the Virgin Mary as container of the Trinity: her body opens to display what very often looks like a "throne of grace" inside: a majestic God the Father, the crucified Son, and the iconic dove of the Holy Spirit.[90] The Magdalene of the confraternal banner invokes both the divine authority of the Throne of Grace and the sacred enclosure of the *Vierge ouvrante*; the image foregrounds her special relationship to Christ in a manner that evokes his identity as both God in Trinity and human flesh born of a virgin tabernacle. The banner's visual echoes of these well-known late medieval iconographic constructions thus display the saint's sacred identity by intimating her closeness to a trinitarian God and to the feminine enclosure that bore that God's divine hypostasis. The theological vision of the Digby saint play resembles that signified by the visual logic of Aretino's banner. Represented in both the dramatic text and the visual image is a gendering of sacred power that is locatable not in Magdalene herself but rather

Figure 13. *Saint Mary Magdalen with a Crucifix*. Processional banner of the Disciplinati Company of S. Maria Maddalena of Borgo Sansepolcro by Spinello Aretino. Reproduced by permission of the Metropolitan Museum of Art, Gift of the Estate of Francis M. Bacon, 1914. (13.175a.)

in her multiple ties to a trinitarian Jesus who is the fully human product of maternal feminine flesh. Just as the Mary Magdalene of both representations draws upon the sacred resources offered by her relationship
to Jesus and Mary, the God of each is also doubly gendered, masculine
and feminine.

If an Italian confraternal banner predating the Digby play by nearly
a century seems too remote a tool for elucidating the gender relationships of the play's sacred figures, the symbolic and rhetorical strategies
of several late medieval East Anglian texts indicate that attention to
genders roles and redemptive theology can also be found much closer
to the Digby play's home. Julian of Norwich's famous elaboration in
A Revelation of Love of a god who is both father and mother offers
compelling evidence of the ways in which expressions of East Anglian
religious culture probed the symbolic and salvific implications of the gender categories comprising a fully human deity. Andrew Sprung assesses
the implications of Julian's theology: "To posit a double-gendered God
is a way to overrride the binary oppositions of male and female, God
and man, to locate both lack and plenitude in both parties and thus
to refuse to limit, define, control either party."[91] In dramatic contexts
more directly related to the Digby saint play, the morality *Wisdom* elaborates on the traditional feminine identification of Sapientia to construct a Christ as Wisdom who absorbs this femininity into a masculine
God of majesty.[92] The play's "ambivalence—or condensation—of gender reflected in the alternating masculine and feminine identity . . . of
Sapientia" is also relevant to passages in the *Mary Magdalene* that similarly designate Christ as "sovverreyn sapyens" and "Son of Sapyens" (709,
886).[93] The subtle mingling of gender identities and attributes between
the sapiential Christ and Anima exhibited by *Wisdom* furnishes an East
Anglian dramatic precedent for the Digby play's analogously shifting
symbolic construction of Christ as the masculine lord and king who is
also the feminized flesh of the virgin's womb.

Although conceptions of the deity made available in these important late medieval East Anglian texts establish contemporary cultural
currency for the Digby play's constructions of gender in the sacred
realm, they only partly illuminate Mary Magdalene's contribution to
that text's gendered vision of salvation. How could this vision become
such an important dimension of this dramatic hagiography? I want to
speculate on this difficult subject for a moment and tender a response to
what must remain an unanswerable question. Over two decades ago

Marjorie Malvern suggested that the Mary Magdalene of the Digby saint play exhibits a kinship with the Magdalene of second-century apocryphal and Gnostic writings such as the *Gospel of Mary* and *Pistis Sophia*, which represent the figure as feminine counterpart to Christ and wisdom goddess who rules over the material world.[94] Subsequent work on women's religious culture and feminine spirituality in the Middle Ages has made Malvern's proposal worth revisiting. Mary Magdalene is in fact linked with what Barbara Newman terms "the shadowy survival of gnostic ideas" in the fourteenth-century beguine text known as *Schwester Katrei*, which circulated under Meister Eckhart's name.[95] Read by monks and nuns as well as beguines and translated into Latin by a Benedictine, *Schwester Katrei* is informed by many Free Spirit ideas, the heresy with which Marguerite Porete was said to have been allied.

What makes the text interesting for our purposes, however, is the special role accorded Mary Magdalene in Sister Catherine's version of beguine piety. In the text Mary Magdalene occupies the position of teacher, critiques the authority of Peter, renders unnecessary the sacramental interventions of priests, and lays claim to a virile womanhood, a pure virginity—and maidenhead.[96] In her analysis of *Schwester Katrei* Newman cites the Digby saint play's conflation of the penitent saint and the mother of Jesus (for example, 1899–1904) to illustrate the medieval symbolic logic that remade Mary Magdalene's spiritual virginity as indistinguishable from that of the Virgin Mary herself.[97] Although we need not invoke a Gnostic-influenced beguine text to explain the Digby play's fusion of Mary Magdalene and the Virgin Mary, dramatic characterization of the saint nevertheless offers provocative points of contact with *Schwester Katrei*, which in turn may hint at a larger cultural context for the more polemical features of this dramatic hagiography. Emphasizing the saint's roles as preacher, teacher, and virgin and stressing her distance from and superiority to clerical ministrations, *Mary Magdalene* attests to the possibility that the spiritual authority accorded the saint by the drama is meaningful not simply in relation to the play's internal logic of gender relations but also in terms of a specific cultural context.

The Digby text need not exhibit heretical allegiances for us to speculate on its possible connections, if not specifically to *Schwester Katrei*, then to beguine spirituality more generally. As Newman has shown, Mary Magdalene was "a virtual patron saint" for beguines' metaphoric elaborations of the soul's loving relationship to Jesus.[98] Of late, the possibility that beguine influences migrated across the channel from the

Low Countries to East Anglia has been frequently hypothesized, if not proven. As I noted in Chapter 2, small beguinelike communities have been identified in late medieval Norwich, though virtually nothing is known about them. The existence of groups of women living in late medieval East Anglia as *mulieres sanctae* is fully consistent with the region's hospitable late medieval reception—through commercial, religious, and intellectual channels—of continental spiritual influences. The prospect of East Anglian female communities sharing traits with the beguines also finds support in Jocelyn Wogan-Browne's notice that in the later Middle Ages "eastern England and north-west France and Flanders are a single region for many purposes."[99] Though by no measure a heterodox text, *Mary Magdalene* nevertheless plays at the margins of a number of ideas that had currency in alternative spiritualities and theologies presented in hybrid works such as the *Book of Margery Kempe*, Julian's *Revelation*, and *Schwester Katrei* as well as in insular heterodox movements such as Lollardy. It makes Mary Magdalene the saintly counterpart of a Christ who is constituted as a masculine Godhead and a feminine manhood, and endows this "flowyr of wommanned" (1747) and mirror image of the Virgin Mary with the masculine functions of preacher, teacher, governor, and spiritual guide. At the same time, the play seems to underwrite its theological adventurousness with the conservatism of a social vision that plants itself, as we have seen, squarely on the side of the domestic values endorsed by official ideologies of the late medieval Church and lay society.

5

Bodies, Theater, and
Sacred Mediations

Quem quaeritis in sepulchro, o Christicolæ?
Ihesum Nazarenum crucifixum, o cœlicola.
Non est hic, surrexit sicut predixerat; ite, nuntiate quia
surrexit a mortuis.
—*Regularis Concordia* (c. 965–75)

CHRISTIAN DRAMA IN THE WEST begins with the recognition of a lost body. Early ritual enactments of the *Visitatio sepulchri* such as that recorded in Æthelwold's *Regularis Concordia* elaborated the *quem quaeritis* trope from the Easter liturgy, embellishing with gesture and song the gospel accounts of the Marys who seek, but do not find, the body of Christ at the tomb.[1] At its culminating moment medieval East Anglian theatrical tradition felicitously returns to the scene of Christian ritual drama's beginnings and to the scriptural and liturgical witness most famously identified with that lost body, returns, that is, to Mary Magdalene, whose experience epitomized longing for the corporeal form of the sacred registered in that body's absence: "Non est hic."[2] The absent body whose revelation marked the turning point of the *Visitatio sepulchri* furnishes the subject matter of much medieval English drama. It influences the theology and aesthetics of the biblical cycles, and through a powerful symbolic condensation provides the nomenclature for the York plays: *Corpus Christi*. That body also underwrites ideologies of representation in East Anglian dramas of saints and miracles such as the Croxton *Play of the Sacrament*, the N-Town *Mary Play*, and the Digby *Magdalene*, in all of which it offers a locus of "doubt, disbelief, and evidential testing" that the resources of theater are ideally suited to explore.[3] Mary Magdalene is the most memorable witness to the absent divinity of the Gospels, the *Visitatio sepulchri*, and medieval English vernacular theater; as David Damrosch notes, she stands in for all Christians "denied direct contact with Christ's body."[4] Because her experience—in scripture, liturgy, and drama—is founded upon the dynamic relationship of divine absence and presence, it also encodes issues that were central to practices of representing the sacred in the religious theater of late medieval England.

Scholars have long recognized the self-reflexiveness of medieval English theater, its tendency not only to comment on the social processes, institutions, and groups that brought it into being but also to draw attention to its own theatricality.[5] With its angelic messengers, flaming pagan temple, sailing ship, moving clouds, heavenly apparitions, and bodily encased demons, the Digby *Mary Magdalene* has provided an important touchstone of medieval English theatricality at its flamboyant best. Yet the play's awareness and exploitation of its own spectacular resources, what Sarah Beckwith in a different context has termed the "artifice . . . [and] . . . crude made-ness" of drama's sacred images, has been less fully appreciated.[6] This chapter uses the Digby saint play to open an investigation of relationships between theatricality, theology, and aesthetics in Middle English drama. The ideological and symbolic complexity of the late medieval Magdalene, I argue, finds especially apt representation in vernacular religious drama. Dramatic engagement with the symbolism of Mary Magdalene has important implications for late medieval East Anglian devotional theater, the construction of the feminine religious subject, and the contested religious climate of late medieval and early Tudor England.

Theology, Theatricality, and the Saint Play

The metatheatricality and dramatic aesthetic of the Digby *Magdalene* are inextricably bound up with the play's commitment to a materiality that embraces dramatic constructions of the deity and encounters with religious knowledge. The play's interest in a human, corporeal Christ of feminine birth, figured in its Marian focus and in the symbolic conflation of the Virgin Mary and Mary Magdalene, finds a dramaturgical counterpart in this hagiographical theater of visual and experiential proof. "Showing," as Mimi Still Dixon has noted, is the play's operative dramatic metaphor, realized in an emphasis on personal, even bodily, cathecting with sacred truth.[7] As a source of knowledge and illumination, "showing" can be contrasted to the abstruse "covnnyng of clerke" (806) whose efficacy in communicating heavenly mysteries is twice rejected by the Digby play's Christ. Even the founder of the Church, Saint Peter himself, promotes the primacy of "very experyens" over the learned patristic opinion implied in the king of Marseilles's eager request for a declaration of the "sentens" of his newly acquired faith: "[G]oo vesyte þe stacyons, by and by; / To Nazareth and Bedlem, goo wyth delygens, / And be yower own inspeccyon, yower feyth to edyfy" (1846, 1848–50). Peter's directive comments, in Laura King's phrase, on a dramaturgy of "real presence" that insists "that the 'experyens' of the play cannot be abstracted. . . . *Mary Magdalene* is a play on a sacred subject whose truth refuses to be transcendent."[8]

At the same time, the Digby saint play articulates an alternative conception of a deity who is recognized principally not by his corporeal signs but his divine power, intimating that its own spectacular visual and material resources are susceptible to critique as conduits of sacred knowledge. The god to whom Mary Magdalene is so physically connected in both scripture and the play's dramaturgy is paradoxically more often characterized as a remote sapience, divine illumination, and supreme ruler. It is a god who, even in Mary Magdalene's own characterization, at times bears a greater resemblance to the omnipotent deity of late medieval and early Tudor reformers than to the sacrificial god of human flesh that was a staple devotional icon of late medieval religion and spirituality.[9] Whereas the incarnational deity of one strand of the Digby play's complex narrative underwrites a sacramental dramaturgy, the imperial god that I have just described points in the direction of a more cautious dramatic aesthetic. Despite the play's frequent insistence on the power of "shewing" and corporeal apprehension of sacred truths, its Jesus also challenges that materialist hermeneutic: "Blyssyd be þey at alle tyme / That sen me nat, and have me in credens" (699–700). His recollection of Christ's parting words to doubting Thomas in John 20:29 is entirely out of place at the point in the play's conflated biblical and hagiographical narrative in which he utters it: Mary Magdalene has just been spectacularly purged of seven demons, and the Bad Angel, as the stage direction reports, has just entered "into hell wyth thondyr" (s.d. 691). Jesus' admonition about the relationship between sight and belief is offered, I think, as a telling response to Mary Magdalene's explanation of her own inner transformation: she asserts that her direct, bodily experience of Jesus' mercy has enabled her to believe the pronouncements of sacred texts: "Now may I trost þe techeyng of Isaye in scryptur, / Wos report of þi nobyllnesse rennyt fere abowt!" (697–98). It is against such brazenly corporeal testimonials that Jesus cautions, suggesting that neither direct experience nor the performative resources of theater can be counted on to provide reliable access to sacred knowledge.[10]

Recognizing the Digby saint play's investments in the sources and interpretation of sacred knowledge enables us to assess the variable uses to which its dramatic spectacle is put. Most of the theatrical effects associated with Mary Magdalene's progress to spiritual perfection reinforce the play's construction of the saint as contemplative and visionary: her angelic visitations; her ceremonial, dreamlike apparition to the king and queen of Marseilles; her heavenly "halsy[ng] . . . wyth angellys wyth reverent song" (s.d. 2030). In the major spectacles involving Mary Magdalene, even the exorcising of her seven devils, Christ significantly figures as dramaturg and stage manager, ordering the messenger angels and priests who will fulfill his divine bidding, specifying visual effects ("goo yow before hyr wyth reverent lyth" [1593]), and revealing himself from heaven (s.d. 1348). But the play also employs spectacle just as ambitiously in devilish and pagan contexts that are not in Jesus' obvious control. The pagan realm of Marseilles is the site for much of this activity, which includes the garbled rites of "Sentt Mahownde" performed by presbiter and his boy; idols that "tremyll and quake" (s.d. 1553); and the cloud that descends from heaven, setting the pagan temple on fire (s.d. 1561). If Mary Magdalene's conversion is accomplished, as Jesus states, through the "inward mythe" of her "contryssyon" (686–87), the conversion of the king of Marseilles is in large measure the work of spectacular "shewings" that progressively wear down his resistance to the Word of God that Mary Magdalene preaches at their first encounter. In the contrast resulting from these distinct modes of apprehending sacred truth, the Digby dramatist inscribes the difference between bodily and "ghostly" forms of knowing, which late medieval spiritual texts such as Hilton's *Scale of Perfection* and commentaries on the efficacy of religious images established in hierarchical terms: bodily or carnal knowing being a necessary and acceptable manner of apprehension for those unable to obtain knowledge of the sacred in other ways.

What I am suggesting, then, is that the spectacular resources of *Mary Magdalene* metatheatrically reinforce central tensions in the play's spiritual and aesthetic vision. In this vision, spectacle is both a medium of conversion and the dramatic signature of demons and lecherous pagan priests; the scriptural word is alternately endorsed yet exposed as ineffective in the work of Christian evangelism; and early Christians are enjoined to pursue a faith without corporeal signs yet are shown bearing witness to the powerful influence that the physical presence of the deity has upon belief. It is not surprising that the play should express ambivalence about the spiritual efficacy of spectacle nor that its employment of a sacramental dramaturgy should sometimes be at odds with its christological preoccupations and its stated epistemological concerns.[11] For the questions articulated through these tensions were important sites of struggle in late medieval culture: how can the sacred be recognized and known? how can—or should—sacred knowledge be embodied in corporeal forms?

A comparison of *Mary Magdalene* with the Chester cycle's play of the *Coming of Antichrist* illuminates the historical and cultural significance of the Digby drama's metatheatricality, enabling us to see how ostensibly discrete elements of the play's spectacle engage broader concerns about the uses of religious art. Such a comparison is amply justified on historical, narrative, and theatrical grounds. Although precise dating of medieval English dramatic texts is always a vexed issue, the contemporaneity of the two plays can be established through dialectal, codicological, and documentary evidence. The Digby editors propose the end of the fifteenth century as the date of composition for the play whose single manuscript witness is several decades later (1515–30).[12] Dramatic records from the city of Chester place the composition of *Antichrist*, or at least its incorporation into the Chester cycle, in the last part of the fifteenth century, when the Harley List of Guilds (c. 1500) indicates its assignment to the city's hewsters or dyers.[13]

These two plays exhibit similarities of genre and structure arising from their common ties to hagiographic narrative. The Chester *Antichrist* adopts the conception of that figure which Adso of Montier-en Der's *Libellus de Antichristo* (c. 954) had provided for later medieval centuries: Adso organized his life along the lines of a saint's vita.[14] The Chester cycle's *Antichrist* can properly be seen as a perverse or negative version of the hagiographic narrative structure and conventions that the Digby saint play offers in authentic form.[15] As saints' lives, both plays depict the *imitatio Christi* that was a distinguishing feature of hagiographic genres. Whereas the Chester *Antichrist* represents that saintly *imitatio* as a dangerous, comic mimesis of the life of Christ necessarily intended to deceive the pretender's potential adherents, *Mary Magdalene* fulfills the imperative of hagiographic narrative that revealed the inevitable conformity of saints' vitae to the one life, the master narrative, to which they were all assimilated.[16] The Digby play renders that saintly mimesis of Christ more complicated, however, by also incorporating an abbreviated version of the life of Christ into Mary Magdalene's dramatic vita, thereby offering a serious counterpoint to the Chester play's similarly condensed yet parodic manifestation of the same subject.[17]

Finally, the Digby *Magdalene* and the Chester *Antichrist* employ similar dramatic techniques and theatrical effects. Each exploits a variety of rhetorical styles and dramatic modes, ranging from broad comedy to high seriousness, with frequent recourse to awe and amazement directly related to their dramatized miracles. In fact, Peter Travis's description of the Chester *Antichrist* as "a melee of dramatic activity, of histrionic to-ings and fro-ings, ups and downs," could readily be taken for an account of the Digby saint play, which similarly exhibits active "descendings from heaven, deaths, . . . resurrectings, and ascendings back to heaven," paralleling the "hypermobility" that distinguishes the *Coming of Antichrist* among the Chester pageants.[18]

These temporal, generic, and theatrical links between the Chester *Antichrist* pageant and *Mary Magdalene* establish grounds for proposing interpretive connections between the two plays as well. Each text strongly emphasizes visual experience as a source of proof of sacred presence, the saint play through its recourse to "shewings" and the "antisaint" play through a dramatic action focusing on the opportunities and dangers that sight affords Christian believers who seek reinforcement of their faith.[19] In each instance this emphasis on seeing as a mode of spiritual cognition underscores an epistemological tension between rival sources of religious authority. Both plays juxtapose an official, learned procedure for acquiring religious knowledge with the sudden, unpredictable force of illuminating vision and other corporeal modes of apprehension. In the Digby *Magdalene* it is clerkly exposition and "covnnyng" that are subject to such scrutiny (804–6, 1364–65), in *Antichrist* "prooffes of disputacon" "by right and reason" (318, 327). An important addition that the Chester pageant makes to the traditional Antichrist legend reinforces this contrast. The play stages conversion of the four kings as a potential outcome of a scholastic disputation conducted between Antichrist and the prophets Enoch and Elias; but rather than resolve that dispute through logical argument, the play provides for its decisive termination with the miraculous appearance of the eucharistic sign in the bread that Elias consecrates for the dead bodies raised by Antichrist. For both plays, the tension between these rival epistemologies points to a tension between the respective spiritual efficacies of word and image. Beckwith's assertion that Corpus Christi theater is "animated by, and thoughtful about, rather than polarized between" its verbal and visual media applies here as well.[20] This tension dominates the dramatic conflict of *Antichrist*, and it is reinforced by the play's structural position in the cycle, which provides the spectacular histrionics of *Antichrist* as the counterpoint to the intensely verbal, scriptural focus of the *Prophets of Antichrist* preceding it.[21] The Digby saint play treats the conflict between word and image more obliquely, suggesting that scripture by itself can only partly inspire conversion and that writing, as illustrated in the plottings of Christ's enemies, is vulnerable to manipulation and misinterpretation.

In detailing these noteworthy points of contact between the *Coming of Antichrist* and *Mary Magdalene*, I by no means intend to elide important differences between the two plays. For example, *Antichrist* provides the narrative and temporal climax to an ambitious dramatic examination of the imperative to "behold and believe." It offers retrospective evaluation of the rhetorical and theatrical strategies employed throughout the Chester cycle while also anticipating the resolution of its own theological and aesthetic tensions in the *Last Judgement* play.[22] By contrast, *Mary Magdalene* deploys its metatheatrical interests in a more limited world-historical sphere and colors its examination of spiritual cognition and corporeal knowing with a distinctly gendered cast. Still, the juxtaposition of the two plays nonetheless foregrounds resemblances between the questions that each poses about "sensible" signs promising access to and reliable measures of sacred truth. Within the contours of their respective hagiographic narratives, the two plays make apprehension and interpretation of such signs central to the dramatic encounter. In *Antichrist* truth and falsehood are fundamentally at issue in the play's repeated stagings of empirical proofs capable of both masking and exposing the deceptions of the archdeceiver, with nothing less than the salvation of humankind at stake. The Digby play is more concerned with the role that sensible signs play in constituting and authenticating individual religious experience, for example, confirming Mary Magdalene's inner contrition in the bodily expulsion of the seven demons who materially signify her sin, or corroborating that her angelic messengers are beneficent and her visions free of "frawd." In both cases this semiotic self-awareness bears witness to religious drama's capacity to exploit "the tension between outward form and inner thing, . . . sign and signified, . . . visible and invisible" that was central to its sacred subject matter and to sacramental theology.[23] Such awareness necessarily raises questions about the spiritual efficacy, the truth and falsehood, of the sensible signs of theater itself.[24]

By depicting a Jesus who serves as master of ceremonies for some of the play's most dazzling visionary effects and yet promises his blessing to those that "sen me nat, and have me in credens" (700), *Mary Magdalene* inscribes its paradoxical relationship to the sacramental dynamic of medieval religious theater.[25] Peter Womack correctly invokes the saint play as providing a "model of theatrical communication" whose structure, representational conventions, and strategies of audience engagement typify the dramatic aesthetic that increasingly would be challenged by reformist conceptions of both theater and the deity in the decade following the play's probable copying in MS Digby 133.[26] If *Mary Magdalene* epitomizes the overlapping representational and religious gestures that underwrite medieval dramatic sacramentality, it does so not as the culminating moment of a coherent theatrical tradition nor, as Womack states in a different context, "a naive expression of a unified cosmos," but rather as "a sophisticated iconographic attempt to assemble, or reassemble, such a unity in the face of . . . [a] felt disintegration . . . generated by the crisis in the religious culture as a whole."[27] I argue that Mary Magdalene's scriptural and legendary experiences with sacred corporeality and divine inspiration provide apt material for enacting the dramatic encounter with the sacred.[28] In this formulation the Digby saint play's visual hermeneutics does not endorse the sacramental potential of medieval theater as much as it interrogates this potential's advantages and risks. In this process the historical moment of performance, the drama's interest in sacred *imitatio* and visual illumination, and the metatheatricality that *Mary Magdalene* shares with the Chester *Antichrist* pageant all play significant roles.

The representational dilemmas of medieval religious drama are figured in the parodic, sacred *imitatio* of the Chester *Antichrist* play. Travis has argued that the play faces head on the charges that iconoclasts as well as critics of sacramentality leveled against religious art. To the anxious iconophobe the pageant offers ostensible corroboration of all that was feared about the difficulty of distinguishing the deceptive carnal sign from the spiritual truth it signified: the play underscores Antichrist's role as "master of the dramatic image" by making him an appealing comedic figure in his own right. It stages the unreliability of human judgment and sense perception in discerning the false *imago dei* from the real thing. Then, having conceded "everything to the iconoclasts," the play reinstates the authority of the sacred sign—and purifies the dramatic image itself—when the four kings are converted from their faith in Antichrist through "that prynt that ys . . . pight" upon the eucharistic wafer that Elias consecrates before their eyes (579).[29] Its dramatic world now cleansed of the "sorcerye, wytchcraft, and nygromancye" (598) that Antichrist represents in both theological and aesthetic terms, the Chester cycle confidently moves on in the *Last Judgement* pageant to assert the spiritual authority of its own status as religious image by self-consciously appropriating two central icons of late medieval devotional art: the symbols of the Passion and the suffered, bleeding body of Christ.[30]

The theological and representational shifts signaled by these images underscore their visual and dramatic power. The *Judgement* pageant's recourse to nonscriptural devotional themes at the dramatic moment when Christ explains his salvific intervention in human history marks a stunning departure for a cycle whose self-authorization is consistently bound up with scripture. Even more important, as Travis notes, is the radically different Christology signified by these devotional icons. In place of the "aloof, powerful, and . . . severe" divine king who otherwise dominates Chester's conception of the deity, the *Judgement* play here offers the naked materiality of the corporeal sacrifice that lovingly effected the Redemption of human kind.[31] The famous verbal and visual austerities of the Chester cycle give way to an almost gruesome insistence on the salvific spectacle: "Nowe that you shall appertlye see / freshe blood bleede, man, for thee— / . . . / Behould now, all men! / Looke on mee / and see my blood freshe owt flee / that I bleede on roode-tree / for your salvatyon" (421–22, 425–28). Although the four evangelists will still have the cycle's last word (24.677–708), the *Judgement* play provides iconic confirmation of the sacred potential of material images in the unfolding of the dramatic action itself.[32] The scene of Last Judgement restores Antichrist's fraudulent yet seductive *imago dei* to its proper signification as the incarnational likeness that linked humanity with divinity and in the process validated other sorts of images.[33] The good souls of the *Judgement* pageant are rewarded with eternal bliss in heaven, not simply because they practiced the corporeal works of mercy but because in doing so they recognized that divine image, as Jesus states, in "the leaste of myne / that on yearth suffered pyne" (637–38). The damned, by contrast, can only testily respond to Jesus' ultimate reprimand of their neglect by revealing their moral failure of vision and understanding: "When was thou naked or harborlesse, / hongrye, thyrstie, or in sycknes; / eyther in any prysoun was? / Wee saw thee never a-could" (629–32). Framed by the debate on sacred images that the Chester cycle conducts in its final pageants and anticipated by Antichrist's deceptions, the *Judgement* play's emphasis on the proper significance of that image likeness confirms the common terms that linked incarnational theology, dramatic aesthetics, and late medieval religious practice.

The Digby saint play also puts idolatrous images at issue in one of the most notable additions that the playwright made to the saint's legendary vita. *Mary Magdalene* stages its own "parodic image of drama" in the scenes that introduce the pagan religious customs of Marseilles before the land and its people are converted through the saint's apostolic mission.[34] Here the occasion for self-critique is furnished not by Antichrist's false *imitatio* of the deity but by his not-so-distant, medieval cousin Mahowne, the all-purpose subject of pagan religious belief that medieval texts associate with an exotic Eastern other.[35] Worship of Mahownde in the Digby play exhibits the same mocking exposure of performative, ritual elements of late medieval religious culture that reformist polemic and drama identified with an idolatrous theater, what Peter Womack describes as "the pageantry of the saints, the magical bones and phials of dubious blood, the theatricality of the liturgy, the superstitious populace—an impure mixture of magical belief, deception, and buffoonery."[36] As if anticipating such reformist discourse, the worship of the pagan gods in the Marseilles episode is animated by all of these motifs. It is a sacrifice replete with intercessory prayers to "Sentt Mahownde" (1205); promises of "grett pardon" (1206); "relykys brygth— / Mahowndys own nekke bon! / . . . [and] Mahowndys own yeelyd" (1232–33, 1237); and image worship accompanied by the offering of "besawnt of gold, rych and rownd" (1218). Mahownde is celebrated by "prystys and clerkys, of þis tempyll" (1178) in the doggerel Latin office "Leccyo mahowndys" (1186–97), performed in liturgical vestments and sung in treble (1183, 1227).

The Digby play's energetic dramatic portrait of pagan religious practices comes to a speedy termination once the apostle Mary Magdalene inquires about the king of Marseilles's "goddys." It takes only her brief utterance of a Latin verse from Psalm 27 (1552–53) to cause the "mament," or idol, to "tremyll and quake" (s.d. 1553) and a vernacular prayer to the "hye name Jhesus" (1554–61) to finish the job: "Here xall comme a clowd from heven, and sett þe tempyl on afyer, and þe pryst and þe cler[k] xall synke" (s.d. 1561). Despite the efficiency with which Mary Magdalene, like Enoch and Elias in the Chester *Antichrist*, "does down" her spiritual adversary and reveals the falsehood of the king's pagan deity—"A! Owt! For angur I am þus deludyd!" he exclaims (1562)—the rites of worship and material religious practices that these scenes perform bear too many resemblances to the real, orthodox Christian thing to warrant simple dismissal as the comic exposure of false pagan faith by true Christian belief.[37] Rather, in venturing into a realm of pagan religious practice that looks dangerously like a late medieval Christian one, the Digby play intimates the idolatry of the material, theatrical trappings of such religion, and perhaps even of theater itself, and significantly figures the demise of such suspect sacred representation in a divinely inspired conflagration of temple and priest.[38]

To that violent outcome, however, the Digby *Mary Magdalene* also proposes a measured alternative. Just as the *Antichrist* pageant purges the dramatic image of its potential deceptions, enabling the restoration of sacramental signs and devotional icons to their proper significations, so does the Digby play recuperate its fraudulent sacred rites by staging a ritual correction of its idolatrous pagan theater: that is, the ceremony in which the hermit priest who discovers Mary Magdalene in the "wyldyrnesse" brings her the eucharistic *viaticum*, accompanied by two angels ("Hic aparuit angelus et presbiter cum corpus domenicum" [s.d. 2100]). Through his angelic messengers, Jesus directs this final "playlet" from on high. He specifies what the angels shall say to the priest ("My body in forme of bred þat he bere, / Hur for to hossell, byd hym provyde" [2079–80]), while they, in turn, describe the appearance of the ritual action:

> Syr pryst, God cummav[n]dytt from heven region
> 3e xall go hosyll hys servont expresse,
> And we wyth yow xall take mynystracyon
> To bere lyth before hys body of worthynesse. (2085–88)

Although the difference between the two ceremonies is clear, the parodic pagan rite also echoes in the proper Christian one. Using virtually the same words as did his counterpart in Marseilles, the hermit priest prepares for the sacramental service by donning liturgical garments: "In a westment I wyll me aray, / To mynstyr my Lord of gret hynesse" (2090–91).[39] The earlier service and the god that it honors produce nothing, a failure imaged in the king of Marseilles's vain attempt to elicit from the dumb idol some sign of spiritual power: "Lord, I besech þe grett myth, / Speke to þis Chrisetyn þat here sestt þou! / Speke, god lord, speke!" (1540–42). But the symbolic focus of this final rite and play-within-the-play is Christ's "body in form of bred," the eucharistic sacrament in which the sacred truly inheres in material substance. Like the Chester *Antichrist* and *Judgement* pageants, *Mary Magdalene* moves to symbolic and narrative closure by forging a link between its dramatic aesthetic, the theology of the Sacrament, and its own visual resources.

Theater, as Womack asserts, "is idolatrous in its essential nature because it works by setting up false images with the intention that they should be taken for truths. . . . However assiduously it proclaims Protestant doctrine, the theater is still a *Catholic kind of thing* in its suspect reassigning of substance: a brown paper effigy is a dragon; some base fellow is Christ; wine is blood."[40] This account of theater's essentially idolatrous nature illuminates the inherent contradictions of a reformist drama that denounced the idolatry it conflated with late medieval religion in the very medium that required the slippery, idolatrous transferral of sign and substance. In so doing, it articulates a critical position to which the Digby saint play and the Chester *Antichrist* bear late medieval witness, as they expose the risks and opportunities that attend the playing of ever potentially idolatrous spectacles on sacred subjects.

The two plays thus afford complex and at times contradictory perspectives on the spiritual efficacy of such spectacles; if they appear to stake their largest claims on behalf of a sacramental theater, they do so not as partisan responses to heterodoxy or what in the sixteenth century would become institutionally sponsored critiques of such supposed idolatry.[41] Rather, as Beckwith has argued in an analysis of the sacramentality of Corpus Christi theater that can be more broadly applied to vernacular drama on sacred subjects, the potent contradictions that such theater generates are "intrinsic to symbolic formation as such, and a component part of the sacramental culture enacted in these plays."[42] Sacramentality involves not a prescriptive set of dogmas that drama is either for or against but the understanding and reading of signs, the "sheer opacity" rather than the "transparency" of their meaning.[43] In "the symbolic understanding of sacramentality that is central to" Corpus Christi theater's "elucidation" of ritual subject and object, Beckwith explains, "it is the change in the person, not in the ritual object, that is the significant and transformative moment."[44]

By calling attention to the ways that meaning is created through the sacramental encounter, Beckwith's analysis of the symbolic complexities of sacramentality in vernacular religious theater can explain why "knowing," "seeing," and "understanding" furnish the operative metaphors for spiritual enlightenment in the plays we have been examining as well as why acts of interpretation and discernment are privileged in those dramatic moments when the sacred assumes the sign's material form. This understanding of dramatic sacramentality also calls attention to vernacular theater's capacity to expose the potential for contradictions between its form and the subject matter that authorizes it, contradictions that are frequently generated at the point where the dramatic necessity of "showing forth" intersects with theological and institutional understandings of the sacred encounter and sacred image. For example, the Chester *Last Judgement* pageant responds to the *Antichrist* play's implicit critique of dramatic religious art with a series of powerful devotional signs, which were themselves validated by the incarnational likeness between God and humankind that animated medieval theologies of the image. But when Christ invokes that likeness at the moment of judgment, faulting the damned souls who failed to recognize it, and him, "in the leaste of myne," he points to an understanding of the *imago dei* that also furnished one of the basic arguments employed by late medieval iconoclasts in the condemnation—and destruction—of religious images: namely, that the true image of God should be recognized and worshiped in his actual human likeness and not in the dead and graven images of devotional art that fraudulently represented him.[45] In a related vein the Croxton *Play of the Sacrament* offers a critique of the material excesses of the sacramental culture promoted for and by late medieval lay society, but it does so in the very dramatic medium that epitomized that culture's emphasis on the spiritual efficacy of mingling the mundane and the sacred.[46]

In the intersecting histories of medieval English drama and vernacular religious culture, *Mary Magdalene* is properly located in the same ideological and aesthetic climate that prompted the critique and recuperation of sacramentality and religious images enacted in the final plays

of the Chester cycle. Viewing the saint play in this light revises the
genealogy of late medieval metatheatrical discourse, linking the Digby
play not only to the closing pageants of the Chester cycle but also
to other texts with which it is not customarily associated: the *Tretise
on Miraclis Pleyinge*, the *Play of the Sacrament*, the Late Banns of the
Chester cycle, and the 1576 directive from the Commissioners of York
to the Wakefield Burgesses prohibiting representation of the deity and
the sacraments of baptism and eucharist.[47] The extended analogy that I
have drawn between *Mary Magdalene* and the Chester *Antichrist* play
acquires further significance in light of shifting semiotic valences of
the Antichrist figure in the early decades of the sixteenth century and
the consequent mobility that must have characterized dramatic reception of the Chester play from its late fifteenth-century addition to the
Chester cycle through its final performance in 1575. Changing significations of Antichrist during this period range from essentially medieval constructions of the figure as a "future eschatological deceiver and
tyrant" to reformist understandings that identified Antichrist not only
with the doctrine and hierarchy of the Roman Church, as was the case
with John Bale, but also more broadly with deceptiveness of embodied
ritual and representation that reformers associated with all things
Catholic, including, and perhaps especially, sacred drama.[48] The variable
reception of the Chester Dyers' pageant occasioned by these divergent
understandings of Antichrist, moreover, points to larger patterns of
accommodation and negotiation that characterized relations between
medieval religious traditions and reformist approaches to both theater
and images in the sixteenth century.[49] Such patterns are probably also at
work in the other Digby saint play, the *Conversion of Saint Paul*, where
they may bear witness to the shadowy early modern textual transmission of the Digby plays.[50]

What is the special relevance of Saint Mary Magdalene's social,
spiritual, and gender identities to the apparent ideological commitments of her late medieval dramatic vita? I want to propose that the
tension between theology and aesthetics that marks cultural uses of
dramatic and other religious images in this period is fundamentally
congruent with the symbolic construction of Mary Magdalene herself,
whose late medieval identities are similarly informed by the tensions
that dominate a sacramental aesthetic: how can the spiritual be bodied
forth in the physical? how can the divine be placed on the same level
as the human?[51] To be sure, all medieval saints performed the central

function of mediating between the sacred and profane realms. But the legendary medieval Mary Magdalene stands out among the holy doctors, confessors, helpers, martyrs, and virgins who populated the calendars and litanies of saints because she performed these acts of mediation not only in scripturally documented moments but also in the startlingly intimate encounters with the deity upon which her complex identity was founded. As a cultural symbol, the late medieval Magdalene was as overdetermined as Antichrist, another loaded signifier for political, religious, and aesthetic conflict. Precisely because her symbolic meanings in biblical history and legend repeatedly bridge—and transgress—the boundaries of sacred and profane, she emerges as a site of controversy in the very period when critiques of late medieval sacramental culture, as well as sacred drama and religious images, would increasingly be articulated. The aesthetic and religious questions put into play by the self-reflexive spectacle of *Mary Magdalene* mirror late medieval cultural struggles over the role of the feminine in religious culture and spiritual experience. Like dramatic forms, feminine bodies, tropes, and symbols pose opportunities for and obstacles to accessing the sacred.[52]

Mary Magdalene and the Body of Resurrection

Apart from the Incarnation and the virgin birth, the Resurrection and the biblical scenes marking its immediate aftermath (the Supper at Emmaus, the doubt of Thomas) provided medieval English dramatists with the most direct occasions for probing the material fact of divine carnality. These events defining the beginning and ending of Christ's earthly life inspire dramatic moments of great doubt, wonder, and amazement, as characters such as Joseph and the apostles reluctantly ask: can a virgin give birth to the human Son of God? can that God-man rise from the dead? As it interrogates Christianity's founding corporeal mysteries, medieval English drama highlights the physical, feminine presences that enabled or attended them, drawing upon exegetical, apocryphal, legendary, and devotional resources to fill in the fragmented picture that the Scriptures sketched of these presences. Of the corporeal mysteries, dramatic versions of the Incarnation and the virgin birth have attracted most scholarly attention, probably because those events evoke a suppressed sexual narrative that implicates femininity in a robust comic and visually challenging theater.[53] But medieval English drama's scenes of Resurrection are similarly marked, indeed strongly defined, by the feminine presence that Mary Magdalene represents.

Even when they also incorporate elements from the other three gospel accounts, such as the journey of the Marys to the tomb (Matt. 28:1–6; Mark 16:1–6; Luke 24:1–10) or Jesus' appearance to the women who have sought him there (Matt: 28:9–10), all of the Middle English dramatic versions of the Resurrection—in the Digby saint play, the biblical cycles, and the meditative texts preserved in Bodleian Library MS e Museo 160—stage the risen Christ's appearance to Mary Magdalene, uniquely recounted in John 20. This commonality of representation among English dramatic versions bears out Cullen Murphy's claim that Mary Magdalene's "fixed image . . . in the Christian imagination is as the original witness, if not to the Resurrection of Jesus itself, then to the core circumstances . . . in which the Resurrection stories are embedded."[54]

From their common acknowledgment of this "fixed image," dramatic scenes of the Resurrection and its aftermath fashion various interpretations of the significance of Mary Magdalene's role as witness, differences that parallel those of the gospel accounts. The biblical cycles, for example, dramatize contrary responses to the veracity of her testimony. Building on the apostolic role that *Passion Play I* establishes for Mary Magdalene by including her at the Last Supper, the N-Town compilation includes Resurrection episodes that carefully reinforce the authority of feminine witness—of the three Marys generally and Magdalene specifically. This interest is typified in Peter's effort to assuage Thomas's doubts by invoking "[r]ecord of Mawdelyn and of her systerys too (379.306)."[55] The Towneley cycle, by contrast, follows Mark 16:11 and Luke 24:10–11 to develop the disciples' disbelief, even going so far as to place a very anachronistic Paul among the disciples who first hear Mary Magdalene's report: "Trist ye it and knawe / He is rysen, the soth to say" (367.3–4). True to his role the man who would "suffer not a woman to preach" launches into a four-stanza tirade about the unreliability of woman's speech: "And it is wretyn in oure law, / 'Ther is no trust in womans saw'" (368.29–30).[56]

Medieval English dramatic versions of the Resurrection also take divergent approaches to Mary Magdalene's meeting with the risen Jesus. As we have seen, the Digby play challenges the notion—implicit in Jesus' reproof of her touch (John 20:17)—that Mary Magdalene was so attached to his humanity that she was insufficiently cognizant of his divinity. Instead, the Digby saint proclaims Jesus' Godhead shortly after he identifies himself to her: "O, þou dereworthy Emperowere, þou hye dyvyne!" (1086). The York Winedrawers' play *Christ's Appearance to Mary Magdalene* takes a similarly abrupt turn, but here Mary Magdalene's quick recognition of the "comely conquerour . . . man and saueour" (358.86, 88) provokes Jesus' elaborate romantic and chivalric allegorization of the body of his Passion (358.94–109).[57] In the meditative drama known as *Christ's Resurrection*, Magdalene's reproof is largely self-generated; she reprimands herself for the "slewth and . . . necligence" that have kept her from attending her "masters sepulcre" with sufficient "dewty" and "diligence." If she had, she reasons, she "shuld haue seyn his vprisinge gloriose / . . . of þe which desirose / I am, and nedes must bee" (203–11).[58]

Despite such lively variations, these Resurrection episodes nevertheless commonly recognize Mary Magdalene's intimacy with Jesus, especially her physical attachment to his body. The account in John 20 provided the basis for this emphasis by showing a Magdalene who seeks her absent beloved even while she stands in his unrecognized presence. In the Towneley *Resurrection*, Mary Magdalene asserts her intention to "bere" that lost body with her "[u]nto myn endyng day" (353.593–94). Disguised as a gardener, Jesus queries her longing, delaying the moment of revelation: "Why, what was he to the. . . ?"(353.603). The Towneley play figures the forbidden physical encounter in precise corporeal terms— Magdalene asks Jesus if she may "negh the nere / And kys thi feete" (353.609–10)—as it does her joyful announcement of her encounter: "with hym spake I bodely / . . . I am as blyth in bloode and bone / As euer was wight" (354.640, 644–45).

Mary Magdalene's attachment to Christ's body is articulated very differently in the York cycle, where the woman's encounter with the resurrected Jesus anticipates the graphic dramatic image of doubting Thomas.[59] In the York Winedrawers' play the body that Magdalene seeks—and that Jesus teasingly withholds from revelation—is the suffered, salvific body of his Passion. Mary Magdalene identifies the object of her search as "[m]i lorde Jesu and God verray, / Þat suffered for synnes his sides bleede" (356.28–29). Jesus employs the idiom of Passion meditations as he queries her intent:

> What wolde þou doo with þat body bare
> Þat beried was with balefull chere?

þou may noght salue hym of his sare,
His peynes were so sadde and seere. (357.50–53)

and as he reveals himself to her, turning the laconic "Maria" of John's gospel into a speech that resembles those delivered from the cross in lyric expressions of the Passion:

Marie, of mournyng amende thy moode,
And beholde my woundes wyde.
Þus for mannys synnes I schedde my bloode,
And all þis bittir bale gonne bide.
Þus was I rased on þe roode
With spere and nayles that were vnride,
Trowe it wele, it turnes to goode
Whanne men in erthe þer flessh schall hyde. (357.62–69)

When this atypical exposure of his flesh elicits Mary Magdalene's recognition ("A! Rabony, I haue þe sought, / Mi maistir dere, full faste þis day" [357.70–71]), Jesus is quick with his reprimand: "Goo awaye Marie, and touche me noȝt" (357.72). But rather than proceed with the explanation offered in John 20:17 ("I am not yet ascended to my Father"), the York Jesus speaks instead of his majesty and his redemption of humankind and then surprisingly solicits Mary Magdalene's further attention: "And therfore, Marie, speke nowe with me, / And latte þou nowe be thy grette [weeping]." She accepts his invitation, suggesting that, like Thomas, she reaches out at that point to grope the orifices that he has so emphatically exposed to her: "Mi lorde Jesu, I knowe nowe þe, / Þi woundes þai are nowe wette." But her gesture provokes a reprise of the "noli mi tangere" and earns her second reprimand (one that hardly seems deserved, under the circumstances): "Negh me noght, my loue, latte be! / Marie my doughtir swete. / To my fadir in Trinité / Forþe I stigh noȝt yette" (358.78–85). Despite Jesus' belated assertion of his divine nature, Mary Magdalene remains fixated on his human body and the visible signs of its Crucifixion: "woundes [that] hath made þi body wete, / With bloode þat was þe withinne" (358.112–13).[60]

In the N-Town *hortulanus* scene, the representation of Mary Magdalene's bodily connection to Jesus occurs in the larger dramatic context in which their relationship has been developed in *Passion Play I*. Mary Magdalene's anointing of Jesus during the Last Supper and his

subsequent expulsion of seven "[w]yckyd spyritys" from her "bodyly
bowre" (270–71.176–77), in fact, furnish the prominent signatures by
which she identifies herself in both the Resurrection and *hortulanus*
scenes, directly associating her own bodily boundaries with her physical contact with Jesus in the house of Simon.[61] In the N-Town Resurrection sequence, the Magdalene who resolves to "towch" Jesus as she
approaches the tomb with the other Marys (360.37) and who asks permission to kiss his "holy fete" (367.41) is thus, as far as her construction
by the manuscript is concerned, already an intimate of the risen Christ.
The particularities of that relationship also inform their post-Resurrection
encounter. Jesus may assert his unapproachability—"Towche me not as
ʒett, Mary" (367.42); but he implies only deferral, not prohibition of
that contact, promising benefits that his ascent "to hevyn towre" will
bring directly to her.[62] Sounding a bit like the Joseph of the N-Town
Mary Play, who explained to his bride that he had to "go laboryn in fer
countré, / With trewth to maynteyn oure housholde so" (110.467–68),
the risen Jesus promises Mary Magdalene that he will "ordeyn . . . [her]
a place" in heaven, where he goes to his Father and to "merth, and joye,
and grett solace, / And endeles blys to brynge ʒow to" (367.50–53). Perhaps it is this familiarity and talk of a shared future that prompts Mary
to express her happiness in marital terms: "So grett a joy nevyr wyff had
non" (368.73)—and to characterize her encounter with Jesus in language
that hints at the intimacy of a forbidden kiss: "Mowth to mowth, þis
[is] sertayn, / I spak ryght now with Cryst Jesus" (368.92–93).

Other Middle English dramatic versions of Magdalene's encounter
with the risen Jesus put their own stamp on the dominant theme of
body. The Chester plays offer the sparest rendering, yet even in Chester,
which of all the biblical cycles is least engaged with feminine dimensions
of the life of Christ, Mary Magdalene is clearly the lovelorn follower of
Jesus, whose poignant rejection, "Mary, touche not my body," is reinforced by his triumphal appearance: "Tunc veniet Jesus alba indutus
baculumque crucis manibus portans."[63] In the Digby saint play Mary
Magdalene's previous encounters with Jesus, like those of the N-Town
compilation, lend familiarity to its representation of her longing by the
tomb. She tells the Jesus whom she has yet to recognize that she has
promised to have her "specyall Lord" with her because she is "hys lovyr"
(1067–68). Once he reveals himself, she wants to reconnect with him,
bodily, for old times' sake, declaring her intention rather than asking
permission to make contact: "Lett me anoynt yow wyth þis bamys

sote! / Lord, long hast þou hyd þe from my spece, / Butt now wyll I kesse þou for my hartys bote!" (1071–73). In the meditative Resurrection drama preserved in Bodleian MS e Museo 160, the loving Mary at the tomb becomes the *sponsa* of the Song of Songs, alternating her paraphrase of the Bride's longing with direct quotations from the Latin biblical text (570–601), whose allegorical potential is here overshadowed by the corporeal object of her desire. She tells one of the other Marys that she must "render thankes immortalle" to his "Godhed . . . Os I am bound of dewtee" (643–44) but also joyfully reports that "he callit me 'Mary', by my name, / And spak with me homlye" (655–56).

The personal, corporeal tie to the deity signified by this "homeliness" marks Mary Magdalene's witness to the Resurrection, inscribing the defining moment of Christian belief in these dramas as a feminine, physical encounter with the sacred.[64] As they elaborate on scriptural story, Middle English dramatic versions of the Resurrection foreground aspects of Mary Magdalene's composite identity—her feminine spiritual authority and attachment to Christ's body—that problematically sanctioned the contested tradition of her apostolate. Perhaps not as metaphorically bold as the scriptural exegesis that figured Mary Magdalene as the surrogate mother for Christ's second birth from the tomb, the emphases of these dramatic moments nonetheless bring into the scene of Resurrection lingering reminders of the mixing of sacred and profane that dramatic treatments of the Incarnation also exploit, a mingling of spirit and matter that Jesus' resurrection was supposed to sort out: "Noli me tangere, nondum enim ascendi ad Patrem meum."[65] The Virgin Mary paradoxically epitomizes the fleshly transgression of spiritual boundaries at the beginning of Jesus' earthly life but mitigates the potential for feminine pollution of the sacred through her own virginal body. As physical intimate and witness of Jesus' resurrection, Mary Magdalene provides no comparable mitigation, since, despite the many symbolic and linguistic grounds on which she could be linked to the Virgin and virginity, she was never completely dissociated from the carnal taint conferred upon her by her composite scriptural identity. Consequently, for late medieval religious culture and its vernacular theater, she signifies the enduring pressures that a corporeal femininity exerted upon understandings of scriptural history, institutional religion, and personal devotion.

These pressures are provocatively articulated in *De Maria Magdalena*, a widely disseminated twelfth-century homily that enjoyed exceptional popularity in the late Middle Ages. Attributed to Origen in the medieval and early modern period but now recognized as being of uncertain authorship, Pseudo-Origen's *De Maria* survives in at least 185 manuscripts. The homily, which Saxer calls "one of the most beautiful texts of the Magdalene literature," was translated into the major European vernaculars and went through many early printed editions in Latin as well as English, French, Italian, Provençal, Czech, and Dutch.[66] Probably composed in France between 1150 and 1175, *De Maria Magdalena* is most likely of Cistercian origin. Its earliest manuscripts are from Cistercian monasteries; early texts circulate with works by or attributed to Bernard of Clairvaux; and a monastic provenance is also strongly suggested by the homily's rhetorical address to "fratres."[67] In the later Middle Ages the homily's migration from a monastic provenance to a broader clerical and lay sphere reflects the widening of venue that characterizes late medieval constructions of spirituality and religious practice more generally, as lay society increasingly appropriated texts and behaviors that were originally the province of professed religious. Twelfth-century spiritual texts that emphasized an inner, affective piety, such as *De Maria*, played an important role in this process.[68]

The medieval English fortunes of *De Maria* are bound up with Alceste's elusive reference, in the *Legend of Good Women*, to Chaucer's having made "Origines upon the Maudeleyne."[69] The probability that Chaucer produced a now-lost translation of the homily is strengthened by evidence of the work's wide distribution in late medieval England. Saxer has identified at least twenty-four fourteenth- and fifteenth-century manuscripts of English provenance.[70] *De Maria Magdalena* appears in prominent manuscripts connected with the devotional and textual community based at the Carthusian monastery at Sheen and neighboring Brigittine house at Syon. Along with portions of *Poor Caitiff*, Thomas à Kempis's *De imitatione Christi*, and devotional and theological works by Augustine, Jerome, Anselm and Bernard, it is also included in Magdalen College, Oxford MS 93, the commonplace book that John Dygoun, recluse at Sheen, wrote in his own hand in 1438.[71] Rosemary Woolf concluded that despite the homily's widespread dissemination, medieval vernacular writers left little evidence indicating that they were significantly influenced by it. But recent work on *De Maria* provides terms not only for reconsidering Chaucer's likely engagement with the text but also for hypothesizing its broader relevance to constructions of Mary Magdalene in late medieval culture.[72]

Based on John 20:11–18, *De Maria Magdalena* preeminently associates Mary Magdalene with the lost body of Christ, whose absence she queries and laments at the tomb: "Now . . . she could feel no consolation for that sorrow because she could not find his body" ("Nunc . . . se de isto dolore consolari non poterat quia corpus defuncti non inveniebat" [324]).[73] Overcome by tears and rendered insensate by her loss, the homily's Mary bears out the criticism that patristic and clerical commentators discerned in the risen Jesus' reprimand: that she is all absorbed with his humanity and insufficiently attentive to his divinity. The transgressions articulated in *De Maria*, however, involve much more than the specter of Magdalene's putative disbelief. Rather, the homily's "celebration of corporeality," its insistence on the radical physicality of the mourning woman's relationship to her lost love, allows "a profound mingling of her spirit and Christ's dead body, a recombination that merges male and female, divinity and humanity, death and life."[74] The narrator's address to the risen Christ typifies this mingling:

Finally as Joseph [of Arimethea] placed your body in the tomb, Mary in a similar manner buried her spirit with you and so indissolubly joined it with your body that she could no more separate her living soul from her living body than separate her loving spirit from your dead body. For the spirit of Mary was greater in your body than in her own. While she was seeking your body, she was also seeking her spirit, and when she had lost your body, she lost her spirit with it. (336)[75]

Such gender slippage as *De Maria Magdalena* exhibits, moreover, also characterizes the narrator's relationship to the mourning woman. As King argues, one of the homily's most innovative features is the monastic narrator's imaginative rhetorical and affective occupation of Mary Magdalene's embodied self.[76] It was not unusual for monks and other male religious to identify with Mary Magdalene as a model of penitence and devotion to Jesus. The narrator of *De Maria*, for example, promotes just such an identification when he exhorts: "Let us imitate, brothers, the affection of this woman. . . . Learn from Mary how to love Jesus and how to hope in Jesus and, by seeking him, how to find Jesus" (340).[77]

What is especially distinctive about the substance and the rhetoric of these minglings is the scriptural hermeneutics on which they are founded. Like many accounts of Mary's seeking Christ at the tomb, *De Maria Magdalena* draws heavily upon the Song of Songs to characterize the Magdalene's emotional involvement and search for her absent beloved. She is the anxious *sponsa* of the canticles, who seeks and does not find, calls but gets no answer, languishes in love with an unmatched grief. But rather than invoke allegorical interpretations of the Song through which Mary Magdalene's relationship to the risen Christ was regularly articulated in Christian exegetical traditions, the homily exhibits instead a remarkably literal treatment of the scriptural text. In the senses defined and promoted by masculine clerical culture, both the Mary Magdalene of the homily and its narrator are bad readers, that is, each reads "as a woman . . . with a gross carnality, resistant to the spiritual sense."[78] The homily's enactment of Mary Magdalene's desire thus constitutes not simply a rejection of traditional hierarchies of spirit and flesh but of the allegorical hermeneutic that customarily displaced such longing to "an abstract or transcendent realm."[79] The text's refusal to spiritualize Mary Magdalene's carnal longings turns the resurrected deity of John 20:17 who reproached the longing woman into a neglectful, offending lover who himself merits the narrator's reproach:

O desire of her soul, why do you ask her 'Why do you cry, [whom] do you seek?' . . . You know that she searches only for you, loves only you, has forsaken all things for you, and yet you ask 'Whom do you seek?' Sweet master, why do you unsettle the mind and spirit of this woman who totally depends upon you, who totally rests in you, who totally hopes in you, who totally despairs over you? (333–34)[80]

Critiquing Jesus' failure to provide an appropriate response to the woman's longing, the narrator also defends at great length Mary Magdalene's thoroughly physical attachment to her beloved until Christ's "Maria" brings the homily's literary and theological excesses to an end. As King notes, that word—and name—"redraws the boundaries between [Christ] . . . and Mary" and reinstates other differences eroded by Mary's corporeal identification with Jesus and the homily's passionate displacement of the allegorical hermeneutic.[81]

Although the complicated history of *De Maria Magdalena* in Western spirituality is just beginning to be illuminated, it seems clear that the homily made available to late medieval religious and lay devotees alike a spiritual model that was congruent with emphases of the dramatic *hortulanus* scenes that we have examined.[82] As a medium of religious knowledge, drama by its very nature is fundamentally incompatible with the privileging of the spiritual over the material that was central to the allegorical hermeneutic scrutinized in *De Maria Magdalena*. This inescapable materiality makes drama a medium ideally suited to exploiting the central tensions activated by Mary Magdalene's witness to the Resurrection.

Bodies That Matter

The scriptural and legendary Mary Magdalene examined in this study never transcends the bodiliness and the physical acts that constituted such a crucial aspect of her late medieval identity. In this respect the symbolism of the late medieval Magdalene recalls Caroline Walker Bynum's well-known formulation about the spiritual lives of later medieval female saints and holy women: that they sought to reach God not by rejecting the physicality with which women were regularly identified but "by sinking more fully into it." For these women, "body is not so much a hindrance to the soul's ascent as the opportunity for it."[83] Even in her ascetic withdrawal, the spiritual progress of the late medieval Magdalene involves not an opposition to flesh but a dynamic relationship to her own bodiliness, what Bynum has described as "elaborate changes rung upon the *possibilities* provided by fleshliness."[84] Late medieval visual representations of Mary Magdalene capture the inescapable corporeality—of tears, hair, and touch—for which she was famous, consistently rendering her spiritual state in precise bodily terms.[85] Images of Mary Magdalene's legendary life as preacher and hermit, for example, evoke the physicality of her renounced sexual past in hauntingly disparate ways. Whereas the elegant and colorfully attired gentlewoman at an outdoor pulpit in the late fifteenth-century painting "Mary Magdalene Preaching" (fig. 12) links the ease and luxury of her former life to her current evangelical mission, Donatello's famous ravaged penitent in a hair cloak conveys a very different preoccupation: one is a mirror of physical beauty, the other of mortified flesh.[86] The fluid relationship of Mary Magdalene's bodiliness to her spiritual state is similarly confirmed in two contrasting images also illustrating scenes from her eremitic life. In one late medieval woodcut the angels who lift up the ascetic saint for her daily feedings with heavenly manna struggle to hoist her sheer mortal weight, the angel in charge of her lower half becoming completely inverted in that effort (fig. 14).[87] Quentin Massys's painting of Mary Magdalene in the desert shows that same bare flesh covered only by flowing hair, but his saint is waiflike, meager, and frail, recalling the image of a body rendered nearly transparent by fasting (fig. 15). Such was the case with Marie d'Oignies, who was discovered to be so slender at her death that people could see right through her thin flesh.[88]

East Anglian versions of the life of Mary Magdalene elaborate on the physicality that was central to the saint's relationship to Jesus in her conflated biblical vita. Bokenham's legend not only emphasizes the physical closeness of Mary Magdalene to Jesus but also, as Delany has shown, "exudes a general physicality, often of a calculatedly repulsive kind," represented by Lazarus's deadly stench or Martha's twelve-year flux. Mary's hermit existence in Bokenham's life is "a cluster of reminders of physicality" that point to what is ultimately at stake in his legend, the relation "between physical and spiritual components in the difficult doctrine of incarnation."[89] The Digby saint play similarly foregrounds Mary Magdalene's corporeality in particular but also materiality in general. Her spiritual journey from sinner to hermit saint is sharply inflected by her evolving relationship to physical desires and needs. The daughter of Cyrus who rejoices in her freedom from "poverte" and "streytnes" (96–97) experiences a mortal fall that is imaged in terms of consumption, the "soppys in wynne" (536) that Curiosity offers to soften

Figure 14. *The Ecstasy of Mary Magdalene.* Woodcut. Rosenwald Collection, Photograph © 2002 Board of Trustees, National Gallery of Art, Washington, D.C.

Figure 15. *Mary Magdalene*, by Quentin Massys. Reproduced by permission of the Philadelphia Museum of Art: The John G. Johnson Collection.

her resistance to his overtures.[90] Whether it is present or absent, physical consumption occupies an important role in the Digby play, dominating the involuntary poverty into which Mary Magdalene is thrown in Marseilles when she finds herself suffering "hongor, threst, and chelle" (1613), marking her flight to the desert as an abandonment of "wordly fodys" (2000), providing the elaborate image of angelic feeding with heavenly manna that accompanies her spiritual ascent, and culminating in her reception of the Eucharist by Jesus' command (2078–80).

The allusion to the Virgin Mary's assumption complicates the dramatic scene of the Digby saint's heavenly ascent by its very evocation of Marian symbolism: whereas the Virgin's body is assumed into heaven once and for all, the body of Mary Magdalene is brought up only to come down again to earth. The Digby saint's material attachments are epitomized in the striking gesture with which she concludes her mortal life, mingling an affectionate farewell to the world with anticipation of the sacred rewards that await her: "Lord, opyn þi blyssyd gatys! / Thys erth at thys tyme fervently I kysse!" (2113–14). In traditional versions of the saint's vita such as that of Jacobus, Mary Magdalene dies in the church where she has received the Eucharist. Instead, the Digby play shows the woman leaving life, not from within the confines of institutional religion, but from her chosen wilderness; it makes reception of the Eucharist her penultimate rather than her final act; and it caps the drama's repeated emphasis on the capacity of the divine to enter the quotidian through visions, signs, and wonders with a spectacular act that symbolically connects Mary's heavenly *transitus* with homage to the entire material realm.

Marjorie Malvern attributes the Digby saint's final gesture to the play's modeling of a "dualistic split between body and soul" that echoes Gnostic constructions of the saint and the cosmos: in this reading Mary Magdalene acts as goddess of life and fertility in a play that casts Gnostic darkness as human mortality and ignorance of Christian teaching.[91] Rather than polarize matter and spirit, the dominate symbolic strategies of the saint play, I suggest, more often underscore the continuities that Christian incarnational and sacramental theology established between them and are perhaps are more aptly characterized by a different trope: transubstantiation. Narrative and scenic structures of repetition and recursion reinforce the symbolic and theological significance of the many transformations that the drama enacts—of bower to garden; valentines to Jesus; sops in wine to earthly alms, heavenly manna, and Eucharist;

humble anointing servant to evangelical apostle—changes that are all a function of the internal transformation experienced by Mary Magdalene herself. Significantly, the play images the central change in her internal condition with a bodily alteration: the expulsion of the "sevyn dyllys" that "dewoyde from þe woman" by Jesus' command in the house of Simon. Like the "sacerdotal ritual action" in which matter was, in Miri Rubin's phrase, "transformed into something quite different," Jesus' priestly act purges and sanctifies the saint's body, which, like the transubstantiated bread of the Sacrament, retains its original appearance but also becomes the locus of her new sacred power.[92]

The rendering of spiritual change in material form that is so central to Mary Magdalene's experience in the Digby play has an aesthetic counterpart in the medium of sacred drama itself. The religious drama of late medieval England enacts its own versions of transubstantiation, making ideas and images of the sacred available in mundane and carnal forms. Dramatic reification of sacred reality risks crossing the boundaries of both ritual and sacrament, just as Mary Magdalene continually transgresses the boundaries of sacred and profane. In this sense the Digby saint, like the Chester Antichrist, can be seen as a condensed figure for sacred drama itself.

6

Conclusion

Towche me natt, Mary.

—Digby *Mary Magdalene*

LATE MEDIEVAL VERNACULAR drama in England bears witness to the cultural circulation of a Mary Magdalene who brought to the sacred encounter an emphasis on physicality, feminine agency, and experiential authority. Yet the spiritual and ideological example she represented was vulnerable to challenge on all of these counts. The late fifteenth- or early sixteenth-century *Lamentatyon of Mary Magdaleyne*, which Thynne first published as the lost Chaucerian translation of "Origines upon the Maudeleyne," presents one such effort. The *Lamentatyon* is by no means a straightforward translation of Pseudo-Origen's *De Maria Magdalena*; rather, it is a verse critique of the homily's central emphases: its insistence on physicality, appeal to lived experience over scriptural authority, and play with gender boundaries. As an imaginative response to the homily's spiritual and intellectual transgressions, the *Lamentatyon*, as King observes, provides a rejoinder that proceeds without any discernable "theoretical or methodological justification."[1] Such was not the case, however, in the far-more-public debate about the identity of Mary Magdalene that English and continental humanist biblical scholars and churchmen carried on between 1518 and 1521, roughly a decade after the Latin text of *De Maria Magdalena* was published in London (1504–8) and during the very period in which the Digby play is believed to have been copied in its current unique manuscript witness (1515–30).[2] These late medieval appearances of Mary Magdalene in vernacular theater, popular Latin homily, and humanist controversy can be seen as parallel responses to the same set of issues: each addresses the authority of scripture, the significance of feminine religious symbols, and corporeal means of accessing the sacred.

Most immediately at stake in the so-called Magdalene controversy, which Richard Rex terms a "'dry run' for the Reformation debates over scripture, tradition, and authority," was the composite scriptural identity of the symbolic figure who underwrote the dominant hagiographic construction of Mary Magdalene in the Middle Ages.[3] By the early decades of the sixteenth century, Mary Magdalene had been recognized for centuries in the West as the *peccatrix sanctissima* who had renounced worldly pleasures and whose attachment to Jesus mingled erotic and spiritual love. She was the exemplar of contemplative yet passionate devotion who also brought the physicality of feminine flesh to the moment of recognition at the scene of Christ's resurrection. The narrator of *De Maria Magdalena* succinctly articulates this composite identity when he says to the weeping Mary of John 20: "This is Jesus who has withdrawn from you. . . . Once he loved you; once he defended you from the Pharisees [Luke 7:44] and gently justified you to your sister [Luke 10:41]. Once he praised you when you anointed his feet with oil, washed them with tears and wiped them with your hair [Luke 7:47]. . . . Once he sought you and, when you were absent, directed you through your sister to come to him [John 11:28]."[4]

First published in 1518, Jacques Lefèvre d'Étaples's *De Maria Magdalena et Triduo Christi Disceptatio* challenged the tradition of biblical interpretation that had produced the Mary Magdalene of the Origenist homily.[5] Lefèvre employed a humanist reading of scripture's literal and historical senses to maintain that the sinful woman who anointed Christ in Luke 7 and the other Gospels, the Mary Magdalene who had witnessed the Resurrection in all the Gospels, and the sister of Martha and Lazarus were three different women. His critique of the single Magdalene put at issue the very point upon which the saint's story depended. In the lively exchange that Lefèvre inspired (twenty treatises by the early 1520s), humanist biblical scholarship questioned the foundations of Church teaching based on custom (*consuetudo*) and authority (*auctores*), prying apart the three women who comprised the mythic Mary Magdalene and challenging the optimistic synthesis of sinner, lover, and contemplative that was so central to her late medieval identity.[6] In three treatises written within six months of the publication of Lefèvre's *Disceptatio*, John Fisher, bishop of Rochester and chancellor of Cambridge University, provided the most able response to the humanist challenge.[7] Arguing on behalf of a tradition of scriptural interpretation based on the authority and consensus of the entire Church, Fisher understood

that the hermeneutic conflict over Mary Magdalene put at stake important devotional and institutional issues: "I immediately thought of how
many difficulties would confront the whole Church if Lefèvre's opinion
were ever to be accepted. How many authors would have to be rejected,
how many books would have to be changed, how many sermons formerly preached to people would now have to be revoked! And then,
how much uneasiness would arise among the faithful, how many occasions for loss of faith. They will soon doubt other books and narratives,
and finally the mother of us all, the Church, who for so many centuries
has sung and taught the same thing."[8]

Humanist critics made the single Magdalene's infamous sexuality a
special point of contention, wishing to sever its links with her equally
well-known identities as contemplative and divine witness.[9] They expressed revulsion at the way the figure's mythic sexuality polluted—and
confused—the boundaries of the sacred. According to Hufstader, Lefèvre
and Josse Clinchtove were "exaggeratedly" concerned to protect the reputation of the Mary who was Martha's sister, and consequently that of
Martha herself.[10] In his preface to the second edition of Lefèvre's *De
Maria Magdalena* Clinchtove asserted his support for the belief that
"Mary sister of Martha was not that common whore, but a holy, un-
defiled virgin."[11] The conflated identities of the single Magdalene also
confounded Clinchtove's sense of fairness regarding the relationship of
innocence and repented sin, further motivating his desire to distinguish
among the biblical women comprising her. He extolled Mary the contemplative because she was "said never to have sunk into the stains of
vice. Is she not given greater praise for virtue than the one who, after
a fall, is said to have been raised up by the merciful grace of God
and washed from her filth?"[12] Advocating the humanists' position more
crudely, Willibald Pirckheimer condemned those who "snatch" the single Magdalene "from her deliverer Lefèvre and thrust her with most
disgraceful harlots into a stinking brothel—when it would rather be
more becoming in such a doubtful matter to follow the opinion which
approaches closer to piety."[13]

Besides its methodological objections to traditional biblical hermeneutics, the humanists' critique of the single Magdalene also rejected
the conflation of the sexual and the spiritual that she represented, the
figure's *sordes* and *lutum* posing too great a problem for the "opinion
which approaches closer to piety."[14] It is easy to see in this contempt
for the sinner turned saint the vilification of feminine flesh that was

basic to misogynist discourse and to the nascent clerical culture that had influenced Gregory the Great's consolidation of several biblical women in the single Magdalene in the first place. Significantly, humanist biblical scholars of the early sixteenth century inscribed their initial critiques of medieval traditions of scriptural exegesis on the lives and bodies of female saints whose fundamental association with sexuality and whose closeness to Jesus balanced Marian purity with alternative models of feminine holiness. Lefèvre's challenge to the idea of Saint Anne's *trinubium*, or three marriages, which he appended to the second edition of his *Disceptatio*, further illustrates this ideological position.[15] More than traditional misogynist opinion about fleshly feminine pollution was at issue in the humanists' need to purify the contemplative Mary from all taint of sin. Specifically, the question of exactly what was "becoming" to piety, what requirements the practice of piety might present not simply to the fleshly female sinner but sinners in general, also motivated the reformers' critique.

What motivated Lefèvre was a belief "that perfection in holiness is consonant with ethical perfection." Though neither he nor his cohort disputed that Jesus had justified and sanctified the sinner of Luke 7 who washed his feet with her tears and dried them with her hair, they contended that superior holiness, "the realized image of God" in humankind, was not something that could emerge, as the vita of the single Magdalene would have it, in one sudden transformative act. Rather, holiness must be "intrinsic to all that went before." For Lefèvre, this theological point had important philosophical ramifications. He subscribed to the Aristotelian ideal of contemplation as the highest good of human life, a good that could be attained only by the withdrawal of its seeker from external affairs and the rigorous pursuit of intellectual and moral virtue.[16] Contemplation was a discipline that required preparation through pursuit of a hierarchical program of knowledge, beginning with natural philosophy, economics, and ethics and progressing through Aristotle's *Metaphysics*, the reading of scripture, and the church fathers. Then, Lefèvre observes, "Once these studies have purified the mind and disciplined the senses (and provided one has extirpated vice and leads a suitable and upright life), then the generous mind may aspire to scale gradually the heights of contemplation, instructed by Nicholas of Cusa and the divine Dionysius and others like them."[17]

Lefèvre's version of the cognitive ascent to contemplation involves three kinds of knowledge: experience, ratiocination, and intellection.

Experience occupies itself with sense perception; intellection focuses on "divine and eternal things, archetypes in the mind of God"; ratiocination mediates the two, abstracting universals from sense experience. Of these, "only reason and intellect are capable" of true knowledge; "pursuit of divine things by sense and imagination leads to idolatry and error."[18] Long before the Magdalene controversy, Clinchtove had similarly characterized the contemplative ascent in terms that bode ill for the fate of the worldly, penitent, contemplative Mary Magdalene: "Contemplative happiness is defined as that which, when our minds are already purified and joined to the highest beings of nature through the study of wisdom, carries us away by the love of those beings. . . . Through the contemplation of wisdom (the mind must) be joined to the most transcendent, divine, and praiseworthy aspects of being, to which indeed the mind is not joined by nearness or presence in space, but by inward consideration and the raising of the mind to meditating heavenly things."[19] The contemplative ideal espoused by Lefèvre and Clinchtove attenuates emotion and the material realm as a whole, for the things of sense are grounds for error. Not surprisingly, the ideal of pious *otium* fashioned by humanist scholars would deem singularly "unbecoming" the example of the penitent contemplative in feminine flesh whose spiritual successes were founded, not on a rarified ascent to the divine, but on her proximity to and familiarity with the sacred body, love, and pain.

Contemplating the Magdalene controversy from this distance, we may find it difficult to comprehend the percolation of such international academic and religious furor over a saint whose cult had reached its height several centuries earlier. But as the fleshly paragon of interior piety and divinely approved contemplation, the *unica* Magdalene represented larger intellectual, symbolic, and ideological issues for the churchmen and philosophers involved in the controversy. Their debates about the saint illustrate a trait that Peter Brown observes of men in antiquity, but it is equally applicable to these sixteenth-century biblical scholars: "the ingrained tendency . . . to use women 'to think with.'"[20] The humanists and their opponents used Mary Magdalene to think about, and think through, the sexual politics of the traditional and reformed churches, epistemologies of the sacred, the gendering of religious subjectivities, and the proper goals of theology and philosophy. Nor was the scholarly treatise the only venue in which such thinking was expressed. Northern European painters, influenced by the Magdalene controversy, produced new visual images of the saint that do not simply take sides in the debate but rather reinvent it in their own medium, employing ideas about the composite Magdalene's worldliness to problematize the relationship between the religious and the secular in representational art.[21]

The embedding of Mary Magdalene in early sixteenth-century cultural controversy is further complicated by the hybrid intellectual and religious climate in which battles over her identity were fought and by the long-term fortunes of the intellectual positions and ideological differences that the controversy engaged. Lefèvre may have objected to the theological and philosophical implications of the single Magdalene, and to the complementarity of reformed sin and sanctity that her conflated identity espoused, but he was not ill disposed to the idea of feminine spiritual authority.[22] In addition to his scholarly work on Aristotle and his involvement in biblical translation and scriptural exegesis, Lefèvre actively engaged in identifying and promoting the visionary theology of medieval women mystics, including Hildegard of Bingen, Elisabeth of Schönau, and Mechtild of Hackeborn.[23] Defending the authenticity of female revelations on the basis of patristic authority, Lefèvre found in the mystics models of Christian eloquence, moral instruction, and divine illumination that supported his search for a rarified, otherworldly contemplation and his belief "that piety was a simple, affective wisdom rather than a syllogistic science."[24] Significantly, Lefèvre shared his interest in feminine mystical revelations with his most important opponent in the Magdalene controversy, John Fisher, who exhibited a hybrid religious sensibility of his own. Although Fisher's theological writings consistently invoked the authority of scriptural, patristic, and papal traditions, they also appealed to the writings of Mechtild, Hildegard, Elisabeth of Schönau, and Bridget of Sweden.[25] Such hybridity was characteristic of a group of educated, elite clerics like Fisher and his counterparts at Syon and Sheen, who were drawn simultaneously to an ascetic, monastic piety and to the new learning, seeing the potential for renewal of the Church through that learning and the power of the printing press.[26]

Lefèvre eventually abandoned his work on the mystics, devoting more than the last decade of his life to the study of scripture.[27] But Fisher remained deeply invested in the theology and hermeneutic traditions that he had defended on behalf of Mary Magdalene. As Duffy notes, this position probably explains his receptivity to the Holy Maid

or Nun of Kent, Elizabeth Barton, the twenty-eight-year-old Benedictine nun, visionary, and prophet who opposed Henry VIII's effort to
divorce Katherine of Aragon in order to marry Anne Boleyn.[28] Barton's
opposition to the royal divorce was the logical outgrowth of an eight-
year ministry, through which she sought to counter the influence of
reformist teaching by emphasizing the virtues of the sacraments; the
importance of traditional cultic practices, such as worship of the saints,
prayers for the dead, and pilgrimages; and the Church's theological
authority and privileges.[29] In the eyes of the authorities, however, these
orthodox religious positions took on dangerous political overtones when
Barton's revelations articulated prophecies that foresaw Henry's loss of
his kingdom. In April 1534 she was hanged at Tyburn along with a number of her supporters for treason and inciting insurrection.

Barton's virtual disappearance, until recently, from the scene of this
revolutionary moment in English political and religious culture attests
to successful efforts by sixteenth-century authorities and reformers to
erase her from the historical record, a success that is reflected in the total
suppression of the books and pamphlets in which accounts of her life
as well as her revelations are known to have circulated.[30] But it is clear
that before her ill-fated involvement in Henry's divorce crisis, Barton
found a receptive audience for female spiritual and visionary authority
in early sixteenth-century England. Her evolution from defender of
orthodoxy to political opponent of the king was facilitated by a continental tradition of women's political prophecy, associated especially
with Bridget of Sweden and Catherine of Siena, of which Barton is the
sole English representative.[31] The sermon preached against her at Paul's
Cross in November 1533 reports that her somatic revelations were attended by several thousand people.[32] Her execution terminated a popular visionary career that, besides putting her into contact with papal
legates, influential Brigittine and Carthusian communities at Syon and
Sheen, and even London merchants and their wives, had brought powerful figures such as Thomas More and John Fisher to her defense.[33]

According to the official government records that are now the principal source of information about Barton's religious and political
involvements, Fisher and Barton shared more than similar opinions
about the royal divorce. The so-called great book of Barton's revelations, compiled by her confessor and advisor, Dr. Edward Bocking, is
reported to have contained heavenly communications that the visionary received from Mary Magdalene.[34] Although Protestant propaganda

subsequently claimed that the illuminated letter that was the source of some of these revelations was the work of a monk named Hawkhurst, Fisher appears to have accepted them, since Cromwell reproached him for "sending his chaplain to her on 'idle questions, as of the three Magdalens.'"[35]

In sarcastically linking the Nun of Kent and Mary Magdalene, the polemical literature produced in the context of Barton's demise invokes a legacy of reformist biblical hermeneutics that looks back to Fisher's early involvement with the Magdalene controversy. Unfortunately, there is no record of what Fisher might have learned from Barton about the identity of the Magdalene. Still, the Protestant propaganda provides some idea of the role Mary Magdalene played in Barton's visionary and spiritual project, which seems to have been to reinforce her positions on religious issues and mirror her visionary insight. In the 1533 "Sermon against the Holy Maid of Kent and Her Adherents," which draws on material from Barton's "great book," Mary Magdalene is credited with advising a London widow to dedicate money hidden by her dead husband to the purchase of church ornaments and, more important, with informing Barton about the outcome of one of her petitions involving a certain soul: "'It hath pleased my Lord God that, through your petition, ye have by the mercy of my said Lord saved the soul of him which was sometime my servant from eternal damnation, that he should have gone unto, if ye had not helped him . . . and now he is in eternal joy and everlasting salvation.'"[36] Mary Magdalene's prescience in this matter would hardly have seemed irregular to Barton, who is reported to have prophesied the eternal fate of Henry VIII himself.[37] Barton's visionary experience imitated that of her sacred correspondent; in one of her visions she was miraculously transported to a mass at Calais, where she received the Eucharist from an angel who took it from the hand of a priest about to give it to Henry VIII.[38] For all her adherence to traditional religious beliefs and practices, Barton's spiritual example pushed at the limits of orthodoxy in other ways. Less than a year before her death for treason, Henry Man, the prior of Sheen, "declared that the knowledge of her pious works was more edifying to his soul than anything he had read in Holy Scripture"—not an insignificant endorsement, coming from a member of the university educated, intellectual, and spiritual elite who dominated the leadership of the Carthusian and Brigittine orders in the early sixteenth century.[39] Like the literal, corporeal challenge that Mary Magdalene's experience presents to the allegorical hermeneutic in Pseudo-Origen's homily, Man's privileging of Barton's "pious works" over scripture risks preempting biblical authority in favor of the woman's more local wisdom.

Barton's ultimate fortunes in the conflict over Henry VIII's divorce set in stark relief the difference between abstract clerical disagreements fought in print about theological and philosophical dimensions of the identity of Mary Magdalene, and official political suppression of female spiritual authority that challenged powers of the state and royal will. While the virtual erasure of Barton's prophetic religious activity from histories of English politics of the 1520s and 1530s bears witness to the long-term impact of that suppression, it also points to the vitality and threat of a feminine visionary authority that could call up such zealous, effective opposition.[40] As moments of ideological struggle, the Magdalene controversy and the affair of the Holy Nun of Kent illustrate the special problem that feminine spirituality and authority—whether legendary, symbolic, or historically real—could pose to dominant religious and political institutions on the eve of reformation. John Fisher well understood that the Magdalene controversy portended the demise of the Church as he knew it. The humanists' effort to uncover the "authentic" identities of the biblical women comprising the *unica Magdalena* signaled the fracturing of the overdetermined symbol who was identified not only with the continuity of the erotic and the divine, as King points out, but with the range of issues that deeply animated English religious drama during the same period: the sacralizing of the material realm, the role of gender in salvation history, and the scriptural foundations of women's religious and evangelical authority.[41] It is hardly coincidental that the efforts of reformist thinkers to attenuate the corporeal dimensions of religious belief and spiritual experience found fertile sites of critique in both sacred drama and the Magdalene figure.

The sixteenth-century Magdalene controversy is sometimes cited with approbation by contemporary feminist historians of religion and women in early Christianity. In these discussions Lefèvre d'Étaples emerges interestingly as a champion of the Magdalene's true identity who tried to "clear the slur" from her name and was "excommunicated for his pains."[42] Sympathy for the humanist position on the part of some scholars stems from a like effort to pry the "authentic" Mary Magdalene from a troubling association with female sexual sin that was the long legacy of Gregory's conflation of Luke's sinner, the woman named Mary Magdalene who witnessed Christ's resurrection in all the Gospels, and

Mary of Bethany. Whereas the humanists wished to secure the purity of Mary of Bethany as a contemplative ideal in the service of an other-worldly piety, contemporary scholars seek to establish the purity of Mary-Magdalene in order to reclaim her from a fifteen-hundred-year-old mistaken identity as a fallen woman, recuperate her apostolic role as "disciple of Christ and herald of the 'New Life,'" and restore to the biblical figure the power and position that the Gospels accorded her.[43] But Lefèvre and the other humanists were hardly intent on distancing Mary Magdalene from the sexual taint of female flesh, and their views of the three Marys reaffirm traditional misogynist understandings of female sexuality. By asserting Mary Magdalene's difference from Luke's penitent sinner, the contemporary recuperation of the historical Magdalene in its own way reinforces the reformers' perception that the attachment of female sexuality and eros to holiness can only be unsuitable—with important consequences for the relationships between flesh and spirit, femininity and divinity.

What is missed or marginalized in these originary appeals to the authentic Mary Magdalene is the theological and affective complexity that is exceptionally well articulated in the late medieval dramatic versions of the saint that we have examined. The conflation of the Last Supper and the anointing of Christ in the house of Simon the Pharisee in N-Town *Passion Play I* startlingly results in Mary Magdalene's simultaneous creation as intimate of Jesus, penitent, and apostle, an identity that is reinforced by the dramatist's careful inclusion of Mary Magdalene among the disciples in the episodes extending from the Last Supper through the arrest of Jesus. In the Digby saint play, Jesus similarly links Mary Magdalene's apostolate to her identity as the sinful woman when he announces:

> Butt now of my servantt I remembyr þe kendnesse;
> Wyth heuenly masage I cast me to vesyte;
> Raphaell, myn angell in my syte,
> To Mary Mavdleyn decende in a whyle,
> Byd her passe þe se be my myth,
> And sey she xall converte þe land of Marcyll. (1366–71)

Recalling his earlier praise of Mary Magdalene's gesture in the house of Simon ("She wassheth my fete and dothe me servyse" [667]), Jesus here suggests that the great spiritual authority he is about to confer on

Mary—"Alle þe land xall be techyd alonly be the" [1381]—is a direct
reward for the kindness his "servantt" showed him there. Mary Magdalene's identity as apostle may have been founded in her witness to the
Resurrection, but Jacobus's *Legenda aurea* had further sanctioned the
notion that her legendary role as preacher in Marseilles stemmed from
her intimate contact with Jesus at the anointing: "No wonder, that the
mouth which had pressed such pious and beautiful kisses on the Savior's
feet should breath forth the perfume of the word of God more profusely
than others could." This "oral-pedal" connection, as Delany notes,
underwrites the saint's evolution from lover to preacher—and a parallel
evolution from body to Word—as "erotic kissing [gives way] to pious
kissing and is finally transformed by contact with Jesus into the vehicle
of gospel."[44]

Contemporary ideological critiques of Gregory's composite Magdalene correctly point to the purposes that this figure fulfilled for a burgeoning ecclesiastical hierarchy seeking to establish its authority and
contain the feminine spiritual power hinted at in the Gnostic gospels.
But local instances of the symbolism of the late medieval Magdalene in
the N-Town and Digby plays also reveal the contradictions and impre-
cisions of symbolic formation itself, the ways in which symbols, as Beckwith states, "do not so much express meaning as encourage the creative
attribution of multiple meanings to themselves."[45] These late medieval
symbolic incarnations of Mary Magdalene complicate the identification
with sins of the flesh that resulted from Gregory's clerical agenda for the
figure, showing the active cultural making of meaning that she inspired.
Conflating intimacy, contemplation, and evangelism, late medieval versions of the *unica Magdalena* bring flesh and materiality to a religion
of presence, a religion that placed feminine bodies at its two defining
moments as agent and witness of divinity. Like Christ and his virgin
mother, Mary Magdalene is an apt symbol for this religion of Word and
flesh and, also like her sacred counterparts, a rich vehicle for examining
the vexed yet dynamic relationship between the two.[46]

Late medieval East Anglia's feminine religious culture and commitment to sacred drama coalesce in the figure of Mary Magdalene. This
book has detailed symbolic, social, and textual features of that culture,
and it has argued that East Anglian drama, especially the Digby saint
play, provides crucial access to it. The arguments advanced in this book
facilitate an expanded view of the ideological and social work of vernacular theater, a learned theater of theological argument in which the

medium itself is implicated in the theater's competing profane and sacred investments. Evidence examined in this book produces a newly detailed picture of the ways that medieval dramatic texts actively questioned fundamental cultural assumptions about gender in the secular and sacred realms. This investigation of theater, gender, and religion in the late medieval drama of saints also has established the deeply shared interests of medieval English theater and a wide range of spiritual texts, with important implications for current conceptions of medieval vernacular religion, English literature, and literary history.

It is felicitous and significant that late medieval East Anglian texts that are also major, even unique, documents in English literary history repeatedly employ Mary Magdalene to probe central questions about late medieval religious experience, representing the challenges and opportunities that the saint's feminine spiritual authority and defining corporeal identity posed for theologies of Redemption, the institutional church, and Christian society on the eve of the Reformation. In both the Short and Long Texts of her *Revelation*, Julian of Norwich invokes Mary Magdalene's scripturally authentic witness to the Crucifixion as a touchstone for the affective yearnings that provide the basis for her daring theological explorations. Margery Kempe makes Mary Magdalene her sacred companion and alter ego, appropriating the saint's closeness to Jesus, sinful past, renounced sexual nature, and reconstituted virginity as her own, and basking in the light of her borrowed sanctity. Osbern Bokenham gives the life of Mary Magdalene the central position in his all-woman hagiography and exploits her legendary and symbolic complexity to support his arguments for a female apostolate and a feminine genealogy of secular rule in fifteenth-century England. In the Macro and Digby morality play *Wisdom*, the corporeal experience of Mary Magdalene shadows that of Anima, the soul whose fallen spiritual state is paradoxically imaged in a bodily expulsion of demons that mirrors the saint's own purgation. The compiler-reviser of N-Town *Passion Play I* includes Mary Magdalene at the Last Supper not only in an effort to establish her apostolic authority along with that of the other disciples but also as part of a larger pattern of alteration and interpolation that likewise brought the *Mary Play* and the *Assumption of the Virgin* into that compilation, as if in a late medieval effort to write a dramatic version of salvation history that gives equal time to its major feminine interventions. The "cycle" that emerges from this effort may stand out among its counterparts because of its feminine spiritual interests. Yet this feature also marks its congruence with other East Anglian dramatic initiatives to juxtapose feminine and masculine foundations and structures of authority, such as that enacted in the competing examples of Saint Anne and Herod in the Digby *Killing of the Children*.[47]

In its sheer encyclopedic scope and symbolic complexity, the Digby *Mary Magdalene* epitomizes the interests and commitments of these dramatic and nondramatic texts, reinforcing their efforts to acknowledge Mary Magdalene's privileged role in traditional religion and bearing witness at the same time to their impulse to push at the margins of religious and social orthodoxies. Seen through the lens of the Digby saint play and the feminine religious culture of the region, these other East Anglian Magdalene texts conduct a sustained cultural dialogue—in visionary literature, spiritual autobiography, hagiography, and drama—about the contributions of feminine spiritual experience, authority, and corporeality to late medieval theology and religious practice. Mary Magdalene is the organizing symbol who presides over much of this dialogue, exposing its assumptions and risks, bearing witness, through her own semiotic multivalence, to the contested, overdetermined symbolic systems of late medieval religion, and giving East Anglian religious culture on the eve of the Reformation this distinctive signature.

The issues explored in this book about the late medieval Magdalene still press on the Western cultural and historical imagination, paralleling the longevity of the saint herself as a subject for scholarly investigation, religious devotion, and aesthetic representation. While I was working on this book, two highly successful commercial feature films, both nominated for Academy Awards, underscored this connection for me. Set in a brutally strict Calvinist community in the Scotland of the 1970s, *Breaking the Waves* tells the story of a simple but paradoxically wise young woman who talks to God and whose shattering personal experience explores the relationship between sexuality, fleshly mortification, and sanctity.[48] The would-be mystic of *Breaking the Waves*, whose sexual excesses are both penance and pathway to the miraculous, is a prostitute saint. If *Breaking the Waves* frames religious issues in distinctly sexual terms, the film *Elizabeth* frames sexual issues in religious terms.[49] Focusing on the tumultuous religious and political culture in the years leading up to and following the coronation of Elizabeth I in 1558, the film depicts the young queen's struggle to establish political authority in an intensely divided religious culture, a political authority that is, moreover, deeply implicated in her personal, marital situation. Elizabeth consolidated that authority, the film suggests, by shrewdly apprehending her culture's psychic longing for the powerful, chaste protectoress that it lost when the Reformation established a religion in which the Virgin Mary played no part. In a gesture that distinctly recalls the medieval opinion that virginity is not a physical state but a cultural construction that can be claimed and deployed for important social and political ends, Elizabeth makes herself a virgin queen.[50] These historically specific images of Bess the saintly whore and Elizabeth the virgin queen inflect contemporary representations of gender's relationship to religious culture with the same questions that the late medieval Magdalene posed for clergy and laity, governments and communities, ecclesiastical authorities and pious women: can sexuality and sanctity coexist in one being? can the flesh provide access to God? is virginity a physical state or a spiritual condition? is feminine spiritual authority grounded in a fleshly identity? As the opportunities and dangers afforded by the prospect of redrawing the boundaries of sacred and profane continue to claim our attention, the example of these late medieval Mary Magdalenes remains instructive.

Abbreviations

BMK	*The Book of Margery Kempe*, ed. Meech and Allen
CCMET	*Cambridge Companion to Medieval English Theatre*, ed. Beadle
CD	*Comparative Drama*
CELMM	*A Critical Edition of the Legend of Mary Magdalena from Caxton's "Golden Legende" of 1483*, ed. Mycoff
EDAM	Early Drama, Art, and Music
EETS	Early English Text Society
e.s.	extra series
ELH	*English Literary History*
JEGP	*Journal of English and Germanic Philology*
JEH	*Journal of Ecclesiastical History*
JMEMS	*Journal of Medieval and Early Modern Studies*
JMRS	*Journal of Medieval and Renaissance Studies*
LMRP	*The Late Medieval Religious Plays of Bodleian MSS Digby 133 and e Museo 160*, ed. Baker, Murphy, and Hall
MÆ	*Medium Ævum*
MEFRM	*Mélanges de l'École Française de Rome. Moyen Age*
MET	*Medieval English Theatre*
MLQ	*Modern Language Quarterly*
MS	*Mediaeval Studies*
NA	*Norfolk Archaeology*
n.s.	new series
o.s.	original series
PL	*Patrologiae cursus completus: Series latina*, 221 vols., ed. J.-P. Migne
RWMEA	*Religious Women in Medieval East Anglia*, by Gilchrist and Oliva
RORD	*Research Opportunities in Renaissance Drama*
SAC	*Studies in the Age of Chaucer*
SP	*Studies in Philology*
s.s.	supplementary series
STC	*Short-Title Catalogue of Books Printed in England . . . 1475–1640*, ed. Pollard and Redgrave

Notes

Introduction

1. This formulation is adapted from Miri Rubin's description of the function of the symbolic in religious cultural systems. See *Corpus Christi*, 5–10. See also Beckwith's discussion of the function of the symbolic in culture and society; *Christ's Body*, 1–6.

2. This usage does not imply an argument about periodization. I am largely sympathetic to the concept of an "early English" drama that incorporates the "medieval" because it has the advantage of more accurately representing the temporal frame in which much "medieval" drama was produced, that is, well into the second half of the sixteenth century. Beadle discusses aspects of nomenclature in his "Preface" to *CCMET*, xiii. Subsuming the medieval within a more broadly conceived early English drama, however, also has its drawbacks. Although the theater traditionally designated as medieval may gain some cultural capital by being severed from the pejorative connotations of that term, the concept of an "early English" drama all too easily elides the differences of medieval forms, practices, and symbolic systems. The difficulty of navigating the historical divide is noted by Marcus, "Tudor Drama, 1490–1567," 132–34.

3. Ashley, "Popular Culture." See also Clopper's discussion of the philology of medieval dramatic and theatrical terminology in *Drama, Play, and Game*, 1–24.

4. Clopper, "*Communitas*: The Play of Saints."

5. For examples of the former, see Norland, *Drama in Early Tudor Britain*, 3–15; and Twycross, "Theatricality of Medieval English Plays."

6. Watson includes plays among the kinds of writing communicating "theological information to an audience" that may be embraced by the catchall term. See "Censorship and Cultural Change," 823–24, n. 4. Important recent studies approaching Middle English dramatic texts in these terms include Beckwith, *Signifying God*; Nissé, "Reversing Discipline"; and idem, "Staged Interpretations."

7. On the coherence of East Anglian dramatic traditions, see Coldewey, "East Anglian Tradition"; and Scherb, *Staging Faith*.

8. Gibson, *Theater of Devotion*.

9. See Coletti, "'*Paupertas est donum Dei*,'" 372–73.

10. For recent interventions in the study of the relationship between medieval and Renaissance drama, see Emmerson, "Contextualizing Performance"; O'Connell, "Shakespeare and the Mysteries"; and Womack, "Shakespeare and the Sea of Stories."

11. For an innovative account of the significance of that vernacular tradition, see Wogan-Browne et al., eds., *Idea of the Vernacular*.

12. See Lerer, *Chaucer and His Readers*; Watson, "Politics of Middle English Writing," 345–52; and essays by Cannon ("Monastic Productions"); Lerer ("Caxton") and Cummings ("Reformed Literature") in Wallace, *Cambridge History*. Knapp discusses the use of genealogical and filial tropes in literary histories; see "Hoccleve and Chaucer Revisited," 247–49. Cannon argues that the laureate narrative was reproduced in linguistic histories of English and established as authoritative in lexical enterprises such as the *Oxford English Dictionary* and *Middle English Dictionary*. See "Making of Chaucer's English."

13. Summit, *Lost Property*, 11.

14. Cannon, "Monastic Productions," 341. See also Wogan-Browne et al., "Introduction," *Idea of the Vernacular*, xiii–xvi. From its inception the laureate account of English literary production was complicated by the cultural circumstances that attended its rise to preeminence. Lawton maps instances of resistance to the laureate narrative on the part of the fifteenth-century writers who perpetrated it; see "Dullness and the Fifteenth Century." Recent efforts to situate Chaucer in relation to "a much wider movement towards the mother tongue" in the late fourteenth century put forward alternative authorial groupings based on common interventions in vernacular textual practice, for example, privileging Chaucer's connection with writers such as Langland and Julian of Norwich rather than his role as progenitor of a line of English poets. This characterization of the Chaucerian project underscores the poet's participation in "political and ideological contexts," such as the debate on Bible translation, from which his principal achievements were once considered largely independent. See Olson, "Geoffrey Chaucer," 580–81.

15. The implications of a medieval English literary history seen from the perspective of the vernacular are surveyed by Evans et al., "The Notion of Vernacular Theory"; and Watson, "Politics of Middle English Writing."

16. Although Lerer acknowledges that his arguments about fifteenth-century England's genealogical literary history necessarily exclude other manifestations of the period's literary culture, his catalog of what is left out (the Scottish Chaucerians, Malory, monastic and courtly historiography, and the "drama of the northern towns") still elides most of the texts mentioned here. See *Chaucer and His Readers*, 5. The two donor portraits illustrated on the cover of *The Idea of the Vernacular* effectively depict late medieval writing's parallel laureate and nonlaureate traditions. One portrait, a rare presentation miniature involving two women, shows the gentry widow Joan Luyt presenting a copy of the *Hours of the Guardian Angel* (Liverpool Cathedral, MS Radcliff 6) to Elizabeth Woodville, Edward IV's queen. The other donor portrait shows Lydgate offering a copy of the *Fall of Princes* (Huntington Library, MS 268), probably to Humphrey Duke of Gloucester. As the editors note (xi–xii), despite differences of gender, the two donors and their patrons occupy analogous positions with respect to their social and cultural relationships and the textual occasion.

17. On the gendered hermeneutics of the vernacular, see Copeland, "Why Women Can't Read." On the feminization of lay reading, see Gillespie, "*Lukyng*

in haly bukes." On the role played by gender in the commissioning and address-ing of texts to audiences, see Millett, "English Recluses"; and Bartlett, *Male Authors, Female Readers*.

18. For instance, Nissé contends that Hoccleve promoted a gendered liter-ary model that found in masculine chivalric practice a paradigm for reading and writing capable of countering the feminized vernacular valorized by Lollard translation and interpretation. See "Gender, Heresy, and Hoccleve's Literary Politics."

19. Warren, *Spiritual Economies*, 134–62; Delany, *Impolitic Bodies*, 44–69 and 127–59. The relationship between Lydgate and Bokenham as hagiographers is also discussed by Winstead, *Virgin Martyrs*, 112–46.

20. See Moore, "Patrons of Letters"; Beadle, "Literary Geography"; Hanna and Edwards, "Ellesmere Chaucer"; Delany, *Impolitic Bodies*, 3–28; and Edwards, "Lydgate Manuscripts." Coldewey links traditions of East Anglian drama to larger patterns of literary production in the region. See "East Anglian Tradition."

21. An inventory of the books of John Paston drawn up before 1474 states: "Item, a boke off Troylus whyche William Bra [. . .] hathe hadde neer x yer & lent it to Da[. . .] Wyngfelde, & jbi ego vidi." See *Paston Letters and Papers*, 1: 517. For Anne's bequest of the *Othea*, see *Testamenta Eboracensia*, 4: 152. Anne's ownership of *Speculum Devotorum* is noted by Lester, "Books of a Fifteenth-Century English Gentleman," 217, n. 89. For discussions of MS Harley 4012, see Wilson, "Middle English Manuscript," 299–301; and Dutton, "Piety, Politics, and Persona."

22. On Baret and Lydgate, see Gibson, "Bury St. Edmunds," 72–73, n. 103. For Baret's bequest to Bokenham, see Tymms, ed., *Wills and Inventories*, 35. On the Drurys, Baret, and the Ellesmere Manuscript, see Hanna and Edwards, "Ellesmere Chaucer," 15–19.

23. Gibson, *Theater of Devotion*, 67–106.

24. Hanna and Edwards, "Ellesmere Chaucer," 18; Tymms, ed., *Wills and Inventories*, 35.

25. See Hanna and Edwards, "Ellesmere Chaucer," 16–17. For a discussion of Suffolk ownership of Arundel 119 and speculation that it might have been commissioned by Alice Chaucer, wife of William de la Pole and granddaughter of the poet, see Meale, "Case of Alice Chaucer," 92–93.

26. See Hanna and Edwards, "Ellesmere Chaucer," 18; and Beadle, "Monk Thomas Hyngham's Hand." The trail leading from MS Arundel 119 through Suffolk ownership and ending with East Anglian dramatic texts takes a final interesting twist with the argument that Duke William and his wife, Alice Chaucer, are the objects of the contemporary political satire of *Wisdom*. See Marshall, "Satirising of the Suffolks in *Wisdom*."

27. Beadle, "Preface," *CCMET*, xiv. For an analysis of the archival effort in early drama studies, see Coletti, "Reading REED"; and the issue of *MET* (17 [1995]) devoted to this topic.

28. See Beadle, "Bases for Critical Enquiry"; Badir, "Resurrection at Bev-erly Minster"; Ashley, "Popular Culture"; Beckwith, *Signifying God*; and Clop-per, *Drama, Play, and Game*.

29. Ashley, "Sponsorship, Reflexivity, and Resistance," 12. See also Sponsler's seminal "Culture of the Spectator." Case studies of the variable cultural reception of dramatic performances include Emmerson, "Contextualizing Performance"; and a seventeenth-century example analyzed by Chartier, "From Court Festivity to City Spectators."

30. Tydeman, *English Medieval Theater*, 8–9.

31. See also Nissé's discussion of the York plays' affinities with heretical discourses of ecclesiology and exegesis; "Staged Interpretations." The capacity of medieval dramatic texts to critique dominant systems of belief is analyzed by Emmerson, "Eliding the Medieval," 29; and Sanok, "Performing Feminine Sanctity."

32. Gibson presents the Bury St. Edmunds hypothesis in *Theater of Devotion*, 107–35. See also her related studies, "Bury St. Edmunds"; and "Play of *Wisdom*." Although aspects of the Bury hypothesis have been challenged, Gibson's argument about the affinities of monastic values and practices with the East Anglian environment for cultural performances is beyond dispute. For other evidence of dramatic and festive performances in late medieval East Anglia, see Beadle, "Medieval Drama of East Anglia"; idem, "Plays and Playing at Thetford"; Wright, "Medieval Theatre in East Anglia"; idem, "Community Theatre"; Sugano, "N-Town Playbooks"; Galloway and Wasson, eds., *Records of Plays and Players*; and Galloway, ed., *Records of Early English Drama: Norwich*.

33. Cf. a recent groundbreaking effort to situate the Towneley plays in sixteenth-century Yorkshire. See Palmer, "Recycling 'The Wakefield Cycle.'" The only East Anglian plays that can be tied to specific records of performance are the early sixteenth-century Norwich Grocers' Plays. See Davis, "Introduction," *Non-Cycle Plays*, xxii–xxxvi; and Clopper, *Drama, Play, and Game*, 155–57.

34. Although my analysis of drama's dialogue with contemporary religious texts and practices assumes its reception by audiences whose horizons of expectation include familiarity with the terms of such a dialogue, I have tried to refrain from speculative commentary on audience response.

35. See Strohm, *Theory and the Premodern Text*, xv.

36. See Beadle, "York Cycle." Boehnen notes that the "lens of close textual analysis" is "precisely the experience most alien to our imagined medieval audience"; "Aesthetics of 'Sprawling' Drama," 327. On the relative importance of dramatic text and spectacle, see Runnalls, "Were They Listening or Watching?" For a recent discussion of the "protean quality of medieval plays" with respect to their manuscript and performative contexts, see Symes, "Early Vernacular Plays."

37. The Chester plays survive in five complete copies, all the work of sixteenth- and early seventeenth-century antiquarians. In addition to the complete version of the play in the Macro manuscript, a substantial fragment of *Wisdom* appears in Bodleian Library MS Digby 133.

38. Bevington, *Medieval Drama*, 967. The attribution of the Chester plays to Higden appears in the Post-Reformation Banns of the cycle; *Chester Mystery Cycle* (ed. Mills), 4, line 6. Colophons to the two extant biblical plays from Coventry attribute the correction and recent translation of the plays to Robert Croo in 1534. See *Two Coventry Corpus Christi Plays*, 109, 148. On the authorship of Middle English dramatic texts, see Clopper, "Civic Religious Drama," 115–16.

The most frequently noted owners of Middle English plays are the monk Hyngham, who laid claim to the Macro texts of *Mankind* and *Wisdom*, and Myles Blomefylde, who wrote his name or initials on three of the dramatic texts in Bodleian Library MS. Digby 133. See Beadle, "Monk Thomas Hyngham's Hand"; and *LMRP*, xii–xv.

39. Womack, "Medieval Drama," 8, 4.

40. Spiegel here invokes Pierre Machery's idea that "history functions as the text's unconscious." See *The Past as Text*, 35.

41. Strohm, *Theory and the Premodern Text*, 110.

42. Twycross, "Theatricality of Medieval English Plays," 54.

43. Beadle, "York Cycle," 86, 100. For a discussion of distinctions between reading and listening as modes of reception by medieval audiences, see Evans, "Addressing and Positioning the Audience," 113–114.

44. Beadle, "York Cycle," 91–92; and idem, "Bases for Critical Enquiry," 106–7, 110–111.

45. Mills, "Chester Cycle," 115.

46. See Henry, "Dramatic Function"; and Meredith, "Performance, Verse, and Occasion." Commenting on the importance of knowing contexts of dramatic performance, Meredith concedes: "If the context does not exist, the only way to lift the play off the page may be the text itself" (205).

47. One anonymous reader proposed the alternative metaphor of "concentric circles" to describe the rhetorical structure of this book's arguments, placing the Digby saint play in the central circle, East Anglian spirituality in the middle, and medieval religious culture in the outside circle. Whatever metaphor is most apt, I am grateful to this reader for calling my attention to the rhetorical complexity of this book's overlapping arguments.

48. The following is only a partial list: Voaden, *God's Words, Women's Voices*; idem, ed., *Prophets Abroad*; Wogan-Browne et al., eds., *Medieval Women: Texts and Contexts in Late Medieval Britain*; Renevey and Whitehead, eds., *Writing Religious Women*; Wogan-Browne, *Saints' Lives and Women's Literary Culture*; Winstead, *Virgin Martyrs*; and Warren, *Spiritual Economies*. Wogan-Browne's wide-ranging bibliographical essay provides an immensely useful account of the state of the field. See "'Reading Is Good Prayer.'"

49. Other important studies include Saxer, *Le culte de Marie-Madeleine en occident*; Garth, *Saint Mary Magdalene in Medieval Literature*; Malvern, *Venus in Sackcloth*; Pinto-Mathieu, *Marie Madeleine dans la littérature du Moyen Age*; and three important collections: Duperray, ed., *Marie Madeleine dans la mystique, les arts et les lettres*; Geoffroy and Montandon, eds., *Marie Madeleine: Figure mythique*; and an issue of *MEFRM* 104 (1992). See also the comprehensive literature review by Jansen, *Making of the Magdalen*, 11–14.

50. I take the term "unruly diachrony" from Strohm. See *Theory and the Premodern Text*, 93. For other considerations of the relationship of the study of the medieval past to present concerns, see Dinshaw, *Getting Medieval*; and Watson, "Desire for the Past."

51. See Murphy, *Word According to Eve*; and Schaberg, "How Mary Magdalene Became a Whore."

52. For discussion of some of these contemporary manifestations, such as Kazantzakis's *Last Temptation of Christ* and *Jesus Christ Superstar*, see Haskins, *Myth and Metaphor*, 366–400. On August 2, 2003, a Google search of "Mary Magdalene" yielded thousands of hits, including websites dedicated to elaborating the saint's complex meanings and demonstrating her relevance to the contemporary world. See, for example, < www.magdalene.org >. My completion of this book has serendipitously coincided with Mary Magdalene's coming to prominence in American popular culture. In Dan Brown's best-selling thriller, *The DaVinci Code*, the murder mystery revolves around the identity and authority of the biblical Magdalene. Other works by Margaret George (a novel, *Mary, Called Magdalene*) and Margaret Starbird (*The Woman with the Alabaster Jar*) have also claimed the attention of feature writers for the *Washington Post* (see Roxanne Roberts, "The Mysteries of Mary Magdalene," July 20, 2003, section D: 1, 5). For now, for me, unpacking the cultural significance of this current attention to the biblical and legendary saint must remain the focus of a separate endeavor.

Chapter 1

1. The relevant scriptural passages are Matt. 27:56–61 and 28; Mark 15–16; Luke 7:37, 8:1–4, and 10:38–42; and John 19:25 and 20:1–10. For discussions of the processes by which Mary Magdalene assumed this composite biblical and legendary identity, see Jansen, *Making of the Magdalen*, 18–46; Haskins, *Myth and Metaphor*, 3–32; and Malvern, *Venus in Sackcloth*, 16–29. Gregory's foundational construction appears in *Homily 33*, *XL Homiliarum in Evangelia*, PL 76: 1238–46.

2. "I yeve to þe Chirche of Seynt Stevyn my legende Auri to be scheued in some deske in þe qwer for them þt will rede þ[erin] and lerne." See Harrod, "Early Wills in the Norwich Registries," 335; and Tanner, *Church in Late Medieval Norwich*, 39.

3. *CELMM*, 95–96. Throughout this book I cite Mycoff's edition of Jacobus's vita because Caxton's text is roughly contemporary with the Digby play. On the late medieval popularity of the *Legenda aurea*, see Seybolt, "Fifteenth-Century Editions"; idem, "*Legenda Aurea*"; and Reames, "*Legenda Aurea*", 4.

4. *CELMM*, 40–41; Clopper, *Drama, Play, and Game*, 240–43; and Grantley, "Source of the Digby *Mary Magdalen*." Middle English versions of the life of Mary Magdalene also appear in the Auchinleck MS (Edin. Advoc. Libr.), the *South English Legendary*, the *Northern Homily Cycle*, the *Scottish Legendary*, Osbern Bokenham's *Legendys of Hooly Wummen*, John Mirk's *Festial*, the *Speculum Sacerdotale*, the *Gilte Legende* (a Middle English translation of the *Légende dorée*, a French version of Jacobus's legendary), and the *Golden Legend* published by Caxton in 1483 (a translation based on Jacobus's Latin text, the *Legénde dorée*, and the *Gilte Legende*). For a list of manuscripts containing these texts and printed editions, see D'Evelyn, "Saints' Legends," 610–11.

5. On the uses of medieval sacred biography for contemporary social commentary and critique, see Staley, *Dissenting Fictions*, 39–82.

6. Malvern, *Venus in Sackcloth*, 100–101.

7. See Young, *Drama of the Medieval Church*, 1: 443–44 (Tours); and 2: 432–438 (Benediktbeuren). For overviews of Mary Magdalene's appearances in medieval drama, see Kane, "Mary of Magdala"; Garth, *Mary Magdalene in Medieval Literature*; Chauvin, "Role of Mary Magdalene"; Malvern, *Venus in Sackcloth*; and Pinto-Mathieu, *La Madeleine dans la littérature du Moyen Age*, 189–279. For a list of influential twelfth-century commentaries on Mary Magdalene's witness to Christ's resurrection, see Saxer, "L'homélie latine," 671–672.

8. Brief references to performances involving Mary Magdalene also appear in the early sixteenth-century account books (1506–7) for Magdalen College, Oxford. See Alton, "Academic Drama in Oxford," 46. In 1504 a bequest of red damask and silk mantles was made to the church of St. Mary Magdalene, Taunton, Somerset, for the "'Mary Magdaleyn play' at the sepulcher service." See Lancashire, *Dramatic Texts and Records*, no. 1435. Lancashire also corrects (no. 1793) the mistaken attribution of a Mary Magdalene play to Thetford Priory, Norfolk.

9. D'Ancona, ed., *Sacre Rappresentazione*, 1: 391–425. On the uniqueness of the Digby play, see Chauvin, "Role of Mary Magdalene," 159–63. *La vie de Marie Magdaleine*, an early sixteenth-century French play based on the *Legenda aurea*, focuses on Mary Magdalene's apostolate in Marseilles.

10. A Cornish play on the life of St. Meriasek is also extant. See also Wright, "Ashmole Fragment." The scarcity of extant texts of saint plays in England should be contrasted to the situation in medieval France, where a comparatively large corpus of surviving texts attests to an extensive tradition of scripted drama based on the lives of the saints. See Muir, "Saint Play in Medieval France."

11. See Jeffrey, "English Saints' Plays."

12. *LMRP*, xlvi. The text of *Mary Magdalene* is on pp. 24–95. All citations of the Digby saint play refer to line numbers of this edition.

13. Weimann, *Shakespeare and the Popular Tradition*, 57. See also Happé, "Protestant Adaptations," 207.

14. Coldewey, "Digby Plays," 110; Grantley, "Saints' Plays," 273.

15. See Grantley, "Saints' Plays," 273–4.

16. See Mead, "Four-fold Allegory," 281, n. 6; Jeffrey, "English Saints' Plays," 75–76; and Davidson, "Digby *Mary Magdalene*," 72. For other studies that represent the Digby saint as a universalized Christian subject, see Coletti, "Design"; Bush, "*Locus* and *Platea* Staging"; and Scherb, "Worldly and Sacred Messengers."

17. See King, "Sacred Eroticism"; Milner, "Flesh and Food"; and Dixon, "'Thys Body of Mary.'"

18. Sanok suggests that rather than pointing to idiosyncrasies of historical preservation, the spare documentary record of the performance of saint plays in late medieval England may be evidence of a determined "exercise in forgetting" the plays' challenges to societal norms and cultural values. See "Performing Feminine Sanctity," 275. See also Cowling, "Fifteenth-Century Saint Play."

19. Davidson, "Middle English Saint Play," 31; Wasson, "Secular Saint

Plays," 241–42. See also Wickham, "Staging of Saint Plays," 100–101; Jeffrey, "English Saints' Plays," 69; and Johnston, "What If No Texts Survived?," 6–7. Chambers first compiled records of saint plays; see *Medieval Stage*, 2: 379–80.

20. Clopper, "*Communitas*," 81. Clopper presents an abbreviated version of this argument in the broader context of medieval clerical and lay performative traditions in *Drama, Play, and Game*, 127–37; for an inventory of records that have been seen as evidence of saint play production in England, see 299–306. As Clopper notes, the word "drama" does not even appear in the *Middle English Dictionary*.

21. For further contributions to the debate about the English saint play, see Davidson, "British Saint Play Records"; and Clopper, "Why Are There So Few Saint Plays?"

22. Paraphrased in Jeffrey, "English Saints' Plays," 72.

23. For medieval saints in particular, see Vauchez, *Sainthood in the Later Middle Ages*; and Weinstein and Bell, *Saints and Society*. For specific illustrations of the social and political functions of hagiographic narrative and saints' cults, see Farmer, *Communities of Saint Martin*; Ashley and Sheingorn, *Writing Faith*, 1–21; idem, eds., *Interpreting Cultural Symbols*; and Blanton-Whetsell, "St. Æthelthryth's Cult."

24. Geary, "Saints, Scholars, and Society," 15.

25. See Sponsler, "Culture of the Spectator"; Ashley, "Popular Culture"; and idem, "Sponsorship, Reflexivity, and Resistance." Studies focusing on ideological dimensions of medieval performance in specific local contexts include Badir, "Resurrection at Beverly Minster"; Beckwith, *Signifying God*; and Pappano, "Judas in York."

26. Bush, "*Locus* and *Platea* Staging"; Scherb, "Worldly and Sacred Messengers"; Mead, "Four-Fold Allegory"; and Jeffrey, "English Saints' Plays."

27. Bush, "*Locus* and *Platea* Staging," 149, n. 25; 156. See also Mead, "Four-fold Allegory," 281.

28. Scherb, "Worldly and Sacred Messengers," 9. Scherb states (2) that the playwright's identification of "the *logos* and the reception of the Eucharist in the latter half of the play . . . can stress the unity of Latin Christendom through the medium of the Host as it had become sacramentally administered by the late medieval Church." Recent critiques of the development of the Eucharist as a symbol of unity have made clear how that process was fraught with conflict at many levels. See Rubin, *Corpus Christi*; and Beckwith, *Christ's Body*.

29. Bush, "*Locus* and *Platea* Staging," 147.

30. See Happé, "Protestant Adaptation"; White, ed., *Reformation Biblical Drama in England*; and Jeffrey, "English Saints' Plays," 70–73. In 1535 Henry VIII prohibited the interlude of Thomas the Apostle at York, suggesting official anxiety about the sedition that might arise from people congregating in festive celebration. See Wickham, "Staging of Saint Plays," 102.

31. See Gibson, *Theater of Devotion*, 40.

32. Records from early sixteenth-century Boxford, Suffolk, document the mounting of an ambitious dramatic production, but nothing in those records corresponds to any extant East Anglian dramatic text. See *Records of Plays and Players*, 137–38.

33. Beadle, "Literary Geography," 94–95.

34. This account of St. Peter and Paul, Salle draws upon Cautley, *Norfolk Churches*; Pevsner, *Northeast Norfolk and Norwich*, 307–9; the 1955 church guide for Salle written by C. L. S. Linnell; and Parsons, *Salle*.

35. Nichols, *Seeable Signs*. All but three of the forty-two seven-sacrament fonts built in late medieval England appear in East Anglian parish churches.

36. On cultural manifestations of late medieval East Anglia's economic prosperity in religion, literature, and art, see Nichols, *Seeable Signs*; idem, *Early Art of Norfolk*; Beadle, "Literary Geography"; and Gibson, *Theater of Devotion*. For an overview of surviving artifacts, see Lasko and Morgan, eds., *Medieval Art in East Anglia*.

37. Such parallels frequently formulate a link between historicism's effort to recover a lost past and the psychoanalytic modeling of subjectivity in loss and mourning. This topic has been pursued most notably by Louise Fradenburg. See "'Voice Memorial'"; "'Be Not Far from Me'"; "'So That We May Speak of Them'"; and "Psychoanalytic Medievalism." See also the critique of medieval historicism's "narcissistic mirroring" of its proponents' desire for their own lost origins by Margherita, *Romance of Origins*, 100. Recent contributions to the debate include Patterson, "Chaucer's Pardoner"; and Scala, "Historicists and Their Discontents."

38. Strohm, *Theory and the Premodern Text*, 153, 160 (the latter citing Ernesto Laclau and Chantal Mouffe, *Hegemony and Socialist Strategy* [London: Verso, 1985], 3). Fradenburg questions the new historicist privileging of variety as yet another form of mystification; see "'Be Not Far from Me,'" 45, n. 7.

39. See Spiegel, "Towards a Theory of the Middle Ground," in *Past as Text*, 53.

40. Ibid., 43, 53. See also Patterson, "Chaucer's Pardoner," 679.

41. Julian of Norwich, *Book of Showings*, 1: 201. On the dating of the Short and Long Texts, see Watson, "Composition."

42. On the relationship of Kempe's *Book* to the historical and material worlds of fifteenth-century England, see Aers, *Community, Gender, and Individual Identity*, 73–116; Beckwith, *Christ's Body*, 78–111; and Staley, *Dissenting Fictions*.

43. This portrait is fashioned from the "Introduction" by editors Colledge and Walsh to *A Book of Showings*, 1: 33–38, 43–59. Late medieval testamentary bequests to an anchoress named Julian, an anchoress at the church of St. Julian, and the anchoress Julian at the church of the same name are discussed by Tanner, *Church in Late Medieval Norwich*, 200, n. 29. See also Dunn, "Hermits, Anchorites, and Recluses." For discussion of this documentary evidence and what is—or is not—known about Julian, see Jantzen, *Mystic and Theologian*, 15–27; and Bauerschmidt, *Julian of Norwich*, 203–12. On the ways that traditions of editing the texts of the *Revelation* have constructed Julian as author, see Barratt, "How Many Children Had Julian of Norwich?"

44. *BMK*, xlviii–li, 358–75. Only one of the documents—an account roll of the Trinity Guild of Lynn (358)—refers to a Margery Kempe. Assumptions about the historical existence of Margery Kempe take their most intriguing turn in efforts to explain her thought and behavior as symptoms of a mental disorder.

For example, see Farley, "Her Own Creature." Preoccupation with authenticating the personality constructed by Kempe's *Book* is itself symptomatic of the attempt to come to terms with mystical experience, which in some sense is impossible to authenticate. See Beckwith, "Problems of Authority."

45. Colledge and Walsh, "Introduction," *Book of Showings*, 1: 1–18. On the only known fifteenth-century attestation of Julian's Long Text, the extracts that appear in London, Westminster Archdiocesan Archives MS, see Kempster, "Question of Audience."

46. De Worde's extracts appear in *BMK*, 353–57. For discussions of the annotations and early sixteenth-century printed editions, see Lochrie, *Translations of the Flesh*, 203–35; Staley, *Dissenting Fictions*, 96–98; and Summit, *Lost Property*, 126–38.

47. Jones cites the one exception of the Trinity Guild record from Lynn. See "Margery Kempe and the Bishops," 379. See also Staley, *Dissenting Fictions*, 173–74.

48. *LMRP*, xxxvi–xl. For discussion of East Anglian dialectal features in a larger cultural and literary context, see Beadle, "Literary Geography," 89–94. Beadle's map of scribal locations for Norfolk play manuscripts places the *Magdalene* scribe in the southeastern quadrant of the county.

49. *LMRP*, xxx–xxxiii. See also Baker and Murphy, "Late Medieval Plays."

50. *LMRP*, xii–xv; and Baker and Murphy, "Books of Myles Blomefylde."

51. *LMRP*, xiii–xiv. See also Gibson, "Bury St. Edmunds."

52. Baker and Murphy, "Late Medieval Plays," 164–66. See also Hill-Vásquez, "Mediatory Styles," 158–64.

53. Ritchie, "Suggested Location," 52; Johnston, "*Wisdom* and the Records," 94.

54. Coldewey, "Digby Plays" (Chelmsford); Davidson, "Middle English Saint Play," 74–75 (Norwich); Bennett, "*Mary Magdalene*" (King's or Bishop's Lynn); Wickham, "Staging of Saint Plays," 113–15 (Ipswich); Ritchie, "Suggested Location" (Lincoln). King's Lynn and Norwich present intriguing candidacies for the play's local auspices. A major port for much of East Anglia, including the wealthy cloth-producing Stour valley, King's Lynn was an international market for luxury foodstuffs and other commodities. See Owen, ed., *Making of King's Lynn*; and Green, *Town Life*, 2: 402–26. Alternatively, Tanner's vivid portrait of late medieval Norwich's prosperous religious culture gives added appeal to the hypothesis linking the Digby *Magdalene* to that thriving, international East Anglian town, which by the 1520s was second only to London in wealth and population. See *Church in Late Medieval Norwich*; and Pound, "Social and Trade Structure."

55. See Coletti, "'*Paupertas est donum Dei*,'" 340–41; and idem, "Sociology of Transgression."

56. All of the Digby plays establish such a rhetorical stance. In *Mary Magdalene* the hermit priest steps out of character at the end of the play to address the dramatic audience: "Sufferens [sovereigns] of þis processe, thus enddyt þe sentens / That we have playyd in yower syth" (2131–32). The Poeta figure of the Digby *Conversion of Saint Paul* recognizes his audience as an "honorable and

wurshypfull congregacyon." The Poeta of the Digby *Killing of the Children* addresses "Honorable souereignes" who have witnessed the play's performance. See *LMRP*, 13, line 361 (*Paul*); 114, line 551 (*Killing*). The fragmentary dramatic epilogue preserved in the late fifteenth-century commonplace book of Robert Reynes, churchwarden of Acle, Norfolk, thanks "wursheppful soueryens þat syttyn here in syth, / Lordes and ladyes and frankelens in fay." See *Non-Cycle Plays*, 123, lines 1–2. Other instances of rhetorical address to "sovereyns," i.e., "masters," "sirs," or "excellent people," appear in *Mankind*, the *N-Town Plays*, the *Play of the Sacrament*, and the Brome *Abraham and Isaac*. I thank Doug Sugano for calling this rhetorical feature of East Anglian drama to my attention and for providing me with his inventory of examples.

57. Brown, *Popular Piety*, 181–201; Rubin, "Imagining Medieval Hospitals"; idem, *Charity and Community*; and Orme and Webster, *English Hospital*. For an in-depth study of the networks of poverty and charity, social ambition and piety, that informed the activities of one influential late medieval East Anglian hospital, St. Giles's, Norwich, see Rawcliffe, *Medicine for the Soul*. On ideologies of poverty and charity in the Digby saint play, see Coletti, "'Paupertas est donum Dei,'" 357–69.

58. *RWMEA*, 69.

59. A leprosarium dedicated to Mary Magdalene was established outside the city walls at Norwich before 1119. From 1286 to the end of the Middle Ages, this leprosarium held an annual three-day fair around the time of the saint's feast on July 22, but there is little late medieval evidence of the hospital's activities. See Rawcliffe, *Hospitals of Medieval Norwich*, 41–47. The Mary Magdalene hospital at King's Lynn was an important institution of the town through the end of the Middle Ages. See Owen, ed., *Making of King's Lynn*, 106–16. There were also hospitals dedicated to Mary Magdalene at Yarmouth (Rawcliffe, *Medicine for the Soul*, 105, 221) and Thetford (Martin, *History*, 90–92).

60. Rawcliffe, *Medicine and Society*, 1–28; idem, *Medicine for the Soul*, 103–8.

61. Rawcliffe, *Hospitals of Medieval Norwich*, 13–32.

62. Rawcliffe, *Medicine and Society*, 1–28; Duffy, *Stripping of the Altars*, 310–13.

63. For a discussion of the representation of these deaths in light of medieval medical knowledge, see Keyser, "Examining the Body Poetic," 145–58.

64. Maltman, "Light in and on the Digby *Mary Magdalene*," 274. Maltman astutely observes: "[N]o other medieval play makes such extensive use of beds" (258).

65. A connection between the saint play and the cultural functions of the late medieval hospital might also account for the "deyntys delycyows" over which the king of Flesh claims "grett domynacyon" (335). These spices and medicines are the "comfortatywys" ("comforting medicines") that he uses "aȝens alle vexacyon" (340). Baker, Murphy, and Hall note a resemblance to lists in the Croxton *Play of the Sacrament* and John Heywood's *Play Called the Four PP*. See *LMRP*, 201, note to lines 339–43. In terms of the medieval medical model that the play invokes, the king of the Flesh thus declares his attachment to the healing properties of natural remedies to which the vexacious "flesh" could have

recourse. The monastic infirmary at the cathedral priory in Norwich processed pharmaceuticals on the premises and had its own medicinal herb garden. See Rawcliffe, *Hospitals of Medieval Norwich*, 28. For a discussion of aromatics, healing plants, and herbs cultivated in a walled garden for St. Giles's Hospital, Norwich by the sisters who served there, see idem, *Medicine for the Soul*, 51–52.

66. The only specific invocation of medical activity and lore in East Anglian drama is the quack doctor episode involving "Master Brundyche" in the Croxton *Play of the Sacrament*; *Non-Cycle Plays*, 74–78, lines 525–652. See Gibson *Theater of Devotion*, 36–38. Early sixteenth-century charges of riotousness against the residents of the hospital of St. Mary's in the Newark, Leicester, give notice of Robin Hood pageants and spectacles staged within the hospital precinct. See Rawcliffe, *Hospitals of Medieval Norwich*, 68.

67. On the priority of the hospital's spiritual function, see Rawcliffe, *Medicine for the Soul*, 30; and Orme and Webster, *English Hospital*, 49. On the centrality of liturgical function, see Harper-Bill, ed., *Medieval Hospital of Bury St. Edmunds*, 2. As practiced by the moneyed classes of late medieval England, provisions for charitable activity were frequently performative in nature. Alice Chaucer gave a manor to the monks of the Charterhouse in Hull, specifying that in return they were to pray for her soul and that of her late husband, William de la Pole, and to have stone images made in likeness of the duke and duchess, each holding a dish in the right hand and a jug in the left. Summarized from the account in Richmond, "English Gentry and Religion," 139, n. 55.

68. Rawcliffe, *Medicine for the Soul*, 103–32; and idem, "Life, Death, and Liturgy."

69. One of two belonging to St. Giles's, the processional is now British Library MS Add. 57534. Looking rather like minimalist set designs, some of these illustrations and other visual splendors related to the expansion of the church fabric are reproduced in Rawcliffe, *Medicine for the Soul*, between 110–11 and 206–7.

70. Hospital records report performances by players at wealthy venues such as St. Giles's. See Rawcliffe, *Medicine for the Soul*, 120. The late medieval collegiate church may have provided auspices for East Anglian dramatic texts still in search of a local habitation, such as the *Mary Play* and the *Assumption Play* of the N-Town compilation. Influential collegiate foundations with ties to wealthy nobility or citizenries such as the Chapel in the Field, Norwich; the College at Baily End, Thetford; and the College at Rushworth (or Rushford) all pose tantalizing prospects for imagining venues for East Anglian drama. On the Chapel in the Fields, see Taylor, *Index Monasticus*, 48. On the College at Baily End, see Martin, *History of Thetford*, 203–27. On the College at Rushworth, see Bennett, "College of S. John Evangelist." Sugano explores possible connections between collegiate foundations and East Anglian drama; see "N-Town Playbooks," 230–32. See also Coletti, "N-Town Plays," 409. Destruction wrought upon the records of hospitals and collegiate foundations is illustrated by Rawcliffe's notice that new accounts prepared by the post-Dissolution keepers of St. Giles's were wrapped in pages torn from medieval service books; see *Medicine for the Soul*, plate 42.

71. Hughes, *Pastors and Visionaries*. The intersection of contemplative values and lay religion that Gibson and Hughes locate in East Anglian and York, respectively, was obviously not unique to these regions. It is the concentration of extant spiritual and religious texts paralleled by the preeminence and variety of religious institutions that contributes to the prominent positions of the dioceses of Norwich and York in any inventory of religious experience and expression in late medieval England.

72. Gibson, *Theater of Devotion*, 21–30; Tanner, "Reformation and Regionalism"; Farnhill, *Guilds and the Parish Community*; Middleton-Stewart, *Inward Purity and Outward Splendour*.

73. Tanner, *Church in Late Medieval Norwich*, 59–60.

74. Jansen, *Making of the Magdalen*, 6; Wilk, "Cult of Mary Magdalen." Clopper suggests possible mendicant influences on the Digby saint play; see *Drama, Play, and Game*, 246–47.

75. Hale and Rodgers, *Greyfriars of Norwich*, 15–16.

76. Tanner, *Church in Late Medieval Norwich*, 19–20; Hale and Rodgers, *Greyfriars of Norwich*, 17. Tanner notes that twenty-eight of the "famous writers" mentioned in Bale's *Scriptorium illustrium maioris Brytannie catalogue* were from the cathedral priory and friaries of Norwich. See "Reformation and Regionalism," 137.

77. Clark, "Fourteenth-Century Cambridge Theology," 11. Clark (13) calls Norwich a "feeder" for Oxford, London, and especially Cambridge, where it sent its able minds and then welcomed them back.

78. Richmond, "Religion," 187.

79. Moreton, *Townshends and Their World*, 7.

80. Erler, *Women, Reading, and Piety*, 106.

81. Ibid., 68–84, quote at 83. Portions of Purdans's will appear in Harrod, "Norfolk Wills," 335–37. For the will of Richard Ferneys, see Tanner, *Church in Late Medieval Norwich*, 233–34.

82. English people turned to the Low Countries for everything from fine tapestries to manufacturing skills, and in the century after the plague, even found in the lands across the North Sea a source of replenishment for their depleted population. Of 1547 Lowlanders who emigrated to England between 1435 and 1467, 40 percent settled in the East Anglian counties of Norfolk and Suffolk, as well as Kent, Essex, and Surrey. See Barron, "Introduction: England and the Low Countries," 13; and Kerling, "Aliens in the County of Norfolk."

83. Johnston, "Traders and Playmakers," 109.

84. See the instances of sailing ships, water, fire, etc., in Meredith and Tailby, eds., *Staging of Religious Drama*. The extended description (259–62) of a 1496 production of a play on the life of Saint Martin in Seurre indicates a seriousness of purpose and scope of production comparable to those of *Mary Magdalene*. Rich prospects for reading these works in tandem have been outlined by Ashley, "Transgressing Boundaries."

85. See Dillon, "Holy Women and Their Confessors."

86. Dickman, "Margery Kempe and the Continental Tradition," 152.

87. Watson, "Composition," 656. Easton (d. 1397) bequeathed his substantial

library to Norwich Cathedral priory. See Beeching and James, "Library of the Cathedral Church," 71–72. The frequency with which East Anglian notables made bequests to Syon Abbey, the only Brigittine foundation in England, suggests the prominence of the cult of Saint Bridget in the region. See Gibson, *Theater of Devotion*, 20–21; and Dillon, "Holy Women and Their Confessors," 116–17.

88. *BMK*, 22, 136, 150, 168, 169, 217, 219. See Allen's commentary in *BMK*, 268, note for 22/11–12. See also Clark, "Late Fourteenth-Century Cambridge Theology," 3, 13–14.

89. Duffy suggests that donor contact with Syon or its literature may explain the presence of these highly unusual images; see *Stripping of the Altars*, 86. Funded by William Wulcy and his wives Joan and Alice, the screen dates from 1528. See James, *Suffolk and Norfolk*, 160.

90. On such cultural exchange, see Wallace, "Mystics and Followers," 170.

91. The traditional view of medieval English spiritualities has stressed differences from their continental counterparts. See Richmond, "Religion." For critiques of this view, see Watson, "Melting into God"; and idem, "Middle English Mystics."

92. On the late medieval English cults of the Virgin Mary and Saint Anne, especially in East Anglia, see Gibson, *Theater of Devotion*, 137–77; and idem, "Saint Anne." See also Ashley and Sheingorn, "Introduction," *Interpreting Cultural Symbols*, 1–68. Texts associated with Saint Anne comprise nearly 19 percent of the commonplace book of Robert Reynes, a late fifteenth-century church reeve of Acle, Norfolk. See *Commonplace Book of Robert Reynes*, 191–234, 406–32.

Chapter 2

The epigraph is a stage direction after line 992. A red line has been drawn through the stage direction's first line in the manuscript, but the editors do not regard this as a cancellation. See *LMRP*, 57, n. 6.

1. The play identifies the women as Mary Magdalene, Mary Jacobe, and Mary Salome. The Gospels vary in their reports of who approached the tomb to anoint Christ's body. See Matt. 28:1; Mark 16:1; Luke 24:10; and John 20:1.

2. See Coletti, "Design."

3. Schiller, *Iconography of Christian Art*, 2: 184–97; and Woolf, *English Religious Lyric*, 208–9. The "sygnis of the passion" could designate either the instruments of the Passion or the image that Eamon Duffy also calls by the name "arms of the Passion" "in which the hands, feet, and side-hole or pierced heart of Jesus were heraldically displayed against the cross." The image of the wounds of Christ appeared on carved bench-ends, painted glass, grave stones, and woodcuts distributed by the charterhouses. See *Stripping of the Altars*, 246. Duffy includes (fig. 99) a devotional woodcut from Sheen that shows both the five wounds and the more conventional symbols of the Passion.

4. Bush, "*Locus* and *Platea* Staging," 145.

5. Boehnen, "Aesthetics of 'Sprawling' Drama," 341.

6. Erler, "English Vowed Women." See also idem, "Margery Kempe's

White Clothes"; and Harrod, "Mantle and Ring of Widowhood." Evidence of the attire of vowed widows from monumental brasses, including three from Norfolk, appears in André, "Female Head-dresses." In her 1503 will Somerset widow Agnes Burton bequeathed the "mantell lyned with sylke that I was professid yn, to thentent of Mary Magdaleyn play" at the church of Mary Magdalene in Taunton; F. W. Weaver, ed., *Somerset Medieval Wills (1383–1558)*, 3 vols., Somerset Record Society 16, 19, 21 (London, 1901–5), 2:53. Cited in Erler, "English Vowed Women," 177.

7. Late medieval England's most influential vowess was probably Margaret Beaufort, who dedicated herself to chastity while still married to her fourth husband, Thomas Stanley. The public embrace of chastity is best known to postmedieval readers through the example of Margery Kempe, whose eccentric twist on the vowess's attire–her quest for white clothes—seems never to have been officially granted by any of the ecclesiastical authorities from whom she sought approval.

8. Erler, *Women, Reading, and Piety*, 7–26, esp. 8.

9. *RWMEA*, 9, 17. For the number of anchoresses and vowesses, see tables 4 and 5, 97–100.

10. Bishop Walter Suffield's second foundation charter for the hospital; Norfolk Record Office, DCN 43/48. Quoted and translated by Rawcliffe, *Medicine for the Soul*, 242, 244; and for the life of hospital sisters, see 169–76. See also idem, *Hospitals of Late Medieval Norwich*, 69–77; "Hospital Nurses"; and Gilchrist, *Contemplation and Action*, 14, 16–17.

11. *RWMEA*, 94.

12. Rawcliffe, *Hospitals of Late Medieval Norwich*, 73–74.

13. Ibid., 68.

14. Rawcliffe, *Medicine for the Soul*, 21, 169–70.

15. Tanner, *Church in Late Medieval Norwich*, 64–66, 130–31. See also *RWMEA*, 71–74, 95–96. Gilchrist and Oliva have newly identified five groups of nuns who continued to live together in Norwich city parishes after the Dissolution, and individual women whom urban testators described simply as "mother" (table 6, 101).

16. See Mulder-Bakker, "Ivetta of Huy," 228. See also Dor, Johnson, and Wogan-Browne, eds., *Holy Women of Liège*.

17. *RWMEA*, 72. On medieval discourses about lay or "semi"-religious, see Van Engen, "Friar Johannes Nider."

18. Gilchrist, *Gender and Material Culture*, 186–87. On the importance of women's penitentially-focused spirituality in insular culture, see Wogan-Browne, *Saints' Lives and Women's Literary Culture*, 149–50.

19. Cf. the 1379 vow of Isabel Burgh, who promised that "fro yis day forward I sshal ben chast of myn body and in holy chastete kepe me treweliche and devouteliche alle ye dayes of myn lyf." See *Wykeham's Register*, ed. T. F. Kirby, 2 vols., Hampshire Record Society 11 and 13 (London, 1896, 1899), 2: 307–8. Quoted in Erler, "English Vowed Women," 162, n. 23.

20. For Capgrave, see Winstead, *Virgin Martyrs*, 167–80; and idem, "Introduction," Capgrave's *Life of Saint Katherine*, 1–8. For Bokenham, see Delany,

Impolitic Bodies; and Hilles, "Osbern Bokenham's Legendary." See also Warren, *Spiritual Economies*, 134–62.

21. For example, Szövérffy, "'Peccatrix Quondam Femina'"; Kane, "Mary of Magdala"; Chauvin, "Mary Magdalene in Medieval Drama"; Mosco, ed., *La Maddelena*; Dillenberger, "The Magdalen"; Pinto-Mathieu, *Marie-Madeleine dans la littérature*.

22. Ortenberg, "Marie Madeleine dans l'Angleterre Anglo-Saxonne," 13. See also Saxer, *Le culte*, 40; and Jansen, *Making of the Magdalen*, 35.

23. *An Old English Martyrology*, ed. G. Herzfeld, EETS os 116 (London: Kegan Paul, Trench, Trübner and Co., 1900), 126. Cited in Cross, "Mary Magdalene in the *Old English Martyrology*," 16.

24. Ortenberg, "Marie Madeleine dans l'Angleterre Anglo-Saxonne," 16. Ortenberg notes (17) that the *Martyrology* provides the first known use of the *vita eremetica*, which appropriated to the apocryphal history of Mary Magdalene themes from the life of Mary of Egypt. See also Stevenson, "Holy Sinner"; and Magennis, "St. Mary of Egypt." On the *vita eremetica*, see also Jansen, *Making of the Magdalen*, 36–38.

25. Schapiro, "Ruthwell Cross." See fig. 10.

26. Ortenberg, "Marie Madeleine dans l'Angleterre Anglo-Saxonne," 18. Ortenberg (19–20) notes evidence of Carolingian interest in the saint in abbeys that had particularly strong connections with England.

27. Ibid., 24. See Deshman, *Benedictional*, British Library Additional MS 49598, fol. IV–2r. The identity of the Magdalene figure in this image is established by a nineteenth-century engraving that depicts the inscription on her book: "S(an)c(t)a Maria Magdalen"; see J. Gage, "A Dissertation on St. Æthelwold's Benedictional," *Archaeologia* 4 (1832): 1–117. Cited in Deshman, 146.

28. Deshman, *Benedictional*, 151.

29. Ortenberg, "Marie Madeleine dans l'Angleterre Anglo-Saxonne," 25; Deshman, *Benedictional*, 150.

30. Ortenberg, "Marie Madeleine dans l'Angleterre Anglo-Saxonne," 25–31.

31. Jansen, *Making of the Magdalen*, 63. See fig. 1, p. 64.

32. Carrasco, "Christina of Markyate's Psalter"; Caviness, "Anchoress, Abbess, and Queen," 107–13.

33. Carrasco, "Christina of Markyate's Psalter," 73–75; Dalarun, "La Madeleine dans l'ouest de la France."

34. Jansen, *Making of the Magdalen*, 119–20.

35. Alison Binns, *Dedications of Monastic Houses in England and Wales, 1066–1216* (Woodbridge, Eng.: Boydell Press, 1989), 18, 34–38. Cited in Jansen, *Making of the Magdalen*, 120. An inventory of pre-Reformation churches dedicated to Mary Magdalene ranks the saint as the thirteenth most popular, with 187 dedications, after Saint Lawrence in twelfth position with 239 dedications. Among female saints, only the Virgin Mary (number one with 2335) and Saint Margaret (number eleven with 261) are more popular dedicatees. See Francis Bond, *Dedications and Patron Saints*, 16.

36. Religious foundations (i.e., churches, chapels, hospitals, etc.) dedicated to Mary Magdalene appeared during this period in Lynn, Norwich, Wiggenhall,

Pentney, Fordham, Beccles, Thetford, and Ely. See Saxer, *Le culte*, 121–22, 135–36, 146–48, 256–57.

37. Bede, *Ecclesiastical History of the English People*, ed. and trans. B. Colgrave and R. A. B. Mynors (Oxford, 1969), 398. Cited in Deshman, *Benedictional*, 123. See also Wogan-Browne, "Rerouting the Dower"; and Blanton-Whetsell, "St. Æthelthryth's Cult."

38. Deshman, *Benedictional*, 123. See also the discussion of this image by Blanton-Whetsell, "*Imagines Ætheldredae*," 59–62.

39. Blanton-Whetsell, "St. Æthelthryth's Cult," 273, 317, n. 37.

40. Wogan-Browne, "Rerouting the Dower," 30. See also Blanton-Whetsell, "Shrine of St. Æthelthryth."

41. Images of Etheldreda appear on at least fourteen rood screens and possibly six others, all but four of the combined medieval English total surviving in Norfolk and Suffolk. See Blanton-Whetsell, "*Imagines Ætheldredae*," 94–95.

42. Wogan-Browne, "Rerouting the Dower," 28; see 44–46, n. 10 for an inventory of those lives and other evidence of Æthelthryth's cult in medieval England. Anglo-Norman lives of Saints Catherine and Edward were written by women from Barking Abbey. June Hall McCash has argued that the Anglo-Norman life of Æthelthryth is the work of Marie de France; see "*La vie seinte Audree*."

43. The Anglo-Saxon virgin princesses and royal abbesses include Æthelthryth, Modwenna, Osith; English male ecclesiastical authorities include Edmund of Abington, Thomas à Becket, and Richard of Chicester. Virginal purity and asceticism are represented by the lives of Faith, Catherine of Alexandria, Elizabeth of Hungary, Paphnutius, Paul the Hermit, Edward the Confessor, and Mary Magdalene. See Wogan-Browne, *Saints' Lives and Women's Literary Culture*, 7–10, 170–75; and Blanton-Whetsell, "*Imagines Ætheldredae*," 74–80. The Magdalene vita in the Campsey manuscript is the work of Guillaume le Clerc. See "*La vie de Madeleine*."

44. Duffy, "Holy Maydens, Holy Wyfes," 178–80. Williamson counts seven depictions of Mary Magdalene in Norfolk; "Saints on Norfolk Rood-Screens," 305.

45. Ortenberg, "Marie Madeleine dans l'Angleterre Anglo-Saxonne," 25–31. For the interests of these larger audiences, see Wogan-Browne, *Saints' Lives and Women's Literary Culture*.

46. Now supported by the Redundant Churches Fund, Wiggenhall St. Mary the Virgin is one of four Wiggenhall parishes. St. Mary Magdalene and St. German's still function as parish churches; Wiggenhall St. Peter is in ruins. For St. German's, see *Norfolk Churches Great and Small*, 102–3.

47. Cox, *Bench-Ends*, 127. The identity of many figures on these bench-ends is uncertain. Identifications provided here are based on the Wiggenhall St. Mary the Virgin Church Guide; Nichols, *Early Art of Norfolk*, 356; Bullmore, "Church of St. Mary the Virgin"; and my own inspection. Despite his accurate description of the bench-ends on the north side of the center aisle, Cox inexplicably states (17) that the southern block of benches in the nave represents only male saints and the north block contains representations of the Virgin Mary. He

attributes this (mistaken) difference to the traditional segregation of the sexes in churches, which places men on the south side and women on the north. Aston, citing Cox, repeats this error; see "Segregation in Churches," 274.

48. The difference between the two figures on the bench-end of the nave aisle (fig. 7) is especially noticeable: the figure on the left is much taller than the one on the right and wears a different kind of veil. One figure on the south aisle bench-end is badly damaged.

49. *RWMEA*, 78.

50. Accounts of the foundation and activities of Crabhouse priory are based on the extant register, now British Library Additional MS 4733, which includes notice of events up to 1476. See Bateson, "Register." See also Dashwood, "Deeds and Survey of Crabhouse"; Taylor, *Index Monasticus*, 19; *Victoria History*, 2: 408–10; Thompson, *Women Religious*, 25, 66–67; and Oliva, *Convent and the Community*. Several studies have mistakenly located the later site of Crabhouse in the parish of Wiggenhall St. Mary the Virgin. See Jessopp, *Studies by a Recluse*, 98; and Jordan, *Charities of Rural England*, 122. Gilchrist and Oliva (*RWMEA*, 85) locate the later medieval priory on the site of the private dwelling today known as Crabb Abbey, on the south side of the parish of Wiggenhall St. Mary Magdalene.

51. "Apres ke le avaunt dite crestine de euwe esteyt chayue li seniur ke il visent fet del tenement del avaunt dit lu de Crabhus si entra cum en sun achete; & li tint ben lungtens. . . . Li noun de le seniur esteyt apele Aleyn le fiz Richard de le paroz nostre Dame de Wigenhale" [After the previously mentioned flood of water 'the lord whom they chose dealt with the tenement of the aforesaid place of Crabhouse, entered there as into his purchase, and held it for a long time. . . .; the name of the lord was Alan the son of Richard, of the parish of Our Lady of Wigenhall']; Bateson, "Register," 13, partial translation at 5.

52. Blomefield, *History*, 9: 176–78.

53. The proceedings were conducted at Margery Kempe's church, St. Margaret's in Lynn. Among those attending were Robert Spryngold, whom Kempe's *Book* identifies as the church's influential pastor. See Virgoe, "Divorce of Thomas Tuddenham," 122–25. Tuddenham was a leading political figure in fifteenth-century East Anglia and a patron of John Capgrave. See Pearsall, "Capgrave's *Life of St. Katherine*," 122.

54. Bateson, "Register," 11.

55. The inscription on the heart-shaped brass reads: "Orate pro anima Domini Roberti Kervile Militis de Wygenhale Filii Edmundi Kervile de Wygenhale, cujus cor hic humatur." See Blomefield, *History*, 9: 179–81.

56. Bateson, "Register," 57–63.

57. Jessopp, *Studies by a Recluse*, 93–94. There were three other female convents in this area, at Shouldham, Marham, and Blackborough.

58. "Jadis esteyt une pucele, le quer de ki li seynt espirit mova de quere lu de deserte, ou ele poeyt servir Deu saunz desturbaunce de terriene choce; si trova cest lu ke ore est apele Crabhus, tut savagine et de graunt partie envirun de totes pars nesteyt habitaciun de home"; Bateson, "Register," 12, translation at 5. Bateson notes (3) that earlier documents from Castleacre Priory name Leva,

daughter of Godric of Lynn, as the occupant of an "heremum in australi parte situm juxta Wigehale" (a hermitage located in the southern part near Wiggenhall).

59. Bateson, "Register," 13.

60. *RWMEA*, 77. See also Tymms, ed., *Wills and Inventories*, 73.

61. *RWMEA*, 77, 99.

62. In 1497 Katharine Kerre bequeathed ten shillings to Margaret, a vowess at Crabhouse; Norfolk Record Office, NCC 90-1 Multon. Cited in Oliva, *Convent and the Community*, 47.

63. Between 1350 and 1540, Crabhouse averaged a population of eight nuns; in 1536, on the eve of the Dissolution, it housed eleven. Of the eleven female monasteries in the diocese of Norwich, Crabhouse was among the poorest, in the 1536 valuation ranking only above Flixton. See Oliva, *Convent and the Community*, 41, table 7.

64. Ibid., 174–83.

65. *RWMEA*, 10.

66. See Bateson, "Register": on burials at the convent, 60 (the father and mother of John Wiggenhall "bought a lyverey in the same house [and] ligge togedir in the body of the chirche"); on the Trinity Guild, 59; on corrodians, 42 (from a gift of land and "poy de argent" Aleyn Brid and his wife "usunt lur sustenaunce de la Mesun en tote lur vie").

67. Hillen, *Borough of King's Lynn*, 1: 178; Bateson, "Register," 58–59.

68. Bateson, "Register," 59–62; Virgoe, "Divorce of Thomas Tuddenham," 129–30, n. 14. Wiggenhall presided over the 1436 proceedings related to Thomas Tuddenham's request for an annulment at which both prioress Joan and nun Joan Kervile testified. At the time Wiggenhall would have still held the rectorship at Oxborough, Tuddenham's home. Joan's cousin is not to be confused with John Wiggenhall, abbot of the Premonstratensian monastery at West Dereham, who also testified at the proceedings. He too had ties to Capgrave, who dedicated his *Life of St. Norbert* to him. See Pearsall, "Capgrave's *Life of St. Katherine*," 122.

69. Bateson, "Register," 11–12: "Seniurs & dames, veus & jones, / Francs & serfs & totes en communes, / Ke voliunt oyer & entendre, / En cest escrit pount aprendre / Coment la Mesun de Crabhus / E de totes les fez et lus / Comencerunt; ke uncore sunt. / Et de donurs ke donerunt, / E de terres & tenemens, / De rentes & de feffemens, / Ke alavaunt dit Mesun parteynunt, / Coment & de queus done esteyunt."

70. *RWMEA*, 58.

71. *Testamenta Eboracensia*, 4: 151.

72. Here Mary Magdalene appropriates the function that provided for individuals, usually nuns or women in almshouses and charitable foundations such as *maisons dieu*, to pray on another's behalf. See Gilchrist, *Contemplation and Action*, 150.

73. *RWMEA*, 25.

74. The Church Guide dates the screen on the basis of the garments worn by the figure usually identified as Saint Scholastica, here tentatively corrected to Saint Anne. See also Cotton, "Medieval Roodscreens," 47. Nichols proposes

that the figure may be "one of the other nuns represented elsewhere" in the church; see *Early Art of Norfolk*, 227. Carole Hill first suggested to me that this figure may be Saint Anne, functioning as an icon of pious widowhood. She points out that the figure wears only a black veil (and a red dress), not the Benedictine habit in which Scholastica is traditionally shown. Saint Anne's association with vowed chastity makes her a suitable companion for this gathering of virgins. John Mirk noted that after her three marriages, Anne "would haue no more. But aftyr all her lyue scho ʒaf her to chastyte and to holynes"; *Festial*, 215.

75. See Cotton, "Medieval Roodscreens," 45; and Duffy, "Parish, Piety, and Patronage." Dated but still useful are the inventories compiled by Williamson, "Saints on Norfolk Rood-Screens."

76. Jansen, *Making of the Magdalen*, 134.

77. A fifteenth-century sermon for the feast of John the Baptist succinctly links these two attributes: "[H]e was euer a virgine and ladd an heremytis lyf in desert"; *Speculum Sacerdotale*, 165. Virginia Blanton-Whetsell states that the Baptist illustrates, "as no other male saint [. . .] could, purity of the body"; "*Imagines Ætheldredae*," 103, n. 38.

78. *Life of the Blessed Mary Magdalene*, 84–85. Mycoff translates from the vita erroneously attributed to Rabanus Maurus (*PL* 112: 1431–1508). The vita is extant in at least one English manuscript, Oxford, Magdalen College MS 89. See also Saxer, "'Vie de sainte Marie Madeleine.'"

79. Winstead, *Virgin Martyrs*, 147–56.

80. Oliva, *Convent and the Community*, 71.

81. Binski, "English Parish Church," 2.

82. Ibid., 18.

83. Ibid., 17. Binski's notice of the relation of such groups to material representations can usefully be read in tandem with Katherine French's work on the marking of religious experience in the late medieval parish church by gender, age, and status. See "Women's Parish Guilds"; and idem, "'The Seat by Our Lady.'" See also Raguin and Stanbury, "Introduction," *Women's Spaces*.

84. Binski, "English Parish Church," 2.

85. Ibid., 3.

86. Ibid., 18. Gibson analyzes St. Mary's parish church in Bury St. Edmunds along exactly these lines. See *Theater of Devotion*, 168–77.

87. Duffy, "Holy Maydens, Holy Wyfes," 185. Bokenham's text is known by this editorial title, drawn from the friar poet's account of his work (5038–40). Hilles suggests "Bokenham's legendary" as a simpler alternative. See "Gender and Politics," 189, n. 2. All citations refer to Bokenham, *Legendys of Hooly Wummen*.

88. *Legendys of Hooly Wummen*, 289, no line numbers. Edwards hypothesizes that Bokenham brought his accumulated saints' vitae to the attention of Thomas Burgh, a Cambridge friar who is identified in the manuscript's colophon as the person by—or most likely for—whom MS Arundel was copied in 1447. See "Transmission and Audience," 157–59. Hilles contends, however, that the legendary was intentionally structured according to a controlling design based on Bokenham's deployment of female saints' lives in support of the Yorkist cause. See "Gender and Politics."

89. Mirk, *Festial*, 203–8.

90. Isabella's "synguler deuocyoun" parallels the experience of other late medieval English noble women who were intensely attracted to Mary Magdalene's life and example. The 1439 will of Isabella of Warwick provided for her tomb sculpture to depict Mary Magdalene standing at her head and "leyng my handes a-cross." See Furnivall, ed., *Fifty Earliest English Wills*, 116–17. Anne Harling, Lady Scrope, commissioned an image of Mary Magdalene in painted glass for her parish church in East Harling, Norfolk, perhaps intended to stand in for the patron herself. See Sugano, "Apologies for the Magdalene," 172–74. Margaret of York, niece of Isabella Bourchier, had herself represented as Mary Magdalene in a Flemish Deposition painting around 1500; her *Dialogue de la Duchesse de Bourgogne à Jesus Christ* shows Margaret in the role of Mary Magdalene receiving a vision of the resurrected Christ. See Hughes, *Religious Life of Richard III*, 98, 144.

91. Delany, *Impolitic Bodies*, 89. On Isabella's imprint in Bokenham's life, see Dixon, "'Thys Body of Mary,'" 221–22.

92. Johnson, "Tales of a True Translator," 114.

93. Delany, *Impolitic Bodies*, 44–69, reference to "poetic credo" at 54. For different readings of Bokenham's literary strategies in the prolocutory, see Johnson, "Tales of a True Translator"; Hilles, "Gender and Politics"; and Warren, *Spiritual Economies*, 147–53.

94. Delany, *Impolitic Bodies*, 53.

95. Ibid., 53–54.

96. Ibid., 56. See also Hilles, "Gender and Politics," 203.

97. The "embellished as the month of May" trope that Bokenham invokes was a rhetorical commonplace, to be sure; the poet also employs it in the Aristotelian prologue that introduces his life of Saint Margaret when he declares his inability to compete with the "crafty clerk" Chaucer (83–96), to whom his use of the trope surely also pays homage. In Bokenham's rendering, Isabella's sons resemble Chaucer's Squire (1.89–92), and his own protestations of rhetorical inadequacy echo those of Chaucer's Franklin (5.719–27). Citations refer to the *Riverside Chaucer*.

98. See the related assessment by Hilles, "Gender and Politics," 204–5.

99. The abrupt juxtaposition of the two women in the Magdalene prolocutory is especially intriguing in light of their disparate fortunes in the Wars of the Roses. Elizabeth would see her Lancastrian sympathizing husband John and son Aubrey executed for treason by Isabella's nephew, Edward IV, in 1462. Isabella's husband, Henry Bourchier, earl of Essex, was among those entrusted by Edward with the task of weakening the influence of the Vere family in East Anglia. See Seward, *Wars of the Roses*, 136–38.

100. Edwards, "Bokenham's *Legendys of Hooly Wummen*," 165–66. See also Winstead, *Virgin Martyrs*, 141–46; and Hanna and Edwards, "Ellesmere Chaucer."

101. Riddy, "'Women Talking,'" 113.

102. Investigation of women's textual culture in medieval England is a burgeoning field. Important studies include Meale, ed., *Women and Literature*;

Smith and Taylor, eds., *Women, the Book, and the Worldly*; idem, *Women, the Book, and the Godly*; McCash, ed., *Cultural Patronage*; Robertson, *Early English Devotional Prose*; Taylor and Smith, eds., *Women and the Book*; Lewis, Menuge, and Phillips, eds., *Young Medieval Women*; Wogan-Browne et al., eds., *Medieval Women: Texts and Contexts*; Wogan-Browne, *Saints' Lives and Women's Literary Culture*; Reveney and Whitehead, eds., *Writing Religious Women*; Summit, *Lost Property*; Erler, *Women, Reading, and Piety*; and Krug, *Reading Families*.

103. Instances other than the famous examples of Julian of Norwich and Margery Kempe are collected in Barratt, *Women's Writing in Middle English*. Although recorded in official transcriptions of heresy trials, the statements of Lollard women such as Margery Baxter and Hawisia Mone are sometimes included in this small group of texts. See Tanner, ed., *Heresy Trials*, 41–51, 138–44; and Hanna, "Norfolk Women." For a theoretical and historical analysis of the woman writer's absence in early English textual culture, see Summit, *Lost Property*.

104. Julian of Norwich, *Book of Showings*. Short Text, 1: 201, 255; Long Text 2: 285, 446. I quote here from the Short Text.

105. Baker, *Julian of Norwich's "Showings,"* 15–39.

106. Gilchrist, *Gender and Material Culture*, 186–87, 191.

107. Julian of Norwich, *Book of Showings*. Short Text, 1: 201–2.

108. See Hilles, "Sacred Image," 553–55. Differences between the Short and Long Texts are discussed by Windeatt, "Julian of Norwich." For analyses of the spiritual and theological changes mentioned here, see Watson, "Composition," 642–57; Baker, *Julian of Norwich's "Showings"*; Aers, "Humanity of Christ"; and Staley, "Julian of Norwich."

109. Julian of Norwich, *Book of Showings*, 1: 255.

110. Ibid., 2: 447.

111. Aers, "Humanity of Christ."

112. Gibson, *Theater of Devotion*, 47–65; Beckwith, *Christ's Body*, 45–111; and Renevey, "Margery's Performing Body." For a challenge to this view, see Meale, "Early Ownership and Readership of Love's *Mirror*."

113. *BMK*, 191–97.

114. Eberly, "Margery Kempe."

115. Voaden, "Beholding Men's Members," 184.

116. *BMK*, 6. In Britain, July 23 is the feast of Bridget of Sweden, who would thus also participate in the symbolic authorization of the text. See *Book of Margery Kempe*, ed. Windeatt, 19.

117. On the complex religious polemics of the proems, see Shklar, "Cobham's Daughter," 284–87.

118. Voaden, "Beholding Men's Members," 185.

119. See Voaden, "Beholding Men's Members," 184–86; and Dinshaw, *Getting Medieval*, 159.

120. *BMK*, 49. Margery's familiarity with sexual sin not only established her bond with Mary Magdalene but also gave her intercessory power on behalf of those with similar experience. In the visions in which God thanks her for her contemplations, he singles out her efforts on this front (204). One of the more

unusual points of contact between Kempe's life and that of Mary Magdalene involves their transformation of sexual sinners. The principal focus of Kempe's efforts is her own son, whose conversion from a profligate life resembles the experience of the king of Marseilles in the saint's legendary vita: he goes on "many pilgrimagys to Rome [and] to many oþer holy placys to purchasyn hym pardon, resortyng a-geyn to hys wife [and] hys childe as he was bowndyn to do" (224). In Chapter 4 I discuss Mary Magdalene as a deliverer of sexual sinners in the Digby saint play.

121. *BMK*, 51.

122. Ibid., 176.

123. Ibid., 210.

124. Ibid., 193–94.

125. Ibid., 75. All other quotations in this paragraph appear in *BMK*, 197.

126. Margery's notice that Mary Magdalene "fel down at . . . [Jesus'] feet & wolde a kyssyd hys feet" derives from Pseudo-Bonaventure. See *Nicholas Love's Mirror*, 200–201; and *Meditations on the Life of Christ*, 362–63.

127. Dinshaw, *Getting Medieval*, 162. The resistance to standard exegetical procedure exhibited in Pseudo-Bonaventure's reading of John 20 had a precedent in the homily attributed to Pseudo-Origen, *De Maria Magdalena*, which Pseudo-Bonaventure and Love cite at precisely this point of the text. I discuss the Pseudo-Origen homily in Chapter 5.

128. Dinshaw, *Getting Medieval*, 162–63.

129. Ibid., 163.

130. Ibid., 164.

131. Fletcher, "N-Town Plays," 175.

132. On the staging of this action, see Jones, "Seven Deadly Sins."

133. *Macro Plays*, at line 912. All citations refer to this edition. The stage direction in the Macro manuscript states that "vi small boys in þe lyknes of dewellys" are to emerge from Anima's mantle. Eccles's edition emends this six to seven, a change suggested by Jesus' notice that Anima has as "many deullys" in her soul "[a]s . . . dedly synnys" that she has used (909–10). On the number of devils, see also Riggio, *Play of "Wisdom,"* 288.

134. Damrosch, "*Non Alia Sed Aliter*," 191; Matter, *Voice of My Beloved*, 167; Astell, *Song of Songs*, 174.

135. Scherb discusses the play's preoccupation with internal and external states of being. See *Staging Faith*, 131. On the iconic quality of *Wisdom*, see Bevington, "Stage Picture in *Wisdom*"; and Davidson, *Visualizing the Moral Life*, 83–111.

136. Clark, Kraus, and Sheingorn, "Shifting Constructions," 45. My characterization of the fall of the Mights in this paragraph is based on their discussion (50–55).

137. Butler, *Bodies That Matter: On the Discursive Limits of "Sex"* (New York: Routledge, 1993), 93. Cited in Clark, Kraus, and Sheingorn, "Shifting Constructions," 44.

138. Clark, Kraus, and Sheingorn, "Shifting Constructions," 56. See also Riggio, *Play of "Wisdom,"* 39–47.

139. Clark, Kraus, and Sheingorn, "Shifting Constructions," 54.

140. For analysis of the moral valences of Mary Magdalene's permeable dramatic body in a different historical and ideological context, see Badir, "Iconoclasm and Striptease," 5–6.

141. See references to the "clene" soul at lines 45, 54, 176, 284, 289, 969, 976, and ironically at 494. See also Riggio, *Play of "Wisdom,"* 192.

142. Clark, Kraus, and Sheingorn, "Shifting Constructions," 46–47. See also Riggio, *Play of "Wisdom,"* 197, n. to line 102.

143. On "doubleness" as a sign of femininity and sensuality that could be resignified to work through traditional cultural assumptions about gender, see Watson, "'Yf wommen be double.'" The Macro *Mankind* exploits the idea of humanity's double nature through an elaborate series of gendered tropes. See Epp, "Vicious Guise."

144. Riggio, *Play of "Wisdom,"* 39, 186, n. to line 16.

145. Scherb calls Anima the "place where signs and signifieds coincide." See *Staging Faith*, 131.

146. For discussion of probable auspices and audiences of the play, see the essays by Johnston, "*Wisdom* and the Records"; Gibson, "Play of *Wisdom*"; and Riggio, "The Staging of *Wisdom*."

147. *N-Town Play*, 269–271.626–89. Unless otherwise noted, all quotations, cited by page and line numbers, refer to vol. 1 of Spector's edition. I have used Spector's continuous line numbering for *Passion Play I*. An anonymous woman not identified as a sinner anoints Jesus at the home of Simon the leper in Matt. 26:6–13 and Mark 14:3–9. In Luke 7:36–50 Jesus is anointed by a sinful woman in the home of Simon the Pharisee. John 12:1–8 identifies Christ's anointer as Mary of Bethany.

148. See Coletti, "Purity and Danger"; and Ashley, "Image and Ideology," 115–21.

149. On the trope of Jesus as fruit or flower in the *N-Town Plays*, see Stevens, *Four Middle English Mystery Cycles*, 240.

150. Elsewhere in the *N-Town Play*, the Virgin Mary refers to her birth in Saint Anne's "bowre" (97.64); Angel Gabriel addresses the annunciate Virgin as "Goddys chawmere and his bowre" (122.316); and a doubting Joseph protests Mary's explanation of her pregnancy by asserting he has never come "ʒitt so nyh [her] . . . boure" (125.46).

151. See *N-Town Play*, 2: 562, s.v. beleve, belave 2: "remains, dwells in." Meredith glosses "belevyth" as "believe, have confidence," an interpretation that weakens the inhabitation metaphor that Spector's gloss alternatively strengthens. Meredith also sees the reading of line 14 offered here, in which "I" refers to Mary Magdalene, as a viable, if "odd," alternative to the one he offers: "[He] chose his dwelling-place in my sweet soul." The difference depends upon the meaning of "I-ches," which Meredith renders as a form of the verb "ichesen." See *Passion Play*, 224, n. to line 1685.

152. Voaden, "All Girls Together."

153. Ibid., 83. See Mechtild of Hackeborne, *Booke of Gostlye Grace*, 183–84.

154. *The Ancrene Riwle*, trans. Mary Salu (London: Burns and Oates, 1955), 71, 151. Quoted in McInerney, "Poetics of Enclosure," 162.

155. *BMK*, 87. Hope Allen notes many other points in the *Book* where Kempe discusses her soul "as the habitation of God"; see 301, n. to 87/13.

156. Barratt, *Women's Writing*, 209.

157. McInerney, "Poetics of Enclosure," 176; *Book of Showings*, 2: 595.

158. McInerney, "Poetics of Enclosure," 177, 180. Medieval spiritual traditions encouraging intersubjective relationships that found expression in these kinds of tropes were by no means exclusive to female religious and mystics. Exegesis of the Song of Songs promoted spiritual language and symbolism whose terms figure in various medieval cults and devotions; while the verbal and visual metaphors of this language are gendered, they are also fluid in their application and available to both male and female religious subjects. See Lewis, "Wound in Christ's Side," 212–17, and the sources cited therein.

159. Many unique features of the N-Town plays relate directly to the Virgin Mary's physical role in the Incarnation. These include the Jesse play, the play on the life and betrothal of the Virgin, the *Parliament of Heaven and Salutation and Conception*, and the *Trial of Joseph and Mary*. These plays repeatedly return to the idea, as Mary herself puts it in the *Salutation and Conception*, that "Parfyte God and parfyte man" are united in her body (122.293–94; cf. *Visit to Elizabeth*, 133.70–71). The *Tree of Jesse*, which here substitutes for the Prophets' Play of the other biblical cycles, focuses on the "maydens byrth [that] oure welth xal dresse" (69.120) and presents biblical history with a distinctly Marian slant. The N-Town compilation depicts the Nativity as a miracle worked in feminine flesh; its shepherds and the Magi acknowledge Jesus as the child "Blomyd in a maidenys body" (174.164) and fed "with maydynnys mylk" (177.236). Yet these plays also do not shy away from the practical exigencies of coming to terms with the virgin birth, as the *Trial of Joseph and Mary* and the cherry tree and midwives episodes make clear.

160. *Passion Play*, 225, n. to lines 1696–99. Jesus' familial ties receive more emphasis in the N-Town plays than any of the other English biblical cycles, not only through the inclusion of plays depicting the life of Mary and the Tree of Jesse but also through marginal genealogies such at that appearing on f. 37r. See *N-Town Play*, 1: 70.

161. What the N-Town compiler intended to accomplish with these alterations to biblical narrative has been the subject of considerable debate. See Meredith, "Manuscript, Scribe, and Performance"; idem, *Passion Play*, 7–8; Fletcher, "N-Town Plays"; Prosser, *Drama and Religion*, 110–46, 201–5; and Sugano, "Apologies for the Magdalene." I consider this issue in more detail in a forthcoming essay, "Mary Magdalene and the Poetics of Enclosure in the *N-Town Plays*."

162. Recent biblical scholarship investigates these texts as evidence of women's active, public participation in early Christian communities, opposition to which is probably recorded in the famous Pauline injunctions against women's preaching. See King, "Gospel of Mary"; idem, "Gospel of Mary Magdalene"; idem, "Prophetic Power"; and Marjanen, *The Woman Jesus Loved*. I have been unable to examine the recent consideration of these issues by Ann Graham Brock, *Mary Magdalene, The First Apostle: The Struggle for Authority* (Cambridge: Harvard University Press, 2003).

163. Jansen, *Making of the Magdalen*, 27.

164. Jansen, *"Apostolorum Apostola,"* 77–78.

165. Jansen, *Making of the Magdalen*, 28.

166. Mary Magdalene's testimonials in this episode receive very different treatment in the *Towneley Plays*, where Peter and Paul dismiss Mary Magdalene's "useless carping" and begin a diatribe not only against women's speech but the faithlessness of women in general. See *Towneley Plays*, 1: 367–69, lines 1–64.

167. *LMRP*, xxx, xl. Spector proposes that "substantial portions" of the N-Town compilation may date from the second half of the fifteenth century and that the hand of the main scribe and compiler can be dated "no earlier than the 1490s." See *N-Town Play*, 1: xli, xxii, n. 1. Eccles dates the composition of *Wisdom* between 1465 and 1470; *Macro Plays*, xxx. Baker, Murphy, and Hall (*LMRP*, lxv) suggest that the Digby *Wisdom* fragment was copied between 1490 and 1500. Riggio's argument about the textual priority of the Digby fragment, which she assigns to the 1480s or early 1490s, would place the copying of the Macro *Wisdom* at the end of the century. See *Play of "Wisdom,"* 6–18. Beadle maps the proximity of the scribes of these East Anglian dramatic texts. See "Literary Geography," 101, 107.

168. Gibson, *Theater of Devotion*, 113.

169. See Coletti, *"'Paupertas est Donum Dei,'"* 373–75.

170. *Macro Plays*, xxix.

171. For other relationships between the Digby plays and the N-Town collection, see Gibson, "Bury St. Edmunds," 64–66. For a fuller consideration of these plays' connection through regional dramaturgical traditions, see Scherb, *Staging Faith*.

Chapter 3

The epigraph is from Hilton, *Scale of Perfection*, ed. Bestul, 42; cited by book and chapter numbers in my text and by page numbers in the notes. Bestul's edition is based on London, Lambeth Palace MS 472. Here and elsewhere I emend using de Worde's 1533 edition (*STC* 14045).

1. "For that is the lif that is veri contemplatif, unto bigynne here in that felynge of love and goosteli knowynge of God bi openyng of the goostli iye, whiche schal nevere be loste ne bi taken awey, but the same schal be fulfilled othirwise in the blisse of hevene. This bihight oure Lord to Marie Mawdeleyn, whiche was contemplatif, and He seide . . . that Marie hadde chosen the beste partie, that is the love of God in contemplacion, for it schal nevere be taken awey fro hire" (1.45). *Scale of Perfection*, 82.

2. "I seie not that we schulden departe God fro man in Jhesu, but we schullen love Jhesu bothe God and man—God in man, and man in God; goostli, not fleschli. Thus kennede oure Lord Marie Magdaleyn, that schulde be contemplatif, whanne He seide to hire thus: *Noli me tangere, nondum enim ascendi ad patrem meum* (John 20:17). . . . That is for to seie, Marie Magdelene lovede brennandeli oure Lord Jhesu bifore the tyme of His passioun, but here love was moche bodili and litil goostli" (2.30). *Scale of Perfection*, 208–9.

3. Anselm, *Prayers and Meditations*, 201–6; Bernard of Clairvaux, "Sermon 7," *Song of Songs*, 44; Astell, *Song of Songs in the Middle Ages*, 174. See also Matter, *Voice of My Beloved*, 167. One of the earliest associations of Mary Magdalene with the Bride of the Song of Songs appears in a commentary attributed to Hippolytus of Rome (d. c. 235). Jansen, *Making of the Magdalen*, 28.

4. De Certeau, *Mystic Fable*, 81. See also Lochrie, *Translations of the Flesh*, 73–74.

5. *Cloud of Unknowing* (1981), 44–56; *Love's Mirror*, 118–24. Riehle discusses intended audiences of the *Cloud*. See *Middle English Mystics*, 15–16.

6. The competing attributes comprising the composite Magdalene's identity were not always reconcilable. Among thirteenth-century *mulieres sanctae* and their confessors and clerical authority figures, the ecclesiastics emphasized Mary Magdalene's penitential example, while women saw the saint as a model of amorous contemplation. See Lauwers, "'Noli me tangere,'" 257.

7. See Davidson, "Middle English Saint Play," 94; and Dixon, "'Thys Body of Mary,'" 230–39.

8. A commonality of diction and imagery among the sources for mystical and contemplative writings and the texts themselves in many cases makes difficult the identification of particular sources. See Riehle, *Middle English Mystics*; and for helpful commentary on the terminology of contemplative writings in Middle English, see Hodgson, "Introduction," *Cloud of Unknowing and Related Treatises*, xxix–xli.

9. Smart, *English and Latin Sources*, 90.

10. See Gibson, "Play of *Wisdom*"; and Riggio, ed., *Play of "Wisdom,"* 24–66.

11. Watson, "Censorship and Cultural Change," 853.

12. For an overview of the production of the *Scale* and its place in the canon of Hilton's work, see Clark and Dorward, "Introduction," *Scale of Perfection*, 13–21. See also Minnis, "*Cloud of Unknowing* and *Scale of Perfection*."

13. Clark and Dorward, "Introduction," *Scale of Perfection*, 33. See also Sargent, "Walter Hilton's *Scale of Perfection*." Beadle's survey of late medieval manuscripts in Norfolk assigns five of these manuscripts to East Anglia. See "Literary Geography," 104–5.

14. On the popularity of the *Scale* among these groups, see Hussey, "Audience"; Kaiser, "Mystics," 9–14, 24–25; and Lovatt, "*Imitation of Christ*," 99. Hilton's text circulated in common profit books among the London merchant class. See Scase, "'Common-Profit' Books." For specific illustrations of this audience, see the classic essay by Armstrong, "Piety of Cicely, Duchess of York"; and Hicks, "Piety of Margaret, Lady Hungerford."

15. The work was published again by Julian Notary in 1507 and by de Worde in 1525 and 1533, its printing history in late medieval and early Tudor England thus spanning the *terminus a quo* and *terminus ad quem* for the composition and copying of the Digby play. See *LMRP*, xl. Printed versions of the *Scale* often "found their way" to female courtly and religious readers. See Erler, *Women, Reading, and Piety*, 118, 121–22.

16. Watson, "Thirteenth-Century Anchoritic Devotion," 134–37. See also Gillespie, "*Lukyng in haly bukes*."

17. Carey, "Devout Literate Laypeople"; Sargent, "Introduction," *De Cella in Seculum*, 1. Gillespie attributes this migration of cloistered religious values to reading practices and the *compilatio* and *ordinatio* of devotional miscellanies; see "*Lukyng in haly bukes.*" See also Millett, "*Ancrene Wisse.*"

18. Watson, "Middle English Mystics," 551–54; Swanson, *Church and Society*, 252–308.

19. Copeland, "Why Women Can't Read," 254–62; Watson, "Conceptions of the Word," 95.

20. Gillespie, "*Lukyng in haly bukes,*" 4. Erler discusses the "permeable partition" between the spirituality of professed religious and lay society in the specific context of female reading, book-owning, and literate exchange. See *Women, Reading, and Piety*, 8–15.

21. Gibson, *Theater of Devotion*, 127; see also 107–35.

22. *N-Town Play*, 1: 82.21, 85.99. Subsequent citations in my text refer to vol. 1 of Spector's edition by page and line numbers. "Mary and the Temple" is an episode in the longer play on the early life of Mary that has been incorporated into the N-Town compilation. See *Mary Play*.

23. Gibson, *Theater of Devotion*, 135.

24. The Digby saint's contemplative state exhibits striking likenesses to that of young Mary in the temple: each is visited by angels, fed with delicious heavenly food, and serenaded with hymns celebrating virginity. Each concludes her communion with the spiritual realm by kissing the earth. Cf. "Mary in the Temple" in *N-Town Play*, 1: 92–93, lines 246–77, with *Mary Magdalene*, lines 2019–38 and 2114.

25. Hussey, "Latin and English." The *Scale* was translated into Latin by Carmelite Thomas Fishlake around 1400.

26. "In tercia parte modicum tetigi quod quando per graciam (f. 95v) spiritus sancti consciencia mundata est a sensacione peccatorum, et interior oculus anime apertus est, anima reformata est in sensacionem uirtutum, sicut quando anima veraciter sentit humilitatem in corde, perfectam dileccionem et caritatem ad omnis proximos, pacem et pacienciam, castitatem et mundiciam, cum solacio et leticia de illis, et gloria in consciencia. Et hoc pertinet ad statum hominum perfectorum qui per graciam dei et magnam continuacionem laboris, et per contencionem nocte et die contra peccata vicerunt amaras sensaciones peccatorum, et receperunt per graciam dileccionis ihesu christi dulces sensationes virtutum, et sic in sensacione veraciter reformantur. In quarta parte tetigi de quisbusdam animabus que non solum reformantur ad ymaginem dei in sensacione virtutum, set alcius eciam eleuantur, et ita perfecte reformantur dei dileccione que replentur quod senciunt in cordibus suis, et percipiunt secretas inspiraciones ihesu cristi, et spirituales illuminaciones, celestes confortaciones et graciosas cogniciones, mirabiles consideraciones spirituum bonorum, et occultas percepciones celestium gaudiorum." Quoted from MS York Cathedral Library XVI K 5, fol. 95r–95v in Hussey, "Latin and English," 458–59. Unless otherwise noted, translations are my own.

27. It is tempting to consider how these metaphoric invocations of changing array may have been accompanied by concrete changes of apparel. Magdalene's

first profession of donning humility, for example, might signal the shedding of the attire of her sinful life for more modest or even the quasi-religious garb of the "chaste woman." On clothing as a marker of identity, see Coletti, "Design."

28. When Mary Magdalene employs the metaphor of "enhabiting," or clothing, herself with humility to acknowledge her entry into a new spiritual experience, she invokes the Pauline concept of "putting on" the new man in Christ (Eph. 4:23–24; Gal. 3:27–28; Rom. 13:12–14; Col. 3:9–10). The Pauline tenor of her spiritual project is further suggested by her declaration of purpose upon reaching Marseilles: "For mannys sowle þe reformacyon, / In hys name, lord, I beseche þe, / Wythin þi lond to have my mancyon" (1459–61). Reformation of the soul is also a thematic emphasis that the Macro *Wisdom* derives largely from Hilton's work. See Smart, *English and Latin Sources*, 18–22. The dramatic text here echoes the language of religious profession. The *Liber de modo bene vivendi ad sororem* (*PL* 184: 1199–1306), a late twelfth- or early thirteenth-century treatise of spiritual direction for a nun translated in late medieval England as the *Manere of Good Lyvyng*, advises its addressee: "Therfor, my beloved suster, lete us aray ourself with spirituall ornamentis as charite, humylite, mekenes, obediens and paciens. Thes be þe vestures with þe which we maye please Jhesu Cryste þe celestyall spouse." Quoted from Bodleian Library MS Laud misc. 517 in McGovern-Mouron, "*Liber de modo bene vivendi*," 87, 103.

29. In the *Legenda aurea*, the priest who witnesses Mary Magdalene's celestial elevations is physically incapacitated by his vision of "a secrete celestial place where no man humayn myght come"; *CELMM*, 135, lines 493–95.

30. *Scale of Perfection*, 176. See Clark and Dorward, "Introduction," *Scale of Perfection*, 45.

31. Winstead identifies similar rhetorical and ideological strategies in the prose *Lyf of Saint Katherine*, which represents the saint in spiritual states like those described in *Incendium Amoris* and the *Cloud of Unknowing*. See *Virgin Martyrs*, 162–67.

32. This characterization of Hilton's text is based on Watson, "Visions of Inclusion," 147.

33. Sanok observes that public performance of female saint plays could complicate understandings of the "increasingly interior and meditative nature of late medieval devotion." See "Performing Feminine Sanctity," 284.

34. Hudson, "Lollard Sect Vocabulary," 173–74. See also idem, *Premature Reformation*, 417–20.

35. On the redirection of Catherine's spiritual and social commitments in the Middle English text, see Despres, "Ecstatic Reading." On adaptation, extraction, and collection of Saint Bridget's works, see Ellis, "'Flores ad Fabricandam . . . Coronam.'"

36. Alphonse's *Epistola* was independently translated (BL MS Cotton Julius Fii) before being incorporated into *The Chastising of God's Children*. On the Middle English afterlives of Alphonso's text, see Voaden, "Rewriting the Letter." See also Bazire and Colledge, eds., *The Chastising of God's Children*.

37. Holbrook, "Margery Kempe and Wynkyn de Worde"; Summit, *Lost Property*, 126–38.

38. Lines 1–48, 114–264, 963–92, 1249–1335.

39. Bush, "*Locus* and *Platea* Staging."

40. A comparison of the Digby play's treatment of this moment with the much longer version of this scene in the meditative drama known as *Christ's Burial* from Bodleian Library MS e Museo 160 underscores the saint play's emotional and verbal restraint. One of two meditative dramas with probable Carthusian connections, *Christ's Burial* provides sustained, painful reflection on the body of the crucified Christ by every biblical figure associated with the Crucifixion and Deposition in the literature of Passion meditation. On the dramas from MS e Museo 160, see *LMRP*, lxxiv–xcix and 141–68. Because these meditative dramas have twice been edited in the same volume as the Digby plays (Furnivall in his 1882 edition claimed that the plays in MS. e Museo 160 had once belonged to MS Digby 133), they are sometimes mistakenly identified as Digby plays. See Furnivall, *Digby Plays*, vii.

41. Ashley posits a similar emphasis in the Chester cycle. See "Divine Power."

42. John 11:27: "She saith to him: 'Yes, Lord, I have believed that thou art Christ, the Son of the living God, who art come into this world.'"

43. Riehle, *Middle English Mystics*, 76.

44. *Scale of Perfection*, 206.

45. Park, "Reflecting Christ," 21.

46. *Scale of Perfection*, 212. See also 38–39 (book 1.9).

47. Ibid., 207.

48. Ibid., 137.

49. Park, "Reflecting Christ," 22.

50. *Scale of Perfection*, 68; Park, "Reflecting Christ," 23. Aston relates this stance on meditation to the role of visual images in late medieval devotion. See "Imageless Devotion."

51. The Christocentric additions were once thought to be authorial. Sargent provides a collation and an overview of critical opinion; "Walter Hilton's *Scale of Perfection*," 197. See also Hussey, "Latin and English."

52. Park, "Reflecting Christ," 18.

53. *Scale of Perfection*, 208–9.

54. Park, "Reflecting Christ," 23.

55. *Scale of Perfection*, 207–8.

56. For example, the *Speculum Devotorum*, a fifteenth-century compilation made for female religious, adapts the spiritual program of Suso's *Orologium Sapientiae* to recommend meditation on Christ's humanity to its female audience. See Sargent, "Minor Devotional Writings," 160.

57. Voaden, "Rewriting the Letter." The Middle English version of Alfonso's text survives in a single manuscript of Norfolk provenance (British Library MS Cotton Julius Fii), where it appears with the English translation of Bridget's *Liber celestis*. See Voaden's edition in *God's Words, Women's Voices*. See also Colledge, "*Epistola solitarii ad reges.*"

58. Voaden, *God's Words, Women's Voices*, 61–66.

59. Hodgson, "Introduction," *Deonise Hid Divinite*, xi–xiii. Pepwell's collection has been edited by Gardner, *Cell of Self-Knowledge*.

60. *Scale of Perfection*, 40–41. Hilton's warnings also constitute his rejoinder to the bodily and spiritual enthusiasms that Rolle made the highest goals of contemplative experience. See Clark and Dorward, "Introduction," 24, 30–31, 46. On Rolle's enthusiasms, see Watson, *Richard Rolle*, 66–72.

61. Voaden, *God's Words, Women's Voices*, 7–40.

62. *BMK*, 3. Hope Allen called the "discernment of spirits" "the basic problem" of Margery's life (349, n. to p. 248). In *God's Words, Women's Voices* Voaden argues that women visionaries' successful claims to true revelation depended in part upon their understanding and use of the discourse of *discretio spirituum*. See also Dillon, "Holy Women and Their Confessors," 123–25. Margery's anxieties about the truth of her spiritual visitations constitute some of the more memorable moments of her text. She asks the anchoress Dame Julian "yf þer were any deceyte in" her revelations (42). When Jesus orders Margery to wear white clothes, she offers this conditional assent: "Ʒyf þu be þe spiryt of God þat spekyst in my sowle & I may prevyn þe for a trew spiryt wyth cownsel of þe chirche, I xal obey þi" (76). Margery's abiding concern for the authenticity of her spiritual visitations gets her into trouble with the deity, too, because the risk is not only that she will mistake a false spirit for a true one, but that she will mistake the voice of God for that of the devil. This is precisely what happens when Margery refuses to acknowledge what God has shown her about damned souls: "Sche wolde Ʒevyn no credens to þe cownsel of God but raþar leuyd it was sum euyl spiryt for to deceyuyn hir" (144). In *BMK*, see also 143, 201, 215, 219–20, 248.

63. Bridget of Sweden's *Liber Celestis* reports her regular visitation by her "good angel"; see Sutton and Visser-Fuchs, "Cult of Angels," 233.

64. *A Tretis of Discresyon of Spirites*, in *Deonise His Divinite*, 85. The *Tretis* comments at length (84–88) about the contemplative's vulnerability to deceptions of the world, the flesh, and the devil. See also Alfonso of Jaén, *Epistola solitarii ad reges*, 177; and Rolle, *The Form of Living*, in *Rolle: Prose and Verse*, 7.

65. *Revelationes Gertrudianae ac Mechtildianae*, ed. the Benedictines of Solèsmes, 3 vols. (Paris: H. Oudin Fratres, 1877), 2.355. Quoted in Voaden, "Women's Words, Men's Language," 74. See also the Middle English translation of Mechtild's *Liber*, *The Booke of Gostlye Grace of Mechtild of Hackeborn*, 587.

66. Raphael figures prominently in the Book of Tobit, where he is identified as one of seven angels serving the glory of God (12:15).

67. Voaden, *God's Words, Women's Voices*, 62. This salutation also echoes Gabriel's words to the annunciate Mary, which dramatists sometimes represented in terms of the discourse of *discretio spirituum*. See Ashley, "Noon-Day Demon."

68. Mary Magdalene's declaration of understanding corresponds to the third of Alphonso's seven signs by which a true visionary can be identified: "The iiide signe is in the wheche godly vision is knowyn when the soule beinge in vision bodily or ymaginary and spiritual felis an intellectual supernatural of light of treuþe and than takis trew tokenys of yo thinges seen and wordes and the under stonding of it than clerly is openyd . and the treuþe of yat mater is mad opinn"; *Epistola solitarii ad reges*, 177–78. The experience of the Digby saint generally accords with all of Alphonso's other signs of a true visionary (Voaden,

God's Words, Women's Voices, 49–50), except the one that specified the person's adherence to the guidance of a spiritual director, a lack that is dramaturgically accommodated by appearances of Christ, who fulfills that role for the visionary and contemplative Magdalene.

69. Rolle warned that the devil's false illuminations could create the illusion of angels' song; *Song of Angels*, 68–69.

70. *BMK*, 219–20.

71. Baker, Murphy, and Hall cite here echoes of John 11:4 and 1 Cor. 2:9; *LMRP*, 207. John's account of the raising of Lazarus (11:1–44), however, contains no admonition about the limitations of clerical "covnnyng." Jesus also questions clerical discourses and practices in *Wisdom*, which describes salvific knowledge as both inexpressible and experientially and sensibly based. See *Macro Plays*, 116–17, lines 61–64, 87–98.

72. Lochrie, *Translations of the Flesh*, 86.

73. Quoted and translated in Watson, *Richard Rolle*, 115.

74. *Cloud of Unknowing*, 30.

75. I quote here from de Worde's 1533 edition of the *Scale* (STC 14045, sig. T3v), which renders this passage more forcefully than the manuscript edited by Bestul (212).

76. *BMK*, 135.

77. Bush, "*Locus* and *Platea* Staging"; Mead, "Four-fold Allegory"; Scherb, "Worldly and Sacred Messengers"; King, "Sacred Eroticism," 155–214; Dixon, "'Thys Body of Mary.'"

78. *CELMM*, 135, lines 506–10. Cf. Bokenham's life of Mary Magdalene, which closely follows Jacobus's text at this point. See Bokenham, *Legendys of Hooly Wummen*, 170, lines 6226–27.

79. Dramatic representation of heavenly mysteries here is consistent with mystical discourses about contemplative perfection. Rolle identified sight into heaven as one of four mystical experiences fulfilling the contemplative's aspirations. See Watson, *Richard Rolle*, 67–68.

80. Bevington offers this reading for the difficult lines 2050–51: "The joy in Jerusalem (i.e. the rejoicing of the angels in the heavenly Jerusalem just witnessed), the likes of which I haven't seen for thirty years or more, plainly reveals you (i.e. proves your sainthood)"; *Medieval Drama*, 750.

81. See Dixon, "'Thys Body of Mary,'" 230–39; and Jansen, *Making of the Magdalen*, 116.

82. Radulph Ardentis characterizes her conversion as a response to an inner calling: "Non enim per vocem praedicationis, ut Petrus et Andreas, nec per necessitatem, ut Paulus, sed per solam internam inspirationem vocata fuit"; *PL* 155: 1398. Dixon discusses Mary Magdalene as a figure who "cultivates interiority"; "'Thys Body of Mary,'" 230–31.

83. This passage echoes Odo of Cluny's *In veneratione sanctae Mariae Magdalenae*: "Sed non in toto haec mulier erravit cum dominum hortulanum aestimavit. Sicut enim hortulani officium est noxias herbas eradicare, ut bonae quaeque proficere valeant; ita Dominus Jesus Christus de horto suo, id est de

Ecclesia sua quotidie vitia eradicat, ut virtutes crescere valeant"; *PL* 133: 720. See Mycoff, "Bokenham's *Lyf of Marye Maudelyn.*"

84. Watson, *Richard Rolle*, 22.

85. Ibid., 23. See also Watson's discussions of this issue in "Conceptions of the Word," 102–3; and "Middle English Mystics," 551–54. On the late medieval articulation of spiritual cognition in terms of *scientia* and *sapientia*, see also Simpson, "Affective Knowledge"; and Ghosh, *Wycliffite Heresy*, 8.

86. *BMK*, 219–20. See also Lochrie, *Translations of the Flesh*, 203; and Staley, *Dissenting Fictions*, 86–92.

87. In late medieval religious and epistemological discourses, the term "experience" designates awareness acquired through the perceptions, attributes, and behaviors of the sentient subject, in contrast to knowledge based in official culture as codified in written texts and institutional discourses. The historical and discursive function of medieval "experience" is illuminated by Scott's theoretical discussion of the term; "Experience."

88. Watson, *Richard Rolle*, 22; Vauchez, *Laity in the Middle Ages*, 219–29. Late medieval mystical discourses and practices reveal so much anxiety about their own cultural position precisely because they lent credence to the realm of experience. See Beckwith, "Problems of Authority," 180–81; and idem, *Christ's Body*, 14–21. See also Lochrie, *Translations of the Flesh*, 63–64.

89. On sacred biography and social critique, see Staley, *Dissenting Fictions*, 39–47; and Vauchez, *Laity in the Middle Ages*. Studies focusing on critical functions of sacred biography in late medieval East Anglia include Winstead, *Virgin Martyrs*; Delany, *Impolitic Bodies*; and Jones, "Margery Kempe and the Bishops." For recent work on continental examples, see Dor, Johnson, and Wogan-Browne, eds., *Holy Women of Liège*.

90. Newman, *Virile Woman*, 244–48. The bibliography on this subject is steadily growing; for representative discussions, see Bolton, "*Vitae Matrum*"; McNamara, "Rhetoric of Orthodoxy"; Coakley, "Friars as Confidants of Holy Women"; Mooney, ed., *Gendered Voices*; Bartlett, *Male Authors, Female Readers*; Clark, *Elisabeth of Schönau*; Vauchez, *Laity in the Middle Ages*; and Lauwers, "'*Noli me tangere.*'"

91. Vauchez, *Laity in the Middle Ages*, xix.

92. Angela of Foligno, *Complete Works*, 318.

93. Rubin, *Corpus Christi*, 323.

94. For overviews of these influences, see Haskins, *Myth and Metaphor*, 177–91; and Jansen, *Making of the Magdalen*, 247–85.

95. On "approuyd wymmon" see Voaden, "Company She Keeps," 55–56.

96. *Life of Christina of Markyate*, 116–17.

97. *Revelations of Saint Birgitta*, 25–34.

98. Jansen, *Making of the Magdalen*, 252–55, 275–77, 280–81.

99. Jansen, *Making of the Magdalen*, 288. See also Cannon and Vauchez, *Margherita of Cortona*, 164–67.

100. Hugh of Floreffe, *Life of Yvette of Huy*, 115–17. See also Mulder-Bakker, "Ivetta of Huy," 233–50. Jacques de Vitry consciously modeled his life of beguine

Marie d'Oignies on the vita of Mary Magdalene. See Lauwers, "'*Noli me tangere*.'"

101. Newman, *Virile Woman*, 286, n. 29.

102. Vauchez identifies divine election as an important attribute of late medieval female visionaries who engaged in ecclesiastical politics. See *Laity in the Middle Ages*, 220–22.

103. See Clark, *Elisabeth of Schönau*, 25; and Dean, "Elizabeth of Schönau in England." Dean notes a manuscript (University of Paris MS 790) that once belonged to seventeenth-century antiquarian Kenelm Digby, who also owned the manuscript containing *Mary Magdalene*. See also Kerby-Fulton, "Hildegard and the Male Reader," 4–7.

104. On Elisabeth's angelic communications, see Clark, *Elisabeth of Schönau*, 14, 29, 33, 36, 87, 90; on identification with biblical prophets, see 74, 91, 132.

105. Latin parodies of liturgical rite were a staple of festive Christian discourse, and the dog-Latin of the pagan priest's service finds many parallels in dramatic and other texts; see *LMRP*, 211, n. to lines 1185–1201.

106. Dramatic representation of the effectiveness of Mary Magdalene's petitions ("Good Lord, my preor I feythfully send!" [1560]) resonates with the late medieval interest in the power of individual prayer. See Hughes, *Religious Life of Richard III*, 129–31. Jesus specifically acknowledges this power: "My grace xall grow, and don decend / To Mary my lovyr, þat to me doth call" (1586–87).

107. Lauwers, "'*Noli me tangere*,'" 224, 228. On the problem of Mary Magdalene's silent confession, see also Bériou, "La Madeleine dans les sermons Parisiens," 287.

108. Jansen, *Making of the Magdalen*, 215–18. For Odo of Cluny, see *PL* 133: 715.

109. *Meditations on the Life of Christ*, 170–71. Nicholas Love states that Mary spoke to Jesus "in her herte," telling him of her sins; *Mirror of the Blessed Life of Jesus Christ*, 90–91.

110. Quoted and translated from MS Biblioteca Apostolica Vaticana Borgh. 175, f. 28v, in Jansen, *Making of the Magdalen*, 215.

111. *CELMM*, 137–38, lines 549–71, quote at 560.

112. An eleventh-century life of Mary Magdalene includes a similar exchange: "Sed quia te hominem et dignum in tua locutione nove, idcirco tibi que sum vel que gessi narravi." Quoted from a Brooklyn Museum MS of the Old Testament in Misrahi, "A *Vita Sanctae Mariae Magdalenae*," 339.

113. *CELMM*, 137, line 555. On the manner in which the eucharistic viaticum was transported by priest and acolyte to the sick and dying in the late Middle Ages, see Rubin, *Corpus Christi*, 77–78.

114. Bynum, *Holy Feast and Holy Fast*, 81, 94, 166.

115. Vauchez, *Laity in the Middle Ages*, 237–42; Milner, "Flesh and Food"; Dixon, "'Thys Body of Mary,'" 230–39; Coletti, "Design." The play's reminiscences of medieval women's eucharistic piety should not be construed as an effort to model the devotional behaviors of its contemporary female audiences, as Milner suggests. See the important critique of the scholarly emphasis on medieval women's asceticism by Hollywood, *Soul as Virgin Wife*, 1–39; see also McSheffrey, *Gender and Heresy*, 140–44.

116. On the appropriation of priestly roles by late medieval holy women, especially in eucharistic contexts, see Bynum, *Holy Feast and Holy Fast*, 232–33. Mechtild of Hackeborn's *Liber specialis gratiae*, or *Booke of Gostlye Grace*, made one such example available in late medieval England. See Voaden, "Drinking from the Golden Cup," 113–14.

117. Dixon, "'Thy Body of Mary,'" 230–31.

118. See Dillon, "Holy Women and Their Confessors," 128–29.

119. Beckwith, *Christ's Body*, 95.

120. Sanok, "Mary Magdalene and the *Book of Margery Kempe*."

121. Jansen, "*Apostolorum Apostola*." This article consolidates material from several chapters of Jansen's *Making of the Magdalen*, but see especially chap. 2, "The Vita Apostolica," 49–99.

122. John Mirk briefly mentions it; "De Sancta Maria Magdalena," in *Festial*, 205. A fuller account appears in the Northern Homily Cycle. See Horstmann's edition from B.L. MS Harley 4196 in *Altenglische Legenden*, 82–84, lines 140–59; 261–62. The life of Mary Magdalene in Oxford, Bodleian Library MS Laud 108 of the *Early South English Legendary* contains a longer sermon whose references to God's creation of the universe are reminiscent of Mary Magdalene's Creation sermon in the Digby play. See Horstmann, *Sammlung altenglischer Legenden*, 152–53, lines 198–225. Mary Magdalene's preaching in the *Legenda aurea* is discussed by Blamires, "Women and Preaching," 143–44.

123. *CELMM*, 123, lines 170–83. The connection between Mary Magdalene's pleasant appearance and the effectiveness of her preaching subverts the conventional topos of the destructive allure of women's speech. A tract on women's preaching in B.L. MS Harley 31, an anti-Wycliffite miscellany, observes that "a beautiful woman is more likely to incite desire in her auditors by the sweetness of her speech than she is to extinguish it in them" (Sed mulier pulchra vt est verisimile plus accenderet auditores suauitate sermonis ad libidinem quam illam in eis extingueret). See Blamires and Marx, "Woman Not to Preach," 63.

124. Bokenham, "Lyf of Marye Maudleyn," in *Legendys of Hooly Wummen*, lines 5783–93. Warren discusses Bokenham's treatment of Mary Magdalene's preaching. See *Spiritual Economies*, 151–52. In the dramatic *Vie de Marie Magdaleine*, the saint engages frequently in teaching and preaching, even observing at one point that "La sacree page nous dict" (95, line 1588), but is never shown rehearsing the scriptural text.

125. See "Lyf of S. Kateryne," *Legendys of Hooly Wummen*, 184–85, lines 6748–95. Capgrave's Saint Catherine engages in theological debate and quotes scripture. See Winstead, *Virgin Martyrs*, 173.

126. See Jeffrey, "English Saints' Plays"; Bush, "*Locus* and *Platea* Staging"; Mead, "Four-Fold Allegory"; and Scherb, "Worldly and Sacred Messengers."

127. Scherb, "Worldly and Sacred Messengers," 8. See lines 27–28, 120–28, 217–21.

128. *LMRP*, 250, s.v. "Houkkyn": "to hook, prob[ably] here to fornicate with." Audiences for sermons in late medieval England were commonly of mixed gender, age, and social class. See Spencer, *English Preaching*. Women may have been identified more frequently as the target audience for sermons because

they were denied access to scriptural learning in more official forms. See Blamires, "Limits of Bible Study," 8. Margery Kempe comments on her hunger for sermons in *BMK*, 142.

129. Jeanne Tombu hypothesizes that the painting is the inner right panel of a triptych that also represented Mary Magdalene's profligate worldly life, her anointing of Christ and conversion in the house of Simon, and her witness to the Resurrection. See "Un triptyque." Carolyn Dinshaw and David Wallace use the Magdalene preaching panel to frame an introduction to medieval women's textual culture. See *Cambridge Companion to Medieval Women*, 1–10.

130. Tombu's reconstruction of the triptych includes this image; "Un triptyque, " 311.

131. The left panel of Tombu's reconstructed triptych is labeled "Magdalene hunting with falcon" by Mosco, who reports that it was privately owned and lost during World War II. See *La Maddelena*, 39. The hunting panel included a smaller image in which Mary Magdalene stands before a preaching Christ, who instructs from an identical makeshift pulpit in another outdoor scene. See "Un triptyque," 300.

132. Tombu, "Un triptyque," 301. Mary Magdalene's identical apparel in the various scenes of the triptych was one important clue to its reconstruction. Other representations of Mary Magdalene preaching typically show her in more modest garb; see Jansen, "*Apostolorum apostola.*"

133. On gender segregation in medieval sermon audiences, see Rusconi, "Women's Sermons," 174–79.

134. Vauchez, *Laity in the Middle Ages*, 219–36. See the following essays in Kienzle and Walker, eds., *Woman Preachers and Prophets*: Kienzle, "The Prostitute-Preacher"; Bériou, "The Right of Women to Give Religious Instruction," 134–45; Meussig, "Prophecy and Song," 146–58; and Pryds, "The Case of Rose of Viterbo," 159–72. See also Waters, *Angels and Earthly Creatures*. Discussions of women's preaching with special relevance to late medieval England include Blamires and Marx, "Woman Not to Preach"; and Blamires, "Women and Preaching."

135. Jansen, "*Apostolorum Apostola,*" 60–65.

136. Abelard, *De auctoritate vel dignitate ordinis sanctimonialium*, letter 6, "On the Origins of Nuns." Excerpted and translated by Blamires, ed., *Woman Defamed and Woman Defended*, 234. See also Caviness, "Anchors, Abbess, and Queen," 111.

137. "Quia muliebri sexui nouerat prohibitum publicis auditibus non debere divinum inferre sermonem"; *Sermo de sancta Maria Magdalena* (Paris, B.N. lat. 17637), *Analecta Bollandiana* 69 (1951): 145–47. Quoted in Deremble, "Premiers cycles d'images consacrés à Marie Madeleine," 198, n. 28.

138. "Mystice autem per hoc intelligi dedit quod mulieres maioribus ecclesiae ministeriis manum apponere non debent. Non enim licet eis praedicare vel sacramenta ministrare"; *In die sancto Pasche, Sermones de tempore* (Angers, 1575), 386. Quoted in Lauwers, "'*Noli me tangere*,'" 243, n. 182.

139. Jansen, "*Apostolorum apostola,*" 67–69. The debate is summarized by Blamires and Marx, "Women Not to Preach," 39–42. See also Bériou, "Right of Women"; and Blamires, *Case for Women*, 184–98.

140. Blamires and Marx, "Women Not to Preach," 35. See also Blamires, "Women and Preaching," 138–39.

141. Robert of Basevorn's *Forma praedicandi* maintained that "no lay person or Religious, unless permitted by a Bishop or a Pope, and no woman, no matter how learned or saintly, ought to preach." Quoted from James J. Murphy, *Three Medieval Rhetorical Arts* (Berkeley and Los Angeles: University of California Press, 1971), 122–24, in Blamires and Marx, "Women Not to Preach," 45.

142. Blamires and Marx, "Women Not to Preach," 50–55. See also Bériou, "La Madeleine dans les sermons Parisiens."

143. Vincent of Beauvais, *Speculum historiale,* 1.9, chap. 102: "Sancta Maria Magdalena cum diutius uerbum Dei predicasset maximeque cum ad eis notitiam peruenisset quod Apostolus mulieres in ecclesiis tacere precepisset, contemplationi arctius vacare decontulit." Quoted in Bériou, "La Madeleine dans les sermons Parisiens," 301–2, n. 107.

144. "Privilegia paucorum non faciunt legem communem. Vel dicendum quod non predicauit sed fuit prenuntia resurrectionis Christi. . . . Quondam indiguit uel licuit in ecclesia uti predicatione et magisterio virginum ut Catherine tempore et Magdalene et Cecilie et Lucie etc. Propter necessitatem fidei et ecclesie edificande que tunc novella erat, licuit feminis quod tamen non liceret eis si esset plantata sicut modo, et hoc propter defectum predicatorum." Quoted from Gauthier de Château-Thierry, *De officio predicandi. I. Vtrum conueniat uiris tantum uel uiris et mulieribus,* in Bériou, "La Madeleine dans les sermons Parisiens," 301, n. 106.

145. See Lauwers, "*'Noli me tangere,'*" 245–50. On the implications of women's *exhortatio* as defined by preaching manuals, see Farmer, "Persuasive Voices."

146. Blamires, "Women and Preaching," 136, 142. See also Jansen, "*Apostolorum Apostola,*" 69–80.

147. Pryds, "Case of Rose of Viterbo," 160.

148. Blamires, "Women and Preaching," 142–43. See also Winstead, *Virgin Martyrs,* 66–71.

149. See the important studies by Cross, "'Great Reasoners in Scripture'"; and Aston, "Lollard Women Priests?" The idea that Lollardy afforded women opportunities for literate involvement in religious reading and teaching has been challenged by McSheffrey. See *Gender and Heresy*; and "Literacy and the Gender Gap." For an important new interpretation of the material related to the literate activities of Lollard women, see Krug, *Reading Families,* 114–52.

150. Copeland, "Why Women Can't Read," 254–72. On prohibitions of vernacular preaching and the circulation of vernacular texts put into place by Arundel's *Constitutions* in response to Lollardy, see Watson, "Censorship and Cultural Change."

151. The debate on women's preaching was a subset of the larger conflict involving lay access to vernacular scripture and clerical control over sacred learning and its authorization. See Blamires and Marx, "Women Not to Preach," 44–46. Winstead notes the frequent late medieval construction of anxieties about lay learning through the figure of the "unruly female scholar"; *Virgin*

Martyrs, 138–39. Shklar analyzes Margery Kempe's rhetorical manipulations of the central terms of the debate about gender, religious authority, lay learning, and reform; see "Cobham's Daughter."

152. Brut's opinions appear in several anti-Wycliffite tracts that draw on documents related to his trial for heresy. Blamires and Marx provide an edition of *Utrum liceat mulieribus docere viros publice congregatos* from Harley 31 in "Woman Not to Preach," 55–63. See also their effort (36–38) to untangle Brut's complicated relationship to the tracts assembled in this manuscript. Selections from anti-Wycliffite materials containing Brut's arguments and from the episcopal register of his trial are translated in Blamires, ed., *Woman Defamed and Woman Defended*, 251–60. Aston discusses the notoriety of Brut's case (1391–93). See "Lollard Women Priests?," 53–55.

153. "Confirmatur, nam legitur de beata Maria Magdalena quod publice predicauit in Marcilia et in regione adiacente quam sua predicacione ad Christum conuertit. Quare vocatur apostolorum apostola." Blamires and Marx, "Woman Not to Preach," 56.

154. "[M]ulte mulieres constanter predicaverunt verbum quando sacerdotes et alii non audebant verbum loqui et patet de Magdalena et Martha." Quoted from B.L. MS Harley 31, fol. 219r by Aston, "Lollard Women Priests?," 52, n. 14. This treatise is no. 9 in the inventory of the contents of this manuscript provided by Blamires and Marx, "Woman Not to Preach," 36. Staley cites a Wycliffite gloss on John's gospel (MS Bodley 243) that designates Mary Magdalene as "an example of the true preacher." See *Dissenting Fictions*, 126.

155. "Tercia casus est propter messis multitudinem et metencium paucitatem concessum est mulieribus Marie et Marthe publice predicare. . . ." Blamires and Marx, "Woman Not to Preach," 62.

156. Translated from the *Register of John Trefnant*, in Blamires, ed., *Woman Defamed and Woman Defended*, 258. Lochrie discusses Brut's defense in *Translations of the Flesh*, 110–11.

157. Aston, "Lollard Women Priests?" 55.

158. Ibid., 59–61. For the confessions of Baxter and Moone, see Tanner, ed., *Heresy Trials*, 41–51 (Baxter) and 138–44 (Mone).

159. *BMK*, 126.

160. Ibid., 160.

161. Quoted from MSS Bodley 649 and Laud Misc. 706 in Hudson, *Premature Reformation*, 437.

162. I think that the Digby play's actual or ideal audiences would have recognized Mary Magdalene's scripturally based speeches as sermons. Spencer (*English Preaching*, 108–18) discusses the characteristics by which late medieval audiences would have identified a public discourse as a sermon. These include the presence of a theme or "text," the use of hortatory forms of address (such as "friends," "good cristen men and wymmen," and "worshipful syres and dames"), and scriptural references, exempla, etc. Spencer comments: "People recognize a bona fide sermon by its accordance with what they already know of the Church's teaching and by the circumstances of its delivery. . . . [T]o preach never merely meant 'to construct an argument out of numbered divisions based upon

a sentence of scripture,' but 'to utter a religious and hortatory address, customarily based upon a passage of scripture, provided one were an authorized person in an authorized place at an authorized time'" (117–18). Though necessarily truncated in length and lacking the formal structure of a sermon, the scriptural speeches of the Digby play's Magdalene correspond to Spencer's basic characteristics. In the case of Mary Magdalene's preaching on poverty (1923–38), her hortatory "dere fryndys" creates an expectation of the kind of address that will follow. For the purposes of this discussion, the key issue is whether Magdalene speaks as an "authorized person in an authorized place at an authorized time."

163. High ranking, economically privileged individuals who encountered vernacular scripture were less likely to incur the dangers that members of lower social strata did in the same circumstances. The friar who wrote MS Longleat 4, a collection of passages from the Gospels in English with elaborate commentary, for a well-to-do patron in the early fifteenth century distinguished between the upper classes of the laity, whom he thought "sufficiently well-educated and responsible to be entrusted with Bible translations and commentaries, and the rest of the lay population, who . . . were not." See Spencer, *English Preaching*, 97–98. See also Hudson and Spencer, "Sermons of MS Longleat 4." MS Longleat 4 may have been produced for a female patron. See Meale, "Early Ownership and Readership of Love's *Mirror*," 44–45. McSheffrey discusses the license that high social status conferred on heterodox women. See *Gender and Heresy*, 29–30, 136.

164. Winstead also considers late medieval East Anglian saints' lives in relation to contemporary religious polemic. See *Virgin Martyrs*, 167–77.

165. Watson, "Censorship and Cultural Change," 830.

166. Cross, "Great Reasoners," 373–75. See also Hudson, *Premature Reformation*, 456–72.

167. Houlbrooke, "Persecution of Heresy," 311. On the early sixteenth-century persecution of East Anglian Lollards, see Thomson, *Later Lollards*, 134–38.

168. *English Wycliffite Sermons*, 3: 299. See also Staley, *Dissenting Fictions*, 90–91.

169. Open-air preaching is the norm in visual representations. See Spenser, *English Preaching*, 71, 75–76; and Alexander, "Pulpit with the Four Doctors," 202.

170. Cross, "Great Reasoners," 377–78, 370–71, citing Fox, *Acts and Monuments* (London, 1864). Winstead discusses the use of anti-Lollard rhetoric in Capgrave's *Life of Saint Katherine*. See *Virgin Martyrs*, 176. Wycliffite texts hedged about embracing Mary Magdalene's legendary apostolic role; none of the Wycliffite sermons for Easter week in which Mary Magdalene is prominent mentions her conversion of Marseilles through preaching. See Blamires, "Women and Preaching," 151.

171. The stage direction introducing this speech makes reference to Mary Magdalene's appearance "wyth hyr dysypyll," possibly alluding to Jacobus's statement that the woman preached in Marseilles "cum suis discipulis." See Blamires, "Women and Preaching," 143.

172. Some exegetes and hymnists assumed Mary Magdalene's presence among the disciples at Pentecost. See Jansen, *Making of the Magdalen*, 81–82.

173. Quoted from Cambridge University Library MS Gg. vi 16, fol. 15v, in Spencer, *English Preaching*, 185.

174. Quoted from MS Longleat 4, fol. 1r, in Watson, "Censorship and Cultural Change," 855–56, n. 88.

175. Blamires, "Women and Preaching," 151. Reames argues that patterns of abridgement and selection in late medieval breviaries reveal discomfort with Saint Cecelia's role as preacher. See "*Mouvance* and Interpretation," 181. See also Sanok, "Performing Feminine Sanctity," 286–94.

176. Winstead, *Virgin Martyrs*, 177.

177. Katherine Little, "Reading Women into Lollardy."

178. See Watson, "Censorship and Cultural Change"; and Hudson, *Premature Reformation*, 443–45.

179. Hughes, *Religious Life of Richard III*. See also the discussion of the theological eclecticism of MS Longleat 4 by Hudson and Spencer, "Old Author, New Work," 233. Geoffrey Downes is typical of a kind of late medieval lay person who saw no contradiction between the embrace of traditional material manifestations of religious practice—such as image worship, chantries, and confraternal membership—and the possession of vernacular scriptures and Wycliffite commentaries. See Richmond, "English Gentry and Religion, c. 1500," 122–23.

180. See Gibson, *Theater of Devotion*; and Duffy, *Stripping of the Altars*. Known for the vital presence of institutions and customs that represented late medieval orthodoxies, Norwich nevertheless made a smooth transition to the new Protestant religion. See Tanner, *Church in Late Medieval Norwich*; and idem, "Reformation and Regionalism." Sheppard notes the unorthodox flavor of many traditional late medieval religious practices and the ease with which the Norwich merchant class embraced the new religion. See "Reformation and the Citizens of Norwich."

181. Erler, *Women, Reading, and Piety*, 100–106, quote at 100.

182. Scherb locates such paradoxes in the larger context of East Anglian theatrical tradition. See *Staging Faith*, 202.

183. Spencer, *English Preaching*, 320, 324; Watson, "Censorship and Cultural Change," 859.

184. Sanok, "Performing Feminine Sanctity," 294.

Chapter 4

1. See Velz, "Sovereignty"; Jeffrey, "English Saints' Plays"; Bush, "*Locus* and *Platea* Staging"; Mead, "Four-fold Allegory"; Coletti, "Design"; and Grantley, "Saints' Plays," 278–82. Sokolowski critiques the scholarly impulse to seek unity in the play; see "Power and Torture." For an important discussion of the "iterative structure" and technique of East Anglian theatrical practice, see Scherb, *Staging Faith*, 146–90.

2. "'O blessyd Marie Magdalene, thou art of grete merite and gloriouse, for in the paynes of my delyueraunce thou were my mydwyf, and in al my

necessytes thou hast accomplysshid to me the seruyce of a chaumberer'";
CELMM, 132, lines 409–14.

3. Scholarship has regularly noted but not pursued the significance of these identifications. See Bush, "*Locus* and *Platea* Staging," 151, n. 32; Grantley, "Saints' Plays," 280; Velz, "Sovereignty," 38–39; Davidson, "Middle English Saint Play," 97; Maltman, "Light in and on the Digby *Mary Magdalene*," 271–76; and Scherb, *Staging Faith*, 188. Stephen Page links the presence of Marian elements in the saint play to the battle against heresy in late medieval East Anglia; see "Literature and Culture," 189–95. Dixon recognizes the Virgin Mary as a "muted and complementary female presence in the play"; see "'Thys Body of Mary,'" 234. The fullest discussion of the play's paralleling of penitent saint and mother of Jesus is provided by Laura Severt King, from whom I have borrowed the term "assimilation." See "Sacred Eroticism," 206. My thinking about the Digby saint play has been enriched by King's study, to which my specific debts are acknowledged in subsequent notes.

4. For some important exceptions, see Milner, "Flesh and Food"; and Salih, "Staging Conversion."

5. For the term "spiritual anthropology," see Iogna-Prat, "La Madeleine," 58.

6. See Jeffrey, "Saints' Plays"; Bush, "*Locus* and *Platea* Staging"; Grantley, "Saints' Plays"; Velz, "Sovereignty"; and Mead, "Four-fold Allegory." Sokolowski ("Power and Torture") critiques these studies for entering into complicity with the text's own strategies to conceal the violence and retribution of divine power.

7. Milner also posits the gendered construction of power in the play. See "Flesh and Food," 388.

8. See lines 114, 118, 135, 231, 251, 1261, 1300 ("justyce"), 1306. For references to judgment, see lines 15, 223, 236, 246, 256, 723, 727.

9. Clerical commentary on this episode in Mary Magdalene sermons also emphasizes the theme of judgment. Peter of Celle condemns the pharisee who judged by the old law; *Sermo 60, In festivitate sanctae Mariae Magdalenae*, PL 202: 823. Radulph Ardentis accuses the pharisee of arrogating to himself a false justice that lacked humility and charity; *Sermo 25, In festo beatae Mariae Magdalenae*, PL 155: 1399. Peter of Blois identifies fear of God's terrible judgment as the motivation for Mary Magdalene's penitence; *Sermo 30, De sancta Magdalena*, PL 207: 651.

10. The instability of earthly, masculine power represented by the tyrant figures is suggested in their projection of offenders, "precharsse of Crystys incarnacyon" (28), whom they never confront in the play. Caesar orders the rooting out of all "[c]ontrary to me in ony chansse" (37); Cyrus threatens he will bring to "bale" and "knett . . . in knottys of care" those who scorn his command for obedience (56–58); Herod promises to bring down the fools who "aȝens me make replycacyon" (203); and Pilate to spare none who do "pregedyse aȝen the law" (234).

11. On the social dimensions of Mary Magdalene's sin in the Digby play, see Coletti, "'*Paupertas est donum Dei*'"; and "Sociology of Transgression."

12. Murray discusses evidence for a "fundamental dis-ease with the male body" that is "at odds with conventional evaluation of the theologians, which attributed greater lust and less self-control to women." See "Problem of Male Embodiment," 17. A production of the Digby *Magdalene* by the Poculi Ludique Societas at the University of Toronto in May 2003 suggested how effectively Mary's temptation and fall could be elaborated through gesture, music, and the antics of her seven demons, even though the text treats her moral demise with considerable economy.

13. Here I adapt remarks by Lees, "Introduction," *Medieval Masculinities*, xix.

14. Conventions of theatrical crossdressing on the medieval English stage could produce provocative manipulation of these emphases in performance. Men acting the female parts could interject these scenes of heterosexual wooing with homoerotic valences, further rendering gender categories unstable, especially in light of Mary Magdalene's association with feminine sexual transgression. The unknown auspices of the Digby saint play must put the rein on speculation about such issues, compared to the fuller picture that may be invoked, say, for the York cycle. More detailed knowledge of its social context enables a different assessment of the possibilities for manipulations of gender in performance. See Evans, "Signs of the Body." For a related assessment of the impact of theatrical crossdressing on the performance of female saint plays, see Sanok, "Performing Feminine Sanctity," 286–87.

15. Davenport, "'Lusty fresche galaunts,'" 121. See also King, "Sacred Eroticism," 179–80; and Dixon, "'This Body of Mary,'" 235–36.

16. On the ways in which courtly ideology contributed to the socialization and control of medieval women, see Bloch, *Medieval Misogyny*, 196–97.

17. Notable exceptions are King, "Sacred Eroticism," 191–93; and Scherb, "Blasphemy and the Grotesque," 234–36. My use of "queer" in this context follows Lochrie's observation that the word "is not simply a reconstructed term for homosexual or homoerotic, but a category marking the sexual as the site for a variety of cultural struggles." See "Mystical Acts, Queer Tendencies," 181.

18. Comic repartee in these episodes is illuminated by Marguerita's analysis of the relationship between wooing, aggression, and homosociality in the obscene joke, the pleasures of which depend on feminine absence. See "Women and Riot in the Harley Lyrics," 70–71.

19. The editors gloss "jorn(e)y" as a sexual pun. See *LMRP*, 210–11, 251.

20. Rendering women as "absent presences," theatrical crossdressing once more introduces the prospect for self-conscious dramatic artifice. Might the riotous erotic antics over imaginary women reference the theatrical fact that "male actors can never make sex, gender, or the body fully present," that in the most concrete terms, the feminine is indeed absent from this play so utterly preoccupied with femininity? See Evans, "Signs of the Body."

21. Jacobus de Voragine has Mary of Egypt report: "When they asked me for my fare, I said: 'Brothers, I have no other fare, but take my body in payment for the passage.' So they took me aboard and I paid for my fare with my body"; *Golden Legend*, 1: 227. On the absorption of elements of the life of Mary of Egypt by the vita of Mary Magdalene, see Misrahi, "*Vita Sanctae Mariae*

Magdalenae." See also Karras, "Holy Harlots." In view of the more limited options that Mary of Egypt faced in similar circumstances, the fact that the dramatic Magdalene has wealth at her disposal—the play clearly establishes her comfortable social condition—makes a point that Margery Kempe also understood very well: that a woman's financial independence had direct bearing on her control of her own sexuality.

22. These male characters' preoccupation with femininity marks their own effeminacy, an attribute that by the sixteenth century was associated with excessive attraction to women. Epp discusses the importance of effeminacy in the characterization of the vices in *Mankind*, a play in which women are constantly invoked but always absent. See "Vicious Guise," 304. Epp cites Jonathan Goldberg, *Sodometries: Renaissance Texts, Modern Sexualities* (Stanford, Calif.: Stanford University Press, 1992), 111.

23. Schnell's analysis of the gender discourse of marriage sermons, "in which behavioral rules are given for both sexes," suggests ways of thinking about the rhetorical aims of the Digby saint play and the audience to whom its critique of gender and eros was directed. See "Discourse on Marriage," 776.

24. Salih notes that Mary Magdalene's preconversion sins (sexual trangression, materialism, vanity) as well as her postconversion role as devotee of Christ, are customarily gendered feminine. See "Staging Conversion," 127.

25. Haskins cites a Florentine fertility doll associated with Mary Magdalene. See *Myth and Metaphor*, 454, n. 89. Mary Magdalene's patronage of maternal care is also discussed by Wogan-Browne, *Saints' Lives*, 142.

26. King, "Sacred Eroticism," 208–9. King also suggests (197) that the odd illness of "ȝen sueke" to which the king falls victim soon after he has told Magdalene he will embrace her faith if she helps him and his wife to conceive a child (1576–77), may be a "yearning sickness" or lovesickness. Lovesickness was understood as a physiological disease related to male assumption of feminine behaviors; heterosexual intercourse was its cure. See Bullough, "On Being a Male," 38–39.

27. Jonathan Hughes notes the late medieval gentry's taste for romances, such as *Sir Degrevant, Octavian*, and *Erl of Tolous*, which "advised laymen against renouncing temporal responsibilities for the sake of private feelings." See *Pastors and Visionaries*, 282. As the play's lay hero, the king of Marseilles also resembles Magdalene's father, Cyrus. Each models the behavior of the lay head of household; and each is associated in the text with amorous discourse, physical indulgence in wine and spices, and property and dynasty. Each also takes to his bed. But whereas Cyrus seems to die morally unregenerated, the king of Marseilles, though he fears death (1576–77), instead receives visitations from Mary Magdalene that ultimately lead to his conversion from both paganism and lust.

28. *N-Town Play*, 1: 408, lines 509–14. Subsequent citations of the *Assumption* play in this paragraph refer to page and line numbers in vol. 1 of this edition. Similarities between the two plays have received little attention. Both include heavenly appearances of Jesus to announce the fates of the Virgin and Mary Magdalene through angelic messengers (*N-Town*, 391.109–116; *MM*, 2077–84, 2093–96). The angels who announce Magdalene's apostolate and the

Virgin Mary's impending death both offer assurance that their addressees should not be frightened (*N-Town*: "[A]basche you not, lady" [393.151]; *MM*: "Abasse þe novtt, Mary" [1376]). The palm branch that the angelic messenger presents to Mary in the *Assumption* (393.134) reappears in the Digby saint play as the "palme of grett wytory" that the angel gives to Mary Magdalene shortly before her last communion (2094). Both plays show Jesus responding with angelic dispatch to "sweet prayers" he has received from the two women (*N-Town*, 391.107; *MM*, 2003). More idiosyncratically, both plays illustrate the limitless reaches of divine power by referring to Habaccuk's relieving of Daniel in the lion's den (*N-Town*, 393.147–50; *MM*, 1582–85). Finally, the two plays speak of preparing the dead women's bodies in strikingly similar terms (*N-Town*, 401.332–35; *MM*, 2127–30). A common debt to Jacobus's narrative of the Virgin's assumption in *Legenda aurea* could account for a few (the angelic messengers, the palm of victory) but by no means all of these similarities. The other resemblances are sufficiently distinctive to suggest some common point of contact between these late medieval East Anglian plays deeply committed to representing the most important female actors in salvation history.

29. Emphasis on the Virgin Mary's "concrete physical involvement in human salvation" is a common theme of late medieval piety. See Ellington, *Sacred Body to Angelic Soul*, 47–76; quote at 50. Julian of Norwich put the idea in her own inimitable way in chap. 57 of her Long Text: "Thus oure lady is oure moder, in whome we be all beclosyd and of hyr borne in Crist, for she that is moder of oure savyoure is moder of all þat ben savyd in our sauyour"; *Book of Shewings*, 2: 580.

30. Echoes of a Trinitarian hymn in this speech are noted by the editors; *LMRP*, 206.

31. In the *N-Town Play* see *The Salutation and Conception* (1: 123.333); and *The Visit to Elizabeth* (1: 135.138).

32. Newman, "Intimate Pieties," 78. A fuller treatment of the issues raised in this essay, with fascinating implications for my argument, appears in "Maria: Holy Trinity as Holy Family," chap. 6 of Newman's *God and the Goddesses*, 245–90. See also idem, *Virile Woman*, 206–8. On the theological implications of the Marian trinity, see also Ellington, *Sacred Body to Angelic Soul*, 107–10.

33. Newman, *Virile Woman*, 207. The redemptive anthropology of the Marian Trinity echoes in Brigittine interests in the Virgin Mary's containment of the Trinity, which involved "the vnyon of the trynyte in all wyse undeparted" in Mary's womb and Mary's right to be "partener of al the goodes that myghte be gyuen of god"; *Myroure of Our Ladye*, 266. My attention was drawn to this passage by King's unpublished paper, "Cracks in the Looking Glass."

34. For a different approach to same-sex identifications that emphasizes female homosocial bonding in light of specifically East Anglian texts and practices, see Lavezzo, "Sobs and Sighs."

35. Beckwith, *Christ's Body*, 2.

36. Haskins, *Myth and Metaphor*, 88, 63–67. See also Jansen, *Making of the Magdalen*, 18–35.

37. Gregory the Great, *Homilia 33, PL* 76: 1238–46. On the influence of this homily, see Bériou, "La Madeleine dans les sermons parisiens," 284–86.

38. Haskins, *Myth and Metaphor*, 97. Haskins quotes the phrase "exegetically untenable" from Peter Ketter, *The Magdalene Question*, trans. Reverend Hugo C. Koehler (Milwaukee: Bruce, 1935), 36.

39. For discussions of Mary Magdalene as model penitent in some specific medieval contexts, see Jansen, *Making of the Magdalen*, 199–244; Dalarun, "La Madeleine dans l'ouest"; Lauwers, *"Noli me tangere"*; Bériou, "La Madeleine dans les sermons Parisiens"; and Iogna-Prat, "La Madeleine."

40. Matter, *Voice of My Beloved*, 15. See also Jansen, *Making of the Magdalen*, 29–30; and Haskins, *Myth and Metaphor*, 92–93. Jennings calls the paralleling of the Virgin Mary and Mary Magdalene "common medieval practice"; see "Pseudo-Origen Homily," 150, n. 15.

41. For example, see Szövérffy, *"Peccatrix quondam femina,"* 93, 125–26; Harris, "'Maiden in the Mor Lay'"; Slim, "Music and Dancing," 143; Deremble, "Premiers cycles d'images," 199–200; and Mosco, ed., *La Maddelena*, 34.

42. See Iogna-Prat, "La Madeleine," 53–67.

43. "Venit Maria. Hoc nomen matris est Christi, venit ergo mater in nomine, venit mul-ier. . . . Venit Maria et altera Maria. Non dixit venerunt, sed venit; sub uno nomine venerunt duae mysterio, non casu. Venit Maria et altera Maria. Venit ipsa sed altera, altera sed ipsa, ut mulier mutaretur vita, non nomine; virtute, non sexu." Peter Chrysologus, *Sermo 74, De resurrectione Christi*, PL 52: 409.

44. "Quando non credit, mulier est; quando converti incipit, Maria vocatur, hoc est, nomen eius accipit, quae parturit Christum; est enim anima quae spiritualiter parit Christum." Ambrose of Milan, *De virginitate*, 4.20 (*PL* 16: 27); quoted in Iogna-Prat, "La Madeleine," 60–61.

45. "Nec parvipendendum est patrocinium hujus poenitentis quae, sicut aequivocatur beatae Virgini in vocabulo, sic etiam quodammodo confertur ei in exemplo; nec dedignatur ancillae Domina, adolescentulae regina, Dei Genetrix, ei quae fuerat peccatrix, aequivocari. Utraque siquidem Maria vocatur, quod sonat *maris stella*, quod propter earum exemplum eis congruit. In hoc enim mari magno et spatioso, utraque nobis ducatum luminis praevium praestat." Peter Comester (formerly attributed to Hildebert of Lavardin), *In festo sanctae magdalenae sermo unicus*, PL 171: 677. I have used the translation of Harris, "'Maiden in the Mor Lay,'" 80. The sermon's attribution has been corrected by Bériou; see "La Madeleine dans les sermons Parisiens," 272, n. 10.

46. Jansen, *Making of the Magdalen*, 239–44; Haskins, *Myth and Metaphor*, 141; Harris, "'Maiden in the mor lay,'" 81–82; Maltman, "Light in and on the Digby *Mary Magdalene*," 278, n. 10.

47. "Quia enim per feminam mors mundo illata fuerat, ne semper in opprobrium sexus femineus haberetur, per sexum femineum voluit nuntiare viris gaudia Resurrectionis. . . . Et sicut per beatam Mariam semper virginem quae spes est unica mundi, paradisi portae nobis sunt apertae, et maledictio exclusa Evae, ita per beatam Mariam Magdalenam opprobrium feminci sexus deletum est. . . . Unde bene Maria interpretatur stella maris. Quae interpretatio quamvis Dei genitrici specialiter congruat, per cujus partum virgineum Sol justitiae mundo resplenduit, tamen et beatae Magdalenae potest congruere, quae cum aromatibus veniens ad sepulcrum Domini, prima splendorem Dominicae

resurrectionis mundo nuntiavit." Odo of Cluny, *In veneratione sanctae Mariae Magdalenae*, PL 133: 721. Iogna-Prat discusses the attribution and dating of the sermon. See "La Madeleine," 37–42.

48. Iogna-Prat, "La Madeleine," 58.

49. "Huic questioni usque ad tempora ueri Salmonis, id est Christi, non poterat responderi, sed ipse qui uirginem sanctificauit et Magdalenam a peccatis purificauit, in utraque tantam fortitudinem posuit ut illa esset exemplar innocencie et hec penitencie. Illa fuit luminare maius ut preesset diei, id est iustis, hec fuit luminare minus ut preesset nocti id est peccatoribus." Peter of Reims, "*Mulier fortem quis inveniet?*," in Bériou, "La Madeleine dans les sermons Parisiens," 318–22, quote at 318–19.

50. . "Venit Maria ad sepulchrum, venit ad resurrectionis uterum, venit ad vitae partum, ut iterum Christus ex sepulchro nasceretur fidei, qui carnis fuerat generatus ex ventre; et eum quem clausa virginita protulerat ad praesentem, clausum sepulchrum ad vitam redderet sempiternam." Peter Chrysologus, *Sermo 75, De resurrectione Christi*, PL 52: 412–13.

51. "[R]igat plantas Maria, de horto Mariae natas: Maria, sed Dei genitrix, plantas istas de carne sua et sanguine plantavit. . . . Maria, sed multum peccatrix, de internorum viscerum fonte rigavit: rigavit plane et alius non aqua, sed oleo gratiae; cum Maria in utero, imo in Maria Pater de coelo plantaret, quem Maria Magdalene rigavit aqua, et unxit unguento cum in domo Simonis recumberet." Peter of Celle, *Sermo 60, In festivitate sanctae Magdalenae*, PL 202: 824. On the Mary Magdalene sermons of Peter of Celle, see Kundera, "Models of Monastic Devotion."

52. Iogna-Prat discusses Odo of Cluny's image of Mary Magdalene's spiritual fecundity; "La Madeleine," 46–47. Jansen notes the saint's link to agricultural tropes associated with the Virgin; *Making of the Magdalen*, 241–42.

53. Harris, "'Maiden in the mor lay,'" 80, 87, 73.

54. "Plus commemorant evangeliste de Marie Magdalene quam de Maria mater Domini. Et hoc erat conveniens quia nemo habuit laborem de passione Domini quomodo Maria Magdalene. Illa ploravit juxta sepulcrum et interrogabat Dominus: Mulier, quid ploras? Et ipsa respondit: Dominum meum tulerunt de monumento et nescio ubi posuerunt eum. Mater Domini non sic habuit laborem de suo filio. . . . Nolebat Maria lugere filium suum quia sapiebat per Spiritum sanctum quia impleverat illam filium suum regnaturum in celestibus post lavorem hujus vite." Quoted from P. David, *Un recueil de conférences monastiques irlandaises du VIIIe siècle*, *Revue bénédictine* 49 (1937), in Ortenberg, "Marie Madeleine dans l'Angleterre Anglo-Saxonne," 25–26.

55. Ortenberg, "Marie Madeleine dans l'Angleterre Anglo-Saxonne," 16.

56. "Plures enim sunt in Ecclesia qui errata correxerunt; quam qui errare non noverunt: plures, inquam, justificati quam justi. Plures ergo proficiunt exemplo hujus. De auxilio vero utriusque eloquar, an sileam? Indubitanter verum est quia singulare est beatae Virginis auxilium . . . quasi e quodam sublimi fastigio pro nobis intercedit. Haec vero quae novit figmentum nostrum, totam se effundit in preces, tota provolvitur ad pedes Domini, nec pudet eam vel improbe

petere, donec obtinuerit. Interpellet ergo pro nobis ad Dominum. . . ." Peter Comestor, *In festo sanctae Magdalenae sermo unicus*, PL 171: 677–78.

57. Iogna-Prat, "La Madeleine," 65.

58. Lauwers, "*Noli me tangere*," 257–58. Thirteenth-century Parisian sermons on the saint record her difficult fit with the customary formulation of feminine *status*: virgin, wife, and widow. Humbert of Romans's *Summa* introduced another category, the penitent female sinner, in a chapter titled "Mary Magdalene and Those Like Her." See Bériou, "La Madeleine dans les sermons Parisiens," 305–6, n. 121.

59. Wogan-Browne, "Virgin's Tale," 167–68. Recent studies of the complexities and ambiguities of medieval cultural constructions of virginity include idem, *Saints' Lives and Women's Literary Culture*; Salih, *Versions of Virginity*; and Kelly, *Performing Virginity*.

60. Newman, *Virile Woman*, 30–31.

61. "Humilitas enim sine uirginitate Deo placere potest; uirginitas uero sine humilitate Deo placere non potest. Melior est humilis coniugalitas quam superba uirginitas. . . . Audiui de quadam huiusmodi uirgine que spiritum elationis incitata iactanter ait quod nollet esse similis Marie Magdalene. Ex quo accidit ei quod infra mensem postquam talia dicere presumpsit, uilissimo leccatori adhesit, qui eam honore uirginali spoliauit." Quoted from Jacques de Vitry, *Sermones ad status: sermo ad virgines et iuuenculas 1* (Paris BN Latin 3284, fol. 190ra) in Lauwers, "*Noli me tangere*," 220. On the proud virgin as a ubiquitous motif in virginity literature, see Newman, *Virile Woman*, 29.

62. "Hec enim in litania in capite uirginum ponitur quia fuit apostola, fuit et martyr compassione, fuit predicatrix ueritatis. Quod integritate corporis non meruit, meruit integritate mentis. . . . Dixit beata Virgo (Lc 1, 48): *Respexit Dominus humilitatem ancille sue*, non dixit: 'Respexit uirginitatem ancille,' quia humilitas sine uirginitate ualet, uirginitas sine humilitate non ualet, sed cum humilitate." Eudes de Châteauroux, *De beata Maria Magdalena*, in Bériou, "La Madeleine dans les Sermons Parisiens," 331–37, quote at 336–37.

63. Bériou summarizes this point of the sermon on the theme *Gloria Libani data est ei*; see "La Madeleine dans les sermons Parisiens," 306, n. 122.

64. Mulder-Bakker notes that Mary Magdalene "continually crops up" in Caesarius of Heisterbach's *Dialogus Miraculorum*, where she is linked to the Virgin and other female saints. See "Ivetta of Huy," 233.

65. Ibid., 247.

66. Haskins, *Myth and Metaphor*, 185. See also Cannon and Vauchez, *Margherita of Cortona*, 164–66. Jansen argues that the elaboration of the theme of Mary Magdalene's "reconstituted virginity" in fraternal sermons furnished a model to penitent matrons who longed for the virginal state. See *Making of the Magdalen*, 286–94.

67. *BMK*, 51–52.

68. Heiric of Auxerre, *Homily 1.23*, cited by Iogna-Prat, "La Madeleine," 62–64. On the migration of liturgical pieces from the common of virgins to the mass and office of the feast of Mary Magdalene, see Saxer, *Culte de Marie Madeleine*, 287, n. 9.

69. Maltman links the Marian resonances of this scene to the connections established by the liturgical use of Luke 10:38–42 for the Feast of the Assumption; see "Light in and on the Digby *Mary Magdalene*," 273–75. On the transfer of iconography of the Virgin Mary's assumption to Magdalenian contexts, see Deremble, "Premiers cycles d'images," 199–200.

70. ". . . [C]orrupte per humilitatem et pacienciam et caritatem possunt peruenire ad equalem coronam uel cum uirginibus uel etiam maiorem, sicut et hec beata." Eudes de Châteauroux, *De beata Maria Magdalena*, in Bériou, "La Madeleine dans les Sermons Parisiens," 336. Mary Magdalene is also associated with the celestial crown in a thirteenth-century clerical disputation on the question "'whether a woman can merit the celestial crown . . . by preaching and teaching'" (*Utrum mulier praedicando et docendo mereatur aureolam*). See Blamires, "Women and Preaching," 142. On the crowning of virgins, see Hall and Uhr, "*Aureola super Auream*."

71. Deshman, *Benedictional*, B.L. Additional MS 49598; fol. IV–2r.

72. Ortenberg, "Marie Madeleine dans l'Angleterre Anglo-Saxonne," 29–31.

73. *Speculum Sacerdotale*, 172.

74. Wogan-Browne, *Saints' Lives and Women's Literary Culture*, 149–50.

75. Wogan-Browne, "Virgin's Tale," 167–68; idem, *Saints' Lives and Women's Literary Culture*, 140–42. Duffy mentions a girdle of Mary Magdalene in Brinton, Somerset that was "'sent to women travailing,'" and links this to the "lying-in girdle" whose power to help and heal was attributed to various saints; *Stripping of the Altars*, 384. Jansen discusses the "generative, nutritive, and protective qualities" attributed to Mary Magdalene through her reconstituted virginity; *Making of the Magdalen*, 294–303, quote at 294.

76. Cf. Mary Magdalene: "Ewyn at your wyl, my dere derlyng! / Thowe ȝe wyl go to þe wordys eynd, / I wol neuyr from yow wynd, / To dye for your sake!" (543–46).

77. Haskins, *Myth and Metaphor*, 141.

78. Salih sees the white dress of the Digby saint and Margery Kempe as a sign of both women's "movement away from ordinary womanhood . . . [and] from familiar social and sexual categories"; "Staging Conversion," 130.

79. See Cleve, "Semantic Dimensions"; Erler, "Margery Kempe's White Clothes"; Voaden, "Beholding Men's Members," 179. Salih's notice that white is the color worn by the elect in heaven as well as a color signifying liminal states (of the bride, the novice), is not inconsistent with the idea of spiritual virginity that the Digby play seems to suggest. See *Versions of Virginity*, 217–24.

80. Giselle de Nie notes the use of tropes of conception and birth to signify receiving and hearing the divine word; "'Consciousness Fecund through God.'"

81. The Digby saint's donning of white clothes may also signify some of the contradictions that Carolyn Dinshaw finds in Margery Kempe's longing for the same attire. In each case the sign of symbolic, spiritual virginity evokes the contrary state of the holy woman's bodily identity. Kempe's white clothes call attention to the disjunction "in an orthodox Christianity which establishes

marriage as a sacrament yet always maintains its taint"—a contradiction enacted in the plight of the king and queen. See *Getting Medieval*, 149.

82. King differently posits a continuity between the erotic and the divine in the play; "Christianity's Penitent Prostitutes."

83. Matter, *Voice of My Beloved*; Astell, *Song of Songs*. On Mary Magdalene as the allegorized Bride of the Song, see Haskins *Myth and Metaphor*, 40, 63–67; and Malvern, *Venus in Sackcloth*, 58–67.

84. Dixon makes a similar point but does not link this transformation to allegoresis of the Song of Songs, "'Thys Body of Mary,'" 227–28. Scherb notes the spiritualization of the play's central theatrical images; *Staging Faith*, 176–78.

85. See lines 564–71, 1071, 1074, 352, and 2109. Habits and opportunities afforded by allegoresis probably encouraged the structural and verbal doublings of the play. Ambiguities created by such doublings are not simply ironic, as Dixon suggests ("'Thys Body of Mary,'" 228); rather they offer evidence of the linguistic multivalence that allegory generates but cannot fully contain. For a discussion of the unruly semiotics of allegory in a different context, see Coletti, *Naming the Rose*, 39–72.

86. Bynum, *Holy Feast and Holy Fast*, 261–69.

87. Dixon, "'Thys Body of Mary,'" 229.

88. Newman discusses late medieval spiritual and symbolic strategies that effected similar intimacy, especially through representation of the Virgin's complicated relation to a triune God. See "Intimate Pieties."

89. Dixon, "'Thys Body of Mary,'" 224.

90. Newman discusses both images in "Intimate Pieties," 84–87.

91. Sprung, "Inverted Metaphor," 196–97.

92. Riggio, *Play of "Wisdom,"* 39–47.

93. Riggio, "*Wisdom* Enthroned," 247.

94. Malvern, *Venus in Sackcloth*, 30–56, 114–25.

95. Newman, *Virile Woman*, 181. For an English translation, see *Sister Catherine*.

96. See Newman, *Virile Women*, 172–81.

97. Ibid., 177.

98. Ibid., 286, n. 29; see also 137–67. Mary Magdalene figures as model "fin amant" in the thirteenth-century *Règle des Fins Amans*, a discourse on the beguine life probably originating in Amiens. See "*La Règle des Fins Amans*," 194. On Mary Magdalene in beguine devotion, see also Oliver, "'Gothic' Women," 124; and idem, "Some French Devotional Texts," 257.

99. Wogan-Browne, *Saints' Lives*, 265. Wogan-Browne posits "an as yet unwritten history of exchange and cross-influence in women's thirteenth-century literary culture in the region constituted by the East Anglian coast and north-west Europe" (148). See also Wogan-Browne and Henneau, "Liège." Aspects of the Digby Magdalene that I have been examining reinforce Nicholas Watson's contention that medieval English religious culture would benefit from more comparative study of features that resemble those of corresponding continental movements and practices. See "Middle English Mystics," 544.

Chapter 5

The epigraph is from Young, ed., *Drama of the Medieval Church*, 1: 249.

1. Susan Rankin counts forty-four Easter ceremony texts that include Mary Magdalene. See "Mary Magdalene Scene," 233.

2. Young's *Drama of the Medieval Church* provided the foundational account of theatrical and dramatic elements in these liturgical ceremonies. For two important reassessments, see Hardison, *Christian Rite and Christian Drama*; and Flanigan, "Roman Rite." Michel Kobialka's recent study of representational practices in the early Middle Ages critiques scholarship on liturgical rite and performance, arguing that the *quem quaeritis* and *Visitatio sepulchri* ceremonies need to be evaluated in the context of "spiritual and physical power relations" of monastic culture. See *This Is My Body*, 147.

3. Beckwith, "Ritual, Theater, and Social Space," 63.

4. Damrosch, *"Non Alia Sed Aliter*," 191. On the paradigmatic qualities of Mary Magdalene's experience at the tomb, see Murphy, *Word According to Eve*, 197.

5. See Ashley, "Cultural Readings of the York Cycle Plays"; Beckwith, "Ritual, Theater, and Social Space"; idem, "Making the World"; Lerer, "Culture of Spectatorship"; Jones, "Theatrical History"; and Lawton, "Sacrilege and Theatricality."

6. Beckwith, *"Sacrum Signum*," 275.

7. Dixon, "'Thys Body of Mary,'" 237; King, "Sacred Eroticism," 159.

8. King, "Sacred Eroticism," 160.

9. Cf. the self-description of the deity in John Bale's *A Comedy Concerning Three Laws*: "I am Deus Pater, a substance invisible, / All one with the son, and Holy Ghost in essence. / To angels and man I am incomprehensible; / A strength infinite, a righteousness, a prudence, / A mercy, a goodness, a truth, a life, a sapience." Quoted in Kendall, *Drama of Dissent*, 101.

10. On the relationship between theatrical epistemologies and late medieval and Reformation drama, see O'Connell, *Idolatrous Eye*, 14–35.

11. For a different view of the play's sacramental dramaturgy, see Bush, *"Locus* and *Platea* Staging,"142.

12. *LMRP*, xl.

13. Emmerson, "Reception of the Chester *Antichrist*," 97.

14. Emmerson, "Antichrist as Anti-Saint." Lumiansky and Mills do not posit Adso's *Libellus* as a direct source for the Chester *Antichrist*, but it is clear that the play is dependent upon the conception made popular by Adso. See *Chester Mystery Cycle*, 2: 331.

15. For example, both plays end with the death of their principal subject and the departure of the soul from the body. *Mary Magdalene* images this event in a joyous angelic welcome—"Now reseyve we þis sowle . . . In heven to dwelle vs among" (2119–20). The hermit priest who has brought Mary her final communion declares his intention to "cure" her body "from alle manyr blame" and pass it "to þe bosshop of þe sete / . . . to berye . . . / Wyth alle reverens and solemnyte" (2127–30). In the Chester play, Antichrist's death at the hand of

Archangel Michael is rapidly followed by the work of two demons whose actions fulfill the pretender's dying words: "Nowe bodye and soule both in feare / and all goeth to the devyll" (651–52). Seizing his soul in one gesture and carrying his body "by the toppe . . . and by the tayle" with the next, they expeditiously and unceremoniously carry off both to hell (679, 693). All line citations for *De Adventu Antechristi* refer to Lumiansky and Mills, eds., *Chester Mystery Cycle*, 1: 408–38.

16. For discussions of the congruence of the lives of Christ and Mary Magdalene through such holy mimesis, see Scherb, "Worldly and Sacred Messengers"; and Bush, "*Locus* and *Platea* Staging."

17. As a fraudulent *imago dei*, the Antichrist of the Chester play mimes significant actions from the life of Christ: resurrecting the dead, performing miracles, sending the Holy Spirit to his followers, and even dying and raising himself in cartoonlike fashion: "I dye, I dye! Nowe am I dead!" (133); "I ryse! Nowe reverence dose to mee" (165). Important studies of the Chester *Antichrist* play include Travis, *Dramatic Design*, 223–54; Emmerson, "'Nowe ys common this daye'"; and Martin, "Comic Eschatology."

18. Travis, *Dramatic Design*, 233. Boehnen identifies the Digby play's Augustus Caesar as an Antichrist figure and antisaint who is the inverse of all that Mary Magdalene represents. See "Aesthetics of 'Sprawling Drama,'" 332.

19. In *Antichrist* this emphasis marks the culmination of a thematic interest of all of Chester's post-Resurrection plays; it also characterizes the empirical testing that occurs in these episodes in all the biblical cycles. See Travis, *Dramatic Design*, 199–205, 234–38. Beckwith discusses this aspect of the York plays; "*Sacrum Signum*," 273–76. References to sight and seeing as measures of faith are plentiful in the *Antichrist* play; for example, see lines 11–12, 65–68, 77–80, 154–60, 201–4, 257–60, 384–86, 404–9, 521–28, 545–60, 577–88. The idea of deceptive appearances is central to the medieval legend of Antichrist. Resemblance to the true God would be essential to the pretender's identity, but it is the genius of the Chester pageant to discern the theatrical possibilities of this topos. For an Antichrist play that does not exploit this theme to the same extent as the Chester pageant, see *Antichrist and Judgment Day*.

20. Beckwith, "*Sacrum Signum*," 277. See also O'Connell, *Idolatrous Eye*, 36–62.

21. Emmerson, "'Nowe Ys Common This Daye,'" 106; Travis, *Dramatic Design*, 228–30.

22. Travis, *Dramatic Design*, 201, 226–28.

23. Beckwith, "*Sacrum Signum*," 277.

24. The Chester *Antichrist* and *Mary Magdalene* enter the debate on this subject more obliquely than their rhetorical counterpart, the Wycliffite attack on the physicality of all types of sacred representation in play and performance known as the *Tretise on Miraclis Pleyinge*. The *Tretise* engages reformist biblical hermeneutics, the debate on images, and sacramental theology, all of which probed the efficacy and legitimacy of material embodiments of the sacred. Despite disagreement on specific ideological dimensions of the *Tretise*, recent scholarship exhibits general consensus on these basic points. See Clopper, "Miracula and

the *Tretise*"; Olson, "Plays as Play"; Nissé, "Reversing Discipline"; Hill-Vásquez, "'Miraclis Pleyinge.'" See also Davidson's "Introduction" to *Tretise of Miraclis Pleyinge*, 1–52. For an important analysis of late medieval and early modern theater's relationship to sacramental theology and the debate on images, see O'Connell, *Idolatrous Eye*.

25. Christ's post-Resurrection appearances in the play also stage this paradox. Only the Digby saint play and the Chester cycle combine events from the Gospels of Matthew (28:9–10) and John (20:11–17) to stage Christ's double appearance, first to Mary Magdalene and then to the three Marys. In both cases the two appearances are separated by Mary Magdalene's speech announcing the Resurrection to the other Marys. These episodes in the Chester cycle appear in only two of the cycle manuscripts (H and R) and are printed in the edition of Lumiansky and Mills as Appendix Id, 1: 486–90. The Digby play's treatment of this sequence emphasizes—and the stage directions reinforce—Christ's appearing and disappearing acts (s.d. 1060: "Hic aparuit Jhesus"; s.d. 1095: "Here avoydyt Jhesus sodenly . . ."; s.d. 1124: "Here Jhesus devoydytt aȝen.") This sequence of episodes also interpolates into the basic scriptural accounts from John and Matthew a verbal emphasis on seeing and "shewing." See lines 1092–93, 1110–11, and 1121–24.

26. Womack, "Shakespeare and the Sea of Stories," 179.

27. Womack, "Medieval Drama," 22.

28. Patricia Badir discusses analogous uses of Mary Magdalene in Reformation biblical theater in "Iconoclasm and Striptease." See also her forthcoming study on English sixteenth- and seventeenth-century devotional writing and the figure of Mary Magdalene.

29. Travis, *Dramatic Design*, 240. My account here of the dramatic aesthetic of Chester's *Antichrist* and *Judgement* pageants is summarized from Travis, 228–49. The association of Antichrist with the lie of theatrical representation has a long history. In the twelfth century, Gerhoh of Reichersberg's *De investigatione Antichristi* made the figure a locus for antitheatrical discourse. See Clopper, *Drama, Play, and Game*, 43–44. Several hundred years later the Wycliffite *Tretise on Miraclis Pleyinge* drew upon the same tradition; *Tretise*, 99, lines 197–209. While acknowledging the ideological critique that Antichrist represents, we should remember, as Clopper usefully notes, that the dramatic figure also had immense entertainment value.

30. See the stage directions at line 356 ("Finitis lamentationibus mortuorum, [descendet] Jesus quasi in nube, si fieri poterit, quia, secundum doctoris opiniones, in aere prope terram judicabit Filius Dei. Stabunt angeli cum cruce, corona spinea, lancea, et instrumentis aliis; ipsa demonstrant"); and line 428 ("Tunc emittet sanguinem de latere eius"); *De Judicio Extremo*, in *Chester Mystery Cycle*, 1: 438–63. Line citations in my text refer to this edition.

31. Travis, *Dramatic Design*, 248. On the Chester cycle's conception of the deity, see Ashley, "Divine Power in Chester Cycle." For a discussion of the iconography of the symbols of the Passion and the wounds of Christ in the context of the Last Judgment, see Lewis, "Wound in Christ's Side."

32. Travis, *Dramatic Design*, 246–47.

33. Travis, *Dramatic Design*, 236–37, here citing medieval defenses of images, based on the discussion in Coletti, "Spirituality and Devotional Images."

34. The phrase is from Travis, *Dramatic Design*, 226.

35. The parodic liturgy to Mahownde names the demon Ragnall (1200), who also appears as a minion summoned by Antichrist in the Chester pageant (647).

36. Womack, "Shakespeare and the Sea of Stories," 177. See also Badir, "Iconoclasm and Striptease."

37. Scherb terms the play's representation of pagan religion "inversely Christian." See "Worldly and Sacred Messengers," 6–7. On the function of this parodic dramatic image of religious practice, see also Scherb, "Blasphemy and the Grotesque," 226. Boehnen observes that the Digby saint play both endorses orthodox religious practices and reflects alternatives to them, as it panders to the tastes of a paying audience; see "Aesthetics of Sprawling Drama," 349–51.

38. The genius of iconoclastic dramas such as John Bale's *King Johan*, for example, resides in their "systematic figuration of ecclesiastical office as theater." See Beckwith, *Signifying God*, 149. An East Anglian Carmelite who resided in Norwich before he turned reformer, Bale was surely aware of the dramatic traditions of the region; see Kendall, *Drama of Dissent*, 90. For Bale's parodies of Catholic rites, ceremonies, and ecclesiology, see *King Johan* in *Complete Plays of John Bale*, lines 636–57, 763–68, 1033–51, 1644–90. Jones's observation that antitheatrical rhetoric tends to identify the "accroutrements of . . . theater" with the other also glosses the Digby play's treatment of pagan rite in Marseilles; see "Theatrical History," 240.

39. Cf. lines 1182–83: "Now, boy, to my awter I wyll me dresse— / On xall my westment and myn aray." In reformist polemic, liturgical costume underscored the gap between man and role and associated the priest with the actor; see Beckwith, *Signifying God*, 146–49. As Beckwith notes, the reformation gave ecclesiastical vestments new life as actual theatrical costumes. On the priest as actor, see also Kendall's discussion of the *Apology of John Bale againste a Ranke Papyst*; *Drama of Dissent*, 129–31.

40. Womack, "Shakespeare and the Sea of Stories," 177, his emphasis. See also Badir, "Iconoclasm and Striptease"; and Kendall's analysis of reformers' ambivalent response to and employment of the theater; *Drama of Dissent*.

41. See Beckwith's comments on studies by Lepow (*Enacting the Sacrament*) and Nichols (*Seeable Signs*), which respectively identify the Towneley plays and the East Anglian seven-sacrament font as responses to Lollard eucharistic heresy and other aspects of Lollard doctrine; "Sacrum Signum," 276. The idea that enduring fifteenth- and early sixteenth-century expressions of so-called late medieval traditional religious culture constitute a deliberate reaction to Lollard and other heterodox ideas is most often associated with Duffy's *Stripping of the Altars*.

42. Beckwith, "Sacrum Signum," 265.

43. Ibid., 268. Beckwith theorizes a conception of dramatic sacramentality from a wide array of sources, including Augustinian sign theory, medieval debates about the real presence, contemporary theories of the symbol, and uses

of modern hermeneutics in recent Catholic theology; see 266–68 and the references cited therein.

44. Ibid., 267, 266.

45. A fifteenth-century Wycliffite text chastised those who provided for and worshiped resplendent images of Christ and the saints because they "bryngen þe symple puple in errour of Cristis lif and his apostelis and oþer seyntis . . . and to waste temperal godis and leeue dedis of charite to her pore neyeboris þat ben nedy and mysese, made to þe ymage and lickenesse of God." See *English Wycliffite Writings*, 84. This stress on the human *imago dei* at the moment of judgment when the sins of the damned are explained in terms of their failure to perform corporeal works of mercy is not unique to the Chester cycle, but the context provided by the *Antichrist* pageant here oddly aligns the damned souls' complaints with issues from the debate about images, extending the theme of proper interpretation of corporeal sacred signs to the final moments of human history itself. The invocation of iconoclastic topoi in Capgrave's *Life of Saint Katherine* analogously assigns reformist positions to a sacred being who epitomizes the capacity of the sacred to inhere in a material thing. See Stanbury, "Vivacity of Images."

46. See Hill-Vásquez, "'Miraclis Pleyinge.'"

47. On the Chester Banns and the Wakefield prohibition, see Clopper, "Lay and Clerical Impact," 108–9.

48. Emmerson, "Reception of the Chester *Antichrist*."

49. Ibid., 111. See also White, "Reforming Mysteries' End"; idem, *Theater and Reformation*; O'Connell, *Idolatrous Eye*; and Diehl, *Staging Reform*. The survival of the Croxton *Play of the Sacrament* in a sixteenth-century reformist manuscript analogously signals how literary forms were recast and put to new polemical use. See Jones, "Theatrical History"; and Lerer, "Culture of Spectatorship," 52–55.

50. See Hill-Vásquez, "Reformation Sponsorship." Coldewey argues that the Digby saint plays were revived for Reformation performance at Chelmsford in 1562; see "Digby Plays." See also Baker and Murphy, "Late Medieval Plays of MS. Digby 133."

51. My characterization of these tensions is adapted from comments on Lollard objections to drama by Davidson, "Introduction," *Tretise*, 18; and Kendall, *Drama of Dissent*, 53.

52. For a related discussion of antitheatricality and the feminization of sacred and dramatic images in the sixteenth century, see Diehl, *Staging Reform*, 156–81. See also Epp, "John Foxe."

53. For example, see Gibson, "'Porta Haec Clausa Erit'"; and Coletti, "Purity and Danger."

54. Murphy, *Word According to Eve*, 198–99.

55. All quotations, cited by page and line number, refer to volume 1 of Spector's *N-Town Play*.

56. All quotations, cited by page and line number, refer to volume 1 of Stevens's and Cawley's *Towneley Plays*. Peter disparages Mary Magdalene's "carping" (367.7), and Paul simply asserts, "[W]oman, thou says wrang" (368.17). The

Chester cycle eschews the subject of feminine testimony; only two of the five complete manuscripts of the cycle, BL Harley 2013 (R) and Harley 2124 (H), even include the risen Christ's appearance to Mary Magdalene.

57. All quotations, cited by page and line numbers, refer to Beadle's *York Plays*. On resonances of the Song of Songs in this play, see Astell, *Song of Songs*, 174–75.

58. All line citations refer to the edition of *Christ's Resurrection* in *LMRP*, 169–93.

59. The Towneley and York *Resurrection* plays parallel each other quite closely up to the point of Christ's appearance to Mary Magdalene; Towneley extends the Resurrection play with the episode from John, but York locates it in the separate play of the Winedrawers. Towneley's version is thought to be "a heavily edited version" of its York counterpart. See *Towneley Plays*, 2: 600.

60. Jesus' elaboration of his allegorical identity as the lover-knight directly after his revelation to Mary Magdalene (358.94–109) thus extends the emphasis on body that characterizes their initial exchange.

61. I discuss Mary Magdalene's post-Resurrection speeches in Chapter 2. See *N-Town Play*, 360.9–16, 366.5–6, 368.74–77.

62. The text's relocation of the adverb "not yet" (*nondum*) from the action of ascending in John 20:17 to the action of Mary's touching ("Towche me not as 3ett, Mary") revises the focus on the biblical scene, by looking back to past contact and forward to the touching that has yet to occur.

63. *Chester Mystery Cycle*, Appendix Id, 1: 487.10, s.d. 486.

64. Murphy, *Word According to Eve*, 197.

65. A Wycliffite sermon chides Mary Magdalene at the Resurrection because she "louyde heere fleyssly Crist, and he was not steyede in her herte as a body glorified, as he shal be aftir þe ascencion; . . . [F]or bi his ascension his body shal be goostly knowen, and not by siche fleyssly kissyng as Mary wolde haue kissid Crist"; *English Wycliffite Sermons*, 3: 200. Lochrie argues that female mystics, by insisting on a connection between flesh and word, posed a challenge to dominant social and institutional discourses sanctioned by *Noli me tangere*. See *Translations of the Flesh*, 44.

66. Saxer provides this count of the manuscripts as well as tables of their chronological and geographical distribution and religious affiliations in "L'homélie latine," 667–69, quote at 676. Saxer's more recent tally replaces the 130 counted by McCall, who also includes a list of Latin and vernacular manuscript copies of the homily and vernacular printed editions; see "Pseudo Origen *De Maria Magdalena*," 504–9. A Latin version was printed in London c. 1504–8 (*STC* 18846).

67. Saxer, "L'homélie latine," 675; McCall, "Pseudo Origen *De Maria Magdalena*," 494–95. McCall notes (492) that the homily circulates with two different *incipits*, one of which also invokes this monastic context: "Audivimus [Vidimus] fratres [karissimi] Mariam ad monumentum foris stantem."

68. Constable, "Twelfth-Century Spirituality," 46.

69. *Riverside Chaucer*, F Prologue, line 428. The fullest critical assessment of Chaucer's probable translation and poetic use of the homily appears in King, "Sacred Eroticism," 16–66.

70. According to Saxer's data, fifteenth-century England surpasses all other countries in number of assignable manuscripts. The broadest dissemination of the homily occurs in the fifteenth century; 75 of Saxer's 175 identifiable manuscripts date from this period. See "L'homélie latine," 668.

71. Coxe, *Catalogus*, 49–51. Magdalen College, Oxford MS 93 contains the earliest extant English text of the *Imitatio Christi*. See Lovatt, "*Imitation of Christ*," 101.

72. Woolf, "English Imitations."

73. All line citations refer to the Latin edition and English translation of *De Maria* from Corpus Christi College, Cambridge MS 137, in Delasanta and Rousseau, "Chaucer's *Orygenes upon the Maudeleyne*," 319–42.

74. King, "Sacred Eroticism," 24. The second quotation in this sentence is taken from King's unpublished manuscript, "Chaucer and the Pseudo-Origen *De Maria Magdalena*." Shuger similarly points out the collapsing of identities of Christ and Mary in Origenist texts of the medieval and early modern period. See "Saints and Lovers," 164.

75. "Denique Ioseph posuit in monumento corpus tuum Maria ibi pariter tibi sepelivit spiritum suum, et ita indissolubiliter iunxit quomodo univit eum cum corpore tuo ut facilius [posset] seperare animam suam se vivificantem a vivente corpore suo quam spiritum te diligentem a defuncto corpore tuo. Spiritus enim Marie magis erat in corpore tuo quam in corpore suo. Dumque requiret corpus tuum, requirebat et pariter spiritum suum, et ubi perdiderat corpus tuum perdidit cum eo spiritum suum."

76. King, "Sacred Eroticism," 38–39.

77. "Sequamur [ergo] fratres huius mulieris affectum. . . . Disce a Maria ihesum amare et sperare et querendo ihesum investigare." Monastic homiletic writings on Mary Magdalene are replete with exhortations to male religious to model themselves after the saint. In one visionary account she appeared as "a lady of extreme beauty" to a Carthusian from the monastery at Hinton. "'God keep thee, my lover, Stephen,' she said to the prostrate monk" when he flung himself at her feet. See Dunning, "West-Country Carthusians," 37.

78. Copeland, "Why Women Can't Read," 257. See also Shuger, "Saints and Lovers," 155; and Jennings, "Pseudo-Origen Homily," 149.

79. King, "Sacred Eroticism," 41. See also Shuger, "Saints and Lovers," 156. Allegorical habits of reading were central to monastic constructions of the scriptural text and what Leclercq has called "the love of learning and the desire for God." See the analysis of this hermeneutic in Coletti, *Naming the Rose*, 39–72.

80. "O desiderium animae suae cur interrogas eam quid ploras, [quem] queris? . . . Tu scis quia te solum querit, te solum diligit, pro te omnia contempnit et tu dicis quem queris? Dulcis magister ad quid provocas spiritum huius mulieris et animum eius [que] tota pendet in te, tota manet in te, tota sperat in te, tota desperat de se [*sic*]."

81. King, "Sacred Eroticism," 45.

82. Several Middle English dramatic texts have been directly linked to *De Maria Magdalena*. Baker, Murphy, and Hall posit the homily's influence on the meditative dramas in Bodleian Library MS e Museo 160; see *LMRP*, xc–xciii.

King notes resemblances between the homily and the Digby saint play; "Sacred Eroticism," 174.

83. Bynum, "'. . . And Woman His Humanity'," 172; idem, "Female Body and Religious Practice," 194.

84. Bynum, *Holy Feast and Holy Fast*, 6.

85. Probably no medieval saint, even the Virgin Mary, was more variably represented than Mary Magdalene. See Mosco, ed., *La Maddelena*.

86. See the account of Donatello's Mary Magdalene in Malvern, *Venus in Sackcloth*, 5. For an illustration of Donatello's statue and many other wonderful examples of the wizened, penitent Magdalene, see Mosco, ed., *La Maddelena*, 30, 35–37, 50–51, 53, 54.

87. Antonio Pollaiuolo's "St. Mary Magdalene in Colloquy with Angels," Pieve Sta. Maria Assunta, Staggia, similarly shows the gravity-defying work of angels hoisting up the saint to receive the Eucharist. See Wilk, "Cult of Mary Magdalen," 688.

88. "For soþ, whan hir holy body shulde be washen in hir obyt, she was founden so smalle and lene þurgh infirmite [and] fastynges, þat þe rigge-bone of hir bak was clungen to hir wombe, and as vndir a þynne lynnen clothe þe bones of hir bak semyd vndir þe litil skynne of hir bely." From the Middle English translation of Jacques de Vitry's *Life of Marie d'Oignies*. See Horstmann, ed., "Prosalegenden," 183.

89. Delany, *Impolitic Bodies*, 94.

90. On acts and tropes of consumption in the play, see Coletti, "Design."

91. Malvern, *Venus is Sackcloth*, 114–25, quote at 124.

92. Rubin, *Corpus Christi*, 13.

Chapter 6

1. King, "Sacred Eroticism," 128–54, quote at 131. Skeat dates the authorship of the poem between 1448 and 1506 and provides a history of the text's transmission as a work attributed to Chaucer. See *Lamentatyon*.

2. Davidson was the first to note the temporal coincidence of the play and the Magdalene controversy. See "Digby *Mary Magdalene*," 73.

3. Rex, *Theology of John Fisher*, 65.

4. Delasanta and Rousseau, "Chaucer's *Orygenes upon the Maudeleyne*," 327–28: "Iste est ihesus qui recessit a te. . . . Olim te diligebat, olim te a phariseo defendebat, erga sororem tuam dulciter te excusabat. Olim laudabat te cum pedes eius unguento ungebas lacrimis rigabas, et capillis tergebas. . . . Olim querebat te et cum non adesses; mandavit tibi per sororem tuam ut ad se venires." I have added the gospel references within the quotation.

5. The Magdalene controversy is discussed by Hufstader, "Lefèvre d'Étaples"; Cameron, "Biblical Work of Lefèvre d'Étaples"; Surtz, *Works and Days*, 5–7, 274–89; and Rex, *Theology of John Fisher*, 65–77. None of these treatments of the controversy entertains the importance of gender in it.

6. Hufstader, "Lefèvre d'Étaples," 55–58. This count comes from Rigolot, "Heptameron," 222.

7. Fisher's major publications in the Magdalene controversy were *De unica Magdalena, Libri tres* (Paris: Josse Bade, March 1519); *Eversio Munitionis quam Iodocus Clinchtoveus erigere moliebatur adversus unicam Magdalenam* (Louvain: T. Martens, 1519); and *Confutatio Secundae Disceptationis per Jacobum Fabrum Stapulensem* (Paris: Josse Bade, September 1519). See Hufstader, 36–38.

8. *De unica Magdalena, Libri tres*, f. A3v. Quoted and translated in Hufstader, "Lefèvre d'Étaples," 44. Surtz discusses Fisher's understanding and defense of scriptural tradition in his various polemical works. See *Works and Days*, 100–132. Arguing that Fisher at first was a reluctant contributor who initially may even have supported the idea that the composite Magdalene was two distinct figures, Rex states that the bishop was drawn into the debate by his pastoral concerns. See *Theology of John Fisher*, 72–75.

9. See King, "Christianity's Penitent Prostitutes," 439–440.

10. Hufstader, "Lefèvre d'Étaples," 57.

11. "Et saepe hic Parisiis variis in locis praedicatum Mariam sororem Marthae non fuisse illam publicam Peccatricem, sed sanctam, incontaminatam, et virginem, quod et magis credo." Josse Clinchtove to François du Moulin de Rochefort, *De Maria Magdalena, Triduo Christi, Et ex tribus una Maria* (Paris, 1518). In Rice, ed., *Prefatory Epistles of Jacques Lefèvre*, 403–4.

12. Josse Clinchtove, *Disceptationis de Magdalena, Defensio: Apologiae Marci Grandivallis illam improbare nitentis, ex adverso respondens* (Paris, 1519), f. 7v. Quoted and translated in Hufstader, "Lefèvre d'Étaples," 57.

13. "[V]t diuam Mariam Magdalenen assertori suo Fabro eriperent et cum turpissimis scortis in olidum lupanar detruderent? cum tamen potius deceret in re tam dubia eam sequi opinionem que ad pietatem accederet propius." Pirckheimer's letter to Erasmus, April 30, 1520. Quoted and translated in Surtz, *Works and Days*, 403–4, n. 14.

14. For discussion of methodological strategies and principles of the humanists' critique, see Hufstader, "Lefèvre d'Étaples," 41–55. King suggests that Fisher objected to the humanist position because it eliminated "the paradox, the erotic continuity verging on causality, and the quasi-divinity that the Magdalene had evolved"; "Christianity's Penitent Prostitutes," 440. But Fisher never posed his arguments in these terms. A statue of Mary Magdalene was included among the personal effects he gave to St. John's College, Cambridge, in 1525. See Rex, "The Polemical Theologian," 120. On Fisher's devotion to Mary Magdalene, see also Rex, *Theology of John Fisher*, 68–69.

15. Hufstader, "Lefèvre d'Étaples, 35; see Cameron, "The Attack on Lefèvre," 13–14, 20–21 for other humanist treatments of the topic. While the single Magdalene did not become subject to revisionary biblical scholarship until the early sixteenth century, the idea that Saint Anne, mother of the Virgin Mary, had three marriages—another conundrum of gender in medieval scriptural tradition—had been disputed since the twelfth century. See Ashley and Sheingorn, "Introduction," *Saint Anne in Medieval Society*, 11–12. Fisher agreed with Lefèvre on the issue of Saint Anne's *trinubium*, because, unlike the *unica* Magdalene, it was not universally accepted nor was it confirmed by miracles, based on scripture, or enshrined in liturgy. See Rex, *Theology of John Fisher*, 69–70.

16. Hufstader, "Lefèvre d'Étaples, 55–58, quotes at 58. See also Rigolot, "*Heptameron*," 223–24. The Franciscan Matteo d'Aquasparta (d. 1302), by contrast, singled out Mary Magdalene as a model of scholarly comportment and pious study. See Jansen, *Making of the Magdalen*, 118.

17. Lefèvre d'Étaples, ed., *Politicorum libri octo* (Paris: Henri Estienne, 5 August 1506), ff. 123v–4r. Quoted and translated in Rice, "Jacques Lefèvre d'Étaples," 90–91. See also Rice's "Introduction" to *Prefatory Epistles*, xv–xx.

18. Rice, "Jacques Lefèvre d'Étaples," 101.

19. Lefèvre's and Clinchtove's collaborative edition of the *Nichomachean Ethics* and commentary, *Moralis Iacobi Fabri Stapulensis in Ethicen Introductio* (Paris: Simon de Colines, 1528), f. 52v. Quoted and translated in Hufstader, "Lefèvre d'Étaples," 59.

20. Brown, *Body and Society*, 153. The formula originates with Lévi-Strauss.

21. Harbison, "Lucas van Leyden." Harbison suggests (128, n. 20) that the painting of the preaching Mary Magdalene discussed earlier (fig. 12) was one work generated by the controversy.

22. Lefèvre was a friend of Cornelius Agrippa, whose *De nobilitate et praecellentia foeminei sexus* promoted women's evangelical authority on historical and biblical grounds. See Newman, *Virile Woman*, 226, 237–42.

23. Lefèvre also published works by twelfth-century spiritual writers such as Bernard of Clairvaux, Hugh of St. Victor, Richard of St. Victor, and the mystical writings of Ramon Lull, Jan van Ruysbroek, and Raymundus Jordanus. His edition of the women mystics appeared in a collection with works by three male writers, the *Liber trium virorum [et] trium spiritualium virginum* (Paris, Henri Estienne and Jean de Brie, 1513), which included the first edition of Hildegard's *Scivias*, selections from Elisabeth's visions, letters, and *Liber viarum Dei*—the first printed edition of her work too—and Mechtild's *Liber specialis gratiae*. See Rice, "Jacques Lefèvre d'Étaples," 112–15; and idem, "Introduction" to Lefèvre's *Prefatory Epistles*, xv.

24. Rice, "Introduction" to Lefèvre's *Prefatory Epistles*, xx; and idem, "Jacques Lefèvre d'Étaples," 91–92; 96–100. Lefèvre said that the visionary works of Elisabeth of Schönau "well express the energy of the Spirit and make manifest angelic speech in the simplicity and sincerity of holy visions." Quoted in Clark, *Elisabeth of Schönau*, 27.

25. Rex, "Polemical Theologian," 116–17. See also Duffy, "Spirituality of John Fisher," 210. On similarities between Fisher and Lefèvre, see Rex, *Theology of John Fisher*, 76.

26. Duffy, "Spirituality of John Fisher," 223–25; Bradshaw, "Bishop John Fisher," 10–11.

27. Rice, "Jacques Lefèvre d'Étaples," 103.

28. Duffy, "Spirituality of John Fisher," 210.

29. For recent assessments of Barton's significance, see Watt, "Prophet at Home" and the expanded version of this article in *Secretaries of God*, 51–80. See also McKee, *Dame Elizabeth Barton*; and the full-length biography by Neame, *Holy Maid of Kent*.

30. The effectiveness of the campaign to censor all evidence of Barton's

spiritual activities and prophecies is analyzed by Devereux, "Elizabeth Barton and Tudor Censorship." Devereux (97) compares the total disappearance of all works directly associated with Barton to the survival of virtually all of the condemned books of Tyndale and his circle. For an overview of the sources related to Barton, see Neame, *Holy Maid of Kent*, 18–20; and Watt, "Prophet at Home," 165–67.

31. Watt argues that Barton adopted Bridget of Sweden and Catherine of Siena as role models; "Prophet at Home." Barton is unique among her contemporaries as well as earlier and later English visionaries and holy women in the extent to which she took public, political positions; see Watt, *Secretaries of God*, 78–80. Warren, however, has identified a strong tradition of feminine spiritual involvement—saintly and visionary—in the dynastic politics of fifteenth-century England. See *Spiritual Economies*, 111–33.

32. Whatmore, "Sermon against the Holy Maid of Kent," 465–66.

33. Neame, *Holy Maid of Kent*, 17–18; Watt, *Secretaries of God*, 72. Rex discusses support for Barton among the scholars and opponents of Lutheranism at St. John's College, Cambridge, founded by John Fisher; "English Campaign against Luther," 91–94. Mary Erler's portrait of the community of male clerics and scholars, nuns and vowesses associated with support for Barton provides counterweight to the idea of Barton as a mere eccentric and underscores her connections to mainstream traditions of reading and piety in early Tudor England. See *Women, Reading, and Piety*, 87–96.

34. Devereux, "Elizabeth Barton and Tudor Censorship," 100; Watt, *Secretaries of God*, 57; Whatmore, "Sermon against the Holy Maid of Kent," 470–71.

35. *Letters Relating to the Suppression of the Monasteries*, ed. Wright, Camden Society. Quoted in Whatmore, "Sermon against the Holy Maid of Kent," 471, n. 2. McKee notes that Barton visited Fisher three times at his bishop's seat in Rochester; *Dame Elizabeth Barton*, 27–28.

36. Whatmore, "Sermon against the Holy Maid of Kent," 470.

37. *Calendar of Letters, Despatches, and State Papers, Relating to the Negotiations between England and Spain*, ed. G. A. Begenroth et al. (London, 1862–1947), 4, part 2, no. 1149. Cited in Watt, *Secretaries of God*, 69.

38. Watt, "Prophet at Home," 175.

39. Watt, "Prophet at Home," 169. Man was a member of the intellectual network for whom English mystical works such as the *Scale of Perfection* and the *Cloud of Unknowing* were translated into Latin. Besides Barton's supporters, this group included men such as John Dygoun, the recluse at Sheen, bachelor of civil and canon law, and benefactor of two Oxford colleges who owned a copy of the Pseudo-Origen *De Maria Magdalena*. See Lovatt, "Library of John Blacman," 225–29.

40. Neame, a great Barton sympathizer, suggests that her demise lay not in her prophesies about Henry but in the "possibility that she would have become a successful apostle of a Catholic rebellion against the excommunicate sovereign." See *Holy Maid of Kent*, 17.

41. King, "Christianity's Penitent Prostitutes," 439–40.

42. Haskins, *Myth and Metaphor*, 26, 406, n. 54.

43. Haskins, *Myth and Metaphor*, 16. See also Schaberg, "How Mary Magdalene Became a Whore." Both Haskins and Schaberg analyze the negative impact that the traditional image of Mary Magdalene as the penitent prostitute has had on modern-day women seeking a role in the ministry of the Church. The relationship between feminist historians of the Bible and early Christianity and the political situation of women in the contemporary Church is analyzed by Murphy, *Word According to Eve*. See also Jansen, *Making of the Magdalen*, 335–36.

44. *Golden Legend*, 1: 377: "Nec mirum, si os, quod tam pia et tam pulchra pedibus salvatoris infixerat oscula, caeteris amplius verbi Dei spiraret odorem." Latin text quoted in Delany, *Impolitic Bodies*, 92, 98.

45. Beckwith, *Christ's Body*, 3–4.

46. Shuger ("Saints and Lovers") uses the medieval and early modern Magdalene literature to reassess the historical relationship of eros and sexuality. Shuger argues that in medieval constructions of the erotic, typified in the Pseudo-Origen homily, "sexual desire is an inflection of erotic longing, not its origin or essence" (159); hence sexual desire emerges from spiritual longing, not the other way around. This is why Mary Magdalene's sacred eroticism is carnal, i.e., corporeal, but not necessarily sexual (156–57). In Shuger's analysis the erotic comes to be identified with physical desire only after 1650, when the genitals replace the eye as the locus of erotic longing. The dissociation of sexuality from desire in the medieval literature of spiritual eros is not an act of sublimation; it involves a genuinely different organization of longing in a subject. Neither is the medieval Magdalene a figure for the sacralizing of sexuality, however much her modern interpreters may want to construe her as such. The dichotomy through which Shuger traces the historical construction of desire—between eros, love, and longing on the one hand and sexuality, guilt, and carnality on the other (169, n. 34)—explains why the Digby *Mary Magdalene* takes such a critical stance toward human sexuality but not to the body and desire. The play is singularly attentive to circumscribing proper sexual relations to the nuclear family and to showing how unruly sexual relations—in and outside of marriage, between men and women or men and men—can lead not only to sin (as in the case of Mary Magdalene) or sickness (as in the case of the king of Marseilles) but also to disturbances in social and gender order (the priest and shipman and their boys). Thus statements such as Haskins's observation that the repentant Mary Magdalene represents "the sexuate feminine redeemed and therefore rendered sexless" (141) seem beside the point when applied to late medieval symbolic constructions of the saint such as that of the Digby play, which hints that normative sexual and gender relations are irrelevant to sacred beings. Symbolic figures such as the late medieval Magdalene have much to contribute to the analysis of the historical construction of sexuality.

47. See Coletti, "Genealogy, Sexuality, and Sacred Power."

48. *Breaking the Waves*, dir. Lars von Trier, 1996.

49. *Elizabeth*, dir. Shekhar Kapur, 1998.

50. On these issues, see Hackett, *Virgin Mother*.

Works Cited

Primary Sources

Alfonso of Jaén. "The Middle English *Epistola solitarii ad reges* of Alfonso of Jaén: An Edition of the Text in London, British Library, MS Cotton Julius Fii." In *God's Words, Women's Voices,* ed. Voaden, 159–81.

Angela of Foligno: Complete Works. Trans. Paul Lachance, O.F.M. Mahwah, N.J.: Paulist Press, 1993.

Anselm. *Prayers and Meditations of St. Anselm.* Trans. Sister Benedicta Ward, S.L.G. Harmondworth, Middlesex: Penguin, 1973.

Antichrist and Judgement Day: The Middle French "Jour de Judgement." Trans. and commentary Richard K. Emmerson and David F. Hult. Asheville, N.C.: Pegasus Press, 1998.

Bale, John. *The Complete Plays of John Bale.* Ed. Peter Happé. 2 vols. Cambridge: D. S. Brewer, 1985–86.

Barratt, Alexandra, ed. *Women's Writing in Middle English.* London: Longman, 1992.

Bateson, Mary, ed. "The Register of Crabhouse Nunnery." *NA* 11 (1892): 1–71.

Bernard of Clairvaux. *On the Song of Songs I.* Trans. Kilian Walsh. Cistercian Fathers Series 4. Kalamazoo, Mich.: Cistercian Publications, 1976.

Bevington, David, ed. *Medieval Drama.* Boston: Houghton Mifflin, 1975.

Blamires, Alcuin, ed., with Karen Pratt and C. W. Marx. *Woman Defamed and Woman Defended.* Oxford: Clarendon Press, 1992.

Bokenham, Osbern. *Legendys of Hooly Wummen.* Ed. Mary S. Serjeantson. EETS o.s. 206. London: Humphrey Milford, Oxford University Press, 1938.

Breaking the Waves. Dir. Lars von Trier. October Films, 1996.

Capgrave, John. *The Life of Saint Katherine.* Ed. Karen A. Winstead. Kalamazoo, Mich.: Medieval Institute Publications, 1999.

Cavalca, Domenico. *The Life of Mary Magdalen. Translated from the Italian of an Unknown Fourteenth-Century Writer.* Trans. Valentina Hawtrey. London: John Lane, 1904.

The Chastising of God's Children and the Treatise of Perfection of the Sons of God. Ed. Joyce Bazire and Eric Colledge. Oxford: Basil Blackwell, 1957.

Chaucer, Geoffrey. *The Riverside Chaucer.* 3d. ed. Ed. Larry D. Benson et al. Boston: Houghton Mifflin, 1987.

The Chester Mystery Cycle. Ed. R. M. Lumiansky and David Mills. 2 vols. EETS s.s. 3, 9. Oxford: Oxford University Press, 1974, 1986.

The Chester Mystery Cycle. Ed. David Mills. East Lansing, Mich.: Colleagues Press, 1992.

Clinchtove, Josse. Letter to François du Moulin de Rochefort. *De Maria Magdalena, Triduo Christi, Et ex tribus vna Maria, disceptatio*. Paris, 1518. In *Prefatory Epistles of Jacques Lefèvre d'Étaples*, ed. Rice, 399–406.

The Cloud of Unknowing and the Book of Privy Counselling. Ed. Phyllis Hodgson. EETS o.s. 218. 1944. Reprint, London: Oxford University Press, 1981.

The Cloud of Unknowing and Related Treatises. Ed. Phyllis Hodgson. Analecta Cartusiana 3. Salzburg: Institut für Anglistik und Amerikanistik, Universität Salzburg, 1982.

The Commonplace Book of Robert Reynes of Acle: An Edition of Tanner MS. 407. Ed. Cameron Louis. New York: Garland, 1980.

D'Ancona, Alessandro, ed. *Sacre Rappresentazione dei secoli XIV, XV e XVI*. 3 vols. Florence: Successori Le Monnier, 1872.

Delasanta, Rodney K. and Constance M. Rousseau. "Chaucer's *Orygenes upon the Maudeleyne*: A Translation." *Chaucer Review* 30 (1996): 319–42.

Deonise Hid Divinite and Other Treatises on Contemplative Prayer Related to "The Cloud of Unknowing." Ed. Phyllis Hodgson. EETS o.s. 231. 1955. Reprint with corrections, London: Oxford University Press, 1958.

The Digby Plays. Ed. F. J. Furnivall. EETS e.s. 70. 1896. Reprint, London: Oxford University Press, 1967.

The Digby Plays: Facsimiles of the Plays in Bodley MSS Digby 133 and e. Museo 160. Intro. Donald C. Baker and John L. Murphy. Leeds Texts and Monographs. Medieval Drama Facsimiles 3. Leeds: University of Leeds, 1976.

Elizabeth. Dir. Shekhar Kapur. Channel Four Films, 1998.

English Wycliffite Sermons. Ed. Anne Hudson and Pamela Gradon. 5 vols. Oxford: Clarendon Press, 1983–96.

Furnivall, Frederick J., ed. *The Fifty Earliest English Wills in the Court of Probate*. EETS o.s. 78. London: Trübner, 1882.

Gardner, Edmund G., ed. *The Cell of Self-Knowledge: Seven Early English Mystical Works Printed by Henry Pepwell in 1521*. New York: Cooper Square Publishers, 1966.

Gregory the Great. *Homilia 33*. In *XL Homiliarum in Evangelia*. PL 76: 1238–46.

Guillaume le Clerc. "La vie de Madeleine." Ed. Robert Reinsch. *Archiv* 64 (1880): 85–94.

Harper-Bill, Christopher, ed. *Charters of the Medieval Hospitals of Bury St. Edmunds*. Woodbridge, Eng.: Boydell and Brewer, for the Suffolk Record Society, 1994.

Harrod, Henry. "Extracts from Early Norfolk Wills." *NA* 1 (1847): 111–28.

———. "Extracts from Early Wills in the Norwich Registries." *NA* 4 (1855): 317–39.

Hilton, Walter. *Scala perfectionis*. Westminster: Wynkyn de Worde, 1533. *STC* 14045.

———. *The Scale of Perfection*. Trans. and intro. John P. H. Clark and Rosemary Dorward. Mahwah, N.J.: Paulist Press, 1991.

———. *The Scale of Perfection*. Ed. Thomas H. Bestul. Kalamazoo, Mich.: Medieval Institute Publications, 2000.

Horstmann, Carl, ed. *Altenglische Legenden: Neue Folge*. Heilbronn: Henniger, 1881.

————. "Prosalegenden. Die Legenden der MS. Douce 114." *Anglia* 8 (1885): 102–96.

————. *Sammlung altenglischer Legenden*. 1878. Reprint, Hildesheim: Georg Olms Verlag, 1969.

Hudson, Anne, ed. *Selections from English Wycliffite Writings*. Cambridge: Cambridge University Press, 1978.

Hugh of Floreffe. *The Life of Yvette of Huy*. Trans. Jo Ann McNamara. Toronto: Peregrina Publishing, 1999.

Jacobus de Voragine. *The Golden Legend*. Trans. William Granger Ryan. 2 vols. Princeton: Princeton University Press, 1993.

Julian of Norwich. *A Book of Showings to the Anchoress Julian of Norwich*. Ed. Edmund Colledge, O.S.A., and James Walsh, S.J. 2 parts. Toronto: Pontifical Institute of Medieval Studies, 1978.

Kempe, Margery. *The Book of Margery Kempe*. Ed. Sanford Meech and Hope Emily Allen. EETS o.s. 212. 1940. Reprint, London: Oxford University Press, 1982.

————. *The Book of Margery Kempe*. Ed. Barry Windeatt. Harlow, Essex: Longman, 2000.

King, Karen L. "The Gospel of Mary." *The Complete Gospels: Annotated Scholars Version*. Ed. Robert J. Miller. Sonoma, Calif.: Polebridge Press, 1994.

Lamentatyon of Mary Magdaleyne. Ed. Bertha Skeat. Cambridge: Fabb and Tyler, 1897.

The Late Medieval Religious Plays of Bodleian MSS Digby 133 and e. Mus. 160. Ed. Donald C. Baker, John L. Murphy, and Louis B. Hall, Jr. EETS o.s. 283. Oxford: Oxford University Press, 1982.

Lefèvre d'Étaples, Jacques. *The Prefatory Epistles of Jacques Lefèvre d'Étaples and Related Texts*. Ed. Eugene F. Rice, Jr. New York: Columbia University Press, 1972.

The Life of Christina of Markyate: A Twelfth-Century Recluse. Ed. and trans. C. H. Talbot. 1959. Reprint, Toronto: University of Toronto Press in association with the Medieval Academy of America, 1998.

The Life of Saint Mary Magdalene and of Her Sister Martha. Ed. and trans. David Mycoff. Cistercian Studies Series 108. Kalamazoo, Mich.: Cistercian Publications, 1989.

Love, Nicholas. *Nicholas Love's Mirror of the Blessed Life of Jesus Christ*. Ed. Michael Sargent. New York: Garland, 1992.

Ludus Coventriae; or, the Plaie Called Corpus Christi. Ed. K. S. Block. EETS e.s. 120. 1922. Reprint, London: Oxford University Press, 1960.

Lydgate, John. *The Minor Poems of John Lydgate*. Vol. 1. Ed. Henry Noble MacCracken. EETS e.s. 107. 1911. Reprint, Oxford: Oxford University Press, 1961.

The Macro Plays. Ed. Mark Eccles. EETS o.s. 262. London: Oxford University Press, 1969.

The Mary Play from the N. Town Manuscript. Ed. Peter Meredith. London: Longman, 1987.

Mechtild of Hackeborn. *The Booke of Gostlye Grace of Mechtild of Hackeborn*. Ed. Theresa A. Halligan. Toronto: Pontifical Institute of Medieval Studies, 1979.

Meditations on the Life of Christ: An Illustrated Manuscript of the Fourteenth Century. Trans. Isa Ragusa and ed. Isa Ragusa and Rosalie B. Green. Princeton: Princeton University Press, 1977.

Meredith, Peter, and John Tailby, eds. *The Staging of Religious Drama in Europe in the Later Middle Ages: Texts and Documents in English Translation*. EDAM Monograph Series 4. Kalamazoo, Mich.: Medieval Institute Publications, 1983.

Migne, J.-P. *Patrologiae cursus completus: Series latina*. 221 vols. Paris: Garniére Press, 1844–64.

Mirk, John. *Mirk's Festial*. Ed. Theodor Erbe. EETS e.s. 96. 1905. Reprint, Millwood, N.Y.: Kraus, 1973.

Mycoff, David A., ed. *A Critical Edition of Mary Magdalena from Caxton's "Golden Legende" of 1483*. Salzburg Studies in English Literature. Elizabethan and Renaissance Studies 92: 11. Salzburg: Institut für Anglistik und Amerikanistik, Universität Salzburg, 1985.

The Myroure of Oure Ladye. Ed. John Henry Blunt. EETS e.s. 19. 1873. Reprint, Millwood, N.Y.: Kraus, 1981.

The New Testament: Douay Version. Intro. Laurence Bright. London: Sheed and Ward, 1977.

Non-Cycle Plays and Fragments. Ed. Norman Davis. EETS s.s. 1. London: Oxford University Press, 1970.

The N-Town Play, Cotton MS. Vespasian D.8. Ed. Stephen Spector. 2 vols. EETS s.s. 11, 12. Oxford: Oxford University Press, 1991.

Odo of Cluny. *In veneratione sanctae Mariae Magdalenae*. PL 133: 713–21.

Owen, Dorothy M., ed. *The Making of King's Lynn: A Documentary Survey*. London: Oxford University Press for the British Academy, 1984.

The Passion Play from the N.Town Manuscript. Ed. Peter Meredith. London: Longman, 1990.

Paston Letters and Papers of the Fifteenth Century. Ed. Norman Davis. 2 vols. Oxford: Oxford University Press, 1971, 1976.

Peter of Celle. *Sermo 60. In festivitate sanctae Mariae Magdalenae*. PL 202: 822–25.

Peter Chrysologus. *Sermo 74. De resurrectione Christi*. PL 52: 408–11.

———. *Sermo 75. De resurrectione Christi*. PL 52: 411–14.

Peter Comestor (attributed to Hildebert de Lavardin). *In festo sanctae Mariae Magdalenae. Sermo unicus*. PL 171: 671–78.

Radulph Ardentis. *Homilia 25. In festo beatae Mariae Magdalenae*. PL 155: 1397–1402.

Records of Early English Drama: Chester. Ed. Lawrence M. Clopper. Toronto: University of Toronto Press, 1979.

Records of Early English Drama: Norwich, 1540–1642. Ed. David Galloway. Toronto: University of Toronto Press, 1984.

Records of Plays and Players in Norfolk and Suffolk, 1330–1642. Ed. David Galloway and John Wasson. Malone Society Collections 11. Oxford: Oxford University Press, 1981.

"*La Règle des Fins Amans*: Eine Beginenregel aus dem Ende des XIII Jahrhunderts." Ed. Karl Christ. In *Philologische Studien aus dem romanische-germanischen Kulturkreise: Festgabe Karl Voretzsch*. Ed. B. Schädel and W. Mulertt, 173–213. Halle: Max Niemeyer, 1927.

Revelations of Saint Birgitta. Ed. William Patterson Cumming. EETS o.s. 178. 1929. Reprint, Millwood, N.Y.: Kraus, 1971.

Riggio, Milla Cozart, ed. *The Play of "Wisdom": Its Texts and Contexts*. New York: AMS Press, 1998.

Rolle, Richard. *Richard Rolle: The English Writings*. Trans., ed., and intro. Rosamund Allen. Mahwah, N.J.: Paulist Press, 1988.

———. *Richard Rolle: Prose and Verse from MS. Longleat 29 and Related Manuscripts*. Ed. S. J. Ogilvie-Thomson. EETS o.s. 293. Oxford: Oxford University Press, 1988.

———. *The Song of Angels*. In *Cell of Self-Knowledge*, ed. Gardner, 63–73.

Sister Catherine (Schwester Katrei). Trans. Elvira Borgstädt. In *Meister Eckhart: Teacher and Prophet*, ed. Bernard McGinn, 349–87. Mahwah, N.J.: Paulist Press, 1986.

Speculum Sacerdotale. Ed. Edward H. Weatherly and H. Milford. EETS o.s. 200. Oxford: Oxford University Press, 1936.

Tanner, Norman P., ed. *Heresy Trials in the Diocese of Norwich, 1428–31*. Camden Society, 4th ser., 20. London: Royal Historical Society, 1977.

Testamenta Eboracensia: A Selection of Wills from the Register at York. Vol. 4. Ed. James Raine. Surtees Society 53. Durham: Andrew, 1869.

Thomas à Kempis. *Imitatio Christi. The following of Christ, translated out of Latin into English*. London: 1556. STC 23967.

The Towneley Plays. Ed. Martin Stevens and A. C. Cawley. 2 vols. EETS s.s. 13, 14. Oxford: Oxford University Press, 1994.

A Tretise of Miraclis Pleyinge. Ed. Clifford Davidson. EDAM Monograph Series 19. Kalamazoo, Mich.: Medieval Institute Publications, 1993.

Two Coventry Corpus Christi Plays. Ed. Pamela M. King and Clifford Davidson. EDAM Monograph Series 27. Kalamazoo, Mich.: Medieval Institute Publications, 2000.

Tymms, Samuel, ed. *Wills and Inventories from the Registers of the Commissary of Bury St. Edmunds and the Archdeacon of Sudbury*. Camden Society, 1st ser. 49. London: J. B. Nichols and Son, 1850.

La vie de Marie Magdaleine. Ed. Jacques Chocheyras and Graham Runnalls. Geneva: Droz, 1986.

White, Paul Whitfield, ed. *Reformation Biblical Drama in England: "The Life and Repentaunce of Mary Magdalene" and "The History of Jacob and Esau."* New York: Garland, 1992.

York Plays. Ed. Richard Beadle. London: Edward Arnold, 1982.

Young, Karl, ed. *The Drama of the Medieval Church*. 2 vols. 1933. Reprint, Oxford: Clarendon Press, 1962.

SECONDARY SOURCES

Aers, David. "Altars of Power: Reflections on Eamon Duffy's *The Stripping of the Altars: Traditional Religion in England, 1400–1580*." *Literature and History* 3 (1994): 90–105.

———. *Community, Gender, and Individual Identity: English Writing, 1360–1430*. London: Routledge, 1988.

———. "The Humanity of Christ: Reflections on Julian of Norwich's *Revelation of Love*." In *Powers of the Holy*, Aers and Staley, 77–104.

Aers, David, and Lynn Staley. *The Powers of the Holy: Religion, Politics, and Gender in Late Medieval English Culture*. University Park: Pennsylvania State University Press, 1996.

Alexander, Jonathan. "The Pulpit with the Four Doctors at St. James's, Castle Acre, Norfolk." In *England in the Fifteenth Century*, ed. Rogers, 198–206.

Alton, R. E. "The Academic Drama in Oxford: Extracts from the Records of Four Colleges." Malone Society. *Collections* 5 (1960): 29–95.

André, J. L. "Female Head-dresses Exemplified by Norfolk Brasses." *NA* 14 (1901): 241–62.

Armstrong, C. A. J. "The Piety of Cicely, Duchess of York: A Study in Late Medieval Culture." *For Hilaire Belloc: Essays in Honour of His Seventy-Second Birthday*, ed. Douglas Woodruff, 73–94. London: Sheed and Ward, 1942.

Ashley, Kathleen. "The Bourgeois Piety of Martha in the *Passion* of Jean Michel." *MLQ* 45 (1984): 227–40.

———. "Contemporary Theories of Popular Culture and Medieval Performances." *Mediaevalia* 18 (1995 [for 1992]): 5–17.

———. "Divine Power in Chester Cycle and Late Medieval Thought." *Journal of the History of Ideas* 39 (1978): 387–404.

———. "Image and Ideology: Saint Anne in Late Medieval Drama and Narrative." In *Interpreting Cultural Symbols*, ed. Ashley and Sheingorn, 111–30.

———. "The Specter of Bernard's Noon-Day Demon in Medieval Drama." *American Benedictine Review* 30 (1979): 205–21.

———. "Sponsorship, Reflexivity, and Resistance: Cultural Readings of the York Cycle Plays." In *Performance of Middle English Culture*, ed. Paxson, Clopper, and Tomasch, 9–24.

———. "Transgressing Boundaries, Comparing Dramas in English and French." Paper presented at the Modern Language Association Convention, New York, December 2002.

Ashley, Kathleen, and Pamela Sheingorn. *Writing Faith: Text, Sign, and History in the Miracles of Saint Foy*. Chicago: University of Chicago Press, 1999.

———, eds. *Interpreting Cultural Symbols: Saint Anne in Late Medieval Society*. Athens: University of Georgia Press, 1990.

Astell, Ann. *The Song of Songs in the Middle Ages*. Ithaca, N.Y.: Cornell University Press, 1990.

Aston, Margaret. "Imageless Devotion: What Kind of Ideal?" In *Pragmatic Utopias: Ideals and Communities, 1200–1630*, ed. Christine Carpenter and Sara Rees-Jones, 188–203. Cambridge: Cambridge University Press, 2001.

————. "Lollard Women Priests?" In *Lollards and Reformers: Images and Literacy in Late Medieval Religion*, 49–70. London: Hambledon, 1984.

————. "Segregation in Churches." In *Women in the Church*, ed. Sheils and Wood, 237–94.

Badir, Patricia. "The Garrison of the Godly: Antitheatricality and the Performance of Distinction in Early Modern Hull." *JMEMS* 27 (1997): 285–316.

————. "Representations of the Resurrection at Beverly Minster circa 1208: Chronicle, Play, Miracle." *Theatre Survey* 38 (1997): 9–41.

————. "'To allure vnto their loue': Iconoclasm and Striptease in Lewis Wager's *The Life and Repentaunce of Marie Magdalene*." *Theatre Journal* 51 (1999): 1–20.

Baker, Denise Nowakowsi. *Julian of Norwich's "Showings": From Vision to Book*. Princeton: Princeton University Press, 1994.

Baker, Derek, ed. *Medieval Women*. Studies in Church History. Subsidia 1. Oxford: Basil Blackwell, 1978.

Baker, Donald C., and James L. Murphy. "The Books of Myles Blomefylde." *The Library*. 5th ser., 31 (1976): 377–85.

————. "The Late Medieval Plays of MS Digby 133: Scribes, Dates, and Early History." *RORD* 10 (1967): 153–66.

Barratt, Alexandra. "How Many Children Had Julian of Norwich? Editions, Translations, and Versions of Her Revelations." In *Vox Mystica: Essays on Medieval Mysticism*, ed. Anne Clark Bartlett, Thomas H. Bestul, Janet Goebel, and William F. Pollard, 27–39. Woodbridge, Eng.: D. S. Brewer, 1995.

Barron, Caroline. "Introduction: England and the Low Countries, 1327–1477." In *England and the Low Countries*, ed. Barron and Saul, 1–28.

Barron, Caroline, and Nigel Saul, ed. *England and the Low Countries*. New York: St. Martin's Press, 1995.

Bartlett, Anne Clark. *Male Authors, Female Readers: Representation and Subjectivity in Late Medieval Devotional Literature*. Ithaca, N.Y.: Cornell University Press, 1995.

Bauerschmidt, Frederick Christian. *Julian of Norwich and the Mystical Body of Christ*. Notre Dame, Ind.: University of Notre Dame Press, 1999.

Beadle, Richard. "The Medieval Drama of East Anglia: Studies in Dialect, Documentary Records, and Stagecraft." 2 vols. Ph.D. diss., University of York, Center for Medieval Studies, 1977.

————. "Monk Thomas Hyngham's Hand in the Macro Manuscript." *New Science Out of Old Books: Studies in Manuscripts and Early Printed Books in Honor of A. I. Doyle*. Ed. Richard Beadle and A. J. Piper, 315–37. Aldershot, Eng.: Scolar Press, 1995.

————. "Plays and Playing at Thetford and Nearby, 1498–1540." *Theatre Notebook* 32 (1978): 4–11.

————. "Prolegomena to a Literary Geography of Later Medieval Norfolk." In *Regionalism in Late Medieval Manuscripts and Texts*, ed. Riddy, 89–108.

————. "The York Cycle." *CCMET*, 85–108.

————. "The York Cycle: Texts, Performances, and the Bases for Critical Inquiry." In *Medieval Literature: Texts and Interpretation*, ed. Machan, 105–19.

————, ed. *The Cambridge Companion to Medieval English Theatre*. Cambridge: Cambridge University Press, 1994.

Beckwith, Sarah. *Christ's Body: Identity, Culture, and Society in Late Medieval Writings*. London: Routledge, 1993.

————. "Making the World in York and the York Corpus Christi Cycle." In *Framing Medieval Bodies*, ed. Sarah Kay and Miri Rubin, 254–76. Manchester: Manchester University Press, 1994.

————. "Problems of Authority in Late Medieval English Mysticism: Language, Agency, and Authority in the *Book of Margery Kempe*." *Exemplaria* 4 (1992): 171–99.

————. "Ritual, Church, and Theatre: Medieval Dramas of the Sacramental Body." In *Culture and History, 1350–1600: Essays on English Communities, Identities, and Writing*, ed. David Aers, 65–89. Detroit: Wayne State University Press, 1992.

————. "Ritual, Theater, and Social Space in the York Cycle." In *Bodies and Disciplines*, ed. Hanawalt and Wallace, 63–86.

————. "*Sacrum Signum*: Sacramentality and Dissent in York's Theater of Corpus Christi." In *Criticism and Dissent in the Middle Ages*, ed. Rita Copeland, 264–88. Cambridge: Cambridge University Press, 1996.

————. *Signifying God: Social Relations and Symbolic Act in the York Corpus Christi Plays*. Chicago: University of Chicago Press, 2001.

Beeching, H. C., and Montague Rhodes James. "The Library of the Cathedral Church of Norwich." *NA* 19 (1917): 67–116.

Bennett, Jacob. "The *Mary Magdalene* of Bishop's Lynn." *SP* 75 (1978): 1–9.

Bennett, Rev. Dr. "The College of S. John Evangelist at Rushworth, Co. Norfolk," *NA* 10 (1888): 277–312.

Bériou, Nicole. "La Madeleine dans les sermons parisiens du XIIIe siècle." *MEFRM* 104.1 (1992): 269–340.

————. "The Right of Women to Give Religious Instruction in the Thirteenth Century." In *Women Preachers and Prophets*, ed. Kienzle and Walker, 134–45.

Bevington, David. "'Blake and Wyght, Fowll and Fayer': Stage Picture in *Wisdom*." In *"Wisdom" Symposium*, ed. Riggio, 18–38.

Biller, Peter, and Alaistair Minnis, eds. *Medieval Theology and the Natural Body*. York Studies in Medieval Theology 1. York: University of York Press, 1997.

Binski, Paul. "The English Parish Church and Its Art in the Later Middle Ages: A Review of the Problem." *Studies in Iconography* 20 (1999): 1–25.

Blamires, Alcuin. *The Case for Women in Medieval Culture*. Oxford: Clarendon Press, 1997.

————. "The Limits of Bible Study for Medieval Women." In *Women, the Book, and the Godly*, ed. Smith and Taylor, 1–12.

————. "Women and Preaching in Medieval Orthodoxy, Heresy, and Saints' Lives." *Viator* 26 (1995): 135–52.

Blamires, Alcuin, and C. W. Marx. "Women Not to Preach: A Disputation in British Library MS Harley 31." *Journal of Medieval Latin* 3 (1993): 34–63.

Blanton-Whetsell, Virginia. "*Imagines Ætheldredae*: Mapping Hagiographic

Representations of Abbatial Power and Religious Patronage." *Studies in Iconography* 23 (2002): 55–107.

———. "St. Æthelthryth's Cult: Literary, Historical, and Pictorial Constructions of Gendered Sanctity." Ph.D. diss., State University of New York at Binghamton, 1998.

———. "*Tota integra, tota incorrupta*: The Shrine of St. Æthelthryth as Symbol of Monastic Autonomy." *JMEMS* 32 (2002): 227–67.

Bloch, R. Howard. *Medieval Misogyny and the Invention of Romantic Love.* Chicago: University of Chicago Press, 1991.

Blomefield, Francis. *An Essay Towards a Topographical History of the County of Norfolk.* Completed by Charles Parkin. 2d ed. 11 vols. London, 1805–10.

Blumenfeld-Kosinski, Renate, and Timea Szell, eds. *Images of Sainthood in Medieval Europe.* Ithaca, N.Y.: Cornell University Press, 1991.

Boehnen, Scott. "The Aesthetics of 'Sprawling' Drama: The Digby *Mary Magdalene* as Pilgrims' Play." *JEGP* 98 (1999): 325–52.

Bolton, Brenda. "Thirteenth-Century Religious Women: Further Reflections on the Low Countries' 'Special Case.'" In *Holy Women of Liège*, ed. Dor et al. 129–57.

———. "*Vitae Matrum*: A Further Aspect of the *Frauenfrage.*" In *Medieval Women*, ed. Baker, 253–73.

Bond, Francis. *Dedications and Patron Saints of English Churches.* Oxford: Humphrey Milford for Oxford University Press, 1914.

Bradshaw, Brendan. "Bishop John Fisher, 1469–1535: The Man and His Work." In *Humanism, Reform, and Reformation*, ed. Bradshaw and Duffy, 1–24.

Bradshaw, Brendan, and Eamon Duffy, eds. *Humanism, Reform, and the Reformation.* Cambridge: Cambridge University Press, 1989.

Briscoe, Marianne G., and John Coldewey, eds. *Contexts for Early English Drama.* Bloomington: Indiana University Press, 1989.

Brown, Andrew D. *Popular Piety in Late Medieval England: The Diocese of Salisbury, 1250–1500.* Oxford: Clarendon Press, 1995.

Brown, Peter. *The Body and Society: Men, Women, and Sexual Renunciation in Early Christianity.* New York: Columbia University Press, 1988.

Bullmore, William R., "Notes on the Architecture and Wood-carving of the Church of St. Mary the Virgin, Wiggenhall, in the Hundred of Freebridge Marshland." *NA* 19 (1917): 314–32.

Bullough, Vern. "On Being a Male in the Middle Ages." In *Medieval Masculinities*, ed. Lees, 31–45.

Bush, Jerome. "Resources of *Locus* and *Platea* Staging: The Digby *Mary Magdalene.*" *SP* 86 (1989): 139–65.

Butler, Judith. *Bodies That Matter: On the Discursive Limits of "Sex."* New York: Routledge, 1993.

Bynum, Caroline Walker. *Fragmentation and Redemption: Essays on Gender and the Human Body in Medieval Religion.* New York: Zone Books, 1991.

———. *Holy Feast and Holy Fast: The Religious Significance of Food to Medieval Women.* Berkeley and Los Angeles: University of California Press, 1986.

Cameron, Richard. "The Attack on the Biblical Work of Lefèvre d'Étaples, 1514–1521." *Church History* 38 (1969): 9–24.

Camille, Michael. *The Gothic Idol: Ideology and Image-Making in Medieval Art*. Cambridge: Cambridge University Press, 1989.

Cannon, Christopher. "Monastic Productions." In *Cambridge History*, ed. Wallace, 316–48.

———. "The Myth of Origin and the Making of Chaucer's English." *Speculum* 71 (1996): 646–75.

Cannon, Joanna, and André Vauchez. *Margherita of Cortona and the Lorenzetti: Sienese Art and the Cult of a Holy Woman in Medieval Tuscany*. University Park: Pennsylvania State University Press, 1999.

Carey, Hilary M. "Devout Literate Laypeople and the Pursuit of the Mixed Life in Later Medieval England." *Journal of Religious History* 14 (1987): 361–81.

Carrasco, Magdalena Elizabeth. "The Imagery of the Magdalen in Christina Markyate's Psalter (St. Albans Psalter)." *Gesta* 38 (1999): 67–80.

Cautley, H. Munro. *Norfolk Churches*. Ipswich: N. Adlard, 1949.

Caviness, Madeleine. "Anchoress, Abbess, and Queen: Donors and Patrons or Intecessors and Matrons?" In *Cultural Patronage*, ed. McCash, 105–54.

de Certeau, Michel. *Heterologies: Discourse on the Other*. Trans. Brian Massumi. Minneapolis: University of Minnesota Press, 1986.

———. *The Mystic Fable*. Vol. 1, *The Sixteenth and Seventeenth Centuries*. Trans. Michael B. Smith. Chicago: University of Chicago Press, 1992.

Chambers, E. K. *The Medieval Stage*. 2 vols. Oxford: Clarendon Press, 1903.

Chartier, Roger. "From Court Festivity to City Spectators." In *Forms and Meanings: Texts, Performances, and Audiences from Codex to Computer*, 43–82. Philadelphia: University of Pennsylvania Press, 1995.

Chauvin, Sister Mary John of Carmel. "The Role of Mary Magdalene in Medieval Drama." Ph.D. diss., Catholic University of America, 1951.

Clark, Anne L. *Elisabeth of Schönau: A Twelfth-Century Visionary*. Philadelphia: University of Pennsylvania Press, 1992.

Clark, J[ohn] P. H. "Late Fourteenth-Century Cambridge Theology and the English Contemplative Tradition." In *Medieval Mystical Tradition in England*, ed. Glasscoe (1992), 1–16.

Clark, Marlene, Sharon Kraus, and Pamela Sheingorn. "'Se in what stat thou doyst indwell': The Shifting Constructions of Gender and Power Relations in *Wisdom*." In *Performance of Middle English Culture*, ed. Paxson, Clopper, and Tomasch, 43–57.

Cleve, Gunnel. "Semantic Dimensions in Margery Kempe's 'Whyght Clothys.'" *Mystics Quarterly* 12 (1986): 162–70.

Clopper, Lawrence M. "*Communitas*: The Play of Saints in Late Medieval and Tudor England." *Mediaevalia* 18 (1995 [for 1992]): 81–109.

———. *Drama, Play, and Game: English Festive Culture in the Medieval and Early Modern Period*. Chicago: University of Chicago Press, 2001.

———. "Lay and Clerical Impact on Civic Religious Drama and Ceremony." In *Contexts for Early English Drama*, ed. Briscoe and Coldewey, 102–36.

———. "Medieval Drama." In *Cambridge History*, ed. Wallace, 739–66.

————. "Why Are There So Few Saint Plays?" *Early Theatre* 2 (1999): 107–12.

Coakley, John. "Friars As Confidants of Holy Women in Medieval Dominican Hagiography." In *Images of Sainthood*, ed. Blumenfeld-Kosinski and Szell, 222–46.

Coldewey, John. "The Digby Plays and the Chelmsford Records." *RORD* 18 (1975): 103–21.

————. "The Non-Cycle Plays and the East Anglian Tradition." In *CCMET*, 189–210.

Coletti, Theresa. "'Curtesy doth it yow lere': The Sociology of Transgression in the Digby *Mary Magdalene*." *ELH* (forthcoming).

————. "The Design of the Digby Play of *Mary Magdalene*." *SP* 76 (1979): 313–33.

————. *Naming the Rose: Eco, Medieval Signs, and Modern Theory*. Ithaca, N.Y.: Cornell University Press, 1988.

————. "The N-Town Plays." In *Dictionary of Literary Biography*, ed. Jeffrey Helterman and Jerome Mitchell, 405–14. Detroit: Gale Research, 1994.

————. "'Paupertas est donum Dei': Hagiography, Lay Religion, and the Economics of Salvation in the Digby *Mary Magdalene*." *Speculum* 76 (2001): 337–78.

————. "Purity and Danger: The Paradox of Mary's Body and the Engendering of the Infancy Narrative in the English Mystery Cycles." In *Feminist Approaches to the Body in Medieval Literature*, ed. Linda Lomperis and Sarah Stanbury, 65–95. Philadelphia: University of Pennsylvania Press, 1993.

————. "Reading REED: History and the Records of Early English Drama." In *Literary Practice and Social Change in Britain, 1380–1530*, ed. Lee Patterson, 248–84. Berkeley and Los Angeles: University of California Press, 1990.

————. "Spirituality and Devotional Images: The Staging of the Hegge Cycle." Ph.D. diss., University of Rochester, 1975.

Colledge, Eric. "*Epistola solitarii ad reges*: Alphonse of Pecha As Organizer of Birgittine and Urbanist Propaganda." *MS* 43 (1956): 19–49.

Constable, Giles. "Twelfth-Century Spirituality and the Late Middle Ages." In *Medieval and Renaissance Studies*, ed. O. B. Hardison, 27–60. Chapel Hill: University of North Carolina Press, 1971.

Copeland, Rita. "Why Women Can't Read: Medieval Hermeneutics, Statutory Law, and the Lollard Heresy Trials." In *Representing Women: Law, Literature, and Feminism*, ed. Susan Sage Heinzelman and Zipporah Batshaw Wiseman, 253–86. Durham, N.C.: Duke University Press, 1994.

Cotton, Simon. "Medieval Roodscreens in Norfolk—Their Construction and Painting Dates." *NA* 40 (1987): 44–54.

Cowling, Jane. "A Fifteenth-Century Saint Play in Winchester: Some Problems of Interpretation." *Medieval and Renaissance Drama in England* 13 (2001): 19–33.

Cox, Henry O. *Catalogus Codicum MSS qui in Collegiis Aulisque Oxoniensibus*. 1852. Reprint, Wakefield, Eng.: E. P. Publishing, 1972.

Cox, J. Charles. *Bench-Ends in English Churches*. London: Humphrey Milford, Oxford University Press, 1916.

Craymer, Suzanne. "Margery Kempe's Imitation of Mary Magdalene and the Digby Plays." *Mystics Quarterly* 19 (1993): 173–81.

Cross, Claire. "'Great Reasoners in Scripture': The Activities of Women Lollards, 1380–1530." In *Medieval Women*, ed. Baker, 359–80.

Cross, J. E. "Mary Magdalene in the *Old English Martyrology*: The Earliest Extant 'Narrat Josephus' Variant of Her Legend." *Speculum* 53 (1978): 16–25.

Cummings, Brian. "Reformed Literature and Literature Reformed." In *Cambridge History*, ed. Wallace, 821–51.

Dahmus, John. "Preaching to the Laity in Fifteenth-Century Germany: Johannes Nider's *Harps*." *JEH* 34 (1983): 55–68.

Dalarun, Jacques. "La Madeleine dans l'Ouest de la France au tournant des XIe–XIIe siècles." *MEFRM* 104.1 (1992): 71–119.

Damrosch, David. "*Non Alia Sed Aliter*: The Hermeneutics of Gender in Bernard of Clairvaux." In *Images of Sainthood*, ed. Blumenfeld-Kosinski and Szell, 181–98.

Dashwood, G. H. "Notes of Deeds and Survey of Crabhouse Nunnery, Norfolk." *NA* 5 (1859): 257–62.

Davenport, Tony. "'Lusty fresche galaunts.'" In *Aspects of Early English Drama*, ed. Paula Neuss, 110–28. Cambridge: D. S. Brewer, 1983.

Davidson, Clifford. "British Saint Play Records: Coping with Ambiguity." *Early Theatre* 2 (1999): 97–106.

————. "The Digby *Mary Magdalene* and the Magdalene Cult of the Middle Ages." *Annuale Mediaevale* 13 (1972): 70–87.

————. "The Middle English Saint Play and Its Iconography." In *Saint Play*, ed. Davidson, 31–122.

————. "Saints Plays and Pageants of Medieval Britain." *EDAM Review* 22 (1999): 11–37.

————. *Visualizing the Moral Life: Medieval Iconography and the Macro Moralities*. New York: AMS Press, 1989.

————, ed. *The Saint Play in Medieval Europe*. EDAM Monograph Series 8. Kalamazoo, Mich.: Medieval Institute Publications, 1986.

Davis, Virginia. "The Rule of Saint Paul, the First Hermit, in Late Medieval England." In *Monks, Hermits, and the Ascetic Tradition*, ed. W. J. Sheils, 203–14. Studies in Church History 22. Oxford: Basil Blackwell, 1985.

Dean, Ruth J. "Manuscripts of St. Elizabeth of Schönau in England." *Modern Language Review* 32 (1937): 62–71.

Delaney, Sheila. *Impolitic Bodies: Poetry, Saints, and Society in Fifteenth-Century England*. New York: Oxford University Press, 1998.

Deremble, Colette. "Les premiers cycles d'images consacrés à Marie Madeleine." *MEFRM* 104.1 (1992): 187–208.

Deshman, Robert. *The Benedictional of Æthelwold*. Princeton: Princeton University Press, 1995.

Despres, Denise L. "Ecstatic Reading and Missionary Mysticism: *The Orcherd of Syon*." In *Prophets Abroad*, ed. Voaden, 141–60.

D'Evelyn, Charlotte. "Saints' Legends." In *A Manual of the Writings in Middle English, 1050–1500*, ed. J. Burke Severs, vol. 2, 413–39, 556–635. Hamden, Conn.: Archon, 1970.

Devereux, E. J. "Elizabeth Barton and Tudor Censorship." *Bulletin of the John Rylands Library* 49 (1966–67): 91–106.

Devlin, Dennis. "Female Lay Piety in the High Middle Ages: The Beguines." In *Medieval Religious Women*. Vol. 1, *Distant Echoes*, ed. John A. Nichols and Lillian Thomas Shank, 183–96. Kalamazoo, Mich.: Cistercian Publications, 1984.

Dickman, Susan. "Margery Kempe and the Continental Tradition of the Pious Woman." In *Medieval Mystical Tradition*, ed. Glasscoe (1984), 150–68.

Diehl, Huston. *Staging Reform, Reforming the Stage: Protestantism and Popular Theater in Early Modern England*. Ithaca, N.Y.: Cornell University Press, 1997.

Dillenberger, Jane. "The Magdalen: Reflections on the Image of Saint and Sinner in Christian Art." In *Women, Religion, and Social Change*, ed. Yvonne Yazbeck Haddad and Ellison Banks Findly, 115–45. Albany, N.Y.: State University of New York Press, 1985.

Dillon, Janette. "Holy Women and Their Confessors or Confessors and Their Holy Women?: Margery Kempe and Continental Tradition." In *Prophets Abroad*, ed. Voaden, 115–40.

Dinshaw, Carolyn. *Getting Medieval: Sexualities and Communities, Pre- and Post-modern*. Durham, N.C.: Duke University Press, 1999.

Dinshaw, Carolyn, and David Wallace, eds. *Cambridge Companion to Medieval Women's Writing*. Cambridge: Cambridge University Press, 2003.

Dixon, Mimi Still. "'Thys Body of Mary': 'Femynyte' and 'Inward Mythe' in the Digby *Mary Magdalene*." *Mediaevalia* 18 (1995 [for 1992]): 221–44.

Dor, Juliette, Lesley Johnson, and Jocelyn Wogan-Browne, eds. *New Trends in Feminine Spirituality: The Holy Women of Liège and Their Impact*. Turnhout: Brepols, 1999.

Duffy, Eamon. "Holy Maydens, Holy Wyfes: The Cult of Women Saints in Fifteenth- and Sixteenth-Century England." In *Women in the Church*, ed. Sheils and Wood, 175–96.

———. "The Parish, Piety, and Patronage in Late Medieval East Anglia: The Evidence of Rood Screens." In *The Parish in English Life, 1400–1600*, ed. Katherine L. French, Gary G. Gibbs, and Beat A. Kümin, 133–62. New York: St. Martin's Press, 1997.

———. "The Spirituality of John Fisher." In *Humanism, Reform, and the Reformation*, ed. Bradshaw and Duffy, 205–31.

———. *The Stripping of the Altars: Traditional Religion in England, c. 1400–1580*. New Haven: Yale University Press, 1992.

Dunn, F. I. "Hermits, Anchorites, and Recluses: A Study with Reference to Medieval Norwich." *Julian and Her Norwich*, 18–26. Norwich: Julian of Norwich 1973 Celebration Committee, 1973.

Dunning, Robert W. "The West-Country Carthusians." In *Religious Belief*, ed. Harper-Bill, 33–42.

Duperray, Eve, ed. *Marie Madeleine dans la mystique, les arts et les lettres*. Paris: Beauchesne, 1989.

Dutton, Anne. "Piety, Politics, and Persona: MS Harley 4012 and Anne Harling."

In *Prestige, Authority, and Power in Late Medieval Manuscripts and Texts*, ed. Felicity Riddy, 133–46. York: York Medieval Press, University of York, 2000.

Eberly, Susan. "Margery Kempe, St. Mary Magdalene, and Patterns of Contemplation." *Downside Review* 107 (1989): 209–23.

Edwards, A. S. G. "Lydgate Manuscripts: Some Directions for Future Research." In *Manuscripts and Readers in Fifteenth-Century England*, ed. Derek Pearsall, 15–26. Cambridge: D. S. Brewer, 1983.

———. "The Transmission and Audience of Osbern Bokenham's *Legendys of Hooly Wummen*." In *Late Medieval Religious Texts and Their Translation*, ed. Alastair Minnis, 157–67. Cambridge: D. S. Brewer, 1994.

———, ed. *Middle English Prose: A Critical Guide to Major Authors and Genres*. New Brunswick, N.J.: Rutgers University Press, 1984.

Elkins, Sharon. *Holy Women of Twelfth-Century England*. Chapel Hill: University of North Carolina Press, 1988.

Ellington, Donna Spivey. *From Sacred Body to Angelic Soul: Understanding Mary in Late Medieval and Early Modern Europe*. Washington, D.C.: Catholic University Press of America, 2001.

Elliott, Dyan. "Dress As Mediator between Inner and Outer Self: The Pious Matron of the High and Late Middle Ages." *MS* 53 (1991): 279–308.

———. "The Physiology of Rapture and Female Spirituality." In *Medieval Theology*, ed. Biller and Minnis, 141–73.

Ellis, Roger. "'Flores ad Fabricandam . . . Coronam': An Investigation into the Uses of the Revelations of St. Bridget of Sweden in Fifteenth-Century England." *MÆ* 51 (1982): 163–86.

Emmerson, Richard K. "Antichrist As Anti-Saint: The Significance of Abbot Adso's *Libellus de Antichristo*." *American Benedictine Review* 30 (1979): 175–90.

———. "Contextualizing Performance: The Reception of the Chester Antichrist." *JMEMS* 29 (1999): 89–119.

———. "Eliding the Medieval: Renaissance 'New Historicism' and Sixteenth-Century Drama." In *Performance of Middle English Culture*, ed. Paxson, Clopper, and Tomasch, 25–41.

———. "'Nowe ys common this daye': Enoch and Elias, Antichrist, and the Structure of the Chester Cycle." In *Homo, Memento Finis: The Iconography of Just Judgement in Medieval Art and Drama*, ed. David Bevington et al., 89–120. EDAM Monograph Series 6. Kalamazoo, Mich.: Medieval Institute Publications, 1985.

Epp, Garrett. "John Fox and the Circumcised Stage." *Exemplaria* 9 (1997): 281–313.

———. "The Vicious Guise: Effeminacy, Sodomy, and *Mankind*." In *Becoming Male in the Middle Ages*, ed. Jeffrey Jerome Cohen and Bonnie Wheeler, 303–20. New York: Garland, 1997.

Erler, Mary C. "English Vowed Women at the End of the Middle Ages." *MS* 57 (1995): 155–203.

———. "Margery Kempe's White Clothes." *MÆ* 62 (1993): 78–83.

————. *Women, Reading, and Piety in Late Medieval England*. Cambridge: Cambridge University Press, 2002.

Evans, Ruth. "Introduction to Part Two: Addressing and Positioning the Audience." In *Idea of the Vernacular*, ed. Wogan-Browne et al., 109–25.

————. "Signs of the Body: Gender, Sexuality, and Space in York and the York Cycle." In *Women's Spaces*, ed. Raguin and Stanbury. Forthcoming.

Evans, Ruth, Andrew Taylor, Nicholas Watson, and Jocelyn Wogan-Browne. "The Notion of Vernacular Theory." In *Idea of the Vernacular*, ed. Wogan-Browne et al., 314–30.

Farley, Mary Hardiman. "Her Own Creature: Religion, Feminist Criticism, and the Functional Eccentricity of Margery Kempe." *Exemplaria* 11 (1999): 1–21.

Farmer, Sharon. *Communities of Saint Martin: Legend and Ritual in Medieval Tours*. Ithaca, N.Y.: Cornell University Press, 1991.

————. "Persuasive Voices: Clerical Images of Medieval Wives." *Speculum* 61 (1986): 517–43.

Farnhill, Ken. *Guilds and the Parish Community in Late Medieval East Anglia, c. 1470–1550*. York: York Medieval Press, 2001.

Firth, Catherine. "Village Guilds of Norfolk in the Fifteenth Century." *NA* 18 (1914): 161–203.

Flanigan, Clifford. "The Roman Rite and the Origins of Latin Liturgical Drama." *University of Toronto Quarterly* 43 (1974): 263–84.

Fletcher, Alan. "The N-Town Plays." In *CCMET*, 163–88.

Fradenburg, Louise. "Analytical Survey 1: We Are Not Alone: Psychoanalytic Medievalism." *New Medieval Literatures* 2 (1998): 249–76.

————. "'Be Not Far from Me': Psychoanalysis, Medieval Studies, and the Subject of Religion." *Exemplaria* 7 (1995): 41–54.

————. "'So That We May Speak of Them': Enjoying the Middle Ages." *New Literary History* 28 (1997): 205–30.

————. "'Voice Memorial': Loss and Reparation in Chaucer's Poetry." *Exemplaria* 2 (1990): 169–202.

French, Katherine. "Maidens' Lights and Wives' Stores: Women's Parish Guilds in Late Medieval England." *Sixteenth Century Journal* 29 (1998): 399–425.

————. "'The Seat by Our Lady': Gender and Seating in Late Medieval English Parish Churches." In *Women's Spaces*, ed. Raguin and Stanbury. Forthcoming.

Garth, Helen Meredith. *Saint Mary Magdalene in Medieval Literature*. Baltimore: Johns Hopkins University Press, 1950.

Geary, Patrick. "Saints, Scholars, and Society: The Elusive Goal." In *Saints: Studies in Hagiography*, ed. Sandro Sticca, 1–22. Medieval and Renaissance Texts and Studies 141. Binghamton, N.Y.: Center for Medieval and Early Renaissance Studies, State University of New York, Binghamton, 1996.

Geoffroy, Marguerite, and Alain Montandon, eds. *Marie-Madeleine: Figure mythique dans la littérature et les arts*. Clermont-Ferrand: Presses Universitaires Blaise Pascal, 1999.

Ghosh, Kantik. *The Wycliffite Heresy: Authority and the Interpretation of Texts*. Cambridge: Cambridge University Press, 2002.

Gibson, Gail McMurray. "Bury St. Edmunds, John Lydgate, and the *N-Town Cycle.*" *Speculum* 56 (1981): 56–90.

———. "The Play of *Wisdom* and the Abbey of St. Edmund." In *"Wisdom" Symposium*, ed. Riggio, 39–66.

———. "'*Porta haec clausa erit*': Comedy, Conception, and Ezechiel's Closed Door in the *Ludus Coventriae* Play of 'Joseph's Return.'" *JMRS* 8 (1978): 137–56.

———. "Saint Anne and the Religion of Childbed: Some East Anglian Texts and Talismans." In *Interpreting Cultural Symbols*, ed. Ashley and Sheingorn, 95–110.

———. *The Theater of Devotion: East Anglian Drama and Society in the Late Middle Ages*. Chicago: University of Chicago Press, 1989.

Gilchrist, Roberta. *Contemplation and Action: The Other Monasticism*. London: Leicester University Press, 1995.

———. *Gender and Material Culture: The Archaeology of Medieval Religious Women*. London: Routledge, 1994.

Gilchrist, Roberta, and Marilyn Oliva. *Religious Women in Medieval East Anglia: History and Archaeology, c. 1100–1540*. Studies in East Anglian History 1. Norwich: Centre of East Anglian Studies, University of East Anglia, 1993.

Gillespie, Vincent. "'Lukyng in haly bukes': *Lectio* in Some Late Medieval Spiritual Miscellanies." In *Spätmittelalterliche geistliche Literatur in der Nationalsprache*, ed. James Hogg, 1–27. Analecta Cartusiana 106. Salzburg: Institut für Anglistik und Amerikanistik, Universität Salzburg, 1984.

Glasscoe, Marian, ed. *The Medieval Mystical Tradition in England: Papers Read at Darlington Hall, July 1984*. Cambridge: D. S. Brewer, 1984.

———. *The Medieval Mystical Tradition in England*. Exeter Symposium 4. Cambridge: D. S. Brewer, 1987.

———. *The Medieval Mystical Tradition in England*. Exeter Symposium 5. Cambridge: D. S. Brewer, 1992.

Godden, Malcolm. "Fleshly Monks and Dancing Girls: Immorality in Morality Drama." In *The Long Fifteenth Century*, ed. Helen Cooper and Sally Mapstone, 205–28. Oxford: Clarendon Press, 1997.

Goodich, Michael. "The Contours of Female Piety in Later Medieval Hagiography." *Church History* 50 (1981): 20–32.

Grantley, Darryll. "Saints' Plays." In *CCMET*, 265–89.

———. "The Source of the Digby *Mary Magdalen.*" *Notes and Queries* n.s. 31 (1984): 457–59.

Graves, Pamela C. "Social Space in the English Medieval Parish Church." *Economy and Society* 18 (1989): 297–322.

Green, Alice Stopford. *Town Life in the Fifteenth Century*. 2 vols. New York: MacMillan, 1894.

Griffiths, Jeremy, and Derek Pearsall, eds. *Book Production and Publishing in Britain, 1375–1475*. Cambridge: Cambridge University Press, 1989.

Hackett, Helen. *Virgin Mother, Maiden Queen: Elizabeth I and the Cult of the Virgin Mary*. New York: St. Martin's Press, 1995.

Hale, Richard, and Mary Rodgers. *The Grayfriars of Norwich*. Norwich: King Street Publications, 1991.

Hall, Edwin, and Horst Urh. "*Aureola super Auream*: Crowns and Related Symbols of Special Distinction for Saints in Late Gothic and Renaissance Iconography." *Art Bulletin* 67 (1985): 567–603.

Hanawalt, Barbara A., and David Wallace, eds. *Bodies and Disciplines: Intersections of Literature and History in Fifteenth-Century England*. Minneapolis: University of Minnesota Press, 1996.

Hanna, Ralph, III. "The Difficulty of Ricardian Prose Translation: The Case of the Lollards." *MLQ* 51 (1990): 319–40.

———. "Some Norfolk Women and Their Books, ca. 1390–1440." In *Cultural Patronage*, ed. McCash, 288–305.

Hanna, Ralph, III, and A. S. G. Edwards. "Rotheley, the De Vere Circle, and the Ellesmere Chaucer." In *Reading from the Margins: Textual Studies, Chaucer, and Medieval Literature*, ed. Seth Lerer, 11–35. San Marino, Calif.: Huntington Library, 1996.

Happé, Peter. "Protestant Adaptations of the Saint Play." In *Saint Play*, ed. Davidson, 205–40.

Harbison, Craig. "Lucas van Leyden, the Magdalen and the Problem of Secularization in Early Sixteenth Century Northern Art." *Oud Holland* 98 (1984): 117–29.

Hardison, O. B., Jr. *Christian Rite and Christian Drama in the Middle Ages*. Baltimore: Johns Hopkins University Press, 1965.

Harper-Bill, Christopher, ed. *Religious Belief and Ecclesiastical Careers in Late Medieval England*. Woodbridge, Eng.: Boydell Press, 1990.

Harris, Joseph. "'Maiden in the Mor Lay' and the Medieval Magdalene Tradition." *JMRS* 1 (1971): 59–87.

Harrod, Henry. "On the Mantle and the Ring of Widowhood." *Archaeologia* 40 (1844): 307–10.

Haskins, Susan. *Mary Magdalen: Myth and Metaphor*. New York: Harcourt, Brace and Co., 1993.

Henry, Avril. "The Dramatic Function of Rhyme and Stanza Patterns in *The Castle of Perseverance*." In *Individuality and Achievement*, ed. Pickering, 147–83.

Hicks, M. A. "The Piety of Margaret, Lady Hungerford (d. 1478)." *JEH* 38 (1987): 19–38.

Hillen, Henry. *History of the Borough of King's Lynn*. 2 vols. Norwich: East of England Newspaper Co., 1907.

Hilles, Carroll. "Gender and Politics in Osbern Bokenham's Legendary." *New Medieval Literatures* 4 (2001): 189–212.

———. "The Sacred Image and the Healing Touch: The Veronica in Julian of Norwich's *Revelation of Love*." *JMEMS* 28 (1998): 553–80.

Hill-Vásquez, Heather. "The Possibilities of Performance: Mediatory Styles in Middle English Religious Drama." Ph.D. diss., University of Washington, 1997.

———. "The Possibilities of Performance: A Reformation Sponsorship for the Digby *Conversion of Saint Paul*." *Records of Early English Drama Newsletter* 22 (1997): 2–20.

———. "'The precious body of Christ that they tretyn in ther hondis': 'Miraclis Pleyinge' and the Croxton *Play of the Sacrament*." *Early Theatre* 4 (2001): 53–72.

Holbrook, Sue Ellen. "Margery Kempe and Wynkyn de Worde." In *Medieval Mystical Tradition*, ed. Glasscoe (1987), 27–46.

Hollywood, Amy. *The Soul As Virgin Wife: Mechtild of Magdeburg, Marguerite Porete, and Meister Eckhart*. Notre Dame, Ind.: University of Notre Dame Press, 1995.

Horrox, Rosemary, ed. *Fifteenth-Century Attitudes: Perceptions of Society in Late Medieval England*. Cambridge: Cambridge University Press, 1994.

Houlbrooke, R. A. "Persecution of Heresy and Protestantism in the Diocese of Norwich under Henry VIII." *NA* 35 (1970–73): 308–326.

Hudson, Anne. "A Lollard Sect Vocabulary." In *Lollards and Their Books*, 165–80. London: Hambledon, 1985.

———. *The Premature Reformation: Wycliffite Texts and Lollard History*. Oxford: Clarendon Press, 1988.

Hudson, Anne, and H. L. Spencer. "Old Author, New Work: The Sermons of MS Longleat 4." *MÆ* 53 (1984): 220–38.

Hufstader, Anselm. "Lefèvre d'Étaples and the Magdalen." *Studies in the Renaissance* 16 (1969): 31–60.

Hughes, Jonathan. *Pastors and Visionaries: Religion and Secular Life in Late Medieval Yorkshire*. Woodbridge, Eng.: Boydell Press, 1988.

———. *The Religious Life of Richard III: Piety and Prayer in the North of England*. Stroud, Eng.: Sutton, 1997.

Hussey, S. S. "The Audience for the Middle English Mystics." In *De Cella in Seculum*, ed. Sargent, 109–22.

———. "Latin and English in the *Scale of Perfection*." *MS* 35 (1973): 456–76.

Iogna-Prat, Dominique. "La Madeleine du *Sermo in Veneratione Sanctae Mariae Magdalenae* attribué à Odon de Cluny." *MEFRM* 104.1 (1992): 37–70.

James, Mervyn. "Ritual, Drama, and Social Body in the Late Medieval English Town." *Past and Present* 98 (1983): 3–30.

Jansen, Katherine Ludwig. *The Making of the Magdalen*. Princeton: Princeton University Press, 2000.

———. "Maria Magdalena: *Apostolorum Apostola*." In *Women Preachers and Prophets*, ed. Kienzle and Walker, 57–96.

———. "Mary Magdalen and the Mendicants: The Preaching of Penance in the Late Middle Ages." *Journal of Medieval History* 21 (1995): 1–25.

Jantzen, Grace M. *Julian of Norwich: Mystic and Theologian*. New York: Paulist Press, 1988.

Jeffrey, David L. "English Saints' Plays." In *Medieval Drama*, ed. Neville Denny, 69–89. Stratford-upon-Avon Studies 16. London: Edward Arnold, 1973.

Jennings, Margaret. "The Art of the Pseudo-Origen Homily *De Maria Magdalena*." *Medievalia et Humanistica* 5 (1974): 139–52.

Jessopp, Augustus. *Studies by a Recluse*. New York: G. P. Putnam's Sons, 1893.

Johnson, F. R. "The English Cult of St. Bridget of Sweden." *Analecta Bollandiana* 103 (1985): 75–93.

Johnson, Ian. "*Auctricitas*? Holy Women and Their Middle English Texts." In *Prophets Abroad*, ed. Voaden, 177–97.

———. "Tales of a True Translator: Medieval Literary Theory, Anecdote, and

Autobiography in Osbern Bokenham's *Legendys of Hooly Wummen*." In *The Medieval Translator 4*, ed. Roger Ellis and Ruth Evans, 104–24. Medieval and Renaissance Texts and Studies 123. Binghamton, N.Y.: State University of New York Press, 1994.

[Johnson], Lynn Staley. *The Art of the Gawain Poet*. Madison: University of Wisconsin Press, 1985.

Johnston, Alexandra F. "Acting Mary: The Emotional Realism of the Mature Virgin in the N-Town Plays." In *From Page to Performance: Essays in Early English Drama*, ed. John Alford, 85–98. East Lansing: Michigan State University Press, 1995.

———. "Traders and Playmakers: English Guildsmen and the Low Countries." In *England and the Low Countries*, ed. Barron and Saul, 99–114.

———. "What If No Texts Survived?: External Evidence for Early English Drama." In *Contexts for Early English Drama*, ed. Briscoe and Coldewey, 1–19.

———. "*Wisdom* and the Records: Is There a Moral?" In *"Wisdom" Symposium*, ed. Riggio, 87–102.

Jones, Mary Loubris. "How the Seven Deadly Sins 'Dewoyde from þe Woman' in the Digby *Mary Magdalene*." *American Notes and Queries* 16.8 (1978): 118–19.

Jones, Michael. "Theatrical History in the Croxton *Play of the Sacrament*." *ELH* 66 (1999): 223–60.

Jones, Sarah Rees. "'A peler of Holy Cherch': Margery Kempe and the Bishops." In *Medieval Women: Texts and Contexts in Late Medieval Britain: Essays for Felicity Riddy*, ed. Jocelyn Wogan-Browne et al., 377–91. Turnhout: Brepols, 2000.

Jordan, W. K. *The Charities of Rural England, 1480–1660*. London: George Allen and Unwin, 1961.

Kane, John. "Mary of Magdala: The Evolution of Her Role in Medieval Drama." *Studi Medievali* 3d ser., 26 (1985): 677–84.

Karras, Ruth. "Holy Harlots: Prostitute Saints in Medieval Legend." *Journal of the History of Sexuality* 1 (1990): 3–32.

Keiser, George R. "The Mystics and the Early English Printers: The Economics of Devotionalism." In *Medieval Mystical Tradition*, ed. Glasscoe (1987), 9–26.

Kelly, Kathleen Coyne. *Performing Virginity and Testing Chastity in the Middle Ages*. London: Routledge, 2000.

Kempster, Hugh. "A Question of Audience: The Westminster Text and Fifteenth-Century Reception of Julian of Norwich." In *Julian of Norwich: A Book of Essays*, ed. Sandra J. McEntire, 257–89. New York: Garland, 1998.

Kendall, Ritchie. *The Drama of Dissent: The Radical Poetics of Nonconformity, 1380–1590*. Chapel Hill: University of North Carolina Press, 1986.

Kerby-Fulton, Kathryn. "Hildegard and the Male Reader: A Study in Insular Reception." In *Prophets Abroad*, ed. Voaden, 1–18.

Kerling, Nelly J. M. "Aliens in the County of Norfolk, 1436–1485." *NA* 33 (1965): 200–12.

Keyser, Linda Migl. "Examining the Body Poetic: Images of Illness and Healing in Late Medieval English Literature." Ph.D. diss., University of Maryland, 1999.

Kienzle, Beverly Mayne. "The Prostitute-Preacher: Patterns of Polemic against Medieval Waldensian Women Preachers." In *Women Preachers and Prophets*, ed. Kienzle and Walker, 99–113.

Kienzle, Beverly Mayne, and Pamela J. Walker, eds. *Women Preachers and Prophets through Two Millenia of Christianity*. Berkeley and Los Angeles: University of California Press, 1998.

King, Karen L. "The Gospel of Mary Magdalene." In *Searching the Scriptures*. Vol. 2, *A Feminist Commentary*, ed. Elisabeth Schüssler Fiorenza, 601–34. New York: Crossroad, 1994.

———. "Prophetic Power and Women's Authority: The Case of the *Gospel of Mary* (Magdalene)." In *Women Preachers and Prophets*, ed. Kienzle and Walker, 21–41.

King, Laura Severt. "Blessed when they were riggish: Shakespeare's Cleopatra and Christianity's Penitent Prostitute." *JMRS* 22 (1992): 429–49.

———. "Chaucer and the Pseudo-Origen *De Maria Magdalena*." Manuscript.

———. "Cracks in the Looking-Glass: Monastic Rebellion and Marian Models in Syon Abbey's *Myroure of Oure Lady*." Manuscript.

———. "Sacred Eroticism, Rapturous Anguish: Christianity's Penitent Prostitutes and the Vexation of Allegory, 1370–1608." Ph.D. diss., University of California–Berkeley, 1993.

Knapp, Ethan. "Eulogies and Usurpations: Hoccleve and Chaucer Revisited." *SAC* 21 (1999): 247–73.

Kobialka, Michal. *This Is My Body: Representational Practices in the Early Middle Ages*. Ann Arbor: University of Michigan Press, 1999.

Krug, Rebecca. *Reading Families: Women's Literate Practice in Late Medieval England*. Ithaca, N.Y.: Cornell University Press, 2002.

Kundera, Clare M. "Models of Monastic Devotion in Peter of Celle's Sermons for the Feast of Mary Magdalene." In *Models of Holiness in Medieval Sermons*, ed. Beverly Mayne Kienzle et al., 67–84. Louvain-la-Neuve: Fédération Internationale des Instituts d'Études Médiévales, 1996.

Lancashire, Ian. *Dramatic Texts and Records of Great Britain: A Chronological Topography to 1558*. Studies in Early English Drama 1. Toronto: University of Toronto Press, 1984.

Lasko, P., and N. J. Morgan, eds. *Medieval Art in East Anglia, 1300–1520*. Norwich: Jarrold and Sons, 1973.

Lauwers, Michel. "'*Noli me tangere*': Marie Madeleine, Marie d'Oignies et les pénitentes du XIIIe siècle." *MEFRM* 104.1 (1992): 209–65.

Lavezzo, Kathy. "Sobs and Sighs between Women: The Homoerotics of Compassion in the *Book of Margery Kempe*. In *Premodern Sexualities*, ed. Louise Fradenburg and Carla Freccero, 175–98. New York: Routledge, 1996.

Lawton, David. "Dullness and the Fifteenth Century." *ELH* 54 (1987): 761–99.

———. "Sacrilege and Theatricality: The Croxton *Play of the Sacrament*." *JMEMS* 33 (2003): 281–309.

Lees, Clare, ed., with Thelma Fenster and Jo Ann McNamara. *Medieval Masculinities: Regarding Men in the Middle Ages*. Minneapolis: University of Minnesota Press, 1994.

Lerer, Seth. "Caxton." In *Cambridge History*, ed. Wallace, 720–38.

———. *Chaucer and His Readers*. Princeton: Princeton University Press, 1993.

———. "'Representyd now in yower syght': The Culture of Spectatorship in Late Fifteenth-Century England." In *Bodies and Disciplines*, ed. Hanawalt and Wallace, 29–62.

Lester, G. A. "The Books of a Fifteenth-Century English Gentleman, Sir John Paston." *Neuphilologische Mitteilungen* 88 (1987): 200–17.

Lewis, Flora. "The Wound in Christ's Side and the Instruments of the Passion: Gendered Experience and Response." In *Women and the Book*, ed. Taylor and Smith, 204–23.

Lewis, Katherine J., Noël James Menuge, and Kim M. Phillips, eds. *Young Medieval Women*. New York: St. Martin's Press, 1999.

Linnell, C. L. S. *St. Peter and Paul, Salle, Norfolk*. Church guide.

Little, Katherine. "Reading Women into Lollardy." Paper presented at the Thirty-Fifth International Congress on Medieval Studies, Western Michigan University, Kalamazoo, Mich., May 2000.

Lochrie, Karma. *Margery Kempe and the Translations of the Flesh*. Philadelphia: University of Pennsylvania Press, 1991.

———. "Mystical Acts, Queer Tendencies." In *Constructing Medieval Sexuality*, ed. Karma Lochrie, Peggy McCracken, and James Schultz, 180–200. Minneapolis: University of Minnesota Press, 1997.

Lovatt, Roger. "The *Imitation of Christ* in Late Medieval England." *Transactions of the Royal Historical Society*. 5th ser., 18 (1968): 97–121.

———. "The Library of John Blacman and Contemporary Carthusian Spirituality." *JEH* 43 (1992): 195–230.

Lumiansky, R. M., and David Mills, eds. *The Chester Mystery Cycle: Essays and Documents*. Chapel Hill: University of North Carolina Press, 1983.

MacCulloch, Diarmid. "A Reformation in the Balance: Power Struggles in the Diocese of Norwich, 1533–1553." In *Counties and Communities*, ed. Rawcliffe, Virgoe, and Wilson, 97–114.

Machan, Tim William, ed. *Medieval Literature: Texts and Interpretation*. Medieval and Renaissance Texts and Studies 79. Binghamton, N.Y.: Center for Medieval and Early Renaissance Studies, State University of New York, Binghamton, 1991.

Magennis, Hugh. "St. Mary of Egypt and Ælfric: Unlikely Bedfellows in Cotton Junius E. VII?" In *Legend of Mary of Egypt*, ed. Poppe and Ross, 99–112.

Maltman, Sister Nicholas, O. P. "Some Light in and on the Digby *Mary Magdalene*." In *Saints, Scholars, and Heroes: Studies in Medieval Culture in Honor of Charles W. Jones*, ed. Margaret H. King and Wesley M. Stevens, 257–80. Collegeville, Minn.: St. John's Abbey and University, 1979.

Malvern, Marjorie. *Venus in Sackcloth: The Magdalen's Origins and Metamorphoses*. Carbondale: Southern Illinois University Press, 1975.

Marcus, Leah S. "Dramatic Experiments: Tudor Drama, 1490–1567." In *The*

Cambridge Companion to Early English Literature, 1500–1600, ed. Arthur F. Kinney, 132–52. Cambridge: Cambridge University Press, 2000.

Margherita, Gayle. "Women and Riot in the Harley Lyrics." In *The Romance of Origins: Language and Sexual Difference in Middle English Literature*, 62–81. Philadelphia: University of Pennsylvania Press, 1994.

Marjanen, Antti. *The Woman Jesus Loved: Mary Magdalene in the Nag Hammadi Library and Related Documents*. Leiden: E. J. Brill, 1996.

Marshall, John. "'Fortune in Worldys Worschyppe': The Satirising of the Suffolks in *Wisdom*." *MET* 14 (1992): 37–66.

Martin, Leslie Howard. "Comic Eschatology in the Chester *Coming of Antichrist*." *CD* 5 (1971): 163–76.

Martin, Thomas. *The History of the Town of Thetford*. London: J. Nichols, 1779.

Marx, C. W. "British Library Harley MS 1740 and Popular Devotion." In *England in the Fifteenth Century*, ed. Rogers, 207–22.

Matter, E. Ann. *The Voice of My Beloved: The Song of Songs in Western Medieval Christianity*. Philadelphia: University of Pennsylvania Press, 1990.

McCall, John. "Chaucer and the Pseudo-Origen *De Maria Magdalena*: A Preliminary Study." *Speculum* 46 (1971): 491–509.

McCash, June Hall, ed. *The Cultural Patronage of Medieval Women*. Athens: University of Georgia Press, 1996.

———."*La vie seinte Audree*: A Fourth Text by Marie de France." *Speculum* 77 (2002): 744–77.

McGovern-Mouron, Anne. "'Listen to me, daughter, listen to a faithful counsel': The *Liber de modo bene vivendi ad sororem*." In *Writing Religious Women*, ed. Renevey and Whitehead, 81–106.

McInerney, Maud Burnett. "'In the Meydens Womb': Julian of Norwich and the Poetics of Enclosure." In *Medieval Mothering*, ed. Parsons and Wheeler, 157–82.

McKee, J. R. *Dame Elizabeth Barton, OSB: The Holy Maid of Kent*. London: Burns, Oates, and Washbourne, 1925.

McNamara, Jo Ann. "The Rhetoric of Orthodoxy: Clerical Authority and Female Innovation in the Struggle with Heresy." In *Maps of Flesh and Light: The Religious Experience of Medieval Women Mystics*, ed. Ulrike Wiethaus, 9–27. Syracuse, N.Y.: Syracuse University Press, 1993.

McSheffrey, Shannon. *Gender and Heresy: Women and Men in Lollard Communities, 1420–1530*. Philadelphia: University of Pennsylvania Press, 1995.

———. "Literacy and the Gender Gap in the Late Middle Ages: Women and Reading in Lollard Communities." In *Women, the Book, and the Godly*, ed. Smith and Taylor, 157–70.

Mead, Stephen X. "Four-fold Allegory in the Digby *Mary Magdalene*." *Renascence* 43 (1991): 269–82.

Meale, Carol M. "'Oft siþis with grete deuotion I þought what I miȝt do pleysyng to god': The Early Ownership and Readership of Love's *Mirror*, with Special Reference to Its Female Audience." In *Nicholas Love at Waseda*, ed. Shoichi Oguro, Richard Beadle, and Michael Sargent, 19–46. Cambridge: D. S. Brewer, 1997.

————. "Reading Women's Culture in Fifteenth-Century England: The Case of Alice Chaucer." In *Mediaevalitas: Reading the Middle Ages*, ed. Piero Boitani and Anna Torti, 81–101. Cambridge: D. S. Brewer, 1996.

————, ed. *Women and Literature in Britain, 1150–1500*. Cambridge: Cambridge University Press, 1993.

Meredith, Peter. "Manuscript, Scribe, and Performance: Further Looks at the N-Town Manuscript." In *Regionalism in Late Medieval Manuscripts*, ed. Riddy, 109–27.

————. "Performance, Verse, and Occasion in the N-Town *Mary Play*." In *Individuality and Achievement*, ed. Pickering, 205–21.

Meussig, Carolyn. "Prophecy and Song: Teaching and Preaching by Medieval Women." In *Women Preachers and Prophets*, ed. Kienzle and Walker, 146–58.

Middleton-Stewart, Judith. *Inward Purity and Outward Splendour: Death and Remembrance in the Deanery of Dunwich, Suffolk, 1370–1547*. Woodbridge, Eng.: Boydell Press, 2001.

Millett, Bella. "*Ancrene Wisse* and the Book of Hours." In *Writing Religious Women*, ed. Renevey and Whitehead, 21–40.

————. "Women in No Man's Land: English Recluses and the Development of Vernacular Literature in the Twelfth and Thirteenth Centuries." In *Women and Literature in Britain*, ed. Meale, 86–103.

Mills, David. "Drama and Folk-Ritual." In *The Revels History of Drama in English: Medieval Drama*, ed. A. C. Cawley et al., 121–51. London: Methuen, 1983.

————. "The Chester Cycle." In *CCMET*, 109–33.

Milner, Susannah. "Flesh and Food: The Function of Female Asceticism in the Digby *Mary Magdalene*." *Philological Quarterly* 73 (1994): 385–401.

Minnis, Alaistair. "The *Cloud of Unknowing* and Walter Hilton's *Scale of Perfection*." In *Middle English Prose*, ed. Edwards, 61–81.

Misrahi, Jean. "A *Vita Sanctae Mariae Magdalenae* (*B.H.L.* 5456) in an Eleventh-Century Manuscript." *Speculum* 18 (1943): 335–39.

Mittendorf, Ingo. "The Middle Welsh Mary of Egypt and the Latin Source of the *Miracle of the Virgin*." In *Legend of Mary of Egypt*, ed. Poppe and Ross, 205–36.

Mooney, Catherine M., ed. *Gendered Voices: Saints and Their Interpreters*. Philadelphia: University of Pennsylvania Press, 1999.

Moore, Samuel. "Patrons of Letters in Norfolk and Suffolk, c. 1450." *Publications of the Modern Language Association* 27 (1912): 188–207; 28 (1913): 79–105.

Moreton, C. E. *The Townshends and Their World: Gentry, Law, and Land in Norfolk, c. 1450–1551*. Oxford: Clarendon Press, 1992.

Mosco, Marilena, ed. *La Maddelena tra sacro e profano*. Milan: Mondadori, 1986.

Muir, Lynette. "The Saint Play in Medieval France." In *Saint Play*, ed. Davidson, 123–80.

Mulder-Bakker, Anneke B., "Ivetta of Huy: *Mater et Magistra*." In *Sanctity and Motherhood*, ed. Mulder-Bakker, 225–58.

————, ed. *Sanctity and Motherhood: Essays on Holy Mothers in the Middle Ages*. New York: Garland, 1995.

Murphy, Cullen. *The Word According to Eve*. Boston: Houghton Mifflin, 1998.

Murray, Jacqueline. "'The law of sin that is in my members': The Problem of Male Embodiment." In *Gender and Holiness*, ed. Riches and Salih, 9–22.

Neame, Alan. *The Holy Maid of Kent: The Life of Elizabeth Barton, 1506–1534*. London: Hodder and Stoughton, 1971.

Newman, Barbara. *From Virile Woman to WomanChrist*. Philadelphia: University of Pennsylvania Press, 1995.

———. *God and the Goddesses: Vision, Poetry, and Belief in the Middle Ages*. Philadelphia: University of Pennsylvania Press, 2003.

———. "Intimate Pieties: Holy Trinity and Holy Family in the Late Middle Ages." *Religion and Literature* 31 (1999): 77–101.

Nichols, Ann Eljenholm. *The Early Art of Norfolk: A Subject List of Extant and Lost Art*. EDAM Reference Series 7. Kalamazoo, Mich.: Medieval Institute Publications, 2002.

———. *Seeable Signs: The Iconography of the Seven Sacraments, 1350–1544*. Woodbridge, Eng.: Boydell Press, 1994.

De Nie, Giselle. "'Consciousness Fecund through God': From Male Fighter to Spiritual Bride-Mother in Late Antique Female Sexuality." In *Sanctity and Motherhood*, ed. Mulder-Bakker, 102–61.

Nieuwland, Jeannette. "Motherhood and Sanctity in Bridget." In *Medieval Mothering*, ed. Parsons and Wheeler, 297–329.

Nissé, Ruth. "'Oure Fadres Olde and Modres': Gender, Heresy, and Hoccleve's Literary Politics." *SAC* 21 (1999): 275–99.

———. "Reversing Discipline: The *Tretise of Miraclis Pleyinge*, Lollard Exegesis, and the Failure of Representation." *Yearbook of Langland Studies* 11 (1997): 163–94.

———. "Staged Interpretations: Civic Rhetoric and Lollard Politics in the York Plays." *JMEMS* 28 (1998): 427–52.

Norfolk Churches Great and Small. Photographed by Richard Tilbrook and described by C. V. Roberts. Norwich: Jarrold, 1997.

Norland, Howard B. *Drama in Early Tudor Britain, 1485–1558*. Lincoln: University of Nebraska Press, 1995.

O'Connell, Michael. *The Idolatrous Eye: Iconoclasm and Theater in Early-Modern England*. New York: Oxford University Press, 2000.

Oliva, Marilyn. *The Convent and the Community in Late Medieval England: Female Monasteries in the Diocese of Norwich, 1350–1540*. Woodbridge, Eng.: Boydell Press, 1998.

Oliver, Judith. "'Gothic' Women and Merovingian Desert Mothers." *GESTA* 32 (1993): 124–34.

———. "'Je pecherise renc grasces a vos': Some French Devotional Texts in Beguine Psalters." *Medieval Codicology, Iconography, Literature, and Translation: Studies for Keith Val Sinclair*, ed. Peter Monks and D. Owen, 248–62. Leiden: Brill, 1994.

Olson, Glending. "Geoffrey Chaucer." In *Cambridge History*, ed. Wallace, 566–88.

———. "Play As Play: A Medieval Ethical Theory of Performance and the

Intellectual Content of the *Tretise of Miraclis Pleyinge*." *Viator* 26 (1995): 195–221.

Orme, Nicholas, and Margaret Webster. *The English Hospital, 1070–1570*. New Haven: Yale University Press, 1995.

Ortenberg, Veronica. "Le Culte de Sainte Marie Madeleine dans L'Angleterre Anglo-Saxonne." *MEFRM* 104.1 (1992): 13–35.

Page, Stephen. "Literature and Culture in Late Medieval East Anglia." Ph.D. diss., Ohio State University, 1988.

Palmer, Barbara. "Recycling 'The Wakefield Cycle': The Records." *RORD* 41 (2002): 88–130.

Pappano, Margaret Aziza. "Judas in York: Masters and Servants in the Late Medieval English Drama." *Exemplaria* 14 (2002): 317–50.

Park, Tarjei. "Reflecting Christ: The Role of the Flesh in Walter Hilton and Julian of Norwich." In *Medieval Mystical Tradition*, ed. Glasscoe (1992), 17–37.

Parsons, John Carmi, and Bonnie Wheeler, eds. *Medieval Mothering*. New York: Garland, 1996.

Parsons, Walter Langley Edward. *Salle: The Story of a Norfolk Parish, Its Church, Manors, and People*. Norwich: Jarrold and Sons, 1937.

Patterson, Lee. "Chaucer's Pardoner on the Couch: Psyche and Clio in Medieval Literary Studies." *Speculum* 76 (2001): 638–80.

Paxson, James S., Lawrence M. Clopper, and Sylvia Tomasch, eds. *The Performance of Middle English Culture: Essays on Chaucer and the Drama in Honor of Martin Stevens*. Cambridge: D. S. Brewer, 1998.

Pearsall, Derek. "John Capgrave's *Life of St. Katherine* and Popular Romance Style." *Medievalia et Humanistica* 6 (1975): 121–37.

Petrakopoulos, Anja. "Sanctity and Motherhood: Elizabeth of Thuringia." In *Sanctity and Motherhood*, ed. Mulder-Bakker, 259–96.

Pevsner, Nicholas. *The Buildings of England: North-East Norfolk and Norwich*. Harmondsworth: Penguin, 1962.

Pickering, O. S., ed. *Individuality and Achievement in Middle English Poetry*. Cambridge: D. S. Brewer, 1997.

Pinto-Mathieu, Élisabeth. *Marie-Madeleine dans la littérature du Moyen Age*. Paris: Beauchesne, 1997.

Poppe, Erich, and Bianca Ross. *The Legend of Mary of Egypt in Medieval Insular Hagiography*. Dublin: Four Courts Press, 1996.

Pound, J. F. "The Social and Trade Structure of Norwich, 1525–1575." *Past and Present* 34 (1966): 49–69.

Prosser, Eleanor. *Drama and Religion in the English Mystery Plays*. Stanford, Calif.: Stanford University Press, 1961.

Pryds, Darleen. "Proclaiming Sanctity through Proscribed Acts: The Case of Rose of Viterbo." In *Women Preachers and Prophets*, ed. Kienzle and Walker, 159–72.

Raguin, Virginia, and Sarah Stanbury. eds. *Women's Spaces: Patronage, Place, and Gender in the Medieval Church*. Albany: State University of New York Press (forthcoming).

Rankin, Susan. "The Mary Magdalene Scene in the 'Visitatio Sepulchri' Cere-
    monies." In *Early Music History: Studies in Medieval and Early Modern
    Music*. Vol. 1, ed. Iain Fenlon, 227–55. Cambridge: Cambridge University
    Press, 1981.

Rastall, Richard. "Female Roles in All-Male Casts." *MET* 7 (1985): 25–50.

Rawcliffe, Carole. "'Gret crynge and joly chauntynge': Life, Death, and Liturgy
    at St. Giles's Hospital, Norwich, in the Thirteenth and Fourteenth Cen-
    turies." In *Counties and Communities*, ed. Rawcliffe, Virgoe, and Wilson,
    37–55.

———. *The Hospitals of Late Medieval Norwich*. Studies in East Anglian His-
    tory 2. Norwich: Centre of East Anglian Studies, University of East Anglia,
    1995.

———. "Hospital Nurses and Their Work." *Daily Life in the Middle Ages*, ed.
    Richard Britnell, 43–64. Stroud, Eng.: Sutton, 1998.

———. *Medicine and Society in Later Medieval England*. Stroud, Eng.: Sutton,
    1995.

———. *Medicine for the Soul: The Life, Death, and Resurrection of an English
    Medieval Hospital*. Stroud, Eng.: Sutton, 1999.

Rawcliffe, Carole, Roger Virgoe, and Richard Wilson, eds. *Counties and Com-
    munities: Essays on East Anglian History*. Norwich: Centre of East Anglian
    Studies, University of East Anglia, 1996.

Reames, Sherry L. *The "Legenda Aurea": A Reexamination of Its Paradoxical His-
    tory*. Madison: University of Wisconsin Press, 1985.

———. "*Mouvance* and Interpretation in Late-Medieval Latin: The Legend
    of St. Cecelia in British Breviaries." In *Medieval Literature*, ed. Machan,
    159–89.

Renevey, Denis. "Margery's Performing Body: The Translation of Late Medieval
    Discursive Religious Practices." In *Writing Religious Women*, ed. Renevey
    and Whitehead, 197–216.

Renevey, Dennis, and Christiania Whitehead, eds. *Writing Religious Women:
    Female Spiritual and Textual Practices in Late Medieval England*. Toronto:
    University of Toronto Press, 2000.

Rex, Richard. "The English Campaign against Luther." *Transactions of the Royal
    Historical Society*, 5th ser., 39 (1989): 85–106.

———. "The Polemical Theologian." In *Humanism, Reform, and Reformation*,
    ed. Bradshaw and Duffy, 109–30.

———. *The Theology of John Fisher*. Cambridge: Cambridge University Press,
    1991.

Ricci, Carla. *Mary Magdalene and Many Others: The Women Who Followed Jesus*.
    Trans. Paul Burns. Minneapolis, Minn.: Fortress Press, 1994.

Rice, Eugene F., Jr. "Jacques Lefèvre d'Étaples and the Medieval Christian Mys-
    tics." In *Florilegium Historiale: Essays Presented to Wallace K. Ferguson*, ed.
    J. G. Rowe and W. H. Stockdale, 90–124. Toronto: University of Toronto
    Press, 1971.

Riches, Samantha J. E., and Sarah Salih, eds. *Gender and Holiness: Men, Women,
    and Saints in Late Medieval England*. London: Routledge, 2002.

Richmond, Colin. "The English Gentry and Religion, c. 1500." In *Religious Belief*, ed. Harper-Bill, 121–50.

———. "Religion." In *Fifteenth-Century Attitudes*, ed. Horrox, 183–201.

Riddy, Felicity, ed. *Regionalism in Late Medieval Manuscripts and Texts*. Cambridge: D. S. Brewer, 1991.

———. "'Women Talking about the Things of God': A Late Medieval Subculture." In *Women and Literature in Britain*, ed. Meale, 104–27.

Riehle, Wolfgang. *Middle English Mystics*. Trans. Bernard Standring. London: Routledge and Kegan Paul, 1981.

Riggio, Milla. "The Staging of *Wisdom*." In *"Wisdom" Symposium*, ed. Riggio, 1–18.

———. *"Wisdom* Enthroned: Iconic Stage Portraits." *CD* 23 (1989): 228–54.

———, ed. *The "Wisdom" Symposium: Papers from the Trinity College Festival*. New York: AMS Press, 1986.

Rigolot, François. "The *Heptameron* and the 'Magdalen Controversy': Dialogue and Humanist Hermeneutics." In *Critical Tales: New Studies of the "Heptameron" and Early Modern Culture*, ed. John D. Lyons and Mary B. McKinley, 218–31. Philadelphia: University of Pennsylvania Press, 1993.

Ritchie, Harry M. "A Suggested Location for the Digby *Mary Magdalene*." *Theatre Survey* 4 (1963): 51–58.

Robertson, Elizabeth. *Early English Devotional Prose and the Female Audience*. Knoxville: University of Tennessee Press, 1990.

Rogers, Nicholas, ed. *England in the Fifteenth Century*. Proceedings of the 1992 Harlaxton Symposium. Harlaxton Medieval Studies 4. Stamford, Eng.: Paul Watkins, 1994.

Rubin, Miri. *Charity and Community in Medieval Cambridge*. Cambridge: Cambridge University Press, 1987.

———. *Corpus Christi: The Eucharist in Late Medieval Culture*. Cambridge: Cambridge University Press, 1991.

———. "Imagining Medieval Hospitals: Considerations on the Cultural Meaning of Institutional Change." In *Medicine and Charity before the Welfare State*, ed. Jonathan Barry and Colin Jones, 14–25. London: Routledge, 1991.

Runnalls, Graham. "Were They Listening or Watching? Text and Spectacle in the 1510 Châteaudun *Passion Play*." *MET* 16 (1994): 25–36.

Rusconi, Roberto. "Women's Sermons at the End of the Middle Ages." In *Women Preachers and Prophets*, ed. Kienzle and Walker, 173–95.

Russo, Daniel. "Entre Christ et Marie: La Madeleine dans l'art Italien des XIIIe–XVe siècles." In *Marie Madeleine*, ed. Duperray, 173–90.

Saint Mary the Virgin, Wiggenhall, Norfolk. Church guide. London: Redundant Churches Fund, 1989.

Salih, Sarah. "Staging Conversion: The Digby Saint Plays and *The Book of Margery Kempe*." In *Gender and Holiness*, ed. Riches and Salih, 121–34.

———. *Versions of Virginity in Late Medieval England*. Cambridge: D. S. Brewer, 2001.

Sanok, Catherine. "Mary Magdalene and the *Book of Margery Kempe*." Paper presented at the Thirty-Fourth International Congress on Medieval Studies, Western Michigan University, Kalamazoo, Mich., May 1999.

————. "Performing Sanctity in Late Medieval England: Parish Guilds, Saints' Plays, and the *Second Nun's Tale*." *JMEMS* 32 (2002): 269–303.

Sargent, Michael. "Minor Devotional Writings." In *Middle English Prose*, ed. Edwards, 147–75.

————. "The Transmission by the English Carthusians of Some Late Medieval Spiritual Writings." *JEH* 27 (1976): 225–40.

————. "Walter Hilton's *Scale of Perfection*: The London Manuscript Group Reconsidered." *MÆ* 52 (1983): 189–216.

————, ed. *De Cella in Seculum: Religious and Secular Life and Devotion in Late Medieval England*. Cambridge: D. S. Brewer, 1989.

Saxer, Victor. *Le culte de Marie Madeleine en occident des origines à la fin du moyen-âge*. 2 vols. Cahiers d'archéologie et d'histoire 3. Auxerre: Publications de la Société des Fouilles Archéologiques et des Monuments Historiques de l'Yonne; Paris: Librarie Clavreuil, 1959.

————. "L'homélie latine du Pseudo-Origène sur Jean XX, 11–18: Tradition manuscrite et origine historique." *Studi Medievali*, 3d ser., 26 (1985): 667–76.

————. "La 'Vie de Sainte Marie Madeleine' attribuée au pseudo-Raban Maur, oeuvre claravallienne du XIIe siècle." *Mélanges Saint Bernard*. XXIVe Congrès de l'Association bourguignonne de Sociétés savantes, 408–21. Dijon: Marilier, 1953.

Scala, Elizabeth. "Historicists and Their Discontents: Reading Psychoanalytically in Medieval Studies." *Texas Studies in Language and Literature* 44 (2002): 108–31.

Scase, Wendy. "Reginald Peacock, John Carpenter, and John Colop's 'Common-Profit' Books: Aspects of Book Ownership and Circulation in Fifteenth-Century London." *MÆ* 62 (1993): 261–74.

Schaberg, Jane. "How Mary Magdalene Became a Whore." *Bible Review* 8 (1992): 30–37, 51–52.

Schapiro, Meyer. "The Religious Meaning of the Ruthwell Cross." *Art Bulletin* 26 (1944): 232–45.

Scherb, Victor. "Blasphemy and the Grotesque in the Digby *Mary Magdalene*." *SP* 96 (1999): 225–40.

————. *Staging Faith: East Anglian Drama in the Later Middle Ages*. Madison, N.J.: Fairleigh Dickinson University Press, 2001.

————. "Worldly and Sacred Messengers in the Digby Mary Magdalene." *English Studies* 73 (1992): 1–9.

Schiller, Gertrud. *Iconography of Christian Art*. Trans. Janet Seligman. 2 vols. Greenwich, Conn.: New York Graphic Society, 1971.

Schnell, Rüdiger. "The Discourse on Marriage in the Middle Ages." *Speculum* 73 (1998): 771–86.

Scott, Joan W. "Experience." In *Feminists Theorize the Political*, ed. Judith Butler and Joan W. Scott, 22–40. New York: Routledge, 1992.

Seward, Desmond. *The Wars of the Roses*. New York: Penguin, 1996.

Seybolt, Robert Francis. "Fifteenth-Century Editions of the *Legenda Aurea*." *Speculum* 21 (1946): 327–38.

————. "The *Legenda Aurea*, the Bible, and *Historica Scholastica*." *Speculum* 21 (1946): 339–42.

Sheils, W. J. and Diana Wood, eds. *Women in the Church*. Studies in Church History 27. Oxford: Basil Blackwell, 1990.

Sheingorn, Pamela. "The Maternal Behavior of God: Divine Father As Fantasy Husband." In *Medieval Mothering*, ed. Parsons and Wheeler, 77–99.

Shepherd, Simon, and Peter Womack. *English Drama: A Cultural History*. Oxford: Blackwell, 1996.

Sheppard, Elaine M. "The Reformation and the Citizens of Norwich." *NA* 38, pt. 1 (1981): 44–58.

Shklar, Ruth. "Cobham's Daughter: *The Book of Margery Kempe* and the Power of Heterodox Thinking." *MLQ* 56 (1995): 277–304.

A Short-title Catalogue of Books Printed in England, Scotland, and Ireland and of English Books Printed Abroad, 1475–1640. Compiled by A. W. Pollard and G. R. Redgrave. London; Bibliographical Society, 1926.

Shuger, Debora Kuller. "Saints and Lovers: Mary Magdalene and the Ovidian Evangel." *Bucknell Review* 35 (1992): 150–71.

Simpson, James. "From Reason to Affective Knowledge: Modes of Thought and Poetic Form in *Piers Plowman*." *MÆ* 55 (1986): 1–23.

Slim, H. Colin. "Music and Dancing with Mary Magdalen in a Laura Vestalis." In *The Crannied Wall: Women, Religion, and the Arts in Early Modern Europe*, ed. Craig Monson, 139–60. Ann Arbor: University of Michigan Press, 1992.

Smart, Walter K. *Some English and Latin Sources and Parallels for the Morality of "Wisdom"*. Menasha, Wisc.: George Banta, 1912.

Smith, Leslie, and Jane Taylor, eds. *Women, the Book, and the Godly*. Selected Proceedings of the St. Hilda's Conference, 1993, vol. 1. Cambridge: D. S. Brewer, 1995.

————. *Women, the Book, and the Worldly*. Selected Proceedings of the St. Hilda's Conference, 1993, vol. 2. Cambridge: D. S. Brewer, 1995.

Sokolowski, Mary E. "Power and Torture, Laughter and Concealment: Critical Complicity and the Development of a Christian Common Sense in the Digby *Mary Magdalene*." Paper presented at the Thirtieth International Congress on Medieval Studies, Western Michigan University, Kalamazoo, Mich., May 1995.

Spencer, H. Leith. *English Preaching in the Late Middle Ages*. Oxford: Clarendon Press, 1993.

Spiegel, Gabrielle M. *The Past As Text: The Theory and Practice of Medieval Historiography*. Baltimore: Johns Hopkins University Press, 1997.

Sponsler, Claire. "The Culture of the Spectator: Conformity and Resistance to Medieval Performances." *Theatre Journal* 44 (1992): 15–29.

————. *Drama and Resistance: Bodies, Goods, and Theatricality in Late Medieval England*. Minneapolis: University of Minnesota Press, 1997.

Sprung, Andrew. "The Inverted Metaphor: Earthly Mothering As *Figura* of Divine Love in Julian of Norwich's *Books of Showings*." In *Medieval Mothering*, ed. Parsons and Wheeler, 183–99.

Staley, Lynn. *Margery Kempe's Dissenting Fictions*. University Park: Penn State University Press, 1994.

Stanbury, Sarah. "The Vivacity of Images: St. Katherine, Knighton's Lollards, and the Breaking of Idols." In *Images, Idolatry, and Iconoclasm*, ed. Jeremy Dimmick, James Simpson, and Nicolette Zeeman, 131–52. Oxford: Oxford University Press, 2002.

Stevens, Martin. *Four Middle English Mystery Cycles*. Princeton: Princeton University Press, 1987.

Stevenson, Jane. "The Holy Sinner: The Life of Mary of Egypt." In *Legend of Mary of Egypt*, ed. Poppe and Ross, 19–50.

Strohm, Paul. *Theory and the Premodern Text*. Minneapolis: University of Minnesota Press, 2000.

Sugano, Douglas. "Apologies for the Magdalene: Devotion, Iconoclasm, and the *N-Town Plays*." *RORD* 33 (1994): 165–76.

———. "'This game wel pleyd in good a-ray': The N-Town Playbooks and East Anglian Games." *CD* 28 (1994): 221–34.

Summit, Jennifer. *Lost Property: The Woman Writer and English Literary History, 1380–1589*. Chicago: University of Chicago Press, 2000.

Sutton, Anne F., and Livia Visser-Fuchs. "The Cult of Angels in Late Fifteenth-Century England: An Hours of the Guardian Angel Presented to Queen Elizabeth Woodville." In *Women and the Book*, ed. Taylor and Smith, 230–65.

Swales, T. H. "Opposition to the Suppression of the Norfolk Monasteries: Expressions of Discontent, The Walsingham Conspiracy." *NA* 33 (1962): 254–65.

Swanson, R. N. *Church and Society in Late Medieval England*. Oxford: Blackwell, 1989.

Symes, Carol. "The Appearance of Early Vernacular Plays: Forms, Functions, and the Future of Medieval Theater." *Speculum* 77 (2002): 778–831.

Szövérffy, Joseph. "*Peccatrix quondam femina*: A Survey of the Mary Magdalene Hymns." *Traditio* 19 (1963): 79–146.

Tanner, Norman. *The Church in Late Medieval Norwich, 1370–1532*. Toronto: Pontifical Institute of Medieval Studies, 1984.

———. "The Reformation and Regionalism." In *Towns and Townspeople in the Fifteenth Century*, ed. John A. F. Thomson, 129–47. Gloucester, Eng.: Alan Sutton, 1988.

Tanner, Thomas. *Notitia monastica; Or, An Account of All the Abbies, Priories, and Houses of Friers Formerly in England and Wales, and Also of All the Colleges and Hospitals Founded before A.D. MDXL*. 1744. Reprint, with additions by James Nasmith. Cambridge: Cambridge University Press, 1787.

Taylor, Jane H. M., and Leslie Smith, eds. *Women and the Book: Assessing the Visual Evidence*. Toronto: British Library and University of Toronto Press, 1997.

Taylor, Richard. *Index monasticus; Or The Abbeys and Other Monasteries, Alien Priories, Friaries, Colleges, Collegiate Churches, and Hospitals with Their Dependencies Formerly Established in the Diocese of Norwich and the Ancient Kingdom of East Anglia*. London: Richard and Arthur Taylor, 1821.

Thompson, Sally. *Women Religious: The Founding of English Nunneries after the Norman Conquest*. Oxford: Clarendon Press, 1991.

Thomson, John A. F. *The Later Lollards, 1414–1520*. Oxford: Oxford University Press, 1965.

Tombu, Jeanne. "Un triptyque de maître de la légende du Marie-Madeleine." *Gazette des Beaux Arts* 15 (1927): 299–310.

Travis, Peter W. *Dramatic Design in the Chester Cycle*. Chicago: University of Chicago Press, 1982.

Twycross, Meg. "The Theatricality of Medieval English Plays." In *CCMET*, 37–84.

———. "'Transvestism' in the Mystery Plays." *MET* 5 (1983): 123–80.

Tydeman, William. *English Medieval Theater, 1400–1500*. London: Routledge and Kegan Paul, 1986.

Van Engen, John. "Friar Johannes Nider on Laypeople Living As Religious in the World." In *Vita Religiosa im Mittelalter*. Ed. Franz J. Felten and Nikolas Jaspert, with Stephanie Haarländer, 583–615. Berlin: Duncker and Humblot, 1999.

Vauchez, André. *The Laity in the Middle Ages: Religious Beliefs and Devotional Practices*. Ed. and intro. Daniel E. Bornstein. Trans. Margery J. Schneider. Notre Dame, Ind.: University of Notre Dame Press, 1993.

———. *Sainthood in the Middle Ages*. Trans. Jean Birrell. Cambridge: Cambridge University Press, 1997.

Velz, John W. "Sovereignty in the Digby *Mary Magdalene*." *CD* 2 (1968): 32–43.

The Victoria History of the County of Norfolk. Ed. H. Arthur Doubleday and William Page. 2 vols. 1906. Reprint, London: Institute for Historical Research, 1975.

Virgoe, Roger. "The Divorce of Thomas Tuddenham." In *East Anglian Society and the Political Community of Late Medieval England: Selected Papers of Roger Virgoe*, ed. Caroline Barron, Carole Rawcliffe, and Joel T. Rosenthal, 117–31. Norwich: Centre of East Anglian Studies, University of East Anglia, 1997.

Voaden, Rosalynn. "All Girls Together: Community, Gender, and Vision at Helfta." In *Medieval Women in Their Communities*, ed. Diana Watt, 72–91. Toronto: University of Toronto Press, 1997.

———. "Beholding Men's Members: The Sexualizing of Transgression in *The Book of Margery Kempe*." In *Medieval Theology*, ed. Biller and Minnis, 175–90.

———. "The Company She Keeps: Mechtild of Hackborne in Late-Medieval Devotional Compilations." In *Prophets Abroad*, ed. Voaden, 51–69.

———. "Drinking from the Golden Cup: Courtly Ritual and Order in the *Liber specialis gratiae* of Mechtild of Hackeborn." *Mystics Quarterly* 26 (2000): 109–19.

———. *God's Words, Women's Voices: The Discernment of Spirits in the Writing of Late-Medieval Women Visionaries*. York: York Medieval Press, University of York, 1999.

———. "Rewriting the Letter: Variations in the Middle English Translation of the *Epistola solitarii ad reges* of Alphonso of Jaén." In *The Translations of St. Birgitta of Sweden's Works in the European Vernaculars*, ed. Bridget Morris and Veronica O'Mara, 170–85. Turnhout: Brepols, 2000.

———. "Women's Words, Men's Language: *Discretio Spirituum* As Discourse in the Writing of Medieval Women Visionaries." In *The Medieval Translator 5 (Traduire au Moyen Age)*, ed. Roger Ellis and René Tixier, 64–83. Turnhout: Brepols, 1996.

———, ed. *Prophets Abroad: The Reception of Continental Holy Women in Late-Medieval England*. Cambridge: D. S. Brewer, 1996.

Wallace, David. "Mystics and Followers in Siena and East Anglia: A Study in Taxonomy, Class, and Cultural Mediation." In *Medieval Mystical Tradition*, ed. Glasscoe (1987), 169–91.

———, ed. *The Cambridge History of Medieval English Literature*. Cambridge: Cambridge University Press, 1999.

Warren, Nancy Bradley. *Spiritual Economies: Female Monasticism in Later Medieval England*. Philadelphia: University of Pennsylvania Press, 2001.

Wasson, John. "The Secular Saint Plays of the Elizabethan Era." In *Saint Play*, ed. Davidson, 241–60.

Waters, Claire M. *Angels and Earthly Creatures: Preaching, Performance, and Gender in the Later Middle Ages*. Philadelphia: University of Pennsylvania Press, 2003.

Watson, Nicholas. "Censorship and Cultural Change in Late-Medieval England: Vernacular Theology, the Oxford Translation Debate, and Arundel's Constitutions of 1409." *Speculum* 70 (1995): 822–64.

———. "The Composition of Julian of Norwich's *Revelation of Love*." *Speculum* 68 (1993): 637–83.

———. "Conceptions of the Word: The Mother Tongue and the Incarnation of God." *New Medieval Literatures* 1 (1997): 85–124.

———. "Desire for the Past." *SAC* 21 (1999): 59–97.

———. "Melting into God the English Way: Deification in the Middle English Version of Marguerite Porete's *Mirouer des simples âmes anienties*." In *Prophets Abroad*, ed. Voaden, 19–49.

———. "The Methods and Objectives of Thirteenth-Century Anchoritic Devotion." In *Medieval Mystical Tradition*, ed. Glasscoe (1987), 132–53.

———. "Middle English Mystics." In *Cambridge History*, ed. Wallace, 539–65.

———. "The Politics of Middle English Writing." In *Idea of the Vernacular*, ed. Wogan-Browne et al., 331–42.

———. *Richard Rolle and the Invention of Authority*. Cambridge: Cambridge University Press, 1991.

———. "Visions of Inclusion: Universal Salvation and Vernacular Theology in Pre-Reformation England." *JMEMS* 27 (1997): 145–87.

———. "'Yf wommen be double naturelly': Remaking 'Woman' in Julian of Norwich's *Revelation of Love*." *Exemplaria* 8 (1996): 1–34.

Watt, Diane. "The Prophet at Home: Elizabeth Barton and the Influence of Bridget of Sweden and Catherine of Siena." In *Prophets Abroad*, ed. Voaden, 161–76.

————. *Secretaries of God: Women Prophets in Late Medieval and Early Modern England*. Cambridge: D. S. Brewer, 1997.

Weimann, Robert. *Shakespeare and the Popular Tradition in the Theater*. Ed. Robert Schwartz. Baltimore: Johns Hopkins University Press, 1978.

Weinstein, Donald, and Rudolph M. Bell. *Saints and Society: The Two Worlds of Western Christendom, 1000–1700*. Chicago: University of Chicago Press, 1982.

Whatmore, L. E. "The Sermon against the Holy Maid of Kent and Her Adherents, Delivered at Paul's Cross, November the 23rd, 1533, and at Canterbury, December the 7th." *English Historical Review* 53 (1943): 463–75.

White, Paul Whitfield. "Reforming Mysteries' End: A New Look at Protestant Intervention in English Provincial Drama." *JMEMS* 29 (1999): 121–47.

————. *Theater and Reformation: Protestantism, Patronage, and Playing in Tudor England*. Cambridge: Cambridge University Press, 1993.

Wickham, Glynne. "The Staging of Saint Plays in England." In *The Medieval Drama*, ed. Sandro Sticca, 99–119. Albany: State University of New York Press, 1972.

Wilk, Sarah. "The Cult of Mary Magdalen in Fifteenth-Century Florence and Its Iconography." *Studi Medievali*, 3d ser., 26 (1985): 685–98.

Williamson, W. W. "Saints on Norfolk Rood-Screens and Pulpits." *NA* 31 (1957): 299–346.

Wilson, Edward. "A Middle English Manuscript at Coughton Court, Warwickshire, and British Library MS Harley 4012." *Notes and Queries*, n.s. 24 (1977): 295–303.

Windeatt, Barry. "Julian of Norwich and Her Audiences." *Review of English Studies* 28 (1977): 1–17.

Winstead, Karen. "Piety, Politics, and Social Commitment in Capgrave's 'Life of St. Katherine.'" *Medievalia et Humanistica* 17 (1991): 59–80.

————. *Virgin Martyrs: Legends of Sainthood in Late Medieval England*. Ithaca, N.Y.: Cornell University Press, 1997.

Wogan-Browne, Jocelyn. "Analytic Survey 5: 'Reading Is Good Prayer': Recent Research on Female Reading Communities." *New Medieval Literatures* 5 (2002): 229–97.

————. "'Clerc u lai, muïne u dame': Women and Anglo-Norman Hagiography in the Twelfth and Thirteenth Centuries." In *Women and Literature in Britain*, ed. Meale, 61–85.

————. "Rerouting the Dower: The Anglo-Norman Life of St. Audrey by Marie (of Chatteris?)." In *Power of the Weak*, ed. Jennifer Carpenter and Sally-Beth MacLean, 27–56. Urbana: University of Illinois Press, 1995.

————. *Saints' Lives and Women's Literary Culture, c. 1150–1300: Virginity and Its Authorizations*. Oxford: Oxford University Press, 2001.

————. "The Virgin's Tale." In *Feminist Readings in Middle English Literature: The Wife of Bath and All Her Sect*, ed. Ruth Evans and Leslie Johnson, 165–94. London: Routledge, 1994.

Wogan-Browne, Jocelyn, and Marie-Élisabeth Henneau. "Liège, the Medieval 'Woman Question,' and the Question of Medieval Women." In *Holy Women of Liège*, ed. Dor et al., 1–32.

Wogan-Browne, Jocelyn, Nicholas Watson, Andrew Taylor, and Ruth Evans, eds. *The Idea of the Vernacular: An Anthology of Middle English Literary Theory, 1280–1520*. University Park: Pennsylvania State University Press, 1999.

Womack, Peter. "Medieval Drama." In *English Drama*, Shepherd and Womack, 1–32.

————."Shakespeare and the Sea of Stories." *JMEMS* 29 (1999): 169–87.

Woolf, Rosemary. "English Imitations of the *Homilia Origenis de Maria Magdalena*." In *Chaucer and Middle English Studies in Honor of Rossell Hope Robbins*, ed. Beryl Rowland, 384–91. Kent, Ohio: Kent State University Press, 1974.

————. *The English Religious Lyric in the Middle Ages*. Oxford: Clarendon Press, 1968.

Wright, Robert. "Community Theatre in Late Medieval East Anglia." *Theatre Notebook* 28 (1974): 24–38.

————."Medieval Theatre in East Anglia: A Study of Drama and the Community in Essex, Suffolk, and Norfolk, 1200–1580, with Special Reference to Game, Interlude, and Play in the Late Fifteenth and Early Sixteenth Century." Ph.D. diss., University of Bristol, 1971.

Wright, Steven. "Is the Ashmole Fragment a Remnant of a Middle English Saint Play?" *Neophilogus* 75 (1991): 139–49.

Index

Mary Magdalene is abbreviated as "MM."